WITHDRAWN

Hoover Institution Bibliographical Series 54

The French Fifth Republic
Continuity and Change, 1966-1970

The French Fifth Republic
Continuity and Change, 1966-1970
An Annotated Bibliography

A Sequel to
The French Fifth Republic, 1958-1965

Grete Heinz and Agnes F. Peterson

Hoover Institution Press
Stanford University
Stanford, California

The Hoover Institution on War, Revolution and Peace, founded at Stanford University in 1919 by the late President Herbert Hoover, is a center for advanced study and research on public and international affairs in the twentieth century. The views expressed in its publications are entirely those of the authors and do not necessarily reflect the views of the staff, officers, or Board of Overseers of the Hoover Institution.

Library of Congress Cataloging in Publication Data

Heinz, Grete.
    The French Fifth Republic.

    (Hoover Institution bibliographical series, 54)
    Sequel to The French Fifth Republic, establishment and consolidation (1958-1965)
    1. France--Politics and government--1958-
--Bibliography--Catalogs. 2. Stanford University.
Hoover Institution on War, Revolution, and Peace.
I. Peterson, Agnes F., joint author. II. Title.
III. Series: Stanford University. Hoover Institution on War, Revolution, and Peace. Bibliographical series, 54.

Z2180.3.H44   016.3209'44'083   73-20124
ISBN 0-8179-2541-4

DC
412
.Z99
H46

Hoover Institution Bibliographical Series 54
International Standard Book Number 0-8179-2541-4
Library of Congress Catalog Card Number 73-20124
© 1974 by the Board of Trustees of the
    Leland Stanford Junior University
All rights reserved
Printed in the United States of America

CONTENTS

Introduction	vii
Abbreviations	xvii
Part I: Non-serial Publications	3
Part II: Serial Publications	99
Subject Index	105
Author Index	115
Title Index	123

INTRODUCTION

The second volume of this bibliographical compilation on the French Fifth Republic was conceived at the time of President de Gaulle's retirement from the helm of the French government in April 1969. The widely held expectation that this resignation would spark a full-fledged constitutional crisis inevitably culminating in the disintegration of the Fifth Republic proved to be unwarranted. The Fifth Republic as a political regime survived the departure of its founder. Nevertheless, with the death of Charles de Gaulle in November 1970, the alterations introduced in French political life eighteen months earlier became irreversible. A terminal point was reached, marking the closing of a well-defined chapter of contemporary French history, which, for want of a better expression, we shall call the years of "de Gaulle's Republic."

It is the aim of this second bibliographic volume on the Fifth Republic to complement and extend the first volume so as to encompass all documentation available at the Hoover Institution on de Gaulle's Republic. We have therefore included here all material on the three and a half years separating de Gaulle's presidential re-election in December 1965 from Georges Pompidou's official confirmation as his successor in June 1969. We have also complemented and updated the first volume on the origins, establishment, and consolidation of the Fifth Republic by listing all relevant publications that have been added to the library's holdings since the completion of the first volume three years ago. For the year and a half preceding de Gaulle's death, which, strictly speaking, lies outside the scope of the bibliography, coverage has been arbitrarily limited to the process of political and institutional adjustment to Gaullism without de Gaulle and to de Gaulle's personal fate in the days of his retirement.

It is remarkable that France was destined to serve once more as a microcosm in which problems besetting the whole Western world could be observed in condensed and dramatic form. No one would have ventured this prognosis in the tranquil years of 1966 and 1967, when the internal turmoil unleashed in the wake of decolonization had been successfully weathered and the French body politic had given its grudging assent to the Gaullist regime. Having resigned himself to a reduced version of national greatness, de Gaulle could reasonably claim that he had at least laid secure foundations for an exemplary modern democracy, whose international influence would derive less from military might than from his country's inner stability. To quote from his December 1967 year-end message, "Au milieu de tant de pays secoués par tant de saccades, le nôtre continuera de donner l'exemple de l'efficacité dans la conduite de ses affaires." Yet even this modest dream was soon to be shattered. In May of 1968, the Fifth Republic edged to the brink of chaos when revolt broke out against the Gaullist design for a modern democratic society. The bureaucratically planned and centrally controlled modernization program faltered as an upsurge of spontaneous, grassroots discontent manifested itself first among French youth and then quickly spread to large segments of the population. This explosion, short-lived as it was, epitomized some of the major crises of modern civilization. In the earlier years of the Fifth Republic, the vast literature spawned by the Algerian conflict demonstrated conclusively that Western democracies, whether parliamentary or presidential, are incapable of creating political institutions for maintaining close and mutually beneficial ties with pre-industrial peoples and dealing efficiently with economic backwardness. The outpouring of analytic and self-critical writings elicited by the "May events" now offers convincing evidence that, even in the absence of divisive foreign entanglements, strong and relatively effective governments can be brought to a standstill by deep-rooted resistances to rational modernization.

Since no modifications have been introduced in the basic pattern of the bibliography, the introductory remarks to the first volume are equally applicable here and need not be reiterated in full. It should be remembered, however, that the final Gaullist years were dominated by issues that were less central to the traditional collecting areas of the Hoover Institution than those on which the first volume was focused. The library's specialization in questions of conventional and revolutionary warfare, political institutions, political parties, and elections coincided closely with French preoccupations between 1958 and 1965: the Algerian conflict and controversies surrounding the establishment of the new political regime. Between 1966 and 1969, political life was dominated by issues rooted in the social, economic, educational, and ideological spheres, which proved more elusive. Although we have made every effort to explore these areas more fully than in the previous volume, an equal degree of comprehensiveness as in the purely political domain could not be achieved. It should be recognized that Hoover Institution holdings for these years constitute a significant sampling rather than a complete survey of existing publications. Characteristically, over one-tenth of the bibliographical entries (those designated ML) were drawn from the holdings of Stanford University's Main Library, whose recently expanded collections of French government documents (statistical, scientific, and technical, as well as economic and sociological) have been only partially incorporated here.

Parts I and II, the main sections of this volume, give full bibliographical data and brief annotations on 1,144 catalogued works and ninety-one new periodicals (serials identified as current in the first volume are not repeated). Complementing the formal alphabetical arrangement of the main sections is the Subject Index. To assure continuity with the first volume, we have maintained subject headings where at all applicable, even when changes in the relative importance of certain subjects might have justified a different breakdown. The scope and changes in emphasis of the original subject headings, as well as major new headings, will be discussed here. (An introductory note to both the Author Index and the Title Index fully outlines their scope.)

The subject headings that serve as the best general introduction to this bibliography are <u>Bibliographies</u>, <u>Reference works</u>, and <u>Special collections</u>. It is especially recommended that the bibliographies under nos. 679 and 1137 and the reference works under nos. 27 and 276 be consulted. An overall view of the Fifth Republic can be gained under <u>Fifth Republic (general)</u>. Comprehensive English-language works are nos. 37, 336, 646, and 860; the two best French surveys are nos. 906 and 1102. Major developments can also be followed up under such <u>Fifth Republic</u> subheadings as "Algerian conflict," "foreign affairs," "Gaullist policies," "political chronicles and diaries," "political history," and "political institutions." While new publications on the Fifth Republic as an entity have declined quantitatively as its novelty has worn off, a number of definitive, scholarly contributions and perceptive longer-range appraisals are noted in this volume. More general works on the characteristics of French society are under <u>Civilization, French</u> (e.g., no. 297).

Nothing reflects more vividly the shift in preoccupation between the earlier and the final years of de Gaulle's Republic than the drastic reduction in publications listed under <u>Algeria</u>, <u>Algerian nationalism</u>, <u>Algerian question</u>, <u>Algerian revolution</u>, and <u>Algerian war</u>, which between them comprised almost one-third of the entries in the preceding volume. Of interest are a handful of comprehensive histories of the war (nos. 283, 803, 876, 1077), retrospective accounts by key military and civilian policy-makers (nos. 353, 381, 648, 779, 1075), and new documentation on the final months of violence preceding Algerian independence (nos. 296, 427, 1075). An oddity is a personal narrative by a close collaborator of Robert Martel, the French-Algerian extreme rightist (no. 845). Two other works deserve special mention: a relatively serene but nonetheless damning work on French use of torture, published with ten years' hindsight (no. 1104); and a scholarly study on the political, sociological, and legal aspects of Algerian decolonization (no. 392). A welcome addition is the phonograph-record collection on the Algerian war described under 483 (B 1). Disenchantment on the part of the French Left with independent Algeria, whose revolutionary fervor was dampened after Ben Bella's ouster, probably accounts for the paucity of publications, polemical as well as scholarly, and the absence of personal narratives under <u>Algeria, post-independence</u>. Aside from the general work under no. 340, only nos. 718 and 953 make some original contributions to an understanding of post-1962 Algerian politics. An important new documentary and bibliographical source on Algeria and the rest of North Africa is no. 29. Significant additions on the problems of repatriation at the end of the Algerian war are two studies on the resettlement of Algerian Jews in France (nos. 104 and 223) and a survey of the pied-noirs' current status (no. 878). Related subjects treated under <u>Army in Algeria</u>, <u>Civilian-military relations</u>, <u>Decolonization</u>, <u>Military doctrine--"counterinsurgency,"</u> <u>Nationalist opposition to de Gaulle</u>, <u>Organisation de l'armée</u>

secrète, and Trials, political have suffered from comparable neglect, as the French opponents to Algerian independence have resigned themselves to the verdict of history; exceptions are works by American political scientists listed under nos. 597, 730, and 794. The courtroom drama of the Salan and Bastien-Thiry trials is re-created in the above-mentioned phonograph-record collection. Several personal narratives by exiled or recently amnestied O.A.S. figures offer new documentation on operations in France and Algeria and on the assassination attempts on de Gaulle (nos. 406, 706, 1022, 1023, 1059). The latest works by the two most prominent spokesmen of the nationalist opposition to de Gaulle--Georges Bidault and Jacques Soustelle--have little new to say on the subject.

While the Algerian war and its domestic repercussions have faded into history, the outpouring of publications about the founder of the Fifth Republic continues nearly unabated, with sixty-six books primarily devoted to him under the heading Gaulle, Charles de, of which the most comprehensive and most useful as a reference work is no. 906. Little new information transpires in the latest crop listed under "biographies," but reassessments of de Gaulle's political career and doctrine under "political philosophy," such as nos. 69, 394, 608, 709, 832, and 1089, are more enlightening. Of special interest is the wealth of "pictorial works" and "satires and cartoons," particularly the outstanding cartoon collections under nos. 805 and 813. Though they may be only the tip of the iceberg, nos. 756, 1061, and 1075 are the first few "memoirs" by close collaborators and are complemented by scattered new "anecdotes" about de Gaulle that round out the picture of his life and personality. Works that shed the most light on de Gaulle's final years in power are under "and Pompidou" (see nos. 9, 670, 1088). Publications dealing with the period after his resignation as head of state can be found under "retirement," which is described in intimate detail in two books (nos. 212 and 787). Material elicited by his demise can be located under the subheadings "death" and "eulogies." More definitive posthumous evaluations have been listed under "judgments on" and "historical place," of which nos. 709 and 933 are the most notable; "indictments" by his detractors, of which nos. 413 and 868 are typical, update those listed in the previous volume. Important source material appears in a five-volume collection of de Gaulle's speeches (no. 511). Attention should also be drawn to a number of stylistic studies under "language and style," as well as to phonograph records of speeches under nos. 484 (B1, B2) and 889. The final two volumes of de Gaulle's memoirs, undertaken in retirement and cut short by death, give his own version of the Fifth Republic's political history through early 1963. Since de Gaulle's death, research, albeit of a partisan character, has been sponsored by the Institut Charles de Gaulle, which has published a de Gaulle chronology (no. 226) and a preliminary bibliography (no. 885) as well as a periodical, "Espoir" (no. 1171), providing new documentation. A more scholarly bibliographical guide to publications about de Gaulle is no. 679, with 180 works on his role during the Fifth Republic, many of them unpublished theses; the extensive but less reliable bibliography in no. 906 might also be consulted.

Gaullism as a political movement gradually acquiring its own momentum independent of its founder is the subject of two comprehensive studies (nos. 215 and 592) and is covered in systematic fashion by the above-mentioned bibliography no. 679, which also lists source material on the Gaullist parties. Views of individual Gaullist politicians can be found under Gaullists. The Gaullist party, Union pour la nouvelle république (U.N.R.), appears under that heading in the Subject Index, although its exact name was Union pour la nouvelle république—Union démocratique du travail (U.N.R.–U.D.T.) after October 1962. For the period following November 1967, when its name was officially changed again, it appears in the Subject Index as Union des démocrates pour la république (U.D.R.), although the party was in fact called Union des démocrates pour la Cinquième République between November 1967 and June 1968. Scholarly works on the party are represented by nos. 75, 216, and 662; party publications are itemized in no. 217, and related Gaullist organizations are listed in no. 906. The lively controversies surrounding the choice of de Gaulle's successor, which were initiated prior to de Gaulle's retirement and reached their height in 1969, can be traced under Gaullism after de Gaulle. This heading indiscriminately records temperate judgments on changes in post-Gaullist political style and doctrine by flexible Gaullists (e.g., nos. 267 and 315) alongside of bitter indictments of the new French president by the more doctrinaire Gaullist purists (e.g., nos. 316 and 1088).

The general acceptance of the Gaullist political regime, with its reinforcement of the executive branch and the president's personal power, is reflected in the reduced number of both factual and polemical works under Political institutions. The most important studies are listed under Fifth Republic--"political institutions," notably nos. 12, 74, 368, 369, 374, 526, 584, and 927. By an ironic twist of history, an American political scientist's contention (no. 1123) that the Fifth Republic had turned France into a typical Western consensual political community, in which ideological dissensions were disappearing, was evinced in a work completed on the eve of May 1968; undaunted, the author propounded in an epilogue that French universities rather than French politics were out of tune with French society, an interpretation that political developments of the last five years have tended to support. Under Political institutions, major studies on specific features of the Fifth Republic focus on "presidency" (no. 77), "prime minister" (no. 233), "executive-legislative balance" (nos. 524, 766, 890), "executive organs" (no. 309), and "referenda" (no. 1008), as well as "Council of State" (no. 885). Administration, governmental should also be consulted for studies on the executive branch; as a reference tool, no. 452 is indispensable.

Concern about European policy continues at a reduced level of intensity, as can be seen under the headings Common Market, European integration, and European integration, economic. Equally controversial and related issues are debated under International economic relations, especially their "monetary aspects" and "U.S. preponderance." Diminished government concern with foreign aid is reflected in the reduced number of publications listed under Assistance, technical and economic. The only two studies on aid to the newly independent African states (nos. 1005 and 1010) are by an Austrian and an American scholar, respectively. Disinterest in the French Union and the French Community is equally evident, but a few scholarly works give detailed information about the scattered remnants of the French Empire under Overseas departments and territories. Little controversy is generated by de Gaulle's policies toward the Atlantic Alliance or the North Atlantic Treaty Organization. Criticism shifts to Foreign relations--"Canada" and "Israel," the latter coupled with renewed interest about Jews in France. Among works on International relations, nos. 245, 253, 595, and 735 are of special interest. The best descriptions of Foreign policy under de Gaulle are nos. 183, 253, and 286; the most important documentary collections are nos. 474 and 1176-1178.

No letup in publications can be observed with respect to internal political affairs. The pulse of French political life continues to find its principal expression under Elections and Referendums. Extensive documentation comparable to that described in the previous volume of the bibliography is listed under Elections, legislative--"1967 (March)" and "1968 (June)"; Elections, presidential--"1969 (June)"; and Referendums--"1969 (April)." Considerable source material on the 1967 legislative elections was listed under no. 811 (m) in the first volume of the bibliography. Conversely, a number of studies on the December 1965 presidential election, including a major one (no. 422), are found in this volume, as are phonograph records of the presidential campaign speeches (no. 484 [B2]). For more academic discussions, the headings Electoral law, Electoral sociology, and Electoral systems should be consulted. Broader aspects of political behavior can be followed up under Political attitudes, Political philosophy, Public opinion polls, and Sociology, political.

Activities of political organizations are documented to the same extent as in the previous volume under the headings Clubs, political, Organizations, political, and Political parties. As an up-to-date reference tool on the entire spectrum of political organizations, large and small, no. 276 (which continues no. 405 in the first volume) is an invaluable guide. Publications of all political parties up to the end of 1967 are itemized in full in no. 217. In contrast to the earlier years of the Fifth Republic, parties and organizations of the extreme Right have been quiescent; a partisan but useful survey of right-wing politics can be found in no. 361. (Developments in the Gaullist movement have been discussed above.) It was the political Left rather than the Right that was in the throes of internal conflict and reorganization for the period covered by this bibliography. Encouraged by the results of the 1965 presidential election and the parliamentary successes of March 1967, the Left placed its hope of regaining power in increasing collaboration between Communist and non-Communist parties, as can be seen under Political parties--"unification of the Left." Material on the two major political parties of the Left, the Parti communiste français and the Parti socialiste

(S.F.I.O.), is under these headings in the Subject Index, but for other parties, such as the Parti socialiste unifié, the Fédération de la gauche démocrate et socialiste, and the newly founded Parti socialiste (1969-), the Author Index must be consulted. A wide range of documentation is available on the French Communist Party, in addition to the two comprehensive works under nos. 419 and 677. Subheadings such as "ideology," "internal opposition," and "and non-Communist Left" illustrate the party's evolution, which is mirrored especially clearly in the subheadings "and Gauchisme," "and May 1968." What is most characteristic of the period, however, concurrent with the above-mentioned unification efforts, is the proliferation and strengthening of Communist organizations outside the orthodox fold. As in the previous volume, these have been designated under Communist opposition groups. Publications by these groups became so prolific that a further breakdown proved imperative. A rough division between "Trotskyist" (affiliated with the Fourth International) and "Maoist" (or pro-Chinese Communist) was therefore introduced. For an overview of the Trotskyist movement in France, see no. 985; for the Maoists, whose split with orthodox Communism dates back only to the mid-1960's, no systematic study exists, but no. 759 gives some idea of their current status. Other revolutionary groups that do not fall in these two categories are documented under Organizations, political--"Left, revolutionary" and Anarchist groups. Among these ephemeral splinter groups the Ligue communiste (see Author Index) is the only one to have emerged as a recognized political party, making its entrance on the national scene during the 1969 presidential election. The ideological dimensions of the debate within the French Left can best be traced under such headings as Socialism and Marxism, to which developments in International communism provide an essential backdrop. Significant for the newly surfaced ideological currents are both Anarchism and Gauchisme, where the dividing line between the establishmentarian Left and the anti-institutional Left is at its sharpest.

Other facets of domestic affairs are covered under Agriculture, Economic conditions, Economic growth, and Industries. Government intervention can be seen most clearly under Economic policy, Planning, and State and economy, as well as under Social policy. Good overviews of changes in French economic life and society can be obtained from nos. 37, 570, 684, 891, and 1078, to which works under Social groups, such as "cadres," "intellectuals," and "workers," are an important complement.

To do justice to the major preoccupations of the concluding years of de Gaulle's Republic, two new subject headings have been introduced and others expanded in conjunction with them. They are directly or indirectly related to the explosion that shook France between the beginning of May and the end of June 1968. It has been estimated that this short upheaval generated more publications than the French Revolution and nearly as many as World War I or II, despite its much more limited impact on French society. More than 230 of these works are listed in this volume, comprising about 90 per cent of those enumerated in the only bibliography (no. 1137) fully devoted to May-June 1968 plus several works omitted there. No. 1137, which is edited by Professor Wylie, should be consulted also for identification of libraries and research centers in France and the United States with extensive collections on the subject; Hoover Institution holdings, combined with those of the Stanford University Main Library, are probably as comprehensive as those of any other single institution. In addition to the catalogued material, which is described individually in this volume, no. 484 contains ephemeral material collected by on-the-spot observers. To complement regular serial holdings, two sets of microfilms on the daily and weekly press for May through June 1968 were purchased by the Hoover Institution from the Association pour la conservation et la reproduction photographique de la presse (see nos. 482 and 485); the Association's announced microfilm sets on the labor press, the ephemeral revolutionary press, and a selection of special editions on the May events have not yet been completed. These microfilms, as well as Françoise Rougier's thesis listing special periodical issues devoted to the May events, will be available eventually.

In order to deal more effectively with this vast amount of material, a dichotomy was arbitrarily introduced into what, historically, formed a single entity. Material focusing on the political and economic crisis created by the convergence of the student revolt with the strike movement is subsumed under the heading May 1968. Publications more specifically limited to the university crisis are placed under the heading May 1968 student revolt.

For an overview of May 1968, it is suggested that the "major works" culled from the vast number of publications be examined, together with those listed under "history." Other useful guides are "bibliographies," "chronicles," "chronologies," and, especially, "documents and sources." For an analysis of events, subheadings of value are "antecedents, ideological," "causes," and, above all, "interpretations," with a special breakdown by different ideological points of view. Publications are identified as "fictional works," "pictorial works," "poetry," and "satires." Other subdivisions refer to the involvement of various groups in the events, such as May 1968--"and art world," "and Catholic activists," "and P.C.F.," "and political parties," "and trade unions." Actions of the principal protagonists can be followed up under "government response," "participants," "revolutionary groups," and "strikes."

May 1968 student revolt has its own "major works" and "documents and sources." The logic of events is analyzed under "antecedents," "causes," and "interpretations, sociological." Facets pertinent to the student revolt can be studied under "and cultural revolution," "international dimensions," and "university reform." Other breakdowns concern the location or type of institution involved in the revolt: "in lycées," "Nanterre," "Paris, University of," and "provincial universities." The subjective stance of the authors is the guiding thread in such subdivisions as "personal accounts--professors," "professors' views," "student reactions," and "views, hostile." The artificially created categories under May 1968 and May 1968 student revolt should not be viewed as watertight compartments; their purpose, rather, is to serve as a guide through the maze of publications, allowing juxtaposition of works with comparable topics, pretensions, or approaches, without interfering with the more practical function of facilitating retrieval of material on certain well-defined aspects of events such as "Odéon occupation" or "police repression."

The heading most closely related to May 1968 is Education, which received passing attention in the first volume of this bibliography and moved to the forefront of interest and political debate during this period. No claim to completeness can be made, but the range of opinions on educational policy and pedagogic philosophy is fully represented and is supplemented by factual accounts of the French educational system, viewed historically and at its different levels. Education covers the entire French system and should be consulted not only for the comprehensive and informative works on the subject, such as nos. 433 and 811 and those listed under "history," "international comparisons," and "statistics," but also for the polemical works under "democratization" and "proposed reforms" or the more reflective studies under "education and society" or "sociology of," including such penetrating critiques of education in modern society as nos. 94 and 137. Gaullist reforms in the educational structure antedating May 1968 and the more hastily drawn up reforms enacted under the pressure of student demands can be traced under "Gaullist policy" and "reforms, post-May 1968." In conjunction with the university crisis, considerable material has been collected under Education, higher, particularly for the subheadings "Gaullist policy, post-May 1968," "reforms, pre-May 1968," and "reforms, post-May 1968." Education, secondary concentrates on lycée students, the reservoir for future university students, among whom the "social factors" determining success or failure can be observed. An excellent study on the status of lycée professors, no. 1111, deserves special mention. The less controversial primary, adult, and vocational components of the educational system are less fully represented under their individual headings. The younger generation is also the subject of such headings as Social groups--"students," Students, and Youth, in which the young tend to emerge as the new proletariat and the most powerful force for change, though it is amusing to juxtapose this post-May 1968 perspective with the complacent views expressed in the government report of 1967 entitled "Jeunes d'aujourd'hui" (no. 468).

Another heading whose importance was enhanced by the May 1968 events-- events that challenged the widely shared approval of affluent Western societies exemplified by the United States--is Civilization, modern. The forty-seven works assembled under this purposely vague label, some concrete and factual, others in a more philosophical vein, reflect the shift in emphasis from political problems to problems connected with the way of life in industrialized societies. Typifying the range of opinions are glowing affirmations of the potentials of modern technology (no. 938), disillusioned acceptance of its benefits and penalties (such as nos. 49 and 429), and harsh Marxist or non-Marxist condemnation (notably nos. 238, 311, 724, 847). The more purely polemical and negative interpretations are designated under "critique of," Interest in the quality of modern life is also reflected in more concrete headings like <u>Cultural life</u>, <u>Daily life in France</u>, <u>Ecology</u>, <u>Leisure occupations</u>, and in the numerous investigations of different social groups under <u>Sociology, case studies</u> (e.g., nos. 239 and 834).

In a somewhat different sphere, discontent with an overpowerful central government emerges in the headings <u>Autonomist movements</u> and <u>Regionalism</u>, for which the <u>Basque autonomy movement</u> and <u>Brittany</u> are neuralgic points. The urge to strengthen grassroots control can be seen under <u>Decentralization</u> and <u>Local government</u>. Response of the Gaullist government to these challenges, as well as partisan controversies on existing or proposed government policies, can best be followed under <u>Planning, regional</u>, which encompasses Gaullist efforts to correct regional disequilibria and give some power to regional authorities in channeling economic growth. Importants works are nos. 553 and 699. The same concern for grassroots control motivates debates around "autogestion" or workers' participation in plant management, which are found under the heading <u>Industrial relations</u>--"worker participation." In the political arena, <u>Regional reform</u> is the key heading for observing changes in administrative structure, government proposals to shift power away from central authorities, and partisan debates surrounding such reforms. It is characteristic of these years that de Gaulle unflinchingly accepted the defeat of the April 1969 referendum on regional reform as a signal for resignation, recognizing it as the verdict of the French people that he would not be capable of solving the most pressing problems of contemporary French society.

It is too early to predict whether France without de Gaulle and with fewer pretensions to national greatness will produce its own form of national "psychodrama" (Aron's disparaging term for the May revolt), let alone to speculate what specific crisis might trigger the same intensity of concern--and generate as many publications--as the Algerian conflict and May 1968 under de Gaulle's Republic.

We would like to express our thanks to Miss Mary Schofield for her friendly advice and expert cataloguing of the complicated materials listed in this volume. We are also grateful to Ms. Liselotte Hofmann for offering her exceptional skills as editor, bibliographer, and typist, which have greatly enhanced the final stages of our work.

Grete Heinz

Agnes F. Peterson

October 1973

ABBREVIATIONS

C. F. T. C.	Confédération française des travailleurs chrétiens
C. G. T.	Confédération générale du travail
C. N. R. S.	Centre national de la recherche scientifique
F. E. N.	Fédération de l'éducation nationale
F. G. D. S.	Fédération de la gauche démocratique et socialiste
F. L. N.	Front de libération nationale
I. N. S. E. E.	Institut national de la statistique et des études économiques
ML	Main Library (Stanford University)
M. R. P.	Mouvement républicain populaire
O. A. S.	Organisation de l'armée secrète
O. R. T. F.	Office de la radio-télévision française
P. C. F.	Parti communiste français
P. S. U.	Parti socialiste unifié
R. P. F.	Rassemblement du peuple français
S. F. I. O.	Section française de l'internationale ouvrière
S. N. E. - Sup.	Syndicat national de l'enseignement supérieur
U. D. - Ve	Union des démocrates pour la Cinquième République
U. D. R.	Union des démocrates pour la république
U. D. T.	Union démocratique du travail
U. N. E. F.	Union nationale des étudiants de France
U. N. R.	Union pour la nouvelle république
U. N. R. - U. D. T.	Union pour la nouvelle république — Union démocratique du travail

The French Fifth Republic
Continuity and Change, 1966-1970

PART I: NON-SERIAL PUBLICATIONS

1 ADAMAFIO, TAWIA. French nuclear tests in the Sahara. Accra, CPP National Headquarters, Bureau of Information and Publicity [1960]. 11 p.

Sept. 1960 speech by Secretary General of Convention People's Party of Ghana protesting French plans for imminent Sahara underground nuclear test.

2 AFRICAN NATIONAL CONGRESS. An open letter to the French Embassy [Dar es Salaam, concerning the action taken by the French Government in regard to Paul Vergès, a national of Réunion Island]. [Dar es Salaam, 1966] 2 l.

Amnesty plea for Paul Vergès, charged with demanding independence for Réunion Island in articles published by "Témoignage chrétien" 1961-63.

3 AGERON, CHARLES ROBERT. Histoire de l'Algérie contemporaine (1830-1966). 2e éd. . . . Paris, Presses universitaires de France, 1966. 128 p. ("Que sais-je?" 400) Bibliography: p. [127].

Last 20 pages deal with Fifth Republic years (end of Algerian war, independence). On the basis of the country's earlier history, independence is viewed as inevitable.

4 L'agression israélienne et ses conséquences. Par Maurice Bardèche, François Duprat, Pierre Fontaine, Paul Rassinier. Paris, Défense de l'Occident, 1967. xvii, 80 p. (Défense de l'Occident, nouv. sér., 15. année, no. 64) Bibliographical footnotes.

Bardèche's introductory article attacks Israel as creation of "Jewish international capitalism" incapable of maintaining itself except through control of entire Mideast. Among articles on conflict are several identifying by name French supporters of Jewish cause and indicating stand of different political groups. Fontaine and Rassinier equate U.S. and British support of Israel with desire for Jewish control of Near East oil.

5 AILLERET, CHARLES. L'aventure atomique française. Paris, B. Grasset, 1968. 405 p.

Memoirs of general having prime responsibility for development of atomic weapons in Fourth and Fifth Republic. Final 100 pages deal with Fifth Republic, describing preparation of nuclear tests in Sahara 1958-60. Ailleret died in 1968.

6 ALASSEUR, REMY, JACQUELINE FOURASTIÉ, and JEAN GUILHEM. Documents pour l'élaboration d'indices du coût de la vie en France de 1910 à 1965. Sous la direction de Jean Fourastié. Paris, A. Colin, 1970. 642 p. tables (1 fold.). (Ecole pratique des hautes études, VIe section et Laboratoire d'économétrie du Conservatoire national des arts et métiers. Etudes et mémoires 66) Bibliography: p. [633]-635.

Prices for individual items chosen from the 213 included in I.N.S.E.E.'s standard budget are based both on I.N.S.E.E.'s figures and on commercial catalogues. Prices of such services as transportation (railroad, bus, taxi), postage, telephone, laundry, barber, and theater are also covered, and results for different budgets, weighting of items compared.

7 ALBRECHT-CARRIE, RENE. Britain and France; adaptations to a changing context of power. Garden City, N.Y., Doubleday, 1970. xv, 652 p. maps (part col.). Bibliography: p. [626]-634.

Only final pages of this history of Franco-British relations concern Fifth Republic.

8 ALEXANDRE, PHILIPPE. Chroniques des jours moroses, 1969-1970. Paris, Solar, 1971. 307 p.

Political chronicle of first year and a half of Gaullist succession, struggle with de Gaulle's heritage in Gaullist ranks, and gradual change in political style. Books ends with posthumous publication of second volume of "Mémoires de l'espoir."

9 ALEXANDRE, PHILIPPE. Le duel: De Gaulle-Pompidou. Paris, B. Grasset, 1970. 420 p. Bibliography: p. [417]-418.

Journalist's inside account of 25 years' relations between de Gaulle and Pompidou, based on personal testimony (given Sept. 1969-July 1970) of 90 persons, many of them high in government. Names of sources are not given, but utterances, with names, extensively quoted. Main episodes are R.P.F., de Gaulle's return to power, 1965 presidential election, and May 1968-June 1969 period, to which last half of book is devoted, documenting the role of each of the two men and carefully tracing the irreparable split between them. Excellent political history of Fifth Republic, with lively portraits of dozens of Gaullists as well as non-partisan portraits of the two men.

10 ALEXANDRE, PHILIPPE. L'Elysée en péril, 2-30 mai 1968. Avec la collaboration de Raoul Tubiana.... Paris, Fayard, 1969. 335 p. (Grands documents contemporains)

Inside story of May events seen through centers of political action. Author interviewed 160 top government officials, Gaullist and opposition politicians, and trade unionists who played an active role, including Pompidou and Debré. Story centers on Ministries of Education, Interior, Justice, Social Affairs, and Treasury, office of prime minister, Assembly, central offices of C.G.T. and C.F.D.T. Actions of Mendès-France, Mitterrand, Monnerville, de Gaulle during escapade to Baden-Baden to see Massu are followed in detail.

11 ALLIANCE FRANCE-ISRAEL. Hommage au Général Pierre Koenig. Paris, Editions Alliance France-Israël, 1969. 16 p.

At this Jan. 29, 1969 celebration of Koenig's 70th birthday, there are speakers representing both Gaullist and anti-Gaullist views, including Alain Poher. Koenig's own speech appeals for friendlier French policy toward Israel.

12 AMBLER, JOHN STEWARD. The government and politics of France. With Lawrence Scheinman. Boston, Houghton Mifflin, 1971. xiii, 257 p. fold. map. (Contemporary government series) Includes bibliography.

Well-documented, up-to-date work integrating recent research, with many international comparisons. Most of material deals with Fifth Republic. There are chapters on: French political tradition, society and politics, political culture, parties and elections, governmental institutions (dual executive, parliament, administration), political processes, and foreign policy (this chapter was written by Scheinman). Author spent 1969 in France.

13 AMME, CARL H. NATO without France; a strategic appraisal. Foreword by Charles Burton Marshall. Stanford, Calif., Hoover Institution on War, Revolution, and Peace, 1967. xvi, 195 p. illus., maps. (Hoover Institution publications, 67) Bibliographical references.

Includes description of current Gaullist views on Atlantic Alliance and withdrawal of its military forces from NATO. Emphasis is on the use and control of nuclear, particularly tactical nuclear, weapons.

14 AMSTERDAM. MUSEUM FODOR. Parijs mei-juni '68. Tentoonstelling onder auspiciën van het Internationaal instituut voor sociale geschiedenis, Amsterdam '69. [Amsterdam, 1969] xliii p. facsims. Includes bibliography.

Guide to exhibit of material on May 1968 events collected by International Institute of Social History and now available there. In addition to facsimiles of revolutionary appeals, posters, many of them not reproduced elsewhere, there is a chronology, excellent list of abbreviations, and bibliographies on: background of period; pamphlets by participant groups; revolutionary press (45 items); documentary collections (32 items); journalistic reports (14 items); eyewitness accounts (6 items); ideological books, political books, interpretations (46 items); books on universities, labor movement, Internationale situationniste; poems; and special issues of periodicals. Titles of 51 films and 15 records complete this survey.

15 ANALYSES ET DOCUMENTS; FICHES CLASSEES DE DOCUMENTATION. De l'occupation des usines à la campagne électorale. Paris, 1968. [389]-405 p. (Its No. 155, spécial mai 1968)

Intended as fact sheets for workers and revolutionary militants, issue gives facts on two aspects of May-June 1968 struggle: (1) labor movement and strikes--Grenelle agreement, continuation of strikes, tactics of C.G.T., C.F.D.T., P.C.F., and P.S.U.; (2) student activities and student organizations May 13-31.

16 ANALYSES ET DOCUMENTS; FICHES CLASSEES DE DOCUMENTATION. Les grèves sauvages en Europe occidentale. Paris, 1970. 51 p. (Its Nouv. sér., no. 182-183, mars 1970)

Background of wildcat strike movements in France, Italy, Germany, Great Britain, Scandinavia as response to collaboration of trade unions with government, hiring of immigrant workers (15 per cent of French labor force) and women, specific instances of such strikes and their effects on trade unions and economy.

17 ANALYSES ET DOCUMENTS; FICHES CLASSEES DE DOCUMENTATION. Le mouvement de mai: de l'étranglement à la répression. Paris, 1968. [121]-145 p. (Its No. 156 spécial)

June 27, 1968 issue covers government repression of uprising, organization of elections, and continuation of strikes at Renault, Peugeot, and Citroën until ended by labor organizations. Publication's own interpretation of revolution's collapse and need for a more militant avant-garde than reformist P.C.F. is voiced.

18 ANARCHY (periodical). The May days in France. London, 1968. 193-224 p. (Its No. 89, July 1968)

Eyewitness report by British journalist, followed by May 23-June 14, 1968 interviews with Daniel Cohn-Bendit as most vocal exponent of anarchists in revolutionary movement.

19 ANCEL, MARC. La défense sociale nouvelle, un mouvement de politique criminelle humaniste. . . . 2e éd. . . . Paris, Editions Cujas, 1966. 392 p. (Publications du Centre d'études de défense sociale de l'Institut de droit comparé de l'Université de Paris, 1) Bibliographical footnotes.

Completely revised and updated version of 1954 edition. New social defense is a concept of crime prevention to protect both society and criminals, replacing idea of retribution with that of treatment: judicial humanism. Work draws on criminal law reform and research world-wide, with special emphasis on current status of French penology. Author is jurist and vice president of Société internationale de défense sociale.

20 ANDERSON, MALCOLM. Government in France; an introduction to the executive power. Oxford, New York, Pergamon Press, 1970. xii, 217 p. illus. (part fold.), maps. (The Commonwealth and international library. Governments of Western Europe) Includes bibliographical references.

Except for chapter on historical and constitutional background, work concentrates on Fifth Republic political institutions: presidential power, including that of president's immediate assistants; role of prime minister, ministries; relation between government organs and administration (civil service); special jurisdictional problems; regional reform. Government involvement in education, research, recruitment of civil service, role of Ecole nationale d'administration are presented with help of organizational charts. Parliament, pressure groups, elections are viewed only as "political environment." Material goes up to July 1969.

21 ANDERSON, ROBERT T., and BARBARA GALLATIN ANDERSON. Bus stop to Paris: the transformation of a French village. Garden City, N.Y., Anchor Books, 1965. 303 p. Bibliography: p. 291-292. ML

American sociologists' study of village of Wissous, 10 miles south of Paris, in immediate vicinity of Orly airport. Transformation from isolated agricultural community to fringe of Paris suburbia is changing social stratification from local to national lines. Authors lived in village 1957-59.

22 ANDREY, BERNARD, and LOUIS MILLET. La révolution universitaire; l'expérience de l'Institut de psychologie de Grenoble. Grenoble, Bordas, 1968. 75 p. (Collection Etudes supérieures, 5)

Andrey is professor of psycho-pathology and Millet is professor of social psychology and philosophy at Grenoble. Work describes student-faculty efforts at Institute, May-July 1968, to restructure teaching of psychology and allow greater student participation. Includes excerpts from committee reports. Non-violent student revolt erupted May 15.

23 ANDRIEU, RENE. Les communistes et la révolution. Paris, Julliard, 1968. 317 p.

Counter-arguments against conflicting indictment of P.C.F. either for betraying the "revolution," as claimed by leftist and student groups, or for threatening to seize power and plunge country into civil war, as claimed by Gaullists. "Humanité" editor reviews Communist Party's position and actions since 1930's, its attitude toward de Gaulle, upholding of democratic socialism and alliance with left, avoidance of irresponsible incitement to civil war. P.C.F.'s "French road to socialism" is defined with emphasis on the realism of its aims and methods. Work concluded July 1968. Appendices with several television discussion texts, one May 25, 1968.

24 ANDRIEU, RENE, and JEAN EFFEL. En feuilletant l'histoire de France du Front populaire à nos jours. Paris, A. Michel, 1969. 237 p.

Narration by Andrieu, cartoons by Effel. Events are arranged by year up to June 1969. Andrieu is editor of "Humanité."

25 ANDRO, PIERRE, ALAIN DAUVERGNE, and LOUIS-MARIE LAGOUTTE. Le mai de la révolution. Paris, Julliard, 1968. 251 p.

Chronicle of events in France May 1-June 14, 1968, with notes on simultaneous events outside country.

26 ANGELI, CLAUDE, and RENE BACKMANN. Les polices de la nouvelle société. Paris, F. Maspéro, 1971. 132 p. (Petite collection Maspéro, 94)

Collection of articles by "Canard enchaîné" and "Nouvel observateur" journalists, 1969-71, describing structure of police forces, operations whereby track is kept of subversive individuals, and how repression is applied, with case histories of such interventions.

27 L'année politique, économique, sociale et diplomatique. 24-27, 1968-1971. Paris, Presses universitaires de France, 1969-72.

For detailed description of contents of this important reference work, see French Fifth Republic Bibliography, 1. Election results for June 1968 are in 1968 volume and those for 1969 presidential election in 1969 volume.

28 Annuaire de la presse et de la publicité. 80.-84. année; 1968-1971. Paris, Société d'édition de l'Annuaire de la presse, 1969-72.

In addition to classified listing of newspapers, weeklies, monthlies, and information on press associations and journalists, has current facts about government and parliamentary composition, administration of radio-television networks.

29 Annuaire de l'Afrique du Nord. v. 1-9, 1962-1970. Paris, Editions du Centre national de la recherche scientifique, 1962-71.

Year's political and economic developments for region as a whole and Algeria, Morocco, Libya, and Tunisia individually. Chronology of North African events, political, diplomatic, and economic reports, texts of selected government documents. Systematic bibliography of books and articles, book reviews.

30 ANTOINE, GERALD, and JEAN-CLAUDE PASSERON. La réforme de l'Université. Avant-propos de Raymond Aron. Paris, Calmann-Lévy, 1966. 289 p. (Questions d'actualité) Bibliographical footnotes.

Separate essays--"Réforme ou renaissance de l'université" and "Conservatisme et novation à l'université"--the first by the rector of Orleans University and the second by a young sociologist from Nanterre Faculté des Lettres. Antoine uses personal administrative experiences to propose "renaissance" rather than "reform" of universities, centering on solidarity of entire educational system, need for better administration and decentralization, more attention to both professional and intellectual preparation of students. In contrast to this middle educational stand, Passeron insists on crisis of higher education resulting from breakdown of coherent view of university's function developed in 1880's and incoherence of values and reforms proposed from within and outside university, centering around democratization of enrollment and pedagogic methods, better adaptation to economic needs. Passeron presents results of questionnaire on proposed abolition of "agrégation" with over half of faculty respondents opposed to reform. This work is of special interest as one of pre-1968 critiques of higher education.

31 ANTOMARCHI, XAVIER. Le général raconté aux enfants. Dessins de Jean Schoumann. Paris, Julliard, 1968. unpaged. M L

Simplified, tongue-in-cheek pictorial biography of General de Gaulle, through 1968, with illustrations in children's book style.

32 Apprendre à faire la paix; les dimensions nouvelles d'une éducation pour la paix. Paris, Editions Fleurus, 1969. 172 p. (Cahiers d'éducateurs, 8)

Individual contributions by Catholic educators or militants in social action movements on teaching of pacifism and civic responsibility inside and outside schools.

33 Approches pour une régionalisation des universités. Paris, Libertés universitaires régionales, 1968. 40 p. (Document de travail provisoire) M L

Attacking both Communist-dominated university faculties, student leaders for using university crisis as pretext for social upheaval and government for its totalitarian control over education, Libertés universitaires régionales group proposes university decentralization rather than mere deconcentration by shifting control and financial support to local political bodies, private organizations, industry, and families, leaving national Ministry of Education only residual function of supplementing local resources and maintaining educational standards. Creation of private and independent universities is urged as further barrier against state monopoly.

34 Après mai 1968, les plans de la bourgeoisie et le mouvement révolutionnaire. Rédigé par des militants des Comités d'action Sorbonne, Vincennes, Nanterre. Paris, F. Maspéro, 1969. 31 p. M L

Analysis of French bourgeoisie's counteroffensive since May 1968 through educational, industrial, and regional reform, followed by appeal to continue revolutionary movement through elaboration of revolutionary theory which was lacking in 1968, in line with Chinese cultural revolution.

35 APRES-DEMAIN; JOURNAL MENSUEL DE DOCUMENTATION POLITIQUE. Le rôle du président. Paris, 1969. 31 p. (Its June 1969 issue)

On eve of June 1969 presidential election, anti-Gaullist politicians and political scientists, among them André Hauriou and Pierre Avril, discuss Gaullist heritage and possible changes in presidency.

36 ARAUJO, BRAZ JOSE DE. Le Plan Fouchet et l'union politique européenne. Nancy, Centre européen universitaire de Nancy [1967?]. ix, 56, xxix p. (Université de Nancy. Publication du Centre européen universitaire. Collection des mémoires, no. 25) Bibliography: p. [52]-55.

Brazilian student's "mémoire" retraces stages of and press reaction to French proposal to European Community for political union, Nov. 1959 to 1962. Fouchet was French representative on Commission politique, in whose name he presented first version of plan July 1961. Its second version fully expressed de Gaulle's personal views and was defeated Jan. 1962. Subsequent European issues (NATO, British admission to Common Market) are briefly reviewed. Appendix juxtaposes two versions of Fouchet Plan and proposals by other members.

37 ARDAGH, JOHN. The new French Revolution; a social and economic survey of France 1945-1967. London, Secker and Warburg, 1968. xiv, 482 p. 16 plates, illus., maps, ports. Bibliography: p. [463]-465.

Comprehensive and well-informed survey of French postwar economy and society by London "Times" correspondent, concentrating on changes that came to fruition in Fifth Republic years. Politics are treated only incidentally. Book was compiled 1966-67, stopping just short of spring 1968. It is unusually knowledgeable about recent developments and based on a synthesis of on-the-spot investigation, talks with prominent figures in the field, and current studies, with excellent chapters on planning, individual industries and agriculture, the realities of regional and urban planning and decentralization (details on Paris, Grenoble, Toulouse), daily life and leisure, manifestations of Americanization in the French family and youth, birth control. Excellent summaries of status of educational reform and resistance thereto, though imminent explosion is not anticipated. Review of intellectual trends and survey of arts and letters, including movies. Good basic bibliography.

38 ARGENSON, MARC PIERRE, MARQUIS D'. La république fictive. Paris, Promotion et édition, 1967. 160 p.

Evolution from Fourth to Fifth Republic and mystification of 1958 Constitution, which is republican in wording but perverted to fit de Gaulle's personal rule (the "fictitious" republic of title), as author proves for individual articles. Pluses and minuses of Fifth Republic are equitably assessed and constitutional reforms proposed for needs of post-Gaullism.

39 ARMAND, LOUIS. Simples propos. Paris, Fayard, 1968. 311 p. ML

Collected essays, speeches on different aspects of modern civilization--scientific progress, education, technology and technocracy, cultural and technological arguments in favor of European unification.

40 ARMAND, LOUIS, and VALERY GISCARD D'ESTAING. Quel avenir pour l'Europe? Dialogue entre Louis Armand de l'Académie française et Valéry Giscard d'Estaing. Paris, Département des relations publiques de Publicis conseil, 1969. 24 p. ports.

Complete text of discussion between two self-styled liberals (in French sense) and pro-Europeans of urgent tasks of European policy, notably common currency, unification of education. Discussion was sponsored Dec. 19, 1968 by Publicis conseil. Photographs of participants and other members of Council, mainly industrialists.

41 L'armée: service national au service du capital. Paris, F. Maspéro, 1970. 31 p. (Cahiers "Rouge." Document Rouge spécial)

Current conditions of military training and situation of soldiers, followed by Ligue communiste's own proposals for revolutionizing military service.

42 ARNAUD-AMELLER, PAULE. La France à l'épreuve de la concurrence internationale 1951-1966. Paris, A. Colin, 1970. 123 p. (Fondation nationale des sciences politiques. Service d'étude de l'activité économique. Recherches sur l'économie française, 15) Includes bibliography.

Domestic and international causes of French foreign trade disequilibria--mainly low export propensity--at time of growing international exchanges and freeing from government restrictions. Appendices summarize French ties with international economic and monetary organization, legislation on foreign exchange.

43 ARNAUD-AMELLER, PAULE. Mesures économiques et financières de décembre 1958. Paris, A. Colin, 1968. 332 p. illus. (Fondation nationale des sciences politiques. Service d'étude de l'activité économique. Recherches sur l'économie française, 11) Bibliography: p. 305-[311].

Devaluation of franc, freeing of exchanges, balancing of budget at beginning of Fifth Republic, and longer-range (through 1962) successes and failures in promoting economic growth and stabilizing prices as reflected in investment, foreign trade, price level, structural changes in economy for those years. June 1958-Dec. 1962 chronology of social and economic measures.

44 ARNAVON, CYRILLE. Précis et procès des humanités. Paris, Hachette, 1968. 134 p. (Classiques Hachette) ML

Professor of American literature at Nanterre describes shortcomings of language and literature department curricula and proposes ways to make humanities more useful for training of secondary school teachers as well as for students' personal development (e.g., sex education) on the basis of his own experiences. Interesting discussion of place of professor's political opinions in teaching as part of renovation of humanist pedagogy. Specific reforms are proposed for university libraries, administration.

45 ARON, RAYMOND. Aspects sociologiques des notions de quantité et de qualité en fait d'éducation. Paris, Institut international de planification, 1966. ii, 25 p. (Les principes de la planification de l'éducation: conférences et discussions no. 6) ML

Problems of reconciling productivist, humanist, and democratic objectives of education in advanced societies, where "quality education"--though differently defined in each country--is demanded by growing numbers. Conciliation is possible at best in very wealthy societies.

46 ARON, RAYMOND. De la condition historique du sociologue. Leçon inaugurale au Collège de France prononcée le 1er décembre 1970. Paris, Gallimard, 1971. 66 p.

Introductory lecture to course on "Critique de la pensée sociologique" gives personal testimony on Aron's involvement in sociology in relation to French school of Durkheim and Mauss and German Max Weber, with whom Aron shares struggle to balance political and scholarly obligations.

47 ARON, RAYMOND. La défense et la rénovation de l'université française; articles de Raymond Aron parus dans le Figaro, mai-juin 1968. Paris, 1968. 8 p.

Articles appearing in May 15 and 16, June 11-15, 1968 issues of "Le Figaro" express intense dismay at student revolt, but remind of his earlier warnings that French universities faced collapse under onslaught of mass higher education. Includes selected correspondence. For more complete set of articles, see no. 53 below.

48 ARON, RAYMOND. De Gaulle, Israël et les Juifs. Paris, Plon, 1968. 187 p. (Tribune libre)

Dec. 1967 comments on de Gaulle's recent press conference calling Jews a dominating people, a remark that might rekindle anti-Semitism in France. Other chapters reproduce "Figaro" articles on Israel and Jews, his personal relations to Zionism as a non-religious Jew.

49 ARON, RAYMOND. Les désillusions du progrès; essai sur la dialectique de la modernité. Paris, Calmann-Lévy, 1969. xxiii, 375 p. ("Liberté de l'esprit")

Body of work written 1964-65 for Encyclopedia Britannica on modern industrial societies. Dialectics of these societies on either side of the Iron Curtain revolve around three axes: tension between aspirations toward economic, social, and political equality and need for technical and political hierarchy as function of technical efficiency, aggravated by residual racial and ethnic inequalities; conflict between philosophy of liberty, full personality development and strict discipline of industrial organization, weight of mass media (poor prospects for equalization through education, worker self-administration); and finally, tension between universality of modern science, technology, and desire for national independence, even at price of unequal development, anarchic international relations. 1969 preface, 1967 afterword emphasize Aron's scepticism toward all revolutionary ardor, including recent student revolt.

50 ARON, RAYMOND. D'une Sainte Famille à l'autre; essais sur les marxismes imaginaires. Paris, Gallimard, 1969. 319 p. (Les Essais, 146)

Three essays on different facets of present-day Marxism: (1) Nov. 1964 review of Sartre's "Critique de la raison dialectique" as best representative of existentialist version of Marxism, centering on Marx's early writings; (2) lengthy 1967-68 disquisition on Althusser representing a "pseudo-structuralist" interpretation centering on "Das Kapital," which impoverishes Marx's contribution by raising the theory of surplus value to the scientific pillar of philosophical structure and rejecting empirical verification (interesting comments on how existentialist and structural streams of interpretation joined forces in 1968); (3) reproduction of UNESCO lecture, May 1968, commemorating 150th anniversary of Marx's birth.

51   ARON, RAYMOND. L'idée européenne; du discours de Zurich au Marché commun. Zürich, 1968. 16 p. (Winston Churchill memorial lecture 1967/68) "Sonderabdruck aus 'Schweizer Monatshefte' 48. Jahr, Heft 3, Juni 1968."

Talk at 2e Conférence Winston Churchill, Lausanne University, Dec. 8, 1967, tracing Common Market's evolution from a vehicle of utopian hopes to an institution of limited economic, political, and cultural scope, into which British admission has no great significance.

52   ARON, RAYMOND. The industrial society; three essays on ideology and development. New York, Praeger, 1967. 183 p. ML

Translation of "Trois essais sur l'âge industriel" (1966), written 1961-64. Last essay restates in contemporary terms Aron's controversial claim made in 1955 about the end of the age of ideologies in advanced industrial societies and answers his recent critics.

53   ARON, RAYMOND. La révolution introuvable; réflexions sur la révolution de mai. Paris, Fayard, 1968. 187 p. (En toute liberté)

July 1968 exchange between Aron (who gave up sociology chair at Sorbonne Jan. 1968) and Alain Duhamel, in which Aron expresses dismay at recent events, whose "revolutionary" character he dismisses, while admitting that it could easily have destroyed a delicately balanced, basically liberal society like France. Other intellectuals are attacked for their blindly enthusiastic support of student movement, and problems raised by Bourdieu's "Les héritiers" as to anti-democratic elements of French universities realistically assessed. Universities' institutional rigidity and student-professor barriers criticized, but May revolt's proposals seen as wrong approach. Revolution is equated with psychodrama, ideology mere rehash of pre-Marxist socialist utopianism and French-style anarchy, which momentarily caught fancy of large number of Frenchmen. De Gaulle's response to crisis and Gaullist electoral victory presage his eventual defeat. Final section reproduces "Figaro" articles of May 15, 16, and 19, June 4, 5, 10-16, 19, and 28, 1968, assessing political significance of May events and desirability of university reform urged by student revolt. English translation, "The elusive revolution; anatomy of a student revolt" (New York, Praeger, 1969), has introduction reappraising and reconfirming conclusions drawn a year earlier.

FOR ADDITIONAL WORKS BY AND ABOUT RAYMOND ARON, SEE AUTHOR INDEX

54   ARON, ROBERT, ed. L'histoire contemporaine depuis 1945. Avec la collaboration de Henri Amouroux et al. Paris, Larousse, 1969. 400 p. illus. (part col.), ports. (part col.).

Individual chapters on major nations, with good survey of French history during Fourth and Fifth Republic by Pierre Viansson-Ponté, including May 1968 events. Other chapters on European integration, decolonization, daily life, emphasize French concerns and experiences in these fields.

55   ARON, ROBERT, ed. Histoire de notre temps. Textes présentés par Robert Aron. Paris, Plon, 1967. 1 v. facsims.

Large proportion of texts deals with pre-1958 episodes. For Fifth Republic there is personal narrative by Geneviève Bailac about siege of Bab-el-Oued, Mar. 1962, and information about Ben Barka affair by Roger Muratet.

56   Art and confrontation; France and the arts in an age of change. Translated from the French by Nigel Foxell. London, Studio Vista, 1970. 201 p. illus. (Student library) Includes bibliographical references.

Individual essays by nine French art critics (Jean Cassou, Michel Ragon, André Fermigier, Gilbert Lascault, Gérald Gassiot-Talabot, Raymonde Moulin, Pierre Gaudibert, René Micha, and Alain Jouffroy) on relation between painting, sculpture, architecture, cinema, etc. and revolutionary goals of May 1968. Of special interest is the problem of how artists can escape commercial ties without being taken over by society. One essay concerns French art education and need for new creative outlets.

57   ASSELAIN, JEAN CHARLES. Le budget de l'éducation nationale, 1952-1967. Préf. de Hubert Brochier. Paris, Presses universitaires de France, 1969. 270 p. illus. (Travaux et recherches de la Faculté de droit et des sciences économiques de Paris. Série "Sciences économiques," no. 7) Includes bibliography.

General statistics on growth of student population, trends and breakdown of education expenditures over time, unit costs for different types of institutions, statistics on student/teacher ratios, investment in equipment (recent plans), and government financing of scholarships.

58   ASSOCIATION D'ETUDE POUR L'EXPANSION DE LA RECHERCHE SCIENTIFIQUE. Pour une école nouvelle; formation des maîtres et recherche en éducation. Actes du Colloque d'Amiens, mars 1968. Paris, Dunod, 1969. 470 p.

Colloquium attended by 600 educators and educational administrators (list appended) as followup of Association's Colloque de Caen on university reform held in 1966. This volume reproduces reports, debates, final declaration, concluding address by current minister of education, Alain Peyrefitte, concurring with proposals for a "new school." In appendix is communication by Alain Geismar, Syndicat national de l'enseignement supérieur secretary general, criticizing Gaullist reforms embodied in Fouchet university reform and threatening students' street action. Subjects of reports are: (1) goals of education; (2) cultural development of students; (3) administrative restructuring of educational establishments; (4) teacher training; (5) pedagogic innovation and research (comments by Bourdieu on educational system's rejection or recuperation of innovation and need to understand system's internal logic).

59   ASSOCIATION D'ETUDE POUR L'EXPANSION DE L'ENSEIGNEMENT SUPERIEUR. De l'université aux universités; octobre 1968-janvier 1971. Paris, A. Colin, 1971. 815 p. illus. (Its Cahiers des universités françaises, 1)

Documentary source for higher education reform initiated by Faure's Nov. 1968 "loi d'orientation." Antecedents, text of law, subsequent decrees for setting up "unités d'enseignement et de recherches" (U.E.R.) in all academies, election procedures, statutes of some of new units, such as Université de droit, d'économie et de sciences sociales de Paris (Paris now has 13 separate units), organization of newly created Centres universitaires, new regulations on diplomas and curricula. Chronology of decrees, Oct. 1968-Dec. 1970. Previous title of "Cahiers" is "Revue de l'enseignement supérieur."

60   ASSOCIATION EUROPEENNE D'HISTOIRE CONTEMPORAINE. Guide de la recherche en histoire contemporaine, tome 1. Publié avec le concours de l'Institut des hautes études européennes de Strasbourg. Strasbourg, 1970. 176 p.

Listing of research centers and historical journals published in France (p. 71-140), with comparable information for seven other European countries. For each research institution, there are data on location, main purpose, administration, publications.

61   ASSOCIATION FRANÇAISE DE SCIENCE POLITIQUE. L'état de la science politique en France. Débat introduit par Serge

Hurtig. Paris, 1969. 45 l. (Entretiens du samedi no. 10, mars 1969)

Introductory survey of areas of current concern in French political science and political science methodology, with debate on deficiencies in current research. Problems raised are lack of research tools, poor centralization of data, inadequate research models (controversy about intrinsic conservative bias of U.S. models). Main participants are François Goguel, Maurice Duverger, Alfred Grosser, Alain Lancelot, Georges Lavau, Léo Hamon, Bertrand de Jouvenel in addition to Serge Hurtig.

FOR ADDITIONAL MATERIAL ISSUED BY ASSOCIATION FRANÇAISE DE SCIENCE POLITIQUE, SEE NO. 253

62 ASSOCIATION FRANCE-ALGERIE. Colloque sur la migration algérienne en France, 13, 14, 15 octobre 1966. Paris, 1966. 207 p.

Representatives of French and Algerian governments discuss employment, housing, education, health needs, problems of delinquency of Algerian immigrants. As of 1966, there were over half a million in France, about 100,000 of them children. Statistics go up to 1965/66. Included is list of associations active in assisting Algerian immigrants. Organ of Association is monthly "France-Algérie" (see French Fifth Republic Bibliography, 1, no. 1969).

63 ASSOCIATION FRANCE-ISRAEL. France-Israël; le livre de la fidélité. Paris, Association France-Israël, 1971. 317 p.

Affirmations of State of Israel on its 23d anniversary by government spokesmen (Hamon, Catroux, Triboulet) and opposition leaders (Pineau, René Mayer, Jean-Claude Schreiber, General Stehlin). List of supporters appended.

64 ASSOCIATION POUR LA CONSERVATION ET LA REPRODUCTION PHOTOGRAPHIQUE DE LA PRESSE. Catalogue de microfilms reproduisant des périodiques, journaux et revues, no. 8-9, 1969-1971. Paris, A.C.R.P.P., 1969-71. 2 v.

Many of periodical files listed antedate Fifth Republic. Among newspapers and journals compiled in this cumulative catalogue are files for Fifth Republic years unavailable or incomplete at Hoover Institution, such as "L'Avenir de la Bretagne," 1958-67; "Combat," 1944-69; "Economie et humanisme," 1952-69; "Lettres françaises," 1944-69; "Témoignage chrétien," 1944-69. There are also several current regional dailies, such as "La République du Centre," "Voix du Nord."

FOR ADDITIONAL MATERIAL ISSUED BY A.C.R.P.P., SEE NOS. 482, 484 (B), 485, 880, 1137

65 ASTIER DE LA VIGERIE, EMMANUEL D'. Portraits. Paris, Gallimard, 1969. 348 p. ports., facsims.

Portraits and interviews reproduced from monthly "Evénement," 1966-68, of which Astier was editor. In addition to artists, writers, actors, foreign statesmen sketched, there are French political figures: Mendès-France, Marcel Barbu, Louis Vallon, André Malraux, Valéry Giscard d'Estaing, and Edgar Faure. Good photographs. "Evénement" discontinued after Astier's death in 1969. See no. 1172.

66 ASTROLABE (periodical). La droite? Paris, 1972. (Its No. 12, mars 1972)

Responses to questionnaire by 14 respondents on concept of "La droite": its interpretation of human nature, hierarchy, whether reaction or conservatism, ties to fascism, economic liberalism, Catholic integrism, its permanent values. Among respondents are René Rémond, Joseph Folliet, Gabriel Marcel.

67 ATELIER POPULAIRE. Atelier populaire présenté par lui-même, 87 affiches de mai-juin 1968. Paris, Usines, Universités, Union, 1968. 96 p. illus. (Bibliothèque de mai)

Origin of Atelier populaire May 14, 1968, when striking students from Paris Ecole des beaux arts took over its studios. Conception and execution of posters are described. Texts of Atelier's General Assembly resolution and statement of purpose. For most posters, date of conception or occasion identified. Posters are generally colored. Some of full-sized posters at Hoover Library. English edition titled "Posters from the revolution, Paris, May 1968" (London, Dobson Books, 1969).

68 AUBERT, JEAN-PIERRE. Systèmes électoraux et représentation parlementaire; les élections de 1967. Préf. de François Luchaire. Paris, Presses universitaires de France, 1969. 91 p. (Travaux et recherches de la Faculté de droit et des sciences économiques de Paris. Série "Science politique," no. 18)

Hypothetical results for Mar. 1967 legislative elections for four variations of electoral system currently in force: (1) majority vote with two ballots without 10 percent rule, (2) same system with only two top candidates, (3) majority vote with single ballot, and (4) proportional vote. Hypothetical and actual results tabulated and compared, with list of departments and number of deputies as of 1967. Effect of different voting systems on main parties' representation is estimated. For Gaullists, majority vote with single ballot would be most favorable.

69 AUBIER, JEAN MARIE. La république du Général. Paris, Stock, 1973. 285 p.

De Gaulle's conception of political institutions best suited for France before 1958, implementation of his ideas in 1958 Constitution and their partial realization in 11 years of power, response of French people to his "Republic" which in the end gained stability of its own surviving his rule, better adapted to present state of French society and more widely accepted than prior republics. Author is high government official.

70 AUBRAY, GERARD. Georges Pompidou, un portrait. Paris, Fayard, 1969. 1 v. (unpaged).

Campaign biography for 1969 presidential election. Good photographs.

71 AUBURTIN, JEAN. Charles de Gaulle; présentation, repères biographiques, choix de textes, illustrations. [Paris?] Seghers, 1966. 189 p. photogs. (Destins politiques)

Political biography concentrating on pre-1958 years but covering main aims and policies during first seven years of Fifth Republic. Second part of volume reproduces selected 1958-65 speeches.

72 AUCLERT, JEAN PIERRE, and CALVI. Ah quelle année! Paris, Denoël, 1969. 156 p. of illus.

Cartoons illustrating events Oct. 1968-Sept. 1969, including de Gaulle's retirement and man's landing on moon, from leading French newspapers, notably "France-Soir" and "Journal du Dimanche."

73 AVRIL, PIERRE. L'arrondissement devant la réforme administrative. Préf. de R. Drago. Paris, Berger-Levrault, 1970. 183 p. (L'Administration nouvelle) Bibliography: p. 175-179. ML

Historical background of arrondissements, the smallest French administrative units, of which there are now 322 in metropolitan France, list of arrondissements, population, area, number of communes within their boundaries. Average population is

120,000, but range is from 7,000 to over one million. Historical role of arrondissement and possible new function analogous to German "Kreis" as link between central administration and local communities, the smallest possible unit for deconcentration.

74 AVRIL, PIERRE. Politics in France. Translated from the French by John Ross. Baltimore, Penguin Books, 1969. 303 p. (A Penguin original) Includes bibliography.

Good introductory work with important facts and figures on French political and administrative institutions, political parties, emphasizing Fifth Republic's place in historical evolution. French title: "Le Gouvernement de la France" (1969). None of material goes beyond 1967.

75 AVRIL, PIERRE. U.D.R. et gaullistes. Paris, Presses universitaires de France, 1971. 95 p. (Dossiers Thémis, 7. Série Partis politiques et groupes de pression)

Brief survey of Gaullist party since 1958: political recruitment, program of loyalty to de Gaulle, role as government majority party, position on political spectrum, organization and Nov. 1967 statutes of Union des démocrates pour la Cinquième République (U.D.-Ve), representation in National Assembly and Senate, with names of Bureau politique members for 1971, sociological breakdown of Gaullist voters in legislative and presidential elections, change of structure after de Gaulle's retirement. Illustrative documents within text.

76 BABY, NICOLAS, and FRANCIS BERTIN. Politique au lycée? Paris, Beauchesne, 1970. 115 p. (Carrefour des jeunes no. 4) ML

Confrontation between a revolutionary Marxist lycée student, who co-founded Comité d'action lycéen at Lycée Henri IV, and a self-styled counterrevolutionary active in Union nationale des lycéens d'action corporative, with surprising convergence of views as to what is wrong with lycées and government reforms. Both describe participation in May 1968 events, discuss effectiveness of Comités d'action lycéens.

77 BAGUENARD, JACQUES, JEAN-CHARLES MAOUT, and RAYMOND MUZELLEC. Le Président de la Ve République. Présentation générale par Jacques Georgel. Paris, A. Colin, 1970. 111 p. (Dossiers U2, 87) Includes bibliography.

Constitutional provisions, decrees, amendments by referendum affecting election of president, his attributes, powers, possibility of removal, relations with prime minister and cabinet, with parliament, judiciary. Results of June 1969 presidential election and constitutional provisions for interim after de Gaulle's withdrawal.

78 BALOUS, SUZANNE. L'action culturelle de la France dans le monde. Préf. de Maurice Genevoix. Paris, Presses universitaires de France, 1970. 190 p. maps, diagrs. Includes bibliography.

Government efforts to support French language outside France, official and unofficial organizations participating in diffusion of French, French culture, French teachers abroad, French language schools, exports of French books, movies, radio-TV programs, exchange of works of art, artists, foreign students in France. Last section reviews cultural efforts in different parts of world.

79 BANON, GABRIEL, and DANIEL HUGUENIN. Le parti de l'entreprise. Paris, Fayard, 1970. 154 p. illus.

Proposals for business ethics and economic growth most suitable for current economic and political environment, with stress on international dimensions of firms. Authors are active in business management and have international ties.

80 BARBIER, J. B. Le pacifisme dans l'histoire de France; de l'an mille à nos jours. Paris, Librairie française, 1966. 466 p.

Pacifists' disastrous influence in France is traced through World War II and dangers of current widespread anti-militarism as guide to foreign policy in the face of continued Communist threat emphasized.

81 BARDECHE, MAURICE, and FRANÇOIS DUPRAT. La comédie de la révolution mai 1968. Paris, 1968. 96 p. (Défense de l'Occident, juin 1968)

Original version of Duprat's "Les journées de mai 68" (see no. 360).

82 BARETS, JEAN. La politique en révolution. Paris, R. Laffont, 1970. 217 p.

Author is head of political club "Technique et démocratie," some of whose specific proposals for short- and medium-range reform are presented, but these are primarily personal reflections on impasse of modern society, capitalist and Communist model, because of priority given to "administration of things" and production rather than psychological human needs. Students' revolt expressed irrational over rational and material priorities, but these priorities were not shared by workers, so that violence at that stage failed to unify Left. Possibility of widespread diffusion of information now permits participatory democracy and in the future psychological rather than material dissatisfaction may be main spur for action.

83 BARJONET, ANDRE. La C.G.T.; histoire, structure, doctrine. Paris, Editions du Seuil, 1968. 193 p. (Politique, 25) Bibliography: p. [184]-186.

Major part of work devoted to C.G.T.'s stand on economic planning, nationalization, Common Market, trade union unity, ties with Communist Party, May 1968 events. Before resignation from C.G.T. May 23, 1968, author was secretary of its Centre d'études économiques et sociales. Book was concluded after resignation.

84 BARJONET, ANDRE. Le Parti communiste français. Paris, J. Didier, 1969. 234 p. (Collection Forum) Bibliography: p. 233-234. ML

Astute, unpolemical dissection of trends in French Communist Party converting it from a revolutionary Marxist force into a reformist organization, culminating in its anti-revolutionary posture in May 1968. At the same time, its Soviet-oriented formation and dogma incomprehensible to the unbelievers have estranged it from rest of French society. As former party functionary, editor of its "Economie et politique" and C.G.T. official who left party May 1968 when its rejection of revolution became evident, author gives inside account of "democratic centralism" control over affiliated organizations, publishing houses, press, relations with youth and intellectuals.

85 BARJONET, ANDRE. La révolution trahie de 1968. Paris, J. Didier, 1968. 44 p.

Exculpation for resignation from C.G.T. and P.C.F. May 23, 1968, because both organizations failed to exploit revolutionary potential of French situation and were blinded by Stalinist dogmatism against importance of student movement and workers' desire for self-administration. Work concluded June 4, 1968.

FOR ADDITIONAL WORKS BY AND ABOUT ANDRE BARJONET, SEE AUTHOR INDEX

86 BARRAL, PIERRE. Les agrariens français de Méline à Pisani. Paris, A. Colin, 1968. 386 p. illus. (Cahiers de la Fondation nationale des sciences politiques, 164) Bibliography: p. 364-[372].

Only last 50 pages deal with problems of modernized agriculture under Fifth Republic, pressure of various agricultural organizations, and government measures, notably Pisani's 1961-66 efforts to bring farmers out of their ghetto of economic underdevelopment and cultural isolation and into Common Market. Excellent list of sources (publications by and on agricultural organizations, press).

87 BARREYRE, FREDERIC. Les derniers mots du Général. Paris, B. Grasset, 1971. 175 p.

De Gaulle witticisms collected during last years of his life, arranged thematically on May 1968 events and their aftermath, 1969 referendum, relations with Pompidou, last year of office, retirement. These remarks were taken down within de Gaulle's political circle.

88 BARRILLON, RAYMOND. La Gauche française en mouvement. Paris, Plon, 1967. 237 p. maps. (Tribune libre)

Unification moves between P.C.F. and other left-wing parties from 1965 presidential election through 1967 legislative elections, in which these tactics bore substantial fruit. 1967 election results are closely scrutinized and positive and negative arguments for permanent alliance between Fédération de la gauche démocrate et socialiste and P.C.F. are weighed. Sept. 1965-July 1967 chronology of unification moves.

89 BARRILLON, RAYMOND. Servan-Schreiber, pour quoi faire? Réflexions sur quelques données de la vie politique en France. Paris, B. Grasset, 1971. 189 p.

Though primarily concerned with Servan-Schreiber's strategy since assuming leadership of Parti radical in Oct. 1969, head of political information service of "Le Monde" studies prospects of a Centrist alliance within political institutions reinforcing polarization between Gaullists and Communist—non-Communist Left by reviewing Center's successes and failures in years preceding and following de Gaulle's retirement.

90 BASSAN, JEAN. Les nouveaux patrons: Robert de Balkany, Jean Davray, Constantin Dragan, Jean Lefebvre, Pierre Lemonnier, Claude Levy, Jean Mantelet, Antoine Riboud, Lars Schmidt et Maurice Varsano. Paris, Fayard, 1969. 265 p.

Interviews with successful industrialists, builders (Balkany is developer of Parly II apartment project), theater producers, bankers.

91 BASSI, MICHEL. Valéry Giscard d'Estaing. Paris, B. Grasset, 1968. 191 p.

Political biography of head of Républicains indépendants and former finance minister by "Figaro" journalist. Among topics are his relations with Pompidou and de Gaulle, presidential ambitions, political and economic views. Appendices include 1967 public opinion poll on popularity of Républicains indépendants and of Giscard d'Estaing personally, and selected 1966-67 statements and articles by the latter.

92 BATAILLON, MARCEL, ANDRE BERGE, and FRANÇOIS WALTER. Rebâtir l'école. Nouv. éd. revue et mise à jour. Paris, Payot, 1969. vii, 355 p. (Collection Etudes et documents Payot. Série sciences humaines) Bibliographical references included in "Notes" (p. [331]-344).

1967 findings of association of parents, medical and educational experts, Défense de la jeunesse scolaire on flaws in French primary and secondary education, described in concrete detail, giving excellent feeling for actuality of French schools and obstacles to democratization. Some experiments for improving teaching summarized. Good bibliographic references. This revised edition has preface and postscript briefly listing 1968-69 reforms.

93 BAUCHET, PIERRE. La planification française, du premier au sixième plan. Paris, Editions du Seuil, 1970 (c1966). 384 p. (Collection Esprit "La Cité prochaine") ML

Revised edition brings material up to date through 1969, especially data respecting Fifth and Sixth Plan, planning in context of Common Market. For original edition, see French Fifth Republic Bibliography, 1, no. 149.

94 BAUDELOT, CHRISTIAN, and ROGER ESTABLET. L'école capitaliste en France. Paris, F. Maspéro, 1971. 336 p. diagrs. (Cahiers libres, 213-214) Includes bibliographical references.

Severest, perhaps most incisive of the many critiques of French (and to a certain extent Western) education: "La forme scolaire dans l'appareil scolaire capitaliste est directement responsable des modalités dans lesquelles celui-ci concourt à la reproduction des rapports de production capitaliste" (p. 298). Attack concentrates on primary and secondary education system to prove that despite recent "democratization," it has remained a two-track system, the "primaire professionnel" (P.P.) forming the working class and that part of the middle class headed for proletarization, or about three-fourths of students, the "secondaire supérieur" (S.S.) intended for bourgeoisie. Each track has its own ideological and pedagogic concepts, between which transition is nearly impossible. Extending years of school attendance only means extension of P.P. network, as is shown by tables of student flow through newly created curricula. Ideology of P.P. track is "petty bourgeois" (not proletarian) in that it proclaims adaptation to society and individual advancement; that of S.S. track envisages humanist goal of cultivated man. Both tracks are now objects of student protest. Author brings out clearly how segregation between two tracks is completed almost at beginning of primary school years by shunting all those who have not learned to read by six and a half years-- almost all children without early contact with middle-class culture--into P.P. network. Differences in content and spirit of two tracks are exemplified in teaching of French language and literature, history in upper grades. Bourdieu's "Les héritiers" is criticized as too limited in its explanation of educational inequalities, Communist-sponsored plans for educational reform by extension of unified school are attacked as unrealistic and confusing for teachers' unions. No mention of education in Soviet Union, Eastern Europe; only Chinese model presented as form of non-capitalist education.

95 BAUDOT, JACQUES, JEAN-MICHEL DESMOTTES, and CLAUDE VIMONT. Conditions de vie et d'emploi des jeunes travailleurs; résultats de deux enquêtes. Préf. d'Alfred Sauvy. Paris, Presses universitaires de France, 1968. 173 p. tables, charts, maps. (Institut national d'études démographiques. Travaux et documents. Cahier no. 50) ML

First investigation based on sample of 4,292 unmarried male and female workers and apprentices, aged 15-24 (out of total of a million young French workers), on problems of vocational qualification, working conditions, salary, mobility, need for special housing. Second study is limited to 19-year-old workers beginning their military training: adequacy of vocational preparation, relation between families' social status and education.

96 BAUMIER, JEAN. Les grandes affaires françaises, des 200 familles aux 200 managers. Paris, Julliard, 1967. 251 p. Bibliographical footnotes.

Unpolemical description of those members of pre-1939 "ruling families" of French industries still active, such as Michelin, Rothschild, Wendel, and newly rich, such as Marcel Dassault, and Marcel Bleustein-Blanchet. Main part of book centers on transition of power from families to holding companies run by managers (e.g., Schneider, Bull, Pechiney-Saint-Gobain) according to U.S. pattern. Final section presents nationalized industries, similarly run by top-level civil servant managers

(Pierre Massé, Guillaumat, François Bloch-Lainé, etc.), such as atomic energy, utilities, Renault, Caisse des dépots.

97 BEAUFRE, ANDRE. Bâtir l'avenir. Paris, Calmann-Lévy, 1967. 256 p. (Questions d'actualité)

General's reflections on methods of predicting future, likely developments in demography, economics, technology, political institutions, key possibilities in relations between major powers, and best way for each country to plan short- and long-range strategy. No specific recommendations are made for France.

98 BEAUFRE, ANDRE. L'enjeu du désordre. Paris, B. Grasset, 1969. 185 p.

Attempt to interpret May 1968 disorders in framework of adaptation crisis on both sides of Iron Curtain, in which dominant mid-20th century models--Marxism-Leninism, consumption society--were rejected. Author suggests various scenarios of crises breaking out either in Russia, Eastern Europe, Western Europe, or U.S. (least likely) and results if revolution broke out in France, a small nuclear power. Suggestions for timely reforms to forestall chain of events that might lead to nuclear war.

99 BEAUFRE, ANDRE. Strategy of action. Translated from the French by R. H. Barry. New York, Praeger, 1967. 136 p.

Translation of "Stratégie de l'action" (Paris, A. Colin, 1966), which is based on general's work at Institut d'études stratégiques. Military strategy cannot operate in a political vacuum but must be subordinated to political diagnosis and objectives, particularly in the case of currently predominant "indirect" strategy, as exemplified by decolonization conflicts, where limitations are placed on military resources.

100 BECET, JEAN-MARIE. La responsabilité de l'état pour les dommages causés par l'armée aux particuliers. Préf. de Jacques Moreau. Paris, Librairie générale de droit et de jurisprudence, R. Pichon et R. Durand-Auzias, 1969. 411 p. (Bibliothèque de droit public, t. 91) Bibliography: p. [393]-401.

Laws and judicial decisions on responsibilities of army as institution and individuals serving in it in times of peace and war. Includes problems of nuclear weapons regulated by law of Nov. 12, 1965.

101 BECQUET, CHARLES. L'ethnie française d'Europe. Avant-propos de Hervé Lavenir. Préf. de Marcel Thiry. Paris, Nouvelles éditions latines, 1963. 238 p. Bibliography: p. [227]-235.

Belgian professor's argument, based on political theory, sociology, and history, that citizenship of state is not only form of possible cohesion, but that ethnic (that is, linguistic) groups could also form nationalities. Focus on French-speaking groups beyond hexagon and possibility of "Europe des ethnies."

102 BENSAID, DANIEL, and C. SCALABRINO. Le deuxième souffle? (Problèmes du mouvement étudiant). Paris, F. Maspéro, 1969. 67 p. (Cahiers "Rouge." Documents de formation communiste no. 12)

Ideological, organizational, and strategic characteristics of various student revolutionary movements before and after May 1968 from perspective of Ligue communiste's construction of a revolutionary party which can overcome contradictions of student movements.

103 BENSAID, DANIEL, and HENRI WEBER. Mai 1968: une répétition générale. Paris, F. Maspéro, 1968. 232 p. (Cahiers libres, 133)

History of May 1968 events seen from point of view of Jeunesse communiste révolutionnaire and 22 March movement leaders, with inside views on origins and make-up of these and other revolutionary groups: Union des jeunesses communistes marxistes-léninistes (U.J.C.M.-L.) and Fédération des étudiants révolutionnaires (F.E.R.), as well as their relations with older student organizations (Union national des étudiants de France [U.N.E.F.] and Union des étudiants communistes). Weaknesses of these groups are realistically assessed.

104 BENSIMON-DONATH, DORIS. L'intégration des Juifs nord-africains en France. Paris, Mouton, 1971. 263 p. tables. (Publications de l'Institut d'études et de recherches interethniques et interculturelles, 1) Bibliography: p. 241-244.

1966-67 questionnaire study of 629 adult and adolescent Jews who immigrated to France from North Africa, mainly after 1956, two-thirds of them in Paris and vicinity, half from Algeria, the rest from Morocco and Tunisia. Some 125,000 Jews moved from Algeria to France, 15,000 to Israel (subject of earlier study), leaving only 1,000 in Algeria. Questions concern motivation for coming to France, conception of France, problems of installation and integration, evolution of family life, degree of cultural assimilation, attitudes toward Judaism and Israel, anti-Semitism experienced (slight). Better assimilation in France than in Israel.

105 BERARD, JOSEPH. Bel-Abbès: ne jamais oublier. Paris, Pensée universelle, 1971. 93 p.

French-born editor of "Bel-Abbès-Journal" for 1946-62 (Bel-Abbès was seat of Foreign Legion in Algeria) was repatriated to France in 1963. Collection of contributions to repatriate publications, 1965-71, with reflections on current political and cultural events in France and reminiscences of Algeria, probably typical of his compatriots' reactions to life in France.

106 BERGE, ANDRE; ROBIN, GILBERT. Pour l'éducation nouvelle, [par] André Berge. Contre l'éducation nouvelle, [par] Gilbert Robin. Nancy, Berger-Levrault [1968?] 80 p., 80 p. (Pour ou contre, 15)

Berge defends principles of "new" or "active" education in line with Montessori methods, stressing that it is the opposite of unbridled license and indolence for students. Robin condemns various contemporary trends such as psychoanalysis, existentialism as agents of current moral collapse, which he also links with new education and weakening of parental and teacher authority.

107 BERGER, IDA. Tiendront-ils? Etude sociologique sur les étudiants des deux bords du Rhin. Préf. par W. Abendroth. Traduit de l'allemand par Odile Meuvret. Paris, Editions Anthropos, 1970. 267 p.

Results based on replies to questionnaires by 150 social science students at Universities of Marburg (Hesse) and Nancy, fall 1967 and spring 1968. Main concerns are student attitudes toward foreign and domestic policy, religion, professional role of women, as well as students' social background and status identification. Differences between French and German students are slight.

108 BERGERON, ANDRE. Confédération Force ouvrière. Paris, Epi, 1971. 109 p. (Collection Carte blanche)

History of Force ouvrière's scission from C.G.T. in 1947, unions' stand on Soviet Union, European unification, decolonization, wage contracts, employment security, social security, and May 1968 events. Author is Force ouvrière's secretary general.

109 BERGHEAUD, EDMOND. Le premier quart d'heure, ou L'Algérie des algériens, de 1962 à aujourd'hui. Préf. de Joseph Kessel. Paris, Plon, 1964. 223 p.

Political history of first two years of independent Algeria by "France-Soir" reporter.

110 BERNARD, PAUL. Le grand tournant des communes de France; des communautés nouvelles à l'épreuve de l'équipement. Paris, A. Colin, 1969. 349 p. (Collection U. Science administrative) ML

Impact of growth in public expenditures on structure of communal and municipal government, through which much of planning and spending is channelled. Author, subprefect in Central France, reviews legislative reforms introduced during Fifth Republic in institutions of local government, evaluates their effectiveness, and urges a "fédéralisme communautaire" reconciling citizen participation and local autonomy with modernization of local administration.

111 BERNARD, PHILIPPE. La France au singulier. Paris, Calmann-Lévy, 1968. 292 p. (Questions d'actualité) Bibliographical footnotes. ML

Specific features of French society, such as authoritarianism, excessive centralization, and intellectual rigidity, in their historical and current manifestations are related to May 1968 crisis and urgent reforms in political institutions (greater polyarchy), decentralization of social, educational, and economic institutions proposed.

112 BERNARD-BECHARIES, J. F. Le choix de consommation; rationalité et réalité du comportement du consommateur. Préf. de Henri Guitton. Paris, Editions Eyrolles et Editions d'Organisation, 1970. 224 p. (Rythmes économiques. Série activités économiques) ML

Psychological approach to actually observed consumer behavior in place of outdated concept of economic rationality.

113 BERSTEIN, SERGE. La décolonisation et ses problèmes. Nancy, A. Colin, 1969. 96 p. (Dossier "sciences humaines," no. 1. Série: Histoire et géographie, problèmes actuels) Bibliography: p. 85.

Selected texts and statistics bringing together facts of worldwide colonization and decolonization phenomena.

114 BERTOLINO, JEAN. Les trublions; reportage photographique Bertolino-Sipahioglo. Paris, Stock, 1969. 397 p. plates.

Main part of volume concerns May 1968 antecedents: student movements, "groupuscules," discussion of academic reform 1966-67, Nanterre crisis. There are interviews with several Sorbonne professors such as mathematician Laurent Schwartz. Journalist author observed Sorbonne firsthand during May. Excellent photographs.

115 BESANÇON, JULIEN. Les murs ont la parole; journal mural, mai 1968, Sorbonne, Odéon, Nanterre, etc. Citations recueillies par Julien Besançon. Paris, Tchou, 1968. 183 p.

Several hundred one- to three-line graffiti from the walls of the Sorbonne, including all Paris faculties and a few other places like the Odéon and Paris lycées. Location is accurately identified. There are no photographs or drawings.

116 BIDAULT, GEORGES. Le point; entretiens avec Guy Ribeaud. Paris, Table ronde, 1968. 344 p. plates.

Apr.-May 1968 interviews with sympathetic journalist covering Bidault's years of exile (he was in Belgium at time of interviews), attitude toward and possible collaboration with political leaders if he returned to France, reaction to student revolt as of mid-May. In discussions on relations with Third World, European unification, regionalization, Catholic aggiornamento, the dominant themes are still anti-Communism, anti-Gaullism, and bitterness about Algeria.

117 BIDAULT, SUZANNE. Je n'ai pas oublié . . . Paris, Table ronde, 1971. 188 p.

Malicious characterizations, by George Bidault's wife, of French and foreign political figures, including de Gaulle, about whom she has a few unkind anecdotes. Most of recollections are from Bidault's years as diplomat.

118 Bilan de la France, 1945-1970. Colloque de l'Association de la presse étrangère, par Alfred Sauvy et al. Paris, Plon, 1971. 186 p. (Tribune libre)

Individual speeches on specific trends in French society: Sauvy on the youth explosion, Paul Ricoeur on French philosophy, Louis Leprince-Ringuet on French high-energy physics, Alain Savary on developments in the French Left, Léo Hamon on strengths of Gaullist party, its political allies, weaknesses of opposition, in perspective of de Gaulle's withdrawal. Final sections cover information and mass media, with talk on management methods of "Le Monde" by its current editor-in-chief, Jacques Fauvet, and discussions among television and press figures.

119 BITTERLIN, LUCIEN. Histoire des barbouzes. Paris, Editions du Palais-Royal, 1972. 269 p. illus., ports., facsims. (Collection La Verité difficile)

Author, working at the time as official of French radio-TV network, stationed in Algiers, was organizer of this counter-O.A.S. force, which was secretly supported by Délégation générale du gouvernement en Algérie but lacked official status, though its men collaborated with various police and secret service agencies. Politically, the "barbouzes" were tied to the Mouvement pour la coopération en Algérie, founded by Jacques Dauer in 1959. Account covers mainly Nov. 1961 through Mar. 1962, height of civil war in Algeria.

120 BLOCH, PIERRE. De Gaulle ou le temps des méprises. Paris, Table ronde, 1969. 228 p.

Former Socialist parliamentarian's personal experiences in London and Algeria during Résistance. Anecdotes and documents highlight de Gaulle's anti-parliamentarian bias and anti-democratic orientations and personality traits. Among political leaders portrayed are François Mitterrand and Astier de la Vigerie, in addition to various Socialist politicians.

121 BLOCH, ROGER. Histoire du Parti radical-socialiste, des radicaux-socialistes d'hier aux démocrates-socialistes de demain. . . . Paris, Librairie générale de droit et de jurisprudence, 1968. 191 p. (Collection D'hier à demain, t. 1) Bibliography: p. [185]-187.

Party history, through five generations of politicians, from 1890 to 1967. Gives text of 1960 manifesto, 1967 declaration of principles of 57th National Congress, and statement of principles of Fédération de la gauche démocrate et socialiste, to which party adhered in 1966. The work is based mainly on party congress documents.

122 BLOCH-MICHEL, JEAN. Une révolution du XXe siècle, les journées de mai 1968. Paris, R. Laffont, 1968. 128 p. (Collection Contestation)

Sympathetic evaluation of student revolt written in early June 1968. Flaws of Gaullist regime, such as self-satisfaction and authoritarianism, are seen as important factors in mishandling of crisis. Refuting Aron's interpretation of events as mere "psychodrama," author sees them as 20th century revolutionary model.

123 BOCHOT, ARISTIDE. Vivre en son temps et le vrai de Gaulle. 2e éd. Paris, A. Bochot, 1971. 210 p.

Main theme of this polemical work is pernicious influence of Catholic Church in world and French affairs and plea for atheism. One chapter on the "true de Gaulle" aims to shatter de Gaulle's legend as war hero, demonstrates that he secretly followed Catholic Church's injunctions in connection with abandonment of Algeria, Common Market, and that Church is furthering his legend after death.

124 BOISDEFFRE, PIERRE DE. Barrès parmi nous. Nouv. éd., enrichie de témoignages inédits. Paris, Plon, 1969. 252 p. Includes bibliography.

New, revised edition includes reactions to Barrès of contemporaries and later writers and reproduces responses by such figures as Michel Droit, François Revel, Philippe de Saint-Robert. The last stresses that de Gaulle has gone beyond narrow nationalism of Barrès.

125 BOISDEFFRE, PIERRE DE. Lettre ouverte aux hommes de gauche. Paris, A. Michel, 1969. 167 p. (Collection "Lettre ouverte") Includes bibliography.

Reflections on ideological and personality characteristics of traditional French Left and Right, the latter embodied in author's own family. Right's stand is seen as turned to past and its maintenance, pessimistic about human nature, silent and death-oriented in defeat. Left viewed as indifferent to present realities for the sake of future rewards. Main part of book shows how student revolution repudiated both traditions but failed to accomplish anything because it lacked ascetic fervor and self-sacrificing spirit of traditional revolutionary Left. Clear-sightedness of Communist Party's refusal to risk civil war in exchange for possible temporary power is recognized.

126 BON, FREDERIC, and MICHEL-ANTOINE BURNIER. Les nouveaux intellectuels. Préf. de Jean-Pierre Vigier. Paris, Cujas, 1966. 382 p. (Civilisation, 2) Bibliography: p. 369-376. ML

Historical evolution from intellectual liberal heritage to present function in scientific and technical society, followed by detailed description of intellectuals as technocrats and on lower level as technicians (with projections for 1975), extent to which university furthers or blocks growth of this new group, different self-concepts of intellectuals ranging from Marxist through technocratic, the "New Left" being torn between these. Each chapter followed by excerpts from texts representing contrasting views of intellectuals, politicians, businessmen, etc.

127 BON, FREDERIC, and MICHEL-ANTOINE BURNIER. Si mai avait gagné. Facétie politique, graffitis de Wolinski. Paris, J. J. Pauvert, 1968. 125 p. illus. (Collection Enragée)

Spoof on May 1968 in the form of a journalist's diary kept for Mar. 15-June 30, 1968 and uncovered in 2155 under Mont Saint-Geneviève. Humorous later-day annotations, poems attached to text by hypothetical Comité d'action de l'Institut d'histoire révolutionnaire of 2156 projecting events and personalities into future. Civil war continues after May 31, leading to Pompidou's and de Gaulle's forced resignation, takeover by Mitterrand government without further elections, then more strikes and troubles, with Communists being brought into government.

128 BONNECARRERE, PAUL. La guerre cruelle; légionnaire en Algérie. Paris, Fayard, 1972. 430 p.

Fictionalized account of military operations of Third Infantry Regiment of Foreign Legion in Algeria, Nov. 1954-May 1958.

129 BONTE, PIERRE. Bonjour Monsieur le maire. Paris, Table ronde, 1965-69. 3 v. 349 p., 273 p., 395 p. ML

v. 1: Le livre d'or des communes de France. 1965.
v. 2: Promenades à travers 350 communes insolites. 1967.
v. 3: Nouvelles promenades et bonnes adresses. 1969. (L'Ordre du jour)

Short descriptions of several hundred picturesque small communities throughout France chosen from 1,500 visited by reporters for short daily television program on Europe 1. Volumes 2 and 3 also contain useful information on local and regional industries, tourist attractions, festivals, as well as lists of restaurants and gastronomic specialties. No illustrations.

130 Bor'ba Frantsuzskoi kommunisticheskoi partii za edinstvo levykh sil, 1958-1967 gg. Otv. redaktor R. S. Varfolomeeva. Moska, "Mysl'," 1968. 229 p. Bibliographical footnotes.

Five contributions (pre-May 1968) dealing with collaboration of P. C. F. and other left-wing parties 1965-67, history of common front of C. G. T. in labor movement, P. C. F.'s fights against monopoly power and for farmer interests, P. C. F. participation in local government.

131 BORELLA, FRANÇOIS. Les partis politiques dans la France d'aujourd'hui. Paris, Editions du Seuil, 1973. 248 p. (Collection "Politique," 56)

Popular work on evolution of political parties 1958-72, with useful figures on election results for major political tendencies, relation with changing French social structure. Trends in main political parties are surveyed (Gaullists, Centrists, Parti socialiste, Parti communiste, Parti socialiste unifié, Communist opposition groups, and anarchists).

132 BOSC, JEAN JACQUES. Si de Gaulle était petit. Paris, J. J. Pauvert, 1968. 120 p. illus. (Libertés nouvelles, 8)

Captionless cartoons on the theme of a small-scale de Gaulle.

133 BOSSERT, FERNAND. Renseignements statistiques budgetaires 1966; données sur les finances des communes de la France métropolitaine. [n.p.] 1966. 24 p.

Tables giving population (1962 census), local tax rates, indebtedness, taxes collected for 15 largest "communes" in each department, arranged by departments.

134 BOUCHARD, CAMILLE. Les grands courants politiques mondiaux; essai d'analyse contre-révolutionnaire. Paris, 1968. 98 p. (Supplément au no. 10 de Lecture et tradition, mars 1968)

Outline of bi-polar forces in international relations, Gaullist attempt to inject neutralist elements, meaning of these changes for counterrevolution, which is opposed to all these forces. Includes book reviews of 10 recent Catholic counterrevolutionary works.

135 BOUDEVILLE, JACQUES RAOUL, ed. L'univers rural et la planification.... Avec la collaboration de O. Guichard, L. Klatzmann, L. Malassis, P. Massé... etc. Paris, Presses universitaires de France, 1968. viii, 216 p. illus. (Bibliothèque contemporaine) Bibliographical footnotes. ML

First group of contributions concerns interactions between agricultural and industrialized sectors, second deals with orientation of regional planning (Pierre Massé) and its administration (Olivier Guichard). Last section presents research on other countries.

136 BOURDET, YVON. La délivrance de Prométhée; pour une théorie politique de l'autogestion. Paris, Editions Anthropos, 1970. xxx, 285 p. (Sociologie et révolution) Bibliography: p. [251]-285.

Definition of "autogestion" in historical Marxist context and in terms of experiences of Communist world, real possibilities in advanced industrialist societies, on the basis of literature on French workers. Present conditions under both capitalism and Communist model are described as "hétérogestion," against which May 1968 revolt was directed by students and skilled workers.

137 BOURDIEU, PIERRE, and JEAN-CLAUDE PASSERON. La reproduction; éléments pour une théorie du système d'enseignement. Paris, Editions de Minuit, 1970. 279 p. tables, diagrs. (Collection "Le Sens commun")

Fundamental, most significant work on education and society, contributing to understanding of French and international situation. It is a sophisticated dissection of educational establishment both as a universal social institution and as its French variant to prove that compulsory education in Europe and the U.S. has proved a powerful force for social conservation (or reproduction) by excluding from positions of power anyone who lacked the proper relation to the dominant cultural heritage, which was transmitted only by the family. First part by Passeron gives theoretical framework for conclusion that every educational system proceeds by selection and elimination, how aspirations of different social classes are made to coincide with their objective chances for academic success, and how pedagogic methods and exams are geared to the function of justifying this system. Complementary statistics are given on social origins in different university faculties. The illusion of neutrality and independence of school system contributes to its power, although it does have a limited autonomy that preserves it from rapid change. Work makes clear role of school in modern society: "En délégant toujours plus complètement le pouvoir de sélection à l'institution scolaire, les classes privilégiées peuvent paraître abdiquer au profit d'une instance parfaitement neutre le pouvoir de transmettre le pouvoir d'une génération à l'autre et renoncer ainsi au privilège arbitraire de la transmission héréditaire. Loin d'être incompatible avec la reproduction de la structure de rapports de classe, la mobilité des individus peut concourrir à la conservation de ces rapports en garantissant la stabilité sociale par la sélection d'un nombre limité d'individus, d'ailleurs modifiés par et pour l'ascension individuelle, et en donnant par là sa crédibilité à l'idéologie de la mobilité sociale" (p. 205-206). Thus democratization of education has meant only that it now takes more years to persuade those that are socially destined to remain at the bottom of the ladder that their exclusion is legitimate. It is a wastefulness the system has to accept to legitimize transmission of power from one generation to the next. For earlier, more limited formulation of these concepts, see Bourdieu's "Les héritiers" (French Fifth Republic Bibliography, 1, no. 233).

138 BOURDIEU, PIERRE, JEAN-CLAUDE PASSERON, and JEAN-CLAUDE CHAMBOREDON. Le métier de sociologue. Livre I. Paris, Mouton, Bordas, 1968. (Les Textes sociologiques, 1)

Introductory discussion of epistemological problems in sociology, followed by illustrative excerpts from writings of French and other sociologists. Further volumes in preparation.

139 BOURGES, HERVE, ed. La révolte étudiante; les animateurs parlent. Par J. Sauvageot, A. Geismar, et D. Cohn-Bendit. Présentation d'Hervé Bourges. Paris, Editions du Seuil, 1968. 128 p. (L'Histoire immédiate)

Interviews by Bourges, May 20-June 1, 1968, with leading student militants. Former U.N.E.F. vice president Jacques Sauvageot describes role of that organization, Alain Geismar, secretary of Syndicat national d'enseignement supérieur (S.N.E. Sup.) that of the Syndicat, and Daniel Cohn-Bendit that of the Mouvement du 22 mars, of which he is founder. Other documents are text of round-table discussion May 17 on Radio Luxembourg with Geismar, Sauvageot, O. Castro (for Mouvement du 22 mars), dialogue between Cohn-Bendit and Sartre, declarations of principles of the three groups. English translation entitled "The French student revolt; the leaders speak" (New York, Hill and Wang, 1968).

140 BOURJOL, MAURICE. Région et administration régionale; douze ans de réforme administrative. Préf. de M. Georges Vedel. Paris, Berger-Levrault, 1970. 487 p. maps. (Collection L'Administration nouvelle) ML

Comprehensive work on restructuring of local, departmental, and regional institutions, 1958-70, giving factual account of new decrees, proposed laws (complete list in appendix) and implementation, as well as underlying economic and political motivations and their culmination in Apr. 1969 referendum. First part traces administrative reform, second describes current institutional set-up, giving details on administration of Paris region, creation of new departments. Final section concentrates on introduction of Apr. 1969 referendum, on regional reform, alternate proposals by political parties, clubs, and author's own modest proposals which dissociate units intended for regional planning from units for local administration.

141 BOURRICAUD, FRANÇOIS. Universités à la dérive: France, Etats-Unis, Amérique du Sud. Paris, Stock, 1971. 178 p. ML

Disequilibria in French universities leading to May 1968 crisis from relative pre-1950 effectiveness, comparisons with student revolts in U.S. of 1960's and Latin America for past decades, so that universities have become nearly paralyzed. Author fears that French universities are on path of degradation and that disintegration is being accelerated by post-May 1968 government reform permitting greater politization and student participation which reduce universities' effective functioning in research, professional preparation and cultural formation of students.

142 BOUSQUIE, GEORGES. Voici Joinville. 2e éd. Vincennes, 1964. 95 p. illus. plan.

Tourist pamphlet on Joinville, small town on the Marne, between Troyes and Nancy.

143 BOUSSARD, LEON. L'irrintzina, ou Le destin des Basques. Paris, R. Laffont, 1969. 259 p.

Basque culture and history of Basque autonomy movement which reached its highest point in 1968. Journalist author advocates combining population of two million from French and Spanish Basque provinces and granting it autonomy in framework of European unification.

144 BOUTHOUL, GASTON. Avoir la paix. Paris, B. Grasset, 1967. 253 p.

Alternations of war and peace throughout history and new factors introduced by nuclear weapons. Author compares contemporary period with other times of relatively extended peace.

145 BOUYER, CHRISTIAN. L'Odéon est ouvert, tribune libre. Paris, Nouvelles éditions Debresse, 1968. 111 p. plates. (Collection Révolte, 1) Bibliography: p. 90-97.

Personal account by history teacher who was one of organizers of free-for-all forum that replaced theatrical productions at Odéon between May 14 and June 14, 1968, and in which 150,000 persons of every age and belief took part. Appendices reproduce open letter of theater's director, Jean-Louis Barrault, to government defending his continued presence in theater after May 21, texts of Odéon wall inscriptions. Many photographs of inside and outside of Odéon. Bibliography lists records and movies made about May 1968. See also no. 958.

146 BRANCIARD, MICHEL. Société française et luttes de classes. Lyon, Chronique sociale de France, 1967. 2 v. ML

Volume 2 covers 1914-66. Work divided by periods, so that one has brief survey of economic conditions, strikes, facts pertaining to labor movement for period of Fifth Republic. Good listing of major trade unions.

147 BRANDES, V. H., and H. SYLVESTER, eds. Merde; Karikaturen der Mairevolte, Frankreich, 1968. München, Trikont Verlag, 1968. 110 p. of illus. (Trikont aktuell, 6)

Most of cartoons were originally printed in student and worker publications: "L'Action," "L'Enragé," "Lutte ouvrière," "Voix ouvrière." Only a few are posters.

148 BRAU, ELIANE. Le situationnisme; ou la nouvelle internationale. Paris, Nouvelles éditions Debresse, 1968. 189 p. illus. (Collection Révolte) Includes bibliography.

Internationale situationniste was founded 1957, with groups in several European countries. Author gives historical antecedents among surrealist writers and artists, main doctrinal points (revolutionary but anti-Communist, anti-Maoist, for worker councils), describes its part in May 1968 student and worker revolts. Extensive list of principal books, pamphlets, of and on I.S., irregularly appearing issues of "Internationale situationniste" 1958-68. Most influential work by organization is "De la misère en milieu étudiant," Nov. 1966 (see no. 631), edited by University of Strasbourg branch, whose subsequent split the author documents in detail.

149 BRAU, JEAN LOUIS. Cours, camarade, le vieux monde est derrière toi! Histoire du mouvement révolutionnaire étudiant en Europe. Paris, A. Michel, 1968. 347 p. illus., plates. (Histoire du XXe siècle) Bibliographical footnotes.

Sympathetic presentation of intellectual currents and spirit underlying French student revolt (information on other European countries is sketchy) with detailed information not available elsewhere on Internationale situationniste and ideas underlying cultural revolution proclaimed May 1968. Good source for vocabulary of students, texts of songs, wall inscriptions and posters, revolutionary publications, clear delineation of student and other groups (Trotskyist, pro-Chinese Communist, anarchist, Situationist). Includes documents illustrating different points of view, among them an unfamiliar text of discussion June 1 at Sorbonne between Cohn-Bendit and several Jeunesse communiste révolutionnaire leaders on ways to organize revolution through Comités d'action. Good list of abbreviations.

150 BRAUD, PHILIPPE. Les crises politiques intérieures de la Ve République. Paris, A. Colin, 1970. 95, [1] p. (Dossiers U2. Droit public interne, 135) Bibliography: p. 95-[96].

Crises are Algerian conflict, 1962 constitutional reform, opposition challenge to majority rule, Dec. 1965-Mar. 1967, and May 1968 and its sequel through de Gaulle's withdrawal. Each crisis is documented by texts of speeches (mainly de Gaulle's), relevant laws and decrees, press comments, election results.

151 BRESSON, JEAN-JACQUES DE. L'O.R.T.F. dans la nation. Conférence le mardi 18 mai 1971 au Théâtre Marigny. Paris, 1971. 25 p. (Conférence des Ambassadeurs, nouvelle série 54)

Director general of O.R.T.F. gives figures on televsion programming, legal status of O.R.T.F., problems of freedom of speech, educational and entertainment role of medium.

152 BRETAGNE, CHRISTIAN, ed. Ce qu'ils ont dit de lui . . . de Gaulle, 1890-1970. Paris, J. P. Taillandier, 1970. 57 p.

Expressions of grief, eulogies appearing in the wake of de Gaulle's death, roughly organized by (1) inner circle of Gaullist Compagnons de la libération, (2) foreign statesmen, (3) French politicians (majority and opposition) and other prominent figures, (4) ordinary citizens. Alphabetically arranged within each section.

153 BREUSE, EDOUARD. La coéducation dans les écoles mixtes. Paris, Presses universitaires de France, 1970. 160 p. tables. Bibliography: p. 150-153. ML

Current status of and trends toward coeducational schools in France, attitudes of educators, Catholic Church, students themselves toward coeducation and career outlook for women, special pedagogic dispositions and problems, proper ratio of male and female teachers, administrators.

154 BRICHANT, COLETTE DUBOIS. Charles de Gaulle, artiste de l'action. New York, McGraw-Hill, 1969. 284 p. illus., maps, ports. Bibliography: p. 272-275.

Biography and political philosophy of de Gaulle, with illustrative passages from his speeches and writings for each period of his life. Fifth Republic years are treated very briefly. The work is intended as source book for American readers and was written with support of French government.

155 BROCHIER, JEAN JACQUES, and BERND OELGART. L'internationale étudiante. Paris, Julliard, 1968. 315 p. illus.

World-wide student revolts, with 50-page section giving sympathetic account of May 1968 events.

156 BROMBERGER, MERRY, and SERGE BROMBERGER. Jean Monnet and the United States of Europe. Translated by Elaine P. Halperin. New York, Coward-McCann, 1969. 349 p.

Journalists' account of Monnet's efforts for European unification and strengthening of European Communities, final third of volume concerning Fifth Republic through 1968. Interesting sections on Euratom, Fouchet Plan. No documentation or bibliography.

157 BROSSAULT, MICHEL. L'énergie atomique et le droit. . . . Melun, Impr. administrative, 1966. 36 p. (Cour d'appel de Caen. Audience solennelle de rentrée du 16 septembre 1966)

Speech at ceremonial meeting of Caen tribunal, Sept. 1966, reviewing recent French legislation on responsibility for nuclear risks.

158 BRULE, MICHEL, and J. PIRET. Les transformations sociales de la France contemporaine; réflexions sur 20 années de sondages politiques de l'I.F.O.P. Paris, Société française de sociologie, 1965. xi, 65 l. mimeographed. tables. ML

Oct. 1965 summary of results showing general level of satisfaction with political innovations of Gaullism and greater unsatisfaction on economic and sociale plane. Appendix in four parts reproduces questions and results for 1945-65 on: (1) dominant preoccupations of French, (2) opinions on new political institutions and political parties, (3) foreign and Algerian policies, (4) overall assessment of Fifth Republic and de Gaulle.

159 BRUNELLE, LUCIEN, ed. Pourquoi des examens; l'université en question. Textes réunis et présentés par Lucien Brunelle. Paris, SER, 1968. 245 p. ("Réflexions croisées," 1)

Contributions by professors and students on issues of university and lycée teaching raised by May 1968 events, one of issues being value of exams in medical studies. Essay on desirability and need of testing as educational tool by Maurice Reuchlin, director of Institut national d'orientation professionnelle. Other essays deal with new approaches to science teaching in lycées, adult education.

160 BÜNNING, THIES. Entwicklung und Zielsetzung der französischen Wirtschaftsplanung. Inaugural-Dissertation zur Erlangung der Doktor-würde einer Hohen Staatswirtschaftlichen Fakultät der Ludwig-Maximilians-Universität zu München. [München?] 1968. 256 p. tables. Bibliography: p. 244-256.

Underlying assumptions, objectives, and practical results of French planning, econometric input-output analysis of Fourth Plan to show how micro- and macro-economic as well as regional equilibria are used to assure balanced growth. Author draws attention to failures of planning process resulting from irresolvable conflicts of growth and stability, which lead to structural inflationary tendency.

161 BUHIER, ALAIN. Petit dictionnaire de la révolution étudiante. . . . Dessins de Cabu. Paris, J. Didier, 1968. 48 p. illus. (Controverses, 2)

Dictionary includes leading participants in May 1968 events, publications, terms coined during period, localities in Latin Quarter, abbreviations.

162 BUHLER, ALAIN, and ALAIN SABATIER. Le VIe Plan, pourquoi? Paris, Fayard, 1971. 159 p. illus., diagrs.

Popularized version of issues involved in parliamentary debate on VIe Plan (1971-75) by journalists collaborating with Centre national d'information pour la productivité des entreprises. Special chapter on Plan's proposals for Paris, excerpts from comments by trade union, farmer, business representatives on Plan. Good statistics of current economic conditions.

163 BUREL, PIERRE. La crise économique dans les événements de mai 1968. Caudry, France, 1970. 143 p.

Real cause of May 1968 explosion is seen in economic crisis: slowdown in economic growth and high unemployment level (about 500,000 unemployed) in preceding half year. Student protests and demands are also analyzed and found only partially justified.

164 BURNIER, MICHEL-ANTOINE, et al. La chute du général; la prise de l'Elysée par Pompidou. Par Michel-Antoine Burnier et l'équipe d'Edition spéciale Julien Fanjeaux et al. Paris, Editions et publications premières, 1969. 275 p.

Elevation of Pompidou to presidency is told in two sections: history of June 1969 presidential election, with good portrait of major candidates and account of Apr. 1969 referendum preceding it; antecedents of de Gaulle's retirement traced back to problems and dissatisfactions generated in May 1968. Author is not sympathetic to Gaullism but recognizes unreadiness of Left to seize power in 1969.

165 BURON, ROBERT. Les dernières années de la IVe République, carnets politiques. Paris, Plon, 1968. 253 p.

Unrevised diary entries of M.R.P. deputy 1953-May 1958, mainly preoccupied with unresolved problems of decolonization, collapse of Fourth Republic.

166 BURON, ROBERT, JEAN OFFREDO, et al. Demain la politique; réflexions pour une autre société. Paris, Denoël, 1970. 253 p.

Original text by Buron was subjected to discussions of local groups of political club Objectif 1972 and results of these discussions summarized by Offredo for national convention, Feb. 1970, at which other clubs and political parties were represented. Work stresses scientific and industrial changes, best response for socialist-oriented groups, makes specific proposals on education, economics; methods of citizen participation in politics. Interview with Buron, head of Objectif 1972, founded Dec. 1966, in which he defines its aims, structure, relation with political parties.

167 BUY, FRANÇOIS. Les étudiants selon Saint-Marx en Europe et en Afrique. Paris, Les Editions municipales, 1967. 112 p.

1946-65 history of Communist-dominated International Students' Union and related Communist-front student movements, with interesting information on French student syndicalism (U.N.E.F.) and ties with P.C.F., Catholic movements, Algerian student movements. Appendix identifies about 200 French participants, mainly well-known professors, and their political affiliations.

168 BYE, MAURICE. Les problèmes économiques européens. Paris, Cujas, 1970. 404 p.

Based on 1965-67 lectures for license des sciences économiques students, with updating of facts to 1969. Chapters on organization of European communities, Common Market (tariff regulations, legislative harmonization, ties with associated states), and common policies on agriculture, energy, trade with non-members.

169 La C.F.D.T.; pour comprendre une évolution; textes. Ce que nous sommes; entretiens avec René Bonéty, Maurice Bouladoux, Gilbert Declercq, Eugène Descamps, Albert Détraz, André Jeanson, Fredo Krumnow, Edmond Maire. Pref. par Eugène Descamp. Paris, Editions du Seuil, 1971. 184 p. (Politique, 43)

Chronologically arranged texts illustrating history of Confédération française des travailleurs chrétiens, founded 1919, its reemergence in 1964 as Confédération française démocratique du travail, original and new statutes, objectives formulated at congresses on democratic planning, wages, political action. Second part transcribes discussion between Jacques Julliard and eight C.F.D.T. leaders, including its secretary general, Descamps, on union's evolution since breaking Catholic ties, influence of May 1968 in radicalizing organization, relations with political parties of Left.

170 CAERLEON, RONAN. Complots pour une République bretonne, les dossiers secrets de l'autonomisme breton. . . . Paris, Table ronde, 1967. 384 p. plates. (L'Histoire contemporaine revue et corrigée) Bibliography: p. [378]-380.

History of Breton independence movement, concentrating on years of German occupation, which saw abortive coup d'état encouraged by Germans. Current possibilities of greater autonomy in a federalist regime are weighed. Additional information on other cultural and linguistic minorities in France.

171 CAHIERS DU COMMUNISME. Les élections législatives de mars 1967; résultats complets et comparés, commentaires et documents. Paris, 1968. 349 p. tables, diagrs. (Its Supplément)

Results for both ballots of Mar. 1967 legislative election and comparative figures for preceding national election (Nov. 1962) for each department and overseas territories and departments. Communist gains and losses in each department are analyzed to see how well electoral alliances with F.G.D.S. and other left-wing parties were implemented. Speeches by Waldeck Rochet and Georges Marchais at Communist Party central committee's Aubervilliers meeting, Mar. 29-30, 1967, commenting on prospects of political agreements with non-Communist Left.

172 CAHIERS DU COMMUNISME. Le rôle des femmes dans la nation. Paris, 1968. 172 p. illus. (Its Supplément)

Speeches at Ivry conference of P.C.F. reporting on party's activities among women workers in different parts of France.

173 CAHIERS FRANÇAIS. Aspects de la politique sociale française: population et famille; problèmes--travail, emploi; action sociale et santé; logement, jeunesse, justice. Sélection de "notices" inédites ou publiées dans les Cahiers français. Paris, Documentation française [1966?]. 1 v. (various pagings) in folder. (Numéro spécial des "Cahiers français")

Report on four surveys: (1) French demographic evolution through 1965; (2) employment conditions and regulations of wages and working conditions; (3) organization of social security and social welfare, problems of handicapped children and aged, statistics for mortality rates of different groups; (4) housing statistics, problems of youth. Followed by figures for social welfare budget 1964-66.

174 CALVET, MAURICE JEAN. Echec au putsch. Paris, Diffusion EDICEF, 1970. 191 p. map.

In this personal narrative an Armée de l'air officer who served in Algeria 1959-61 relates his personal intervention in opposition to Generals' Putsch Apr. 22-27, 1961.

175 CAMERON, RONDO E., comp. Essays in French economic history. Edited by Rondo Cameron with the assistance of Franklin F. Mendels and Judith P. Ward. Homewood, Ill., Published for the American Economic Association by R. D. Irwin, 1970. xiv, 423 p. illus., maps.

Nothing on Fifth Republic years, but good survey of French archival sources on French economic history in appendix.

176 LE CANARD ENCHAINE (periodical). Le canard de mai. Paris, 1968. 16 p. illus. (Numéro spécial exceptionnel du "Canard enchaîné," juin 1968)

Anthology extracted from its May 22-June 6 issues on May 1968 events, consisting of commentaries and cartoons.

177 LE CANARD ENCHAINE. Dictionnaire Canard 1969. Paris, 1969. 144 p. illus.

Humorous definitions in words, quotations, and drawings, of terms and persons of current interest, with separate section for French Algerian slang words. Includes articles on May 1968 events, with cartoons and fictitious diary of Gaullist television staff member during May.

178 CANAVEZO, ROBERT. Pompi-deux, ou Le petit livre d'or du chaos. Dessins de Calvi. Par Robert Rocca [pseud.]. Paris, Editions de la Pensée moderne, 1969. 252 p. illus., ports., facsims.

Satirical characterization of Pompidou, with wealth of citations and anecdotes and some cartoons, using variations on name (Pompi-d'ou, Pompidoux, Pompi-d'aout, etc.) as themes for different aspects of his political activities. Work concentrates on period between Apr. 1969 referendum and first months of rule. See also his satirical compendium on de Gaulle, no. 516.

179 CAPDEVIELLE, JACQUES, and RENE MOURIAUX, comps. Les syndicats ouvriers en France. Paris, A. Colin, 1970. 126 p. (Dossiers U2, 104) Bibliography: p. 212-122. ML

Factual summary on historical background, ideological divisions of trade unions, current structures, field of action, methods and resources for implementing objectives, main current issues, with short illustrative documents for each section. Has list of main trade unions and their addresses, number of members, names of secretaries, size of budget. Identifies dozen extreme Left worker organizations (addresses, publications) active as of 1969.

180 Le capitalisme français maillon le plus faible de la chaîne impérialiste. Paris, F. Maspéro, 1969. 47 p. (Cahiers "Rouge." Document Rouge, no. 4)

Reasons for devaluation of franc and condemnation of trade unions' lack of militancy in contrast to that of workers themselves advanced by organ of Ligue communiste.

181 CAPITANT, RENE. Ecrits politiques 1960-1970. Préf. de Louis Vallon. Paris, Flammarion, 1971. 432 p. (Textes politiques)

Posthumous collection of selected articles drawn from "Notre République," the organ of left-wing Gaullist Union démocratique du travail. Capitant was cabinet member under Couve de Murville 1968-69; died May 1970. Articles fall into three categories: institutions of Fifth Republic (presidential regime, role of parties, activities of opposition); Gaullist policy (foreign affairs, Algeria, social and economic reforms, notably proposals for worker participation in industry and opposition thereto); deviations from Gaullism, 1966-70. Chronological list of articles.

182 CARADEC, FRANÇOIS, ed. La chienlit de papa. Paris, A. Michel, 1968. 122 p.

Collection of quotations from French and foreign authors which would have been suitable (but were not used) for wall inscriptions during May 1968 events. Arranged alphabetically under key words such as "amour," "enfant," "opinions," etc.

183 CARMOY, GUY DE. Les politiques étrangères de la France, 1944-1966. Paris, Table ronde, 1967. 518 p.

Revised English edition, "Foreign policies of France 1944-68" (Chicago, Chicago University Press, 1970), at ML.

First half surveys main areas of foreign policy during Fourth Republic: defense and alliances, European integration, decolonization. In second part, these issues are reexamined for Fifth Republic and cover: decolonization (Algeria) and cooperation; new military strategies (nuclear weapons, withdrawal from NATO, crisis of Atlantic Alliance) and European policy (European Communities institutions, rejection of British membership, relations with Germany). These areas are updated to 1966. Reversal of Fourth Republic orientation on Atlantic Alliance and European integration is critically assessed and approval for changes by public opinion recognized.

184 CASANOVA, ANTOINE, CLAUDE PREVOST, and JOE METZGER. Les intellectuels et les luttes de classe. Paris, Editions sociales, 1970. 169 p. (Collection Notre temps) Bibliographical footnotes. ML

Reappraisal of proper relations between intellectuals and working class in terms of Communist ideology. Three articles, drawn from Communist organ "Nouvelle critique," are Casanova's "Le statut social des intellectuels," tracing quantitative evolution of this social group, Metzger's "Conscience et situation des ingénieurs et cadres," and Prévost's "Nouvelles réflexions sur l'idéologie gauchiste," which identifies several ideological currents related to May 1968 attacks from Left on P.C.F. and Communist response. In appendix good statistics on social background of French students, successful completion of studies.

185 CASTEL, ROBERT, and JEAN-CLAUDE PASSERON, eds. Education, développement et démocratie, Algérie, Espagne, France, Grèce, Hongrie, Italie, Pays arabes, Yougoslavie. Etudes présentées par Robert Castel, Jean-Claude Passeron. Paris, La Haye, Mouton, 1967. 271 p. (Ecole pratique des hautes études. 6e section. Sciences économiques et sociales. Cahiers du Centre de sociologie européenne, 4) Bibliography: p. [241]-260.

Introductory essay by Pierre Bourdieu on comparability of educational systems. Individual articles by several authors concentrate on experiences outside France, but compare these educational systems with French situation in terms of relative democratization and economic function of education. Excellent critical bibliography for works on French education.

186 CATHALA, FERNAND. Cette police si décriée.... Saverdun, Ariège, Editions du Champ-de-Mars, 1971. 309 p.

Inside view of functioning of regular police services, typical problems arising from conflicting public demands for effective crime prevention and punishment of offenders, on the one hand, and negative public attitude toward police and authorities, which leads to uncooperativeness, on the other. Difficulties of reconciling individual civil liberties and police effectiveness during current crime wave are exemplified. Author has had long service as police commissioner. No political issues are raised.

187 CATHERINE, ROBERT. Le fonctionnaire français; droits, devoirs, comportements. Introduction à une déontologie de la fonction publique. Paris, A. Michel, 1961. 411 p. ML

In addition to basic regulations and rights governing civil and military service, author outlines special qualifications, characteristics of top men in hierarchy. Final section on relations within and between ministries, with parliament, local authorities, private citizens. Work based on lectures at Institut des hautes études d'outremer.

188 CATHERINE, ROBERT, and GUY THUILLIER. Introduction à une philosophie de l'administration. Préf. de Vladimir Janké lévitch. Paris, A. Colin, 1969. 373 p. (Collection U: Série Science administrative) Bibliography: p. 349-362. ML

Reflections on ways in which administrators experience administrative way of life and exercise of power, perceive general interest, flow of time, space, arbitrariness, and anonymity, what qualities are esteemed in civil servants, what tensions arise from demands on them, what constitutes a specific administrative "morality." Extensive bibliography of books and articles on spirit of administration and administrative reform.

189 CATY, GILBERT. La coopération scientifique entre la France et le tiers-monde. Paris, Presses universitaires de France, 1967. 201 p. (Travaux et mémoires de la Faculté de droit et des sciences économiques d'Aix-en-Provence) Includes bibliography.

History and present (post-independence) status of research efforts, especially by Office de la recherche scientifique et technique d'outremer, as well as problems of localized as against centralized research. Figures for French and local research support for African states, 1961-64. Good bibliography of books and articles on technical assistance.

190 CAU, JEAN. L'agonie de la vieille. Paris, Table ronde, 1970. 153 p. (Table ronde de Combat. "Les Brûlots," 15)

Medley of personal and political jottings, whose main theme is that the last hours of democracy, Judeo-Christian morality have struck, as exemplified by youth reactions May 1968, and that a new form of nationalist irrationality and a doctrine of racial supremacy are in the offing.

191 CAUTE, DAVID. Frantz Fanon. New York, Viking Press, c1970. 116 p. (Modern masters) Bibliography: p. 109-110.

Analysis of Fanon's writings and of evolution in his thinking from direct concern (as a doctor) with psychiatric problems to commitment to Algerian revolution and violence as way for oppressed to gain self-respect, discovery of decolonization and its new forms of oppression of masses by native elites in Africa, Antilles.

192 CAVANNA, HENRY, ed. Analyse d'un vertige. [Par H. Arendt et al.] Paris, S.E.P.A.L. (Société d'éditions et de publications artistiques et littéraires), 1968. 230 p. (Les Cahiers de la revue la Table ronde)

Articles on violence, anarchy, meaning of student revolt by French and international contributors, with reference to May 1968 events. Among French contributors are Jacques Ellul and Raymond Boudon, the latter with study on changes in social origins and career prospects of French students, which are viewed as factors in explosion.

193 CAVIGLIOLI, FRANÇOIS, and JEAN-MARIE PONTAUT. La grande cible, 1961-64; les secrets de l'O.A.S. Paris, Paris-Match Mercure de France, 1972. 256 p.

Journalists' account of assassination attempts on de Gaulle by O.A.S. at Pont-sur-Seine, Sept. 1961, and at Petit-Clamart, Aug. 1962, political support for these operations inside France, sequels to these attempts (pursuit, capture of some O.A.S. conspirators, escape of others). Also describes final abortive assassination attempt at Mont-Faron near Nice, Aug. 1964, involving remnant of O.A.S. and Conseil national de la Résistance, with sketches of exiled leadership, among them Susini, Rosfelder, Soustelle, and Bidault.

194 CAYROL, ROLAND. François Mitterrand, 1945-1967. Paris, 1967. 166 p. illus., ports. (Fondation nationale des sciences politiques. Centre d'étude de la vie politique française. Série: Recherches, no. 5)

Objective documentary work on Mitterrand's role in Fourth and Fifth Republic, as presidential candidate Dec. 1965 and head of Fédération de la gauche démocrate et socialiste. Mitterrand speeches are main source.

195 CAZENAVE, MICHEL, and OLIVIER GERMAIN THOMAS, eds. Charles de Gaulle. Paris, Editions de l'Herne, 1973. 370 p. plates, ports. (Cahiers de l'Herne, no. 21, février 1973)

Appreciations, personal encounters, scholarly studies on de Gaulle by 55 politicians, writers, journalists, and political scientists. General theme connecting essays is that de Gaulle's prophetic visions are being neglected by his successor. Includes studies of de Gaulle's oratorical style. List of articles by de Gaulle. Two interviews with Malraux regarding his book on his final interview with de Gaulle, "Les chênes qu'on abat."

196 CENTRE CATHOLIQUE DES INTELLECTUELS FRANÇAIS. Censure et liberté d'expression. Paris, Desclée de Brouwer, 1970. 226 p. (Recherches et débats, no. 68)

Individual contributions on censorship of press, audio-visual mass media, freedom of speech for teachers and students, value of Catholic office for movie censorship.

197 CENTRE DE DOCUMENTATION JUIVE CONTEMPORAINE. BIBLIOTHEQUE. La France de l'Affaire Dreyfus à nos jours. Paris, 1964. 266 p. (Its Catalogue no. 1)

Most of the works listed pre-date 1958, but some items for Fifth Republic appear under anti-Semitic and Fascist tendencies, treatment of Jewish question in French school books, Franco-Israeli relations, place of Jews in French society and culture. Catalogue arranged by subjects, with complete author index.

198 CENTRE DE DOCUMENTATION JUIVE CONTEMPORAINE. BIBLIOTHEQUE. La France [1870-1967]; le Troisième Reich; Israël. Paris, 1968. xi, 254 p. (Its Catalogue no. 2)

Complements Catalogue no. 1 with recently published or acquired books, some in categories listed above.

199 CENTRE DE REGROUPEMENT DES INFORMATIONS UNIVERSITAIRES. Quelle université? Quelle société? Textes réunis par le Centre de regroupement des informations universitaires. Paris, Editions du Seuil, 1968. 221 p. (Collection "Combat")

Topically organized May 1968 documents on the revolt as a whole, protests against specific aspects of university and society, the struggle in action, proposals for university and lycée reform, proposals for social reform. Longest excerpt is from separately printed "Nous sommes en marche," others are from various university committees at Sorbonne, Grenoble, Strasbourg, etc. and different faculties, with a few items from lycées.

200 CENTRE D'ETUDES ET DE RECHERCHES MARXISTES, PARIS. COLLOQUE DES 15 ET 16 MARS 1969. Mouvement de libération nationale, néocolonialisme, développement. Paris, 1970. 4 v. (Cahiers du Centre d'études et de recherches marxistes, nos. 76-79, 1970)

Talks followed by lively discussions on nature of neocolonialism, problems of capitalist and socialist economic aid to underdeveloped countries. Aim of meeting was to demonstrate convergence of interests and natural alliance of socialist countries, international labor movement and national liberation movements as answer to imperialism, rather than opposition between poor and rich nations, insistence on specific roads to socialism. Most of participants are P. C. F. members; the others are African and Latin American Communists.

201 CENTRE INTERNATIONAL DE FORMATION EUROPEENNE, PARIS. Répertoire des périodiques consacrés aux questions européennes. Paris, Presses d'Europe, 1967. 144 p.

In addition to alphabetical listing of periodicals related to European unification, many of them French, repertory lists movements and associated groups for European integration, their publications, leading members, headquarters in different countries.

FOR CENTRE NATIONAL DE LA RECHERCHE SCIENTIFIQUE, SEE NO. 439

202 CENTRE NATIONAL DES DIRIGEANTS D'ENTREPRISE. La participation dans l'entreprise. Paris, Editions du Seuil, 1969. 154 p. Bibliography: p. 147-154. ML

Proposals by organization of upper and middle management for making worker participation a reality. Proposals concern information process, participation in management, in fruits of investment, in selection of management.

203 CENTRE NATIONAL D'INFORMATION POUR LA PRODUCTIVITE DES ENTREPRISES. Les événements de mai-juin 1968 vus à travers cent entreprises; document réalisé au cours des mois juillet et août 1968 à partir de témoignages rassemblés au C. N. I. P. E. Paris, 1968. 67 p.

Propagation of strikes, original features of worker demands, modifications brought about by strikes in relations between workers, "cadres," and management. Based on 115 monographs of typical firms throughout France, mainly using interview technique, but with names of firms withheld.

204 CERTEAU, MICHEL DE. La prise de parole, pour une nouvelle culture. Paris, Desclée de Brouwer, 1968. 167 p. Bibliographical references. ML

"Speaking out" (prise de parole) of May 1968 is seen as principal revolutionary weapon through challenging or rejecting existing rational systems and concepts of man and society. Author looks more closely into challenging of elite-masses concept, traditional pedagogic relations. Appendix reviews major works on May 1968 published in wake of events as transposition from "speaking out" to more orderly interpretation of events.

205 CERUSE, COLONEL [pseud.]. Mes barricades. Paris, Presses noires, 1968. 366 p.

Detective-style account of several episodes during May 1968: Nanterre, occupation of Sorbonne, confrontation of workers and police at Flins. Narrator presented as member of security forces.

206 CESPEDES, ALBA DE. Chansons des filles de mai, poèmes. Paris, Editions du Seuil, 1968. 96 p. ML

Italian-born novelist residing in Latin Quarter portrays different young women involved or indifferent to May 1968 uprising who passed by his window. May events serve as backdrop of poems.

207 CEZEDE, illus. Histoire illustrée du plus illustre des Français. Paris, P. de Meyère, 1968. 135 p. illus.

Satirical epic poem in seven chants relating de Gaulle's life from birth to anticipated death. It is based on standard biographical works, with short excerpts from de Gaulle's memoirs and speeches. Seventh chant deals with current events, particularly foreign policy, 1962-67.

208 CHAFFARD, GEORGES. Les deux guerres du Vietnam; de Valluy à Westmoreland. Paris, Table ronde, 1969. 458 p. (La Table ronde de Combat. Documents et reportage) Includes bibliographical references.

History of conflict shows continuity between French and U.S. strategy of "position of strength" before beginning negotiations and repetition of French misjudgments. De Gaulle's role in later stages of conflict is clarified.

209 CHAFFARD, GEORGES. Les orages de mai, histoire exemplaire d'une élection. Paris, Calmann-Lévy, 1968. 232 p. diagrs. (Questions d'actualité)

Journalist's firsthand account of May 1968 strikes and June 1968 elections in the electoral district of Vendôme (Loir et Cher) 130 miles south of Paris, a typical French rural area, 70,000 inhabitants, with a moderate political tradition. Interesting background on political and economic life in the provinces. Socialist deputy was replaced by Catholic Centrist.

210 CHAMBE, RENE. Le Maréchal Juin, duc du Garigliano. Paris, Presses de la Cité, 1968. 445 p. illus., maps, plates. (Collection Coup d'oeil) Bibliographical footnotes.

Juin, born in Algeria 1889, died Jan. 27, 1967, having been named last French marshal in 1953. Final chapter deals with Algerian war and Juin's attitude toward it, torn between military duty and pied-noir status, effects on old friendship with de Gaulle. Contains letters reflecting disagreements, later reconciliation.

211 CHAPSAL, MADELEINE, and MICHELE MANCEAUX. Les professeurs pour quoi faire? Paris, Editions du Seuil, 1970. 187 p. (Collection L'Histoire immédiate)

Interviews during 1969 with 11 university professors by "Express" reporters. Professors, mostly in humanities, teach at Sorbonne, Vincennes, Nanterre, except for two American professors who compare American and French experiences of student revolt. One is Paul Ricoeur, head of Nanterre, 1968-69. Only one interviewee, Frédéric Deloffrée, Sorbonne professor and secretary general of Syndicat autonome des facultés des lettres, frankly defends traditional authoritarian teaching methods, exams, selection, while others vary in degree of sympathy for student revolt and discuss recent implementation of reforms.

212 CHAPUS, JACQUES. Mourir à Colombey. Paris, Table ronde, 1971. 233 p.

Straightforward reconstruction of de Gaulle's last 10 months in details of daily living, trips to Ireland and Spain, visitors whom author interviewed, information on composition of Memoirs, exact circumstances of death, testament, funeral. No sources cited.

213 CHARDONNET, JEAN. L'université en question. Paris, Editions France-Empire, 1968. 174 p.

Professor of economic geography at University of Dijon pleads for limited university reforms only in those areas where feasibility is assured and need recognized within academic community (more adequate and higher-quality staffing, larger scholarships, better housing and food) and protests against ill-considered bureaucratic "reformitis" of Gaullist regime.

214 Charles de Gaulle. Paris, Plon [1965?]. 127 p. ML

Highly laudatory political biography with ample illustrations covering first seven years of de Gaulle's rule.

215 CHARLOT, JEAN. Le Gaullisme. Paris, A. Colin, 1970. 221 p. tables, diagrs. (Dossiers U2. Série Politique)

First part of book contains chronologically arranged documents for different phases of Gaullism (war years, R.P.F., "traversée du désert, Gaullism in power). For Fifth Republic period, texts consist of de Gaulle's speeches, excerpts from Gaullist party publications. Second part brings together material on Gaullist adherents and voters, with tables for main elections and opinion surveys 1967, 1968, as well as sociological breakdown for Gaullist and left-wing voters and different interpretations of Gaullism.

216 CHARLOT, JEAN. Le phénomène gaulliste. Paris, Fayard, 1970. 206 p. tables, diagrs. (Le Monde sans frontières) Includes bibliographical references.

Scholarly, carefully annotated work, an outgrowth of Charlot's 1967 study on U.N.R., is a major study on Gaullism, which is shown to have become anchored in French political life since 1958 as party resembling British Conservative party. First part of book identifies public, electoral support for Gaullism (both de Gaulle and U.N.R.) and reasons for failure of opposition to make headway before or since May 1968. Second part concentrates on Gaullist organizations in and outside parliament (30 are listed) and major allied organizations (Républicains indépendants), with stress on recent transformations and normalization of relations between Gaullist party and government. Final chapter discusses continuity and change after de Gaulle's retirement and Pompidou's presidential style.

217 CHARLOT, JEAN. Répertoire des publications des partis politiques français 1944-1967. A catalogue of the publications of the French political parties 1944-1967. Paris, A. Colin, 1970. 245 p. (Fondation nationale des sciences politiques. Bibliographies françaises de sciences sociales. Répertoires documentaires, 3)

Listing of nearly 2,000 items organized by political party. For each party, repertory enumerates (1) periodicals issued (general and specialized) and (2) printed reports and pamphlets, chronologically arranged, including statutes, reports of congresses and other meetings, election propaganda, pamphlets under authors, special issues of newspapers and periodicals, with complete bibiliographic information. With few exceptions, cited works are available either at Fondation nationale or at Bibliothèque nationale or both and exact location is given. Separate list of congresses for each party, with reference to relevant items in main listing, as well as index of periodicals by title, author index, careful subject index. Parties are: P.C.F. (487 items), Parti socialiste (427 items), Convention des institutions républicaines, Parti républicain radical et radical-socialites, Fédération de la gauche démocrate et socialiste, M.R.P. (399 items). Some are grouped as follows: Gauche indépendante (Union de la gauche socialiste, Parti socialiste autonome, Parti socialiste unifié); Centrisme (Comité d'études et de liaison des démocrates, Centre démocrate, Centre Progrès et démocratie moderne); Gaullisme (R.P.F., Républicains sociaux, U.N.R., U.N.R.-U.D.T., U.D.-Ve, with only 46 items for Fifth Republic years); and Droite modérée (Centre national des Indépendants et paysans, Fédération nationale des Républicains indépendants).

218 CHARRIERE, CHRISTIAN. Le printemps des enragés. Paris, Fayard, 1968. 429 p.

"Inside" journalism re-creating one of most dramatic periods in French history, focusing on events leading to closing of Nanterre and presenting day-by-day chronicle, May 2-June 21, of multiple facets, major and minor incidents making up the "événements de mai." Story moves back and forth between Nanterre, the Sorbonne, Odéon, various street clashes and demonstrations, strikes and individual factory occupations, abortive student-worker collaboration, cabinet and parliamentary meetings, C.G.T. and industrial leaders, tense relations between de Gaulle and Pompidou, de Gaulle's final intervention and gradual normalization culminating in June 23 elections. Vivid sketches of leading student militants (notably Cohn-Bendit) and human elements explaining their actions, portraits of many trade union and political figures who became embroiled at different stages in the drama. Many quoted accounts of closed meetings, whose authenticity is not documented.

219 CHARZAT, GISELE. Les Françaises sont-elles des citoyennes? Paris, Denoël/Gonthier, 1972. 202 p. (Collection Femme) Includes bibliography.

Facts and figures on political participation of women: voting pattern, membership in political parties and trade unions, under-representation among political leadership. Survey also covers professional role of women, education, cultural activities, current status of women's rights movement.

220 CHATEAU, JEAN. Psychologie de l'éducation. Paris, J. Vrin, 1970. 57 p. Includes bibliographical references. ML

Based on 1969 lectures outlining work of Centre bordelais de recherches en psychologie de l'éducation, of which author is head. Studies in development of intellectual attitudes are stressed.

221 CHEVALLIER, JACQUES. L'enseignement supérieur. Paris, Presses universitaires de France, 1971. 94 p. (Dossiers Thémis 12. Série Institutions administratives) Bibliography: p. 95. ML

Introductory summary of changes in regulations affecting French universities introduced by 1968 "loi d'orientation" and subsequent decrees, followed by texts of law and decrees.

FOR CHEVERNY, JULES, SEE GOURDON, ALAIN

222 CHOMBART DE LAUWE, PAUL HENRY. Pour l'université, avant, pendant et après mai 1968. Paris, Payot, 1968. 176 p. (Etudes et documents Payot) Bibliographical footnotes.

Collection of 10 essays by Centre national de la recherche scientifique sociologist specializing in study of attitudes toward social change. Themes of pre-1968 essays are university's function in social and physical science research, danger of isolating university from society. Essays of 1968 deal with possibility of participation in decision-making process by all members of research team, even students at C.N.R.S., underlying aspirations for university reform and opportunity of realizing them through May revolt.

223 CHOURAQUI, ANDRE. Les Juifs d'Afrique du Nord entre l'Orient et l'Occident. Paris, 1965. 44 p. (Fondation nationale des sciences politiques. Centre d'étude des relations internationales. Série G: Etudes maghrébines, no. 5)

Exodus of Jews from North Africa in wake of Moroccan, Tunisian, and Algerian independence (in Algeria only 4 percent of former Jewish population, or 3,000 Jews, have remained after independence) and effect of influx on French Jewish community, which doubled as a result of immigration.

224 CHRISTIANISME ET REVOLUTION, COLLOQUIUM, PARIS, 1968. Christianisme et révolution, colloque des 23 et 24 mars 1968. Paris, 1968. 182 p.

Participating in colloquium were several moderate and extreme left-wing Christian organizations: Economie et humanisme, La Lettre, Groupe Témoignage chrétien, Frères du monde, Terre entière. Topics are feasibility of Christian's collaboration with Marxists, acceptance of violence in revolutionary practice both in Third World and in France. Originally published as supplement no. 119 of "La Lettre," 1968.

225 CHRISTIN, IVAN. Transformation des liquidités et financement du plan. Contribution à l'analyse de l'expérience française. Préf. de Pierre Llau. Paris, La Haye, Mouton, 1967. 151 p. illus., tables. (Publications de la Faculté de droit et des sciences économiques de Grenoble. Collection du Centre de

recherche économique et sociale. Série Economie du financement. Cahier d'études, no. 1)

Scholarly study of mechanisms for channeling savings into investments in current French economic practice and government incentives for directing them in direction stipulated by Plans, with a minimal inflationary impact. Annexes give statistics through 1963 on movement of savings, public and private financial operations, source and allocation of investment funds.

226   Chronologie de la vie du Général de Gaulle. Paris, Plon, 1973. 342 p.

Reference work compiled by Institut Charles de Gaulle. Two-thirds of chronology deals with Fifth Republic years, giving dates for important official functions such as government meetings, diplomatic encounters, trips within and outside France, speeches, diplomatic messages, press conferences, inaugurations. Entries are all based only on official material, not private records. Chronology useful for French and international events as well.

227   CIERNY, JAN. Generál. [Ze slovenského originál přeložil Zdeněk Dvořáček] Praha, Svoboda, 1967. 187 p. illus., ports.

Ostensibly a biography of de Gaulle, but actually deals primarily with political struggles of Fifth Republic through 1965.

228   CIERNY, JAN. Kto vládne v Paríži. Bratislava, Epocha, t. Pravda, 1971. 254, [1] p. [16] p. of plates. Includes bibliographical references.

Political history of Fifth Republic from its inception, including May 1968 and subsequent debates on renewal of French socialism within Communist and non-Communist Left, possibility of opposition parties' coming to power after de Gaulle's withdrawal.

229   Le cinéma s'insurge, Etats-généraux du cinéma. Paris, Le Terrain vague, 1968. 53 p. illus.

Events leading up to formation of Etats-généraux du cinéma, joining all people concerned with film production--workers, technicians, artists, producers. Strike initiated May 7, 1968, production of documentary movies on current events, cooperation with students, O.R.T.F. strikers. List of 400 signatures on one of its resolutions.

230   CIRET, JEAN-PAUL, and JEAN-PIERRE SUEUR. Les étudiants, la politique et l'Eglise: une impasse? Paris, Fayard, 1970. 144 p. (Points chauds)

Collective reflections by members of Jeunesse étudiante chrétienne on political participation among Catholic lycée and university students, religious faith as a source of political orientation. Appendix reproduces selected statements by Catholic students belonging to range of political parties on these problems.

231   Les citations de la révolution de mai, recueillies par Alain Ayache. Paris, J. J. Pauvert, 1968. 107 p.

Very short excerpts from press, speeches and statements by participants, May 3-31, 1968, evoking highlights of revolution. No sources of statements cited. Final section reproduces slogans from posters and leaflets.

232   CLAASSEN, EMIL MARIA, and LOUIS-FERDINAND PETERS. Rebellion in Frankreich; die Manifestation der europäischen Kulturrevolution. München, Deutscher Taschenbuch Verlag, 1968. 152 p. illus. (DTV-Report)

Good general account of student and worker uprising with background explanations and statistics about French higher education, student and radical movements. German authors were eyewitnesses of events in Paris. Appendix gives samples of revolutionary poetry, leaflets, graffiti, map of Latin Quarter.

233   CLAISSE, ALAIN. Le premier ministre de la Ve République. Préf. de Michel Lesage. Paris, Librairie générale de droit et de jurisprudence, R. Pichon et R. Durand-Auzias, 1972. 436 p. (Bibliothèque constitutionnelle et de jurisprudence, XLV) Bibliography: p. 421-427.

Important work on functioning of pivotal element in Fifth Republic's political institutions, describing situation and jurisdiction of head of government in relation to head of state, his power over ministries and permanent administrative bodies, some of them directly under his control, confrontation with parliament and political parties as titular leader of majority, and contact with public opinion through information media. Expanded doctoral thesis is based not only on published and documentary sources but on interviews with leading government figures, and clarifies evolution in each of these domains in the context of political developments 1958-71, with portraits of four prime ministers: Debré, Pompidou, Couve de Murville, and Chaban-Delmas.

234   CLARK, JAMES MILFORD. Teachers and politics in France; a pressure group study of the Fédération de l'éducation nationale. Syracuse, Syracuse University Press, 1967. xv, 197 p. Bibliography: p. 186-190.

Study on major French teachers' union, which follows pattern of other French pressure groups. There is little material beyond 1961. As of 1961, F.E.N., subdivided into 38 member unions, such as Syndicat national des instituteurs with over 200,000 teachers and Syndicat national de l'enseignement secondaire with 30,000 teachers, represented most elementary and secondary school educators. Author shows how union achieved cohesion and exerted influence on administration and parliament of Fourth and Fifth Republic in shaping school legislation (e.g., 1951 and 1959 laws).

235   CLAUDE, HENRI. Histoire, réalité et destin d'un monopole, la Banque de Paris et des Pays-Bas et son groupe (1872-1968). Paris, Editions sociales, 1969. 304 p. Bibliographical footnotes.

This is largest French industrial bank, very involved in furthering industrial concentration with help of Gaullist government. Author shows degree of control in industrial and commercial spheres under Fifth Republic (e.g., Bull, Hachette) and within European and international areas. Final section analyzes current status of organization after July 1968 reform of banks, which gives separate identity to holding company and shows conflicts between national interest and that of holding company. Nationalization is advocated, in line with P.C.F. policy.

236   CLAVEL, MAURICE. Combat de franc-tireur pour une libération. [Paris?] J. J. Pauvert, 1968. 201 p. (Libertés nouvelles, 17)

Collection of articles originally published in "Combat" and "Nouvel observateur" Nov. 1966-July 1968. Pre-May 1968 articles are mainly reviews of television programs; May-July 1968 editorials give enthusiastic support to students.

237   CLAVEL, MAURICE. Combat de la Résistance à la Révolution, juillet 1968-juin 1970. Paris, Flammarion, 1972. 251 p. (Collection "Textes politiques")

Continuation of "Combat de franc-tireur" with collections of articles from "Nouvel observateur" and "Combat" commenting on political events, television programs, with violent indictment of Gaullism under Pompidou and appeals for a "new" resistance as demanded by youth since May 1968.

238   CLAVEL, MAURICE. Qui est aliéné? Critique et métaphysique sociale de l'Occident. Paris, Flammarion, 1970. 330 p. ML

"Combat" journalist, active supporter of student revolt, reinterprets his favorable response to events by examining their relation to the much-abused term "alienation." First part of work, originally published in "La Nef," criticizes internal contradiction of structuralism, existentialism, and Marxism in explaining alienation. Second part presents in detail views of young and mature Marx, neo-Marxists like Ernest Mandel and André Gorz. Refuting alienation as an economic phenomenon, author sees it as outgrowth of culture born with French political and economic revolution at end of 18th century, which replaced God by man as creator through growing knowledge and power of machines. Marxism, sharing this concept of man, is incapable of transcending alienation. Criticism is concentrated on Marxist theory of surplus value as explanation of alienation.

239   CLERC, PAUL. Grands ensembles, banlieues nouvelles; enquête démographique et psycho-sociologique. Paris, Presses universitaires de France, 1967. 471 p. tables. (Centre de recherche d'urbanisme. Institut national d'études démographiques. Travaux et documents. Cahier no. 49) ML

Questionnaire study of 3,117 households in Paris and its vicinity as well as provinces representing the 343,000 households living in such units all over France. There are 200 such "grands ensembles" (apartment buildings with over 1,000 individual units) in Paris, 105 in provinces. Results of questionnaire cover physical description of dwellings, demographic and social status of inhabitants, opinions about quality of housing, way of life.

240   CLUB JEAN MOULIN. Les citoyens au pouvoir, 12 régions, 2000 communes. Paris, Editions du Seuil, 1968. 190 p. (Collection Jean Moulin)

Proposal published in early 1968, drawing on British and German experiences, to change French administration to 12 regions with eight major urban centers, plus several for Paris vicinity, and 2,000 communes with a minimum of 8,000 inhabitants. Functions and financial resources of these new entities are outlined.

241   CLUB JEAN MOULIN. Que faire de la révolution de mai, six priorités. Paris, Editions du Seuil, 1968. 95 p. (Collection Jean Moulin)

Proposals for institutional reform in six areas on the eve of the legislative elections June 1968: taxation system, worker participation in enterprises, non-governmental control of radio-TV, university autonomy, administrative decentralization.

242   CLUB JEAN MOULIN. Quelle réforme? Quelles régions? Paris, Editions du Seuil, 1969. 77 p. (Collection Jean Moulin)

Arguments for rejecting de Gaulle's regional reforms embodied in Apr. 1969 referendum.

243   CLUB NOUVELLE FRONTIERE. Le dossier du 27 avril. Paris, B. Grasset, 1969. 189 p. maps.

Arguments supporting Apr. 1969 referendum for creating 21 regions and detailed discussion of modalities of reform and its impact on local government, central administration, industry, agriculture, education. Club has Gaullist orientation.

244   COBB, RICHARD CHARLES. A second identity; essays on France and French history. London, New York, Oxford University Press, 1969. xii, 316 p. ports.

Essays by British historian who lived much of his life in France. Most deal with revolutionary episodes of 18th and 19th century French history, with comparison to 1968 revolts. Includes extensive review of David Caute's "Communism and the French intellectual" in which he draws on personal experiences to stress human rather than abstract meaning of Communist party membership.

245   COCATRE-ZILGIER, ANDRE. Diplomatie française et problèmes internationaux contemporains. [Paris?] Editions Cujas, 1970. 262 p.

Collected articles by law professor, 1956-69, criticizing different aspects of de Gaulle's foreign policy and his interpretation of the world situation and French standing: decolonization, Atlantic Alliance, U.N., Israel, Canada. Some articles concern "micronational" problems in South Tyrol, Ireland, Belgium.

246   COGNIOT, GEORGES. La Révolution d'octobre et la France. . . . Paris, Editions sociales, 1966. 95 p. (Notre temps)

Lessons to be drawn from Russian Revolution for French Communism: need for strong party, yet democratic methods for transition to French socialist society.

247   COGNIOT, GEORGES, and VICTOR JOANNES. Maurice Thorez, l'homme, le militant. Préf. de Georges Marchais. Paris, Editions sociales, 1970. 186 p. port. (Collection Notre temps) Bibliographical footnotes.

Personal and political biography by two close collaborators in honor of the 70th anniversary of Thorez's birth (he died 1964). Thorez's determination to combine national and international objectives of French Communist Party and his view of P.C.F. as avant-garde of workers are stressed.

248   COHEN, MAURICE, ed. Le bilan social de l'année 1968; ouvrage collectif. Préf. de Henri Krasucki. Paris, Revue pratique de droit social, 1969. 574 p. plates, facsims.

Detailed, documented work, prefaced by C.G.T.'s secretary general, on gains for workers and other employees arising from Grenelle agreements with respect to wages, working hours, holidays, legal rights, apprenticeships, pensions, etc. outlined for individual industries. List of firms cited, with address, number of employees. Complete texts of principal agreements, laws and decrees (national and regional) by trade group and for important firms such as Renault, Citroën. Introductory chapter reviews state of economy (unemployment, real wages) before and after May 1968.

249   COHEN, STEPHEN S. Modern capitalist planning: the French model. London, Weidenfeld and Nicolson, 1969. x, 310 p. Bibliography: p. 269-302.

Exposition of original features of French planning, its history and mode of operation from First to Fifth Plan. Work also points out the failure of French planning to produce greater economic democracy, as demanded by Left, and carefully documents these critiques. May 1968 is seen as expression of these inadequacies and even a revolt against planning. Author is professor of city and regional planning at University of California, Berkeley. Good bibliography of books and articles, government documents.

250   COHN-BENDIT, DANIEL, and GABRIEL COHN-BENDIT. Obsolete communism; the left-wing alternative. Translated by Arnold Pomerans. New York, McGraw-Hill, 1968. 251 p.

Published in French as "La gauchisme--remède à la maladie sénile du communisme," written several weeks after May 1968 events as challenge to traditional bureaucratic structure in government and labor movements. Analysis covers principal factors in May events, giving authors' views on flaws of modern universities and why Nanterre sociology department was spark of revolt, disagreements with P.C.F. as well as other student and political leaders for their overcautiousness. Rest of work shows vulnerability of Gaullist state, role of C.G.T. and P.C.F. in saving government, bureaucratic character of latter organizations, and failure of revolution in Russia under Lenin. Gabriel is Daniel's older brother and professor in lycée.

251 COIN, JEAN. J'en appelle à cent mille hommes; la crise du P.C. et la révolution manquée. Paris, Plon, 1969. 440 p. (Tribune libre) Bibliographical footnotes.

Violent indictment of P.C.F. and C.G.T. leadership (Marchais, Waldeck Rochet) by former editor of Communist weekly "France nouvelle" who was finally excluded from party for his critique of its stand in May 1968 published in "Combat" on May 29, 1968. This text plus other unpublished proposals submitted to Rochet for reform of party is reproduced in appendix. On theoretical plane, Coin attacks recent P.C.F. program of united front with socialist and radical parties and its advocacy of a "démocratie véritable" as stage to Communism.

252 COLLIARD, JEAN-CLAUDE. Les Républicains indépendants; Valéry Giscard d'Estaing. Préf. de Maurice Duverger. Paris, Presses universitaires de France, 1971. 352 p. (Publications de l'Université de Paris I. Panthéon-Sorbonne. Série Science politique, 1) Includes bibliography.

History of Républicains indépendants (founded Nov. 1962 as splinter group of conservative Centre des Indépendants and operating within Gaullist majority), role of Giscard d'Estaing, party's evolution as reflected in public opinion surveys and its stand on political issues 1962-70, tending to become the nucleus of a new liberal party. Second part focuses on parliamentary representation, elections of 1962, 1967, and 1968, reluctant elaboration of party structures, the Fédération nationale des Républicains indépendants, related club "Perspectives et réalités" and organ "France moderne," as well as formulation of party doctrine. Includes statutes.

253 COLLOQUE DE DIJON, 4TH, 1965. L'élaboration de la politique étrangère; entretiens de Dijon organisées avec le concours de l'Association française de science politique et publiés sous la direction de Léo Hamon. Paris, Presses universitaires de France, 1969. 338 p. tables. (Publications du Centre d'études des relations politiques, Université de Dijon)

Talks on different elements influencing foreign policy: public opinion as expressed in polls, press; labor movement, parliament, personality of individual statesmen and their latitude of movement; military strategy, nuclear weapons, participation of military establishment in foreign policy decisions, and impact of military's anti-Communist bias since 1918. In addition to political scientists and sociologists, Generals Beaufre and Gallois are participants. Some of talks draw on foreign rather than French experience. For earlier Colloques de Dijon, also headed by Hamon, see French Fifth Republic Bibliography, 1, nos. 572, 943.

254 COMBE, MAURICE. L'alibi, vingt ans d'un comité central d'entreprise. Paris, Gallimard, 1969. 330 p. (Collection Témoins) Includes bibliographical references. ML

Study of the operation of a worker-management committee in a diversified metallurgical company, 1945-65. Author, former priest, has been skilled worker in company since 1949 and served on the committee, consulting official committee records for this scholarly work. Two main themes are how the committee functioned or failed to function in providing workers access to managerial responsibility, and how it affected profit-sharing. Conclusion is that management refused to yield in any important area and that committee has strengthened rather than overcome class struggle. No information on May 1968.

255 COMBES, JEAN-FRANÇOIS; EGEN, JEAN. Pour le service militaire [par] Jean-François Combes. Contre le service militaire [par] Jean Egen. Nancy, Berger-Levrault [1968?]. 80 p., 80 p. illus. (Pour ou contre, 14)

Advocate of universal military service proposes reform of military training to make it truly formative, while advocate of professional army insists on need for patriotic civilians with minimum of military preparation for defense of country.

256 COMITE D'ACTION SANTE. Médecine. Ce texte n'est qu'un début.... Paris, F. Maspéro, 1968. 80 p. illus. (Cahiers libres, no. 138)

Survey of current medical needs and reexamination of medical care, particularly doctor-patient relations in context of revolutionary movement. Existing socialized medicine is shown to be minimal medical care, with doctors acting as society's policemen and consumer society determining many medical needs. In place of hierarchized structure of medical profession, autonomous, non-hierarchic medical teams are proposed.

257 COMITE D'ETUDE ET DE LIAISON DES INTERETS BRETONS. Bretagne: une ambition nouvelle. Rennes, Presses universitaires de Bretagne, 1971. 169 p. plates, maps, diagrs.

C.E.L.I.B. was constituted 1950 as regional association and has been active in regional reform. This collective work sums up regional developments already undertaken, how Brittany's assets can best be exploited, and proposes new forms of urbanization, local and regional administration. See also no. 925.

258 COMITE ETUDIANT POUR LES LIBERTES UNIVERSITAIRES. Pour rebâtir l'université; étude réalisée par un groupe de syndicalistes étudiants. Paris, Table ronde, 1969. 176 p. Bibliographical footnotes.

Student revolt is explained as result of overcentralized state control coinciding with susceptibility to revolutionary influence of over-politicized student syndicalism on the part of mass of isolated, unorganized, irresponsible students. C.E.L.U. advocates regionally controlled and financed universities, greater diversity in higher education, more support of "free" Catholic universities. Post-1968 reforms threaten to institutionalize conflict and degrade the system. Appendix includes 1967 C.E.L.U. report on financing education.

259 COMMISSION OF THE EUROPEAN COMMUNITIES. DIRECTORATE GENERAL OF AGRICULTURE. Le Plan Mansholt. Le rapport Vedel. 3e éd. Paris, 1969. 589 p. port. Includes bibliography.

1968 Mansholt memorandum on reform of agriculture within European Economic Community to restrict surpluses, particularly of dairy products, and to shift to large-scale farming. Vedel Commission report summarizes long-range (1965-85) evolution of French agriculture in terms of market for food products, available labor force and capital. Separate propositions for now agricultural policy review extreme alternatives and offer compromise model that takes into account some non-economic objectives as well.

260 COMMISSION TEMOIGNAGES ET ASSISTANCE JURIDIQUE. Ils accusent. Paris, Editions du Seuil, 1968. 285 p.

This is joint commission of U.N.E.F. and Syndicat national d'enseignement supérieur to collect, verify, and publicize facts on police repression. Detailed chronology for May 3-June 27, 1968, followed by reports on different aspects of police repression: use of arms, choice of victims, invasion of private homes, expulsion of foreign students and workers, deaths in Flins and Sochaux, with personal testimonies. List of O.R.T.F. staff dismissed July 1968. Laws and statutes regulating subversive organizations presented. See also no. 1085.

261 COMMUNICATIONS (periodical). Mai 1968; la prise de la parole. Paris, Editions du Seuil, 1968. 183 p. (Its Issue no. 12, 1968) Includes bibliography.

July 1968 articles include contributions by Edgar Morin and Michel Crozier analyzing student movement and elements of university education related to crisis as social psychologists. One article on Internationale situationniste. "Communications" is forum for Centre d'études des communications de masses at Ecole pratique des hautes études. Good bibliography.

262 Conditions de vie et besoins de personnes âgées en France. Enquêtes effectuées sous la direction de Paul Paillat. I. Les citadins âgés [par] Paul Paillat et Claudine Wibaux. Préf. d'Alfred Sauvy. Paris, Presses universitaires de France, 1969. xi, 281 p. tables. (Institut national d'etudes démographiques. Travaux et documents. Cahier no. 52) ML

Institut national d'études démographiques 1964 study undertaken for Fifth Plan. This volume samples urban population born prior to 1900 among those non-institutionalized, with questionnaires to 3,000 persons out of the total of three million. Questions on health, past and present professional activity, resources, housing, contacts with outside world, entertainment.

263 CONESA, GABRIEL. Bab-el-Oued, notre paradis perdu. Paris, R. Laffont, 1970. 221 p. plan. (Collection "Vécu")

Flashbacks on Bab-el-Oued childhood, youth, and adulthood by French Algerian who later wrote for "Journal d'Alger" and "Paris-Match" and left Algeria in 1962. Transformation of carefree European district in Algiers during last months of carnage is presented wholly from French Algerian point of view.

264 CONFERENCE INTERNATIONALE SUR LE CAPITALISME MONOPOLISTE D'ETAT, CHOISY-LE-ROI, FRANCE, 1966. Le capitalisme monopoliste d'état; conférence internationale, Choisy-le-Roi, 26/29 mai 1966. Paris, Economie et politique, revue marxiste d'économie, 1966. 2 v.

Conference organized by P.C.F. and Communist journal "Economie et politique" to study changes in contemporary capitalism. Both French and other European (Western and Eastern) Communists were represented. Volume 1 has text of French speakers, among them Henri Claude, Francette Lazard, André Barjonet, Waldeck Rochet on new planning methods, nationalizations, monopolistic concentration induced by Common Market, lowering of real wages. Volume 2 has texts of foreign speakers and special reports on French wages, agriculture, overseas aid and investment in Fifth Republic.

265 CONNAISSANCE DE L'HISTOIRE (periodical). Les journées de mai. Paris, 1968. 128 p. illus. (No. spécial . . . 56 bis)

Pictorial history, May 3-29, 1968, based on "France-Soir" photographs. Street scenes, plants on strike, portraits of government and university figures, labor leaders.

266 Construire le parti révolutionnaire, construire l'Internationale. Extraits du débat préparatoire au congrès de fondation de la Ligue communiste. Paris, F. Maspéro, 1969. 3 v. 157 p., 114 p., 175 p. (Cahiers "Rouge." Documents de formation communiste nos. 6-7, 8-9, 10-11)

Preliminary debates within "Cercles Rouges" carried on in pages of "Bulletin des Diffuseurs de Rouge" between Dec. 1968 and actual meeting of founding congress, Apr. 1969. Majority tendency favored link with Fourth International. Final volume also contains resolutions of congress and statutes of Ligue communiste.

267 CONTE, ARTHUR. Sans de Gaulle. Paris, Plon, 1970. 202 p.

Adaptations required in French political life after de Gaulle's departure to meet public need for stability and tranquility on constitutional, economic, and international plane. A former Socialist and a Gaullist parliamentarian since 1963, the author advocates a loose bi-party system revolving around Gaullists as large center party and P.C.F. as only strong leftist group.

268 Contradictions capitalistes et crise monétaire. Paris, F. Maspéro, 1968. 31 p. (Cahiers "Rouge." Document Rouge no. 6)

Economic problems at end of 1968 as seen by organ of Ligue communiste.

269 Les contradictions du capitalisme français et leurs solutions bourgeoises. Paris, F. Maspéro, 1969. 30 p. (Cahiers "Rouge." Document Rouge no. 2)

State of French economy, structural and monetary problems on eve of June 1969 presidential election and Ligue communiste's evaluation of Pompidou and Poher with respect to economic policy.

270 Contribution au problème de la construction d'un parti marxiste-léniniste de type nouveau. [Par] A. Badiou, H. Jancovici, E. Terray [et] D. Menetry. Paris, F. Maspéro, 1970. 55 p. (Brochures des Comités d'action)

Jan. 1969 critique by dissident militants of Parti socialiste unifié's tactical and ideological mistakes with respect to May 1968, Soviet invasion of Czechoslovakia, and proposals for founding new type of "anti-revisionist" Marxist-Leninist party with Maoist affinities. Text of Alain Badiou's undelivered speech prepared for P.S.U.'s sixth congress.

271 COPFERMANN, EMILE, ed. Ce n'est qu'un début, continuons le combat. Paris, F. Maspéro, 1968. 143 p. (Cahiers libres 124)

Mouvement du 22 mars viewed through its activities at Nanterre and in factories. Texts of leaflets (May-June 1968) and excerpts from "Tribune du 22 mars."

272 CORBEL, PIERRE. Le Parlement français et la planification. Préf. de Pierre Bauchet. Paris, Editions Cujas, 1969. 398 p. (Cahiers de l'Institut d'études politiques de l'Université de Grenoble, 6) Includes bibliography.

Scholarly work on French planning divided into four parts: (1) characteristics of French planning and its constitutional foundation in Fourth and Fifth Republic, (2) parliamentary control over successive plans, (3) intervention of parliamentarians in plans, (4) planning and legislative jurisdiction. Good bibliography of books and articles.

273 CORNATION, MICHEL. Les regroupements de la décolonisation en Algérie. Paris, Economie et humanisme, Editions ouvrières, 1967. 296 p. illus. (Collection "Développement et civilisations") Bibliography: p. [281]-290.

Population regrouping or resettlement as by-product of Algerian war, 1955-61: characteristics of relocation centers and living conditions therein, official regrouping policy and dissolution during last year of war. Second half of work describes fate of centers after independence, 1962-64: urbanization of uprooted farmers, transformation of relocation centers into rural centers. Bibliography includes studies by various government agencies, government instructions and inspection reports.

274 CORNEC, JEAN; CAPELLE, JEAN. Pour le baccalauréat [par] Jean Cornec. Contre le baccalauréat [par] Jean Capelle. Paris, Berger-Levrault, 1968. 80 p., 80 p. (Collection Pour ou contre, 16)

Supporter of baccalauréat is head of Fédération des Conseils de parents d'élèves, feels exam has useful function and is sufficient control for access to university. Opponent is university administrator who criticizes exam's unreliability, its morbid influence on secondary education, and excessive number of students it attracts to universities. There were 5,000 students passing bachot in 1900, 250,000 candidates and 150,000 passing it in 1968, about one-quarter of those beginning secondary education.

275 COSTON, HENRY. L'abominable vénalité de la presse française. Paris, 1969. 48 p. ("Lectures françaises," no. 142, février 1969)

Historical and current instances of press corruption, the latter mainly related to pro-Israel bias and concealed Jewish influence.

276 COSTON, HENRY, ed. Dictionnaire de la politique française. Tome II. Paris, Librairie française, 1972. 782 p. illus., ports.

Valuable complement to 1967 edition (Tome I) of "Dictionnaire politique" (see French Fifth Republic Bibliography, 1, no. 405) which it updates and corrects. Material goes up to 1971, with many entries on new regionalist organizations, extreme Left ("gauchistes"), new Gaullist groups, new Parti socialiste.

277 COSTON, HENRY, ed. Dictionnaire des pseudonymes. Tome II. Paris, Librairie française, 1969. ("Lectures françaises," no. spécial, décembre 1969)

Continues Tome I (1961) with new entries, alphabetically listed, of pen names, followed by real name and profession, but no other biographical information. Mostly writers, journalists, cartoonists.

278 COSTON, HENRY, ed. Le secret des dieux. Paris, 1968. 340 p. ("Lectures françaises," no. spécial) Bibliographical footnotes.

Wealth of information on investment banks, industrial holding companies, press. Individual contributions, many by Coston, show ties between international finance and French political parties, press. Among individual politicians whose personal links are aired are Pompidou, Defferre, Mendès-France. Strong anti-Semitic orientation among contributors. Index of names mentioned in text.

279 COTTERET, JEAN-MARIE, and CLAUDE EMERI. Les systèmes électoraux. Paris, Presses universitaires de France, 1970. 125 p. ("Que sais-je?" no. 1382) Includes bibliography.

Voting conditions, different types of electoral systems (majority with two ballots, proportional representation), and elections as method of communication between governed and government are viewed through experiences of various countries.

280 COTTERET, JEAN-MARIE, and RENE MOREAU. Recherches sur le vocabulaire du général de Gaulle; analyse statistique des allocutions radio-diffusées, 1958-1965. Paris, A. Colin, 1969. 247 p. diagrs. (Fondation nationale des sciences politiques. Travaux et recherches de sciences politiques, 3)

Texts of all 46 radio-TV addresses between June 13, 1958 and Dec. 31, 1965 (reproduced, with dates, at end of work) were computer-analyzed. Results are alphabetically listed vocabulary of 4,000 words used by de Gaulle, frequency of use, statistics on sentence length, richness of vocabulary. Speeches fall into two classes: appeals and reports, each with its own linguistic pattern. The 10 most frequently used nouns are: France, pays, république, état, monde, peuple, nation, progrès, paix, avenir.

281 COTTIER, GEORGES M. MARTIN. Chrétiens et marxistes; dialogue avec Roger Garaudy. Préf. de M.-D. Chenu. Tours, Mame, 1967. 198 p. Bibliographical footnotes.

Catholic theologian, in spirit of Vatican I, opens dialogue with Marxist Garaudy by analyzing his writings on atheism, religion, and Christianity. Common tenets are faith in human reason and love of truth.

282 COULET, FRANÇOIS. Vertu des temps difficiles. 21 illus. hors texte. Paris, Plon, 1967. 302 p. ML

Memoirs of former diplomat, de Gaulle adjutant in Resistance, reserve officer serving in Algeria 1956-59 as commander of a helicopterized parachutist commando detachment in Kabylia of the Armée de l'air. Extensive description of participation in military operations, encounters with military leaders in Algeria.

283 COURRIERE, YVES. La guerre d'Algérie. Paris, Fayard, 1968-71. 4 v. plates, ports. Includes bibliographies.

v. 1: Les fils de la Toussaint. Préf. de Joseph Kessel. 1968. 450 p.
v. 2: Le temps des léopards. 1969. 612 p.
v. 3: L'heure des colonels. 1970. 630 p.
v. 4: Les feux du désespoir (La fin d'un empire). 1971. 675 p.

Major journalistic work on Algerian war giving balanced reconstruction of the conflict on basis of published studies, fictional works, personal accounts by French and Algerians. Volume 1, after introductory section presenting eyewitness account of Mar. 1962 in Algiers, covers political and military background to outbreak of revolution in Algeria. Volume 2 covers Feb. 1955-Mar. 1957, describing conflict through eyes of French-Algerian fanatics, French administrators and politicians, Algerian nationalists, and men of goodwill trying to prevent the growing violence from creating a permanent breach. Volume 3 concerns military operations Feb. 1957-Apr. 1958, de Gaulle's return to power as seen from Algeria, continuation of war under de Gaulle, barricades insurrection Jan. 1960. Final volume covers sequel of barricades, secret de Gaulle negotiations with Kabylian rebel leader Si Salah, Generals' Putsch, history of O.A.S. from formative stages to Salan's capture and O.A.S. participation in peace agreement, protracted government negotiations with F.L.N., efforts of Mouvement pour la coopération under Jacques Dauer in late 1961 to counteract O.A.S. influence, rue d'Isly shooting Mar. 1962. Includes vivid portraits of Delouvrier, Morin, and Fouchet, the top French representatives in Algeria. Extensive bibliographies for each volume, good photographs.

284 COURRIERE, YVES. La guerre d'Algérie en images. Paris, Fayard, 1972. 278 p. illus.

Photographs accompanied by commentaries, drawn from film "La guerre d'Algérie" by Courrière and Philippe Monnier, serve as pictorial history of the Algerian war.

285 COUVE DE MURVILLE, MAURICE. Intervention, Lille, 25, XI, 1967. [n.p., 1967] 6 l.

Speech on foreign policy problems of past year--Canada, Near East, England and Common Market--at Nov. 1967 Assises nationales of Union des démocrates pour la Cinquième République.

286 COUVE DE MURVILLE, MAURICE. Une politique étrangère 1958-1969. Paris, Plon, 1971. 499 p.

De Gaulle's foreign minister June 1958-June 1968, prime minister July 1968-June 1969, gives historical account and justification of major areas of French foreign policy: relations with Soviet Union and Eastern Europe, U.S.; stand on European political and and economic unification and British admission to Common Market; relations with rest of world, U.N. Chronology of diplomatic events.

287 CRAIPEAU, YVAN. Le mouvement trotskyste en France, des origines aux enseignements de mai 68. Paris, Editions Syros, 1971. 285 p. Includes bibliography.

Main part of work was written in 1947 and presents history of Trotskyism in France before World War II, when author was secretary general of Parti communiste internationaliste. Final 75 pages deal with disillusionment with collectivist model of socialism after 1947, Trotskyist approach to socialism in advanced industrial societies, implications of May 1968, currently active Trotskyist factions, and search for an effective revolutionary party, which Parti socialiste unifié at time of writing approximates more than any other organization.

288 CRAS, HERVE, GEORGES ANDRE CHEVALLEZ, et al. Dossiers de la guerre froide. [Par] J. Mordal [pseud.], G. A. Chevallaz, et al. Verviers, Marabout université, 1969. 386 p. plates, ports. (Marabout université, 177) Includes bibliography.

Four approaches to cold war, 1948-63: military crises (Mordal), diplomatic responses (Chevallez), espionage (R. Gheysen), and psychological warfare (J. de Launay), leading to fragmentation of blocs after decline of conflict.

289 CRAWLEY, AIDAN. De Gaulle; a biography. Indianapolis, Bobbs-Merrill, 1969. 510 p. illus., ports. Bibliography: p. 487-493.

Final 140 pages deal with Fifth Republic: return to power, Algerian conflict, assertion of own political style over party opposition, formulation of own "grand design" in terms of Atlantic Alliance, foreign and military policy. Final chapter assesses significance of May 1968 on de Gaulle's ambitions. No new sources but well-rounded portrait and good condensation of French history. Includes list of works by de Gaulle.

290 CREMIEUX, FRANCIS, ed. La vérité sur la libération de Paris; témoignages de André Carrel et al. Paris, P. Belfond, 1971. 186 p.

Factual information does not go beyond 1944, but Crémieux orients questions to participants, including Chaban-Delmas, Léo Hamon, and several P.C.F. functionaries, to make clear that liberation of Paris did not result in power struggle between Communists and Gaullists and that Resistance, notwithstanding dissensions, was united. Interviews originally took place on Aug. 1964 television broadcast celebrating 20th anniversary of liberation and served as reply to insinuations of American best seller "Is Paris burning?"

291 CRIBIER, FRANÇOISE. La grande migration d'été des citadins en France. Paris, Editions du Centre national de la recherche scientifique, 1969. v. 1, 403 p., tables, plates, maps. v. 2, 32 folded maps. (Centre de recherches et documents cartographiques. Mémoires et documents, no. hors série)

National and regional analysis of how 10 million French citizens spread out for summer vacation, social distinctions in vacation pattern, cost of vacation, accommodations, examination of vacation areas. Pros and cons of concentrated vacations studied (on Aug. 15, 1964, four million Parisians left town). Study based on I.N.S.E.E. samples, 1961-67, of entire French population, railway figures, author's own study of schoolchildren's vacations.

292 CRIDDLE, BYRON. Socialists and European integration; a study of the French Socialist Party. London, Routledge and Kegan Paul; New York, Humanities Press, 1969. xii, 115 p. (Library of political studies) Includes bibliography.

History of S.F.I.O.'s stand on European unification, the Atlantic Alliance, German rearmament. Author concludes that throughout Fourth and Fifth Republic, pro-European sentiments were based on anti-Communism, anti-German feelings rather than socialist economic tenets.

293 CRINON, MONIQUE, DANIEL DUIGOU, and JACQUES GERARD. Lycéens en action. Paris, EPI, 1970. 60 p. ML

History and range of lycée militancy, enumeration of groups and movements currently active in demanding reforms after demise of most Comités d'action lycéens in 1969-70. Lists, with addresses, names of publications of parent associations, teacher unions, youth-oriented political organizations (mainly Trotskyist, Maoist, and anarchist).

294 CROCHAT, MAX. Le marché des eurodévises. Paris, Editions de l'Epargne, 1969. 252 p. (De quoi s'agit-il) Includes bibliography.

Use of eurodévises (not an international currency but an intangible form of dollar credit in national currency) and impact thereof on banking practices, credit and investment policies in France and other European countries.

295 CROS, LOUIS. The "explosion" in the schools. Paris, Sevpen, 1963. 186 p. tables, graphs. (Education and economy) ML

Synthesis of a series of articles on the transformation of French educational needs and methods that appeared in the official publication "Education nationale" in 1957 and 1960, with emphasis on the rapid increase of secondary and university students, introduction of active pedagogic methods. Good tables and graphs showing enrollment increment in past century.

296 CROS, VITALIS. Le temps de la violence. Paris, Presses de la Cité, 1971. 343 p. plates, ports.

Personal narrative by police prefect appointed to post in Algiers Nov. 1961, when civil disorder and O.A.S. activities were at their peak. In appendix: communications of police prefect with General Ailleret, Prime Minister Debré; other police communiqués on state of police strength; some O.A.S. tracts and pirate radio broadcasts.

297 CROZIER, MICHEL. La société bloquée. Paris, Editions du Seuil, 1970. 252 p.

Main part of work focuses on French civilization's blockages in adapting to need for more innovative, flexible, and less authoritarian solutions to human and technological problems and suggests administrative or institutional reforms. Some chapters were added using May 1968 university crisis as illustration of efforts to break down these blockages. Contrary to prevalent views, Crozier, who is research sociologist and professor at Nanterre, sees crisis of advanced societies as fear of most human beings to face freedom within rational choice sanctioned by measurable results of this choice and foresees alliance of revolutionary and conservative forces against needed changes. He did not support students at Nanterre, considers opening up of Grandes écoles to competition as most urgent educational reform. See also no. 1137.

298 CYRILLE [pseud. ?]. Les réprouvés de l'honneur. Porrentruy, Suisse, Editions Occident, 1968. 260 p.

Fictional reconstruction of various episodes in history of O.A.S. before Algerian independence. One long episode postdates independence and shows underground O.A.S. work on Swiss border, confrontation between O.A.S. officer and "piedsnoirs" repatriates who reject collaboration with O.A.S.

299 DAMETTE, FELIX. Le territoire français, son aménagement. Préf. par Jean Fabre. Paris, Editions sociales, 1969. 145 p. tables, fold. col. maps.

Introduction by editor of Communist journal "Economie et politique" explains P.C.F.'s opposition to Apr. 1969 referendum on regional reform: that it would reinforce technocratic and autocratic tendencies under veil of increased regional participation. Main work is detailed, scholarly study of different regions in terms of geographic and economic factors, industrial and demographic trends, with eight regions selected as best suited for basic units of administration: Paris, region surrounding Paris, North, East, West, Garonne, Lyon, Mediterranean. Good tables on regional industries, income.

300 DAN, URI, et al. De Gaulle contre Israël; documents sur l'embargo. [Par] Uri Dan et l'équipe d'Edition spéciale. Paris, 1969. 200 p. (Edition spéciale)

Franco-Israeli relations, centering on purchase of French military equipment ($1-1/2 billion between 1954 and 1969) and abrupt change from policy of friendship to one of neutrality in May 1967, embargo on arms to Israel, second arms embargo Jan. 1969. Covers reactions of French press, political parties, statements by Debré.

301 DANSETTE, ADRIEN. Mai 1968. Paris, Plon, 1971. 473 p. Bibliography: p. 463-464.

Well-rounded history of May-June 1968, covering not only student movement and its origins but political and social aspects of crisis. Original material on mobilization of Gaullist forces at end of May and role of army, disappearance of de Gaulle May 29. Appendices include minutes of May 11 session of Sorbonne's Conseil de l'université on approving Rector Roche's actions during preceding night and May 29 letter of Police Prefect Maurice Grimaud to his staff.

302 DARBEL, ALAIN, and DOMINIQUE SCHNAPPER. Morphologie de la haute administration française. v. 1: Les agents du système administratif. Paris, Mouton, 1969. 160 p. tables, diagrs. (Paris. Ecole pratique des hautes études. Centre de sociologie européenne. Cahiers, 6)

Results of I.N.S.E.E. census on social and cultural background of government employees (agents de l'état), complemented by intensive research on upper echelons of administrative hierarchy of central government. There are chapters on social origins of different ranks of civil servants, attitudes toward and actual fecundity, geographic distribution (tables in appendix). For upper echelon, religious affiliation and differences in social background and in attitudes of men and women also presented.

303 DARTAN, JACQUES. Le défi européen. Paris, Editions sociales françaises, 1968. 111 p. (Collection Survivre, 4)

Dialogue by members of Centre international d'études biosociales on causes of French student revolt, blame being placed on educational system and intellectual climate of Western civilization combining loss of faith in search for objective truth with vacuous Marxism. Orthology, a new movement founded by Léon-David Steiner, is considered only proper instrument for forming intellect.

304 DAUMARD, PIERRE. Le prix de l'enseignement en France. Préf. d'Edgar Faure. Paris, Calmann-Lévy, 1969. 269 p. tables. (Perspectives économiques. Economie contemporaine) Bibliography: p. 262-266.

Introduction by Faure clearly states inadaptability of current educational situation. Main part of work breaks down educational budget into its components, trends in total and unit cost of education (teacher salaries, equipment), expenses by central and local government, families. In 1968 total government expenses were 20 percent of budget, 4 percent of gross national product, and cost for different types of education ranged from Fr. 12,000 for minimum 10-year compulsory education to Fr. 40,000 for university degree. Author shows how near tripling of real expenditures on education between 1955 and 1968 was always ex post response to increases in demand through population explosion and extension of education, and how economic factors contributed to persistence of social inequities in secondary and higher education. Author predicts continued rise in educational costs.

305 DAUPHIN-MEUNIER, ACHILLE. Une université vraiment libre est-elle possible? est-elle souhaitable? Texte de la conférence faite . . . le 22 janvier 1969. Paris, Centre d'études politiques et civiques, 1969. 54 p. (Cahiers du C.E.P.E.C., 39)

Rector of Paris Faculté libre autonome et congérée d'économie, a private, Catholic-oriented school founded July 1968, in response to degradation of public universities, explains how new "loi d'orientation" is useful as instrument of parent and student participation at the Faculté libre.

306 DAVEZIES, ROBERT. Mai 68, la rue dans l'Eglise. Présentation de Robert Davezies. Dessins d'André Scob. Paris, Editions de l'Epi, 1968. 144 p. illus.

July 1968 street interviews with eight Catholics who took part in May 1968 revolt. Author, who is sympathetic to revolt, seeks meaning of recent events in terms of their religious convictions and failures of organized church. Includes appeals signed by prominent Catholics supporting revolution.

307 DAVID, ANDRE. Paroles d'or; les coulisses des "Conférences des Ambassadeurs." Paris, Table ronde, 1969. 291 p.

Inside story of current-events lecture series, "Conférences des Ambassadeurs," 1931-69, by one of its organizers. For Fifth Republic, highlights are speeches by various members of the government, ecumenical discussions, talks on the future of Paris by administrators and planners.

308 DAVRANCHE, MAURICE. Enquête sur la jeunesse. Réalisée par Maurice Davranche et commentée par Georges Fouchard. Paris, Gallimard, 1968. 386 p. (Idées, 167)

Results of May 1967 investigation based on questionnaires answered by 4,700 students, aged 14-20, mostly in Paris area, concerning leisure activities, sports, military service, and temporary work. Authors draw on results to propose reorganization of work during vacations, using university students as staff for adult education program and replacing meaningless military service with voluntary service in underdeveloped countries.

309 DEBBASCH, CHARLES. L'administration au pouvoir; fonctionnaires et politiques sous la Ve République. Paris, Calmann-Lévy, 1969. 218 p. (Questions d'actualité)

Changes in status of civil servants within Fifth Republic's political institutions and in governmental practice, leading to increased representation of high-level civil servants in political leadership, as a function of new laws, Gaullist doctrine. Statistics on links between civil service and cabinet, parliament, educational background of civil servants, impact of Ecole nationale d'administration. Professor of administrative law discusses recent reforms affecting civil service: creation of mission-oriented agencies, decentralization through regionalization and restructuring of communes.

310 DEBBASCH, CHARLES. L'université désorientée; autopsie d'une mutation. Paris, Presses universitaires de France, 1971. 173 p. ML

Main provisions of "loi d'orientation" for French universities promulgated by Edgar Faure as minister of education and further implemented by his successor Olivier Guichard. Law sets new goals and structures for higher education, student-faculty participation in administration, greater autonomy. Includes Faure's presentation speech to National Assembly and text of law. Useful figures for enrollment in university faculties 1900-1970 and in individual universities 1950-70, list of ministers of education 1808-1970, 12 of them under Fifth Republic.

311 DEBORD, GUY. La société du spectacle. Paris, Buchet/Chastel, 1967. 175 p.

Author (French, born 1931) is editor of "Internationale situationniste." This is one of major contributions to protest against affluent society and its creation of pseudo-needs, alienated consumption combining with alienated production. "Le spectacle est matériellement l'expression de la séparation et de l'éloignement entre l'homme et l'homme." Worker councils, not Communism as presently organized, seen as answer to alienation.

312 DEBRAY, PIERRE. A bas la calotte rouge! Paris, Table ronde, 1968. 178 p. (La Table ronde de Combat. "Les Brûlots," 7) ML

Polemical attack on self-styled Marxist Dominican priest Jean Cardonnel, who converted Scriptures into Communist gospel and received support of Catholic Left. Author, defending "integrist" Catholic stand, criticizes Catholic mainstream for adapting to affluent society and blames both revolutionary and reformist elements for failures of Catholic leadership in May 1968. Main part of book concluded Apr. 1968.

313 DEBRAY, PIERRE. Dossier des Nouveaux prêtres. Paris, Table ronde, 1965. 253 p. (Ordre du jour) ML

Michel de Saint-Pierre's novel "Les nouveaux prêtres" (1964) giving unfavorable picture of priest in working-class suburb of Paris, which was attacked by Catholic Left, serves as point of departure for diatribe against leftist clergy and organizations and publications supporting Marxist outlook and pressing for rapid "aggiornamento." Author defends "integrist" Catholic position. Texts of comments, statements by Catholic laymen and clergy on problems raised by novel.

314 DEBRE, MICHEL. Discours, Lille, 12, 26 novembre 1967. [n.p., 1967] 23 l.

Speech by minister of economy and finance on Fifth Republic's achievements: strong government, economic and technological progress, independence, international collaboration. Talk delivered at Nov. 1967 Assises nationales of Union des démocrates pour la Cinquième République.

315 DEBRE, MICHEL. Lettre à des militants sur la continuité, l'ouverture et la fidélité. Paris, Plon, 1970. 31 p.

Speech to Gaullist party members at first anniversary of de Gaulle's defeat, Apr. 1969, reminding them of de Gaulle's position on main political issues and his basic attitudes, which were being maintained under the new government, as well as his flexibility in front of changing realities, calling for openness on such issues as education, European policy, role of parliament.

316 DEBU-BRIDEL, JACQUES. De Gaulle contestataire. Paris, Plon, 1970. 254 p. (Tribune libre)

Politician active on Gaullist Left reviews de Gaulle's career as statesman, 1945-69, and fate of Gaullist organizations to demonstrate that Gaullism's true meaning and de Gaulle's efforts lay in the quest for social justice, national independence, and strong political institutions, not conservatism and anti-Communism. May 1968 is interpreted as result of blockage of De Gaulle's reforms by conservative elements animated by Pompidou, who has been abandoning all de Gaulle's objectives since coming to presidency.

317 DECAUNES, LUC, ed. Réformes et projets de réforme de l'enseignement français de la Révolution à nos jours (1789-1960); étude historique, analytique et critique. . . . Documentation réunie par L. Cavalier. Paris, Institut pédagogique national, 1962. 419 p. (Mémoires et documents scolaires, no. 16) Bibliography: p. 419. ML

For Fifth Republic, the 1959 "Berthoin" reform, the major Gaullist educational reform which raised compulsory school age to 16 and introduced observation cycle for ages 11-13, is dealt with in detail. Complete text of parliamentary proposals, ordinances, decrees (1919-59) in appendix.

318 DECOUFLE, ANDRE. Sociologie des révolutions. . . . Paris, Presses universitaires de France, 1968. 128 p. ("Que sais-je?" no. 1298) Bibliography: p. [127].

Attempt to formulate categories tying together the revolutionary project, revolutionary acts, and revolutionary government which characterized certain historical revolutions (Russian, French, Commune, Chinese), with emphasis on concepts expressed by Sartre in "Critique de la raison dialectique." Counterrevolution is analyzed within the same framework.

319 DEFENSE DE L'OCCIDENT (periodical). Les nouveaux communistes; les partis pro-chinois dans le monde. [Par] Maurice Bardèche et al. Paris, 1968. 104 p. (Numéro spécial, no. 68, janvier 1968)

Introductory article by Bardèche explains crisis of Marxism and international Communism through disappointment in Soviet Union and working class, a rebirth of Spartacism coinciding with anti-white racism. Long article by François Duprat on pro-Chinese Communist elements in France, notably the Union des jeunesses communistes marxistes-léninistes.

320 DEFRASNE, JEAN. La gauche en France de 1789 à nos jours. Paris, Presses universitaires de France, 1972. 127 p. ("Que sais-je?" no. 1464) Bibliography: p. 126-127.

Final 12 pages give succinct account of fate of parliamentary and extra-parliamentary Left in Fifth Republic and disarray after June 1969 presidential election. Author sees three current manifestations of Left: libertarian (Radicals, Socialists, P.S.U.), authoritarian (P.C.F.), and revolutionary (gauchistes).

321 De Gaulle au Quebec. Montréal, Editions Actualité, 1967. 143 p.

Report on de Gaulle's July 1967 visit to Canada and its aftermath, as reflected in Canadian, U.S., and French press. Editor favors independence of Quebec. Includes excerpts from de Gaulle statements and speeches.

322 DEJACQUES, CLAUDE. A toi l'angoisse, à moi la rage, mai 68, les fresques de Nanterre. Paris, E. Nalis, 1968. 1 v. (unpaged). col. illus. (Le Document du mois) ML

Color photographs of unsigned collective paintings on walls of big Nanterre auditorium, each fresco preceded by author's own empathetic response to visual stimulus, vaguely related to themes of revolt, in form of free poems.

323 DEJAY, EDOUARD, PHILIPPE JOHNSSON, and CLAUDE MOLITERNI. Paris, mai/juin 1968, 94 documents. Paris, Editions S.E.R.G., 1968. 48 l. illus.

Seventy (rather than 94) photographs chronologically arranged and described in introductory chronology. Technical quality of pictures is outstanding. Selection of scenes shows no pro-revolutionary bias.

324 DELBEZ, LOUIS. Les grands courants de la pensée politique française depuis le XIXe siècle. Avec une préf. de Pierre Jourda. Paris, Librairie générale de droit et de jurisprudence, R. Pichon et R. Durand-Auzias, 1970. 193 p. Includes bibliographical references.

French political thought is divided into different tendencies: traditional, democratic, socialist and Communist, Catholic, and nationalist, the last being the one in which de Gaulle and Gaullism find a place. Very little current material.

325 DELBREL, MADELEINE. Ville marxiste, terre de mission. Provocation du marxisme à une vocation pour Dieu. Rédigé à Ivry de 1933 à 1957. 2e éd. augm. avec une correspondance et deux textes inédits. Paris, Editions du Cerf, 1970. 276 p. (Foi vivante, 129)

Early instance of open confrontation and dialogue between Catholic faith and Communism in a Communist-dominated, militantly atheist suburb of Paris. Author was a Catholic social worker for Ivry Parish who died in 1964. Actual experiences pre-date 1957, except for exchanges with Ivry's Communist mayor, 1957-70, which are reproduced in introduction.

326 DELIGNY, FERNAND. Les vagabonds et autres récits. Préf. d'Emile Copfermann. Paris, F. Maspéro, 1970. 180 p. ("Textes à l'appui")

Personal account of professional experiences, 1940-67, in helping juvenile delinquents, maladapted and retarded children through highly unorthodox methods of reeducation. Author was incapable of adapting to any institutional framework.

327 DELMAS, CLAUDE. La France et l'Europe. Heule, Belgique, Editions UGA, 1967. 151 p. (Université internationale de sciences comparées, Luxembourg. Centre international d'études et de recherches européennes. Cours 1967) Includes bibliography.

Evolution of French position on economic, military, and political unification of Europe and de Gaulle's views on European integration, "Europe des patries," and application of these ideas to Atlantic Alliance, British membership in Common Market.

328 DELORME, HELENE, and YVES TAVERNIER. Les paysans français et l'Europe. Paris, A. Colin, 1969. 153 p. tables, diagrs. (Fondation nationale des sciences politiques. Travaux et recherches de science politique, 6) Includes bibliography.

Positions of main agricultural organizations (Fédération nationale des syndicats d'exploitants agricoles and Centre national des jeunes agriculteurs) in regard to agricultural Common Market, 1957-68. Positions of different agricultural sectors, as represented by producer associations (wheat, sugar beets, wine, cattle, dairy, etc.), are examined separately. Last section summarizes public opinion surveys of farmers' attitudes toward French European policy, European integration during this period.

329 DEMERON, PIERRE. Les 400 coups de Massu. Paris, J. J. Pauvert, 1972. 41 p. (Extrait du mensuel "Lui" de mars 1972, no. 98)

Indignant response to General Massu's self-justifying account of role in Algerian war in his recent "La vraie bataille d'Alger" (see no. 780) and rejection of alibis for use of torture.

330 DEMONQUE, MARCEL. Les conclusions du Comité Armand-Rueff; texte de la conférence faite au 21e dîner d'information du C.E.P.E.C., le mardi 25 octobre 1960. Paris, Centre d'études politiques et civiques, 1961. 31 p. (Cahiers du C.E.P.E.C., 15)

Industrialist who served on Comité explains obstacles to industrial expansion in French economy and society.

331 DENARIE, PAUL. L'aventure de Concorde. Paris, Presses noires, 1969. 189 p. plates, ports.

Technical and political collaboration and difficulties encountered in preparing the Franco-British supersonic jet plane for commercial flight, 1956-69. Includes names of British and French personalities involved in the project, short biographical sketches of 12 main figures, outline of plane's technical features, orders recorded as of 1969.

332 DePORTE, ANTON W. De Gaulle's foreign policy, 1944-1946. Cambridge, Mass., Harvard University Press, 1968 [i.e., 1967]. xiii, 327 p. Bibliography: p. [289]-292.

No recent material, but stress on continuity in de Gaulle's three foreign policy aims: French independence, link between East and West, restoration of great-power status. Of particular interest are de Gaulle's policy toward Germany and views on Western European alliance.

333 DEPREUX, EDOUARD. Souvenirs d'un militant: cinquante ans de lutte, de la social-démocratie au socialisme (1918-1968). Paris, Fayard, 1972. 608 p. (Les Grandes études contemporaines)

Fifty years' association with Socialist Party, with detailed account of his roles in governments of Fourth Republic, break with S.F.I.O. in protest against Mollet's Algerian intervention, and eventual split of S.F.I.O. and founding of Parti socialiste autonome, later the Parti socialiste unifié, of which Depreux is currently honorary secretary, and about which these memoirs are silent. Interesting inside account of conflicts within Left in final years of Fourth Republic and opposition to de Gaulle in 1958 and 1959.

334 DESHUSSES, JEROME. La Gauche réactionnaire. Paris, R. Laffont, 1969. 145 p.

Argument that the Left (and particularly French Left) is reactionary both in its unwarranted indulgence toward Soviet abuses, which are qualified as "social fascism," and in its anti-technological responses, whereby it joins traditional Right in seeking utopia in past.

335 DEUTSCH-FRANZÖSISCHES JUGENDWERK. Jugend heute. Jeunesse d'aujourd'hui. Bonn, 1968. 87 p. illus.

Photographs of German and French youth selected as winners of Mar.-Oct. 1968 contest sponsored by Jugendwerk (Office franco-allemand pour la jeunesse).

336 DIAMOND, ROBERT A., ed. France under de Gaulle. New York, Facts on File, 1970. 319 p. (Interim history)

Factual journalistic account of 11 years of government by de Gaulle, divided chronologically into years of Algerian war (1958-62), foreign policy years (1963-67), and crisis and conclusion (1968-69). Within each of three sections, whole spectrum of internal politics, economic affairs, and foreign and military policy is topically grouped. Useful quick reference work for events of Fifth Republic.

337 Dictionnaire des personnages historiques français. Paris, Nouvelle histoire de la France, 1968. 131 p. ports.

Includes biographical data on most prominent Fifth Republic personalities.

338 DIENESCH, [MARIE-MADELEINE]. Intervention aux Assises de Lille en novembre 1967. [n.p., 1967] [3] p.

Speech in favor of parliamentary and electoral cooperation with political movements outside Union des démocrates pour la Cinquième République. Talk delivered at Union's Assises nationales.

339 DOMBRET, ROGER. Quatre-vingt-cinq ans de vie et de lutte; des faits... des dates. Bellegarde, Ain, 1966. 169 p.

Treasurer of Fédération française des travailleurs du livre gives history of organization up to 1965, including its stand on political issues at Federation congresses. It belongs to C.G.T., has present membership of 70,000.

340 DOUCY, ARTHUR, and FRANCIS MONHEIM. Les révolutions algériennes. Paris, Fayard [c1971]. iii, 364 p. Includes bibliographical references.

Survey of industrial (detailed chapter on petroleum products), political, agricultural, and educational revolutions in Algeria, 1965-70, based primarily on official sources and interviews with government and party leaders. Chapter on Algerian foreign policy.

341 DRANCOURT, MICHEL. Ces entreprises qui font l'économie française. 2e éd. Paris, Entreprise moderne d'édition, 1969. 39 p. illus., diagrs.

Popular presentation of French standard of living around 1966-67, statistics on major industrial sectors (number of workers, dividends, wages, taxes paid), and comparisons between largest French and foreign firms.

342 DREYFUS, FRANÇOIS. Education nationale; rapport. [Paris, 1967] 32 p.

Educational progress during Fifth Republic: schools constructed, number of students, education budget, structural reforms, remaining problems in adapting French education to needs of modern economy. Speaker is professor at University of Strasbourg and party official of Union des démocrates pour la Cinquième République, at whose Assises nationales, Lille, Nov. 1967, this speech was given.

343 DREZE, JACQUES, and JEAN DEBELLE. Conceptions de l'université. Préf. de Paul Ricoeur. Paris, Editions universitaires, 1968. 136 p. (Citoyens, 1) ML

Five conceptions discussed are those of German university (research community), British university (setting for intellectual growth), American university (symbiosis of research and education, stimulation of social progress), in contrast to Soviet and French universities, which are both government tools. The Napoleonic university is conceived as intellectual molding force, the Soviet university as production tool. Impact of mass university on these different goals is analyzed and need seen for network of diversified institutions.

344 DRON, PIERRE. J.J.-S.S.: attention, danger. Paris, Pensée universelle, 1971. 125 p.

Confused diatribe against Jean-Jacques Servan-Schreiber by German-born journalist, who presents him as symptom of antinational subversion and conspirator for synarchy, under veil of economic renovation. Direct target is the "Manifeste radical."

345 DRUON, MAURICE. L'avenir en désarroi. Paris, Plon, 1968. 119 p. ML

Novelist's condemnation of youth revolt as out of proportion to existing evils in French civilization, blaming this attitude on excessive liberalism of society, universities, but regretting at the same time that youth didn't revolt against failure of older generation to carry through construction of truly supernational, socialist, and humanist Europe.

346 DRUON, MAURICE. Lettres d'un Européen, 1943-1970. Paris, Plon, 1970. 329 p.

Plea for European unification consists of two sets of fictitious letters, one dated London, 1943, the other 1968/70. In the latter, Europe's special role as power for peace and source of new civilization transcending crises of modern society, so deeply experienced by youth, is presented to new generation.

347 DUBAIL, RENE. Au nom des silencieux; chronique des années difficiles (1963-1971). Paris, Editions municipales, 1971. 109 p.

Paris politician (XIIIth district) and supporter of Républicains indépendants comments on local Paris issues, education, economic and political questions, expressing conservative views of "silent majority" in face of rapidly changing society. Chronologically arranged essays originally appeared in municipal journal.

348 DUBOIS, JEAN. Les cadres dans la société de consommation. Paris, Editions du Cerf, 1969. 216 p. ML

Sociological definition of "cadre" seen as a social class, a particular product of advanced industrial, affluent society. Estimates range from 700,000 to three million cadres, with average salary of Fr. 4,000, compared to average worker salary of Fr. 1,000. Second party of study closely analyzes advertisements for suburban apartment complex Parly II to show image of "cadre" as consumer and examines prospects for "cadre" to improve quality of this life.

349 DUCATEL, LOUIS. Face à face avec Pompidou; vers un nouveau contrat social. Paris, Nouvelles éditions latines, 1969. 267 p. Includes bibliography.

Defeated independent candidate in June 1969 presidential election (250,000 votes) explains reasons for candidacy, program for a "Mouvement social et démocratique" attacking technocracy. Includes interview with Pompidou which led to Ducatel's desistance and support for Pompidou on second ballot. Three television interviews May 1969 in appendix.

350 DUCLOS, JACQUES. Anarchistes d'hier et d'aujourd'hui; comment le gauchisme fait le jeu de la réaction. Paris, Editions sociales, 1968. 92 p. (Collection notre temps)

Indictment of anarchist, "gauchiste" elements instigating student rebellion (Cohn-Bendit is assimilated with Bakunin) for victimizing P.C.F. and giving Gaullist government a free hand in exploiting fear of chaos and civil war in June 1968 elections, with radio and television publicity for extremist activities and police acting as agent provocateur. Includes historical material on Marx's conflict with Bakunin.

351 DUCLOS, JACQUES. Que sont donc les communistes? Paris, EPI éditeurs, 1971. 183 p. (Carte blanche)

Overview of history of Communist ideas and French Communism, defense of P.C.F. stand May 1968, restatement of current party program and objectives as expressed in Dec. 1968 manifesto and updated for 1971, relations with other parties of the Left.

352 DUCLOS, PIERRE. L'être fédéraliste.... Préf. de Robert Pelloux et Georges Burdeau.... Paris, Librairie générale de droit et de jurisprudence, 1968. viii, 75 p. (Bibliothèque constitutionnelle et de science politique, t. 30) Bibliographical footnotes.

1964-65 lectures on meaning of federalism as the best form of political organization, its current status in the world in the face of unitarian and nationalist tendencies. Author is prominent theorist of European federalist movement, who sees strengthening of regionalism in France since 1963.

353 DULAC, ANDRE. Nos guerres perdues, Levant 1941, Indochine 1951-1953, Algérie 1958-1960. Paris, Fayard, 1969. 228 p. illus.

Personal account by general who served under Salan in Indochina and as his aide in Algeria 1956-58. Dulac was sent to de Gaulle May 28, 1958, by Salan to block Opération Résurrection landing of Algerian troops in France. Gradual split between de Gaulle and military in Algeria, June 1958-June 1960 (latter is date of Dulac's transfer), and growing military demoralization are retraced. Letters and proclamations of Algerian Gouvernement général, de Gaulle, Salan, 1958-60, in appendix.

354 DUMAZEDIER, JOFFRE. Toward a society of leisure. Translated from the French by Stewart E. McClure. Foreword by David Riesman. New York, Free Press, c1967. ix, 307 p. Bibliography: p. 289-299. ML

Relatively favorable appraisal of development of mass leisure civilization in France in early 1960's (French version, "Vers une civilisation de loisir," published in 1962). It is based on published literature as well as author's own study of Annecy workers' use of leisure. Of special interest are chapters giving facts on impact of increased leisure on family life, vacations, sports, utilization of mass media (movies, radio and television programs, books), and adult education.

355 DUMONT, RENE, and MARCEL MAZOYER. Développement et socialismes. Paris, Editions du Seuil, 1969. 330 p. (Collections Esprit. "Frontière ouverte") Bibliography: p. 321-322.

Successes and failures in both capitalist-oriented and socialist states of Africa, Asia, and Latin America, with lengthy study on Algerian agricultural and industrial development since independence. Authors stress need for diversity in socialist models to fit individual national situation.

356 DUNOYER, PIERRE DE SEGONZAC. Le vieux chef; mémoires et pages choisies. Paris, Editions du Seuil, 1971. 251 p.

Memoirs, texts of speeches by general who headed "Service de formation des jeunes en Algérie" 1959-61 and "Service de l'action sociale des armées" 1961-63. Memoirs stop 1965, but speeches on Algerian question, training of personnel for aid to underdeveloped countries are more recent.

357 DUPEUX, GEORGES. La France de 1945 à 1965. Paris, A. Colin, 1969. 384 p. (Collection U2. Série "Dossiers pour l'histoire contemporaine") Includes bibliography.

Last third of book on Fifth Republic, with chapters on political institutions, major aspects of Gaullist policy, and statistical survey of economic conditions, results of public opinion polls. Illustrative documents appended to each chapter.

358 DUPLEIX, ANDRE. Le socialisme de Roger Garaudy et le problème religieux. Toulouse, Privat, 1971. 111 p. ("Sentiers") Bibliography: p. 111.

Garaudy's recent (Jan. 1970) exclusion from P.C.F. and his prior attempts to update Marxism serve as background to evaluation of his written and oral dialogues with representatives of Christian religion. Author shows what difficulties have been overcome and what mutual demands remain unsatisifed. While sympathizing with Garaudy's efforts, author is doubtful how genuine a Marxist spokesman Garaudy is at present, since his Marxist humanism is rejected by most Marxists as heresy.

359 DUPRAT, FRANÇOIS. L'Internationale étudiante révolutionnaire. Paris, Nouvelles éditions latines, 1968. 223 p. (Collection Points de vue)

Survey of revolutionary student movement all over the world, with stress on Trotskyist impetus everywhere. Long chapter on France identifies main revolutionary currents, leading figures, tactics, and publications of each group.

360 DUPRAT, FRANÇOIS. Les journées de mai 68; des dessous d'une révolution. Introd. et post-face de Maurice Bardèche. Paris, Nouvelles éditions latines, 1968. 219 p.

Originally published in June 1968 issue of "Défense de l'Occident" (see above, no. 81), this history of May events focuses on role of Trotskyist and pro-Chinese Communist opposition groups, notably the Jeunesse communiste révolutionnaire (J.C.R.) and the Fédération des étudiants révolutionnaires (F.E.R.), both Trotskyist, and the Maoist Union des jeunesses communistes marxistes-léninistes (U.J.C.M.-L.), on whose history, leaders, and membership there is considerable information. Author shows foreign support for these groups, infiltration of student and labor movement before May 1968, mobilization of diffuse discontent among youth, relations with established student organizations and political Left, responses of army and splintered rightist groups. Bardèche's introduction and conclusion transcend conspiracy interpretation and see revolt as rejection of formal democracy and dehumanized industrial society.

361 DUPRAT, FRANÇOIS. Les mouvements d'extrême droite en France depuis 1944. Paris, Editions Albatros, 1972. 301 p.

Systematic survey of "nationalist opposition" parties and organizations, in several of which young author was personally active but which are treated objectively, within historial context. Chronologically arranged, chapters cover: nationalist opposition and Algerian war (Jeune nation, Mouvement Poujade, and the organizations specifically defending French Algeria such as Front national français, Front national pour l'Algérie française, Mouvement populaire du 13 mai, and later the O.A.S. and the Conseil national de la Résistance); fragmentation after the collapse of the O.A.S. and the ephemeral Esprit public, Europe-Action, Thiriart's Jeune Europe, Trinquier's A.E.R.S.E., Tixier-Vignancour's 1965 presidential campaign. Final chapters on nationalist student movements and clashes with left-wing students culminating in May 1968 at Nanterre and Sorbonne, with Mouvement Occident in foreground; current (1970) status of extreme Right, in which Ordre nouveau, founded after Occident dissolution, is largest group. Work is complemented by quick survey of ideological currents common to and dividing extreme Right, main rightist publications and those sympathetic to Right, index of organizations, publications, and personalities.

362 DUPUIT, JACQUES-MICHEL. De nouvelles structures politiques et administratives pour la France. Paris, S.E.D.E.I.S., 1969. 172 p. (Futuribles, 10)

Economist's critique of existing distribution of budgetary and administrative responsibilities for different economic functions and poor use of resources resulting from overcentralized planning and production (e.g., nationalized industries). Author proposes redistribution of control to permit greatest possible convergence of individual or collective consumer role and fiscal and administrative responsibility. Local governments, cities, city-regions, small and large regions would each assume as much control as technically feasible; only residue and overall coordination would fall within competence of central government. Influence of American model is admitted by author.

363 DUQUESNE, JACQUES. Les prêtres. Paris, B. Grasset, 1965. 309 p. (La France au présent) ML

Unpolemical survey of condition of lower Catholic clergy and religious orders, currently about 50,000 strong. Based on interviews and letters, it covers changing concept of and self-concept of priests from reassuring traditional image of village "curé" to that of political activist, debates within clergy on proper function, activities of different types of clergy, social background, training, geographic distribution. Special section on religious orders (Jesuits, Dominicans, etc.) with their 8,200 members. Includes several typical interviews.

364 DURANDEAUX, JACQUES. Les journées de mai 1968. Rencontres et dialogues présentés par Jacques Durandeaux. Paris, Bruges, Desclée de Brouwer, 1968. 164 p.

June 1968 taped dialogues between professor sympathetic to student revolt and 11 students from different faculties of Sorbonne regarding students' personal reactions to recent events, some negative.

365 DUROCHER, BRUNO, ed. Poèmes de la révolution, mai, 1968. Paris, 1968. 54 p. (Caractères, 6)

Anonymous poems by students and workers, some narrating specific incidents of revolt.

366 DURRIEU, YVES. Régionaliser la France, capitalisme ou socialisme.... Paris, Mercure de France, 1969. 357 p. maps.

Systematic study of regional reform sponsored by Centre d'études socialistes. First part evolves economic and institutional criteria for harmonious regional development and reviews main plans for regional division, favoring establishment of eight regions. Second part reviews Gaullist measures to diminish regional distortions and inequities, proposals of Sixth Plan. Comparisons with Germany, England, Italy, Yugoslavia, Czechoslovakia, advantages of socialist approach: large public sector, imperative planning, problems created for regional development by Common Market. Study is intended as background for Apr. 1969 referendum.

367 DUVAL, HERVE, PIERRE-YVES LEBLANC-DECHOISAY, and PATRICK MINDU. Réferendum et plébiscite. Paris, A. Colin, 1970. 96 p. maps. (Dossiers U2, 96, Droit public interne; série) Bibliography: p. [94].

Historical antecedents and international comparisons for referenda and plebiscites, which tend to be synonymous. For France, focus is on Oct. 1962 and Apr. 1969 referenda, their legal framework, campaign speeches, comments on issues by political scientists. France has had 16 referenda and plebiscites, six of them on entire constitution, since the French Revolution, and only 1946 and 1969 referenda were turned down.

368 DUVERGER, MAURICE. La Cinquième République. 4e éd. refondue. Paris, Presses universitaires de France, 1968. 292 p. illus. Includes bibliographical references.

Up-to-date, balanced survey of French political institutions. Major sections are: origins and evolution of Fifth Republic, the Executive, parliament, other organs (Conseil constitutionnel, Conseil économique et social, Haute cour), political parties. Changes through 1967 are taken into account in each section, with recently published books and articles incorporated in bibliographies after each section. Discussion of political parties emphasizes "bi-polarization" trend between Gaullists and Fédération de la gauche démocrate et socialiste. For first edition, see French Fifth Republic Bibliography, 1, no. 548.

369 DUVERGER, MAURICE. Institutions politiques et droit constitutionnel. 9e éd. Paris, Presses universitaires de France, 1966. vi, 791 p. ("Thémis": manuels juridiques, économiques et politiques) LL

Last third of volume devoted to institutions of Fifth Republic: the Executive, parliament, judicial and constitutional organs, political parties, updated to 1966. (For 1960 edition, see French Fifth Republic Bibliography, 1, no. 553b.) Of special interest is Duverger's evaluation of tendencies toward two-party system after 1965 presidential election.

370 ECHANGES FRANCO-ALLEMANDS. Allemagne, actualité et perspectives. Journées d'études organisées à Paris les 29 et 30 octobre 1966 par les Echanges franco-allemands. Paris, Presses universitaires de France, 1967. x, 109 p.

Introductory addresses by Alfred Grosser on Federal Republic and George Castellan on Democratic Republic, with discussion in which René Capitant and Léo Hamon defend Gaullist policy toward Germany. Meeting not unsympathetic to Democratic Republic. List of participants.

371 Ecole et société. [Par] Jean Floud, Arthur Halsey, Yves Legoux, Christiane Peyre [et] Pierre Naville. Paris, M. Rivière, 1959. 131 p. tables, graphs. (Recherches de sociologie du travail, 5) ML

Individual contributions on social background of secondary school students nationally and more detailed studies on background of students in Collèges techniques and Centres d'apprentissage as of 1958.

372 ECONOMIE ET HUMANISME. Violences et société. Paris, 1969. 197 p. Bibliographical footnotes.

Individual contributions by six members of Economie et humanisme study group revealing different facets of violence, particularly concealed violence of highly technological societies, which aroused student revolt. Findings of psychology, economics, political science, and sociology as to origin and inevitability of violence are reviewed, with conclusion that violence cannot be condemned categorically and that ethics of non-violence are inadequate. For advanced societies, though not underdeveloped ones, pluralism and participation are seen as means to resolve conflicts non-violently. No attempt is made by this Catholic-oriented group to introduce theological views.

373 EDELMANN, PIERRE W. L. Möglichkeiten und Grenzen der französischen Planifikation; ein Beispiel staatlicher Rahmenplanung in der Marktwirtschaft. Bern, Verlag Herbert Lang, 1971. 199 p. diagrs. (Europäische Hochschulschriften, Serie V, Volks- und Betriebswirtschaft, v. 29) Bibliography: p. 181-199.

Theoretical view of planning within market economy, historical and institutional background of French planning, specific mechanisms for formulating and applying plans. Successes are seen in better coordination of economic policy; failures seen in insufficient control of inflation, business cycles. Substantial, up-to-date bibliography of books and articles from French and international literature.

374 EHRMANN, HENRY WALTER. Politics in France. Boston, Little, Brown, 1968. xv, 368 p. maps. (The Little, Brown series in comparative politics. A country study) Includes bibliographical references.

In line with aim of this series, work explains French politics in terms of political attitudes and behaviors. Chapters on (1) social and economic setting; (2) political socialization; (3) political participation (electoral system); (4) recruitment of political elite (politicians and civil service, de Gaulle's personality); (5) political role of mass media, interest groups, political parties; (6) political institutions of Fifth Republic. Twenty-page July 1968 postscript on May 1968 revolt and June elections, general prospects. Informative and up-to-date references.

375 Eléments de théorie économique marxiste. Paris, F. Maspéro, 1968. 36 p. (Cahiers "Rouge." Documents de formation communiste no. 1)

Short Marxist economics manual. For more extensive version, see Mandel (no. 761).

376 ELGOZY, GEORGES. Lettre ouverte à un jeune technocrate: ou Lettre ouverte à un esprit fermé. Paris, A. Michel, 1968. 162 p. (Collection Lettre ouverte) ML

Diatribe against "omnipotent government," with sharpest barbs against young graduates of Ecole nationale d'administration, the future technocrats. Author has himself been ranked among influential technocrats.

377 ELLUL, JACQUES. Autopsie de la révolution. Paris, Calmann-Lévy, 1969. 354 p. (Liberté de l'esprit)

Important critique by political philosopher of currently accepted ideas on revolution. After examining historical evolution of concept, author shows how revolution since Marx has become an objective in itself, taken for granted as God was in Middle Ages. Concept of betrayed revolution inherent in view of revolution as historical necessity: many kinds of revolutions have succeeded, but in none has the state withered away as predicted by Marx. Revolution has been in the sense of history in that after each revolution the state has controlled more of human condition. Revolution is growth crisis of state, to make it more rational and efficient, and this characterizes modern states, dictatorial or not. Particularly interesting analysis for current period of banalization of revolution into a big festival, an inevitable expression of popular will, forgetting real suffering it engenders. Revolution becomes myth to which Christian intellectuals who want to be in tune with times subscribe. For Ellul, a real revolutionary stand should go against sense of history rather than reinforcing natural trends of modern society, against omnipotent, totally technicized state and in favor of individual responsibility, at expense of efficiency and affluence. Students' stress on irrational does not help this revolution because this demand can be integrated by society.

378   ELLUL, JACQUES. Métamorphose du bourgeois. Paris, Calmann-Lévy, 1967. 303 p. (Collection "Liberté de l'esprit") Bibliographical references included in "Notes": p. [292]-300.

Characterization of "bourgeois" and demonstration that his ideology has been assimilated by entire modern world through acceptance of happiness as supreme human goal. At the same time, process of reification leads to abolition of all values, or nihilism. As a class, bourgeoisie has lost its power, technicians are its natural successors.

379   ELLUL, JACQUES. The political illusion. Translated from the French by Konrad Kellen. New York, Knopf, 1967. xxi, 258 p. Bibliographical footnotes.

Published in French as "L'illusion politique." Title refers to commonly held illusion in Communist and non-Communist world that all problems and values should be politicized, making the state responsible for all solutions and turning all commitments into political commitments. Advanced technology, deluge of information, propaganda media make average man incapable of intelligent decision and press him to conform with state goals. The possibility of French democratic planning is critically examined, and opinions of other French political scientists are confronted. Countervailing, non-political poles of tension are seen as remedy for overpolitization.

380   ELLUL, JACQUES. Violence; reflections from a Christian perspective. Translated by Cecilia Gaul Kings. New York, Seabury Press, 1969. 179 p. Bibliographical footnotes.

Political philosopher and Protestant active in Conseil national de l'église examines current Christian theological interpretations of violence and rejects currently fashionable justification of violence on the basis of Christian ethnics, though recognizing violence as part of natural man and realm of necessity, to be taken into account in realistic assessment of politics. Examples are drawn from position of French Catholic intellectuals in Algerian war. Original French edition pre-dates May 1968.

381   ELY, PAUL HENRI RONAULD. Suez . . . le 13 mai. Paris, Plon, 1969. 504 p. (His Mémoires, 2)

Part one of memoirs contains general's 1956 memorandum to government on Algerian question, based on work of his military staff, among them General Challe. Second part is diary of Suez intervention; third gives background of May 13, 1958, and diary for Apr. 16 to June 3. Final section presents general's personal view of growing misunderstanding on solution of Algerian problem on two sides of the Mediterranean and attitudes of military leaders with whom he was in contact, with stress on de Gaulle's sincerity in handling question and on own disapproval of Generals' Putsch. Ely was military chief of staff Feb. 1956 to Feb. 1961.

382   EMMANUEL, PIERRE. Pour une politique de la culture. Paris, Editions du Seuil, 1971. 204 p.

Poet called upon in 1969 to preside over Commission des affaires culturelles to help in elaboration of Sixth Plan describes Commission's work, contents of its report, comments thereon and gives text of interview with Prime Minister Chaban-Delmas about need to encourage multiplicity of local efforts rather than monolithic state culture. Interesting discussion on need for downgrading intellectualism in French education and overcoming modern society's excessive rationalism. Includes letters received by author as Commission chairman. List of Commission members.

383   ENKIRI, GABRIEL. Militant de base. Paris, Mercure de France, 1971. 151 p. (Collection "En direct")

Personal account of young worker's experiences within C.G.T., gradual disillusionment with P.C.F. because of its acceptance of repression in Hungary and unrealistic response to de Gaulle's return to power. Parallel is drawn with P.C.F.'s conservative stance in 1968.

384   ENKIRI, GABRIEL, and ODETTE POIRIER. Hachette, une expérience syndicale C.G.T.-C.F.D.T. Paris, F. Maspéro, 1970. 24 p.

Account of recently formed C.F.D.T. unit's attempt to undermine C.G.T.'s position as sole spokesman for 3,000 employees of Paris branch of Librairie Hachette after C.G.T. broke up strike and ended plant occupation June 1968. Description of subsequent wildcat strikes backed by C.F.D.T.

385   L'ENRAGE (periodical). Collection des 8 premiers numéros introuvables, mai-juin 68. Paris, J. J. Pauvert, 1968. 8 nos. in 1. illus.

Weekly issues May 24 through July 8, final double issue Aug. 1, supporting cause of revolution by cartoons, mock facsimiles, satires. Pauvert was editor and publisher of this short-lived revolutionary publication.

386   ENSEIGNEMENT CATHOLIQUE. COLLOQUE NATIONAL, PARIS, 1968. Les événements de mai et l'enseignement catholique. Paris, Comité national de l'Enseignement catholique, 1968. 351 p.

Collection of excerpts from most significant documents (reports, proposals) emanating from all levels of Catholic schools in Paris and provinces, May-June 1968, which were sent to Comité national. Major themes: participation in academic community, pedagogic reforms, aims of Catholic education, reactions to May events among Catholic educators and parents. No report on conference itself.

387   EPISTEMON [pseud.]. Ces idées qui ont ébranlé la France (Nanterre, novembre 1967-juin 1968), comprendre les étudiants. Paris, Fayard, 1968. 130 p. (Le Monde sans frontières)

Work by Nanterre psychology professor (presumably Didier Anzieu) composed while author was taking part in discussions at Sorbonne in student-faculty committees and concluded June 1968. Valuable insights into intellectual movements within ultra-liberal Nanterre faculty which contributed to ideas of Mouvement du 22 mars and fresh interpretation of motivation of different students in May, reactions of faculty. As one of first insiders' accounts of revolt, this work had considerable impact.

388   ESSONNE (DEPT.), FRANCE. L'Essonne. Corbeil-Essonnes, 1966. 51 p. illus., double map.

Brochure describing department south of Paris created 1964. Gives geographical and demographic facts, statistics on economy, schools, plans for public investments and new branches of Grandes écoles. Current population of half million is expected to double by 1975. Among important establishments is nuclear center of Saclay.

389   ESTIER, CLAUDE. Journal d'un fédéré; la Fédération de la gauche au jour le jour, 1965-1969. Paris, Fayard, 1970. 273 p.

Author was both secretary general of Convention des institutions républicaines and on executive committee of Fédération de la gauche démocrate et socialiste since its founding July 1965, as well as deputy for Paris district. Among major episodes are 1965 presidential campaign, 1967 election, collaboration with P.C.F. and later joint programs, F.G.D.S.'s unfruitful intervention in May 1968 and failure to rally support for single leftist candidate in June 1969 presidential election, dissolution Oct. 1969.

390 ESTIVALS, ROBERT, JEAN-CHARLES GAUDY, and GABRIELLE VERGEZ. "L'Avant-garde"; étude historique et sociologique des publications périodiques ayant pour titre "L'avant-garde." Avec la collaboration de Geneviève Chazelas. Paris, Bibliothèque nationale, 1968. 144 p. facsims., tables, maps. ([France] Ministère de l'éducation nationale. Comité des travaux historiques et scientifiques. Mémoires de la Section d'histoire moderne et contemporaine, 1) Bibliography: p. 111-121.

Range of opinion, temporal and geographical distribution of French journals issued under title "Avant-garde" since French Revolution, with a few Fifth Republic items. Work concluded prior to May 1968. Complete list of journals.

391 ETIEMBLE, RENE. Parlez-vous franglais? Paris, Gallimard, 1964. 376 p. (Collection Idées, 40) ML

Attack on excessive use of Anglo-Saxon terminology, which is degrading French. Ample illustrations not only of vocabulary borrowed liberally from English (examples from sports, language of childhood and youth, clothing, and cosmetics) but also of perversion of French grammar and syntax. Blame is placed on American military and technical influence, nefarious role of advertising, television; and government is urged to intervene by a form of censorship; Resentment against linguistic invasion is coupled with resentment against pervasiveness of American way of life.

392 ETIENNE, BRUNO. Les problèmes juridiques des minorités européennes au Maghreb.... Paris, Editions du Centre national de la recherche scientifique, 1968. 415 p. graphs. (Publications de la Section moderne et contemporaine du Centre de recherches sur l'Afrique méditerranéenne) Bibliography: p. [333]-398.

Excellent integration of political, sociological, and legal documentation on transformation of a colony with over a million non-Moslems, "Algérie française," into a purely Moslem nation, "Algérie algérienne." First part of this revised 1965 doctoral thesis characterizes French colonization as incapable of assimilating majority of population into French state, with good statistics on population by race, profession, social status. Second part leads from Algerian war and O.A.S. intervention to Evian Treaty. Most original is third part, which surveys treatment of non-Moslem minorities in Arabo-Moslem law in other areas. Fourth section gives details on exodus of European settlers, 1962-66, which left only 100,000 French behind, a few hundred of whom received Algerian nationality; statistics on this French residue, legal provisions for maintaining French nationality. Comprehensive bibliography of books and articles on all aspects of Algerian question, Algerian war, O.A.S., peace negotiations, and transitional period to Algerian independence.

393 EXPOSES ET ENTRETIENS SUR LE MARXISME, CERISY-LA-SALLE, 1967. Le centenaire du Capital; exposés et entretiens sur le marxisme. Paris, Mouton, 1969. 241 p. (Décades du Centre culturel international de Cerisy-la-Salle, nouv. sér., 10) ML

July 11-19, 1967, conference celebrating centennial of Marx's "Das Kapital." Main addresses, followed by discussions, are by François Châtelet (introduction), Henri Denis (rereading "Das Kapital"), Christian Schmidt (Marx and economics), and, on related topics, by Pierre Macherey, Etienne Balibar, Victor Fay, Pierre Kende. Other talks by Kostas Papaioannou on Marx and the state, Catherine Backès on Marxism and psychoanalysis, Luce Irigaray on Marxism and structural linguistics, Serge Jonas on Marx and sociology, Anouar Abdel-Malek on Marxism and national liberation. Final talk by Lucien Goldmann on Marxism and ideology. Speakers are both orthodox Communists and those who accept Marxism critically. One of focal reference points is Althusser's influential reinterpretation of Marx.

394 FABRE-LUCE, ALFRED. L'anniversaire. Paris, Fayard, 1971. 216 p. Includes bibliography.

Reappraisal of de Gaulle's personality, political methods and choices (Algeria, Atlantic Alliance, relations with Soviet Union, nuclear weapons), place in history, with effort to recognize both his stature and his misjudgments, especially in foreign policy. Chapters on de Gaulle's retirement, circumstances of death and reactions thereto in terms of legend-creation. Favorable assessment of de Gaulle's successor.

395 FABRE-LUCE, ALFRED. Le Général en Sorbonne.... Paris, Table ronde, 1968. 143 p. (La Table ronde de Combat. "Les Brûlots," 8)

Firsthand impressions of uninvolved but not unsympathetic observer wandering through Latin Quarter and Sorbonne, with report of mock trial by student militants of André Malraux and de Gaulle as its high point. Though a product of the author's imagination like his earlier "Haute cour," it interweaves typical student rhetoric with the accused's self-defense in which quotes from their own works mingle with extrapolations of their ideas.

396 FABREGUES, JEAN DE. Mauriac. [Paris] Plon, 1971. 307 p. photos.

Biography of novelist active in Catholic liberal movements and ardent admirer of de Gaulle, with some attention to his political ideas and commitments, response to Catholic Church's aggiornamento.

397 FAILLANT DE VILLEMAREST, PIERRE. L'espionage soviétique en France, 1944-1969. Paris, Nouvelles éditions latines, 1969. 316 p. plates, ports.

Cases of Soviet espionage networks revealed in France 1944-69. For Gaullist years, author blames French secret services of concentrating on O.A.S. instead of Communist agents and accuses government of laxness against Communism, willingness to cooperate with Soviet Union. Some of spy incidents involve Polish, Czech, and East German agents, infiltration into Catholic Church via pacifist organizations. Most recent Soviet coup concerns theft of information on Concorde.

398 FAUCHER, JEAN ANDRE. 13 mai 1958-13 mai 1968; la gauche française sous de Gaulle. Paris, J. Didier, 1969. 288 p.

Year-by-year survey of French Left's (in broad sense) political activities. Main events covered are maneuvers preceding 1965 presidential elections, negotiations between Fédération de la gauche démocrate et socialiste and P.C.F. Jan. 1966 to May 1968, Mar. 1967 elections. Not much material for May 1968. Conclusion infers impending split in Radical party and founding of new Socialist party. Author was on Radical party's Commission de politique générale and participated in creation of F.G.D.S. As secretary of political club Atelier républicain, he took part in founding of Convention des institutions républicaines. Name and organization index.

399 FAURE, EDGAR. L'âme du combat; pour un nouveau contrat social. Paris, Fayard, 1970. 350 p. (En toute liberté)

After autobiographical sketch, Faure confronts contributions and shortcomings of classical Marxism, contemporary critique of affluent society by Lefebvre, Touraine, and Marcuse. What he calls the "société technologique de consommation" is defended against superficial criticism. Remedies for alienation lie in greater political participation, with specific proposals for institutional change such as length of presidential mandate, operation of parliament.

400 FAURE, EDGAR. Ce que je crois. Paris, B. Grasset, 1971. 223 p. ML

Experiences as minister of education, July 1968 to June 1969, giving inside story of the many reforms known under the "loi

Faure," e.g., introduction of Unités d'enseignement et de recherche in place of university faculties, changes in primary and secondary schools, student participation in university administration, as well as his struggles against student disorders, conservative misgivings.

401 FAURE, EDGAR. Philosophie d'une réforme. Paris, Plon, 1969. 186 p. (Tribune libre)

Excerpts from Oct. 1968 speeches at U.N.E.S.C.O. conference, before National Assembly and Senate. Minister of education explains genesis of proposed reform of higher education, replies to objections, examines youth, university, and cultural crisis and specific remedies through greater participation and autonomy of university institutions, pedagogic innovations.

402 FAVRE, PIERRE, and MONIQUE FAVRE. Les marxismes après Marx. Paris, Presses universitaires de France, 1970. 128 p. ("Que sais-je?" no. 1408) Includes bibliographical references.

Final chapter on recent currents in French Marxism as represented by Henri Lefebvre and Louis Althusser.

403 FEDERATION GENERALE DE LA METALLURGIE C.F.D.T. Mai-juin 68, accords de fin de grève: le droit syndical, les salaires, la durée du travail, la mensualisation. Paris, 1969. 228 p. (Supplément au Bulletin du militant)

Text or summary of June 1968 agreements reached in more than a hundred firms occupied May-June 1968 (automotive, machinery, aeronautics, steel, electrical, construction) with respect to union rights, wages, working hours, holidays.

404 FERNIOT, JEAN. Mort d'une révolution, la gauche de mai. Paris, Denoël, 1968. 239 p. (Collection Réflexions) Bibliographical footnotes.

History of events from March uprising in Nanterre through June elections, stressing P.C.F.'s and C.G.T.'s share in stifling revolution and their lack of sympathy and understanding for student movement.

405 FERRAND, JEROME. La jeunesse, nouveau tiers état. Paris, R. Laffont, 1968. 104 p. (Collection "Contestation")

Revolt of students and young workers in May 1968 is assimilated to that of third estate in 1789, in that legal restrictions and economic dependence were keeping both classes from positions of responsibility in spite of physical and mental maturity. Beyond proposals for lowering voting age and age of majority, earlier retirement for men in high government and business positions, author urges allowing more participation by youth.

406 FERRANDI, JEAN. 600 jours avec Salan et l'O.A.S. Paris, Fayard, 1969. 342 p.

Title refers to 600 days from Sept. 1960 to Apr. 1962. This is slightly revised diary of Salan's adjutant, who was arrested by his side Apr. 20, 1962. Diary retraces events in Spain and Algeria. Among documents in appendix is letter of Salan of Feb. 1, 1962, to non-Gaullist politicians.

407 FERRARI, PIERRE, and HERBERT MAISL. Les groupes communistes aux Assemblées parlementaires italiennes, 1958-1963, et françaises, 1962-1967. Paris, Presses universitaires de France, 1969. 214 p. diagrs. (Travaux et recherches de la Faculté de droit et des sciences économiques de Paris. Série "Science politique," no. 16) Includes bibliography.

Maisl's contribution shows Communist parliamentary group's attitude toward parliamentary participation, role of such groups under Fifth Republic constitution. Major sections on P.C.F. program in 1962 elections, how candidates fared (41 elected with 22 percent of vote), and what are deputies' geographic and party ties. Place in commissions, methods of work, legislative contributions, participation in parliamentary debates.

408 FEUERSTEIN, PIERRE. Printemps de révolte à Strasbourg; les événements de mai-juin 1968 à l'Université de Strasbourg. Strasbourg, Saisons d'Alsace, 1968. 116 p. illus., plates. (Connaissance de l'Alsace) Bibliography: p. 108-109.

Eyewitness of Strasbourg revolt gives background going back to 1966, when student organization was taken over by adherents of Internationale situationniste. Revolt at University of Strasbourg, with 21,000 students, lasted from May 6 to end of June. Documents are student appeals, cartoons, texts of proclamations by local authorities, whose reassertion began at end of May. Failure of students to win support of workers was flagrant.

409 FIELD, NORMA MOORE. A quest; interpretation of the French student revolt of May-June, 1968. Pomona, Calif., 1969. 120 l. Xerox copy. Bibliography: l. 117-120.

Effective synthesis of works on French civilization and education as background to May crisis, straightforward summary of events at Nanterre, Sorbonne, among workers, and reforms emerging from revolt. This was written as Senior Honors paper at Pomona College.

410 FIELDS, A. BELDEN. Student politics in France; a study in the Union nationale des étudiants de France. New York, Basic Books, c1970. 198 p. (Student movements--past and present, 5) Bibliography: p. 180-188.

All but postscript concluded before May 1968, with field work at Sorbonne going back to Sept. 1963-Feb. 1965, complemented by spring 1966 interviews with student leaders, questionnaires to presidents of local U.N.E.F. chapters. Gives history of U.N.E.F., 1907-64, social background and political sympathies of members, factors conducive to student activism. As of 1967, U.N.E.F. had voluntary membership of 50,000.

411 FIGUERAS, ANDRE. L'affaire du bazooka. Paris, Table ronde, 1970. 208 p. (Collection Histoire contemporaine revue et corrigée)

Further light on attempted assassination of General Salan, Dec. 1956, and information revealed during Salan's trial in 1962 implicating prominent Gaullist politicians.

412 FIGUERAS, ANDRE. Corrida de lieutenant. [n.p.] Editions du Midi, 1967. 168 p. ML

In memory of lieutenant (Bastien-Thiry?) condemned, like bull in ring, to die for refusal to accept national dishonor, seen through eyes of 12 young recruits on shooting squad. General Massu is accused of connivance with Gaullist government and of acting as agent provocateur among activist officers.

413 FIGUERAS, ANDRE. De Gaulle l'impuissant. Préf. de Georges Bidault. Paris, 1970. 171 p.

Balance sheet of nearly 11 years of de Gaulle's rule, pinpointing isolated economic and technological accomplishments on the credit side, against loss of the French empire, economic stagnation, civil strife, demoralization of army, loss of civil liberties, chaos in administration of justice and in education, general incapacity to carry through intentions domestically or internationally. Inveterate de Gaulle opponent blames all these failures on chief of state's intellectual incapacity, inability to create. Gaullism equals impotence.

414 FILOZOF, VERONIQUE [pseud.] Mai 68; images de Véronique Filozof. Paris, Le Temps, 1969. [58] p. of illus.

History of May events in 26 line drawings, with short captions.

415 FLACELIERE, ROBERT. Normale en péril. Paris, Presses universitaires de France, 1971. 117 p.

Plea of recently resigned director of Ecole normale supérieure, Paris, to preserve the school's traditions intact in the face of reforms being applied to the university system, and which so far had spared the Grandes écoles. Resignation came in the wake of violence and damage to school Mar. 20, 1971, which are described in detail. Director defends system of selection by competition, value of preparatory classes (khâgne) as far superior to first years of university.

416 FLORES D'ARCAIS, PAOLO. Il maggio di Parigi; cronologia e documenti delle lotte studentesche e operaie in Francia. Traduzione dal francese di Paolo Flores d'Arcais. Padova, Marsilio, 1968. 192 p. (Libri contro n. 3)

Chronology of events, followed by Italian translation of texts in student publication "Action" (May 2-July 1) and Jeunesse communiste révolutionnaire's "Aujourd'hui," as well as chronologically arranged leaflets of worker and student groups. Final part reports on trip to Nantes by three professors from Nanterre to observe city under worker control.

417 FOCKE, KATHARINA, ed. Europäer in Frankreich; eine Dokumentation, zusammengestellt und eingeleitet. Die Übersetzung besorgten Karlheinz Koppe und Dieter Tepelmann. Köln, Europa Union Verlag, 1966. 215 p. (Europäische Schriften des Bildungswerks Europäische Politik, Heft 10) Includes bibliography.

Results of 1962 public opinion polls in France on European integration, translation of excerpts of articles by pro-European politicians, debates in parliament June-Oct. 1965 on particular aspects of European agreements, interview with Emile Roche, interventions of French members in European parliament Oct. 1965, statements by agricultural, industrial, and labor groups. Final section on reactions to de Gaulle's press conference of Sept. 9, 1965, and views of all presidential candidates on European policy. Chronology of crisis around European agricultural policy.

418 FONDATION NATIONALE DES SCIENCES POLITIQUES. Catalogue général des périodiques reçus par la Fondation nationale des sciences politiques. Préf. de Jean Meyriat. Paris, A. Colin, 1968. x, 402 p. (Bibliographies françaises de sciences sociales. Répertoires documentaires, 2)

Numbered alphabetical listing of 4,323 currently (as of 1967) received periodicals. For each item, place of publication, initial date of periodical, periodicity, gaps, library location. Index by country of publication, with separate index of country or region covered and listings of bibliographical and statistical serials. Newspapers and weeklies not included.

419 FONDATION NATIONALE DES SCIENCES POLITIQUES. Le communisme en France. Paris, A. Colin, 1969. 336 p. tables. (Cahiers de la Fondation nationale des sciences politiques, 175)

Reports presented at its colloquium of Mar. 1 and 2, 1968, on French Communism, not modified to take into account subsequent events. Individual contributions are: G. Lavau, Le Parti communiste dans le système politique; J. Touchard, Introduction à l'idéologie du P.S.F.; F. Bon, Structure de l'idéologie communiste; N. Racine, Le P.C.F. devant les problèmes idéologiques et intellectuels; P. Rossi-Landi, Le P.C.F., structures, composition, moyens d'action; J. Ranger, L'évolution du vote communiste en France depuis 1945; A. Lancelot and P. Weill, Attitude des Français à l'égard du P.C.F. en février 1968; N. Racine, Etat des travaux sur le communisme en France. Much information on evolution of P.C.F. views on culture and religion, composition of party leadership, political attitudes of Communist voters. Final report surveys main works on French Communism, with alphabetical list of over 200 books and articles.

420 FONDATION NATIONALE DES SCIENCES POLITIQUES. L'expérience française des villes nouvelles; journée d'étude, tenue le 19 avril 1969. Paris, A. Colin, 1970. 214 p. (Its Travaux et recherches de science politique, 7)

Conference organized by Fondation nationale on new towns or urban centers, many in Paris region, which are ultimately to have as many as 300,000 to a million inhabitants. Delouvrier, in charge of Paris regional development, states own objectives. Experiences of five towns near Paris and one near Lille, another near Toulouse are described.

421 FONDATION NATIONALE DES SCIENCES POLITIQUES. Guide sommaire des ouvrages de référence en sciences sociales. Paris, A. Colin, 1968. 61 p. (Its Bibliographies françaises de sciences sociales. Répertoires documentaires, 1)

Eleven sections: (1) current general bibliographies, (2) retrospective bibliographies, (3) specialized social science bibliographies, (4) general encyclopedias, (5) chronologies, (6) statistical works, (7) documentary sources, (8) collections of documents, (9) biographic sources, (10) lists of organizations, international and by country, (11) atlases. Has 150 annotated items. Index by title and author.

422 FONDATION NATIONALE DES SCIENCES POLITIQUES. CENTRE D'ETUDE DE LA VIE POLITIQUE FRANÇAISE. L'élection présidentielle des 5 et 19 novembre 1965. Paris, A. Colin, 1970. 548 p. tables, diagrs. (Fondation nationale des sciences politiques. Cahiers, 169) Includes bibliography.

Individual contributions on election campaign: chronology, choice of candidates, propaganda themes and role of press and television, reactions of specific groups (farmers, trade unions, businessmen, Catholics). Second part presents results of detailed attitude questionnaire administered Jan. 1966 on political attitudes and voting in this election. Maps of election results. Extensive bibliography of books, articles, theses.

423 FONTAINE, ANDRE. La guerre civile froide. Paris, Fayard, 1969. 194 p. (Les Grandes études contemporaines)

Reflections on the underlying causes of May 1968 events and the tactics of confrontation, which are equated with Cold War.

424 FONTAN, FRANÇOIS. Orientation politique du nationalisme occitan. Bagnols (Gard), Librairie occitane, 1970. 47 p. ML

Program for national independence, restoration of Occitan language by secretary general of Parti nationaliste occitan. Seven French provinces are considered to make up ethnic unity: Provence, Languedoc, Gascogne, Limousin, Auvergne, Dauphiné, Guyenne. Party is opposed to European unification, sees Gaullism under Pompidou as greater threat to its goals than under de Gaulle, whose regional reform efforts were in the right direction.

425 FONVIEILLE-ALQUIER, FRANÇOIS. Les illusionnaires. Paris, R. Laffont, 1968. 200 p. (Contestation)

Students are accused of having started a hopeless revolution which could not gain mass support and merely led to strengthening of Gaullism by alienating from Left by their tactics and slogans the majority of French citizens. Youth is urged to seek changes through parliamentary methods and accept legitimate accomplishments of affluent society.

426 FOSSAERT, ROBERT. Le contrat socialiste. Paris, Editions du Seuil, 1969. 285 p.

Astute, unpolemical dissection of political setbacks of French Left from 1936 Popular Front through failures in May 1968 crisis and 1969 presidential election. Left's heritage for 1970's is assessed, likelihood of "classical" revolution for which extreme Left has been aiming since May 1968 is discounted. Most promising tactics in society with expansionist tendencies, for which there is government and business support, are exploitation of instability to conquer new centers of power. Socialism should not identify itself with state ownership of means of production but accept society with mixed economy in which there is responsibility, solidarity, human fulfillment. "Socialist contract" of title refers to grass-roots approach to political power whereby political parties would draw up contract for specific reforms elaborated jointly with other groups--trade unions, local and regional bodies--who would share in choices of Left's political candidates. Only thus would P. C. F. be integrated into democratic political model. Author is involved in several socialist political clubs and P. S. U.

427 FOUCHET, CHRISTIAN. Mémoires d'hier et de demain. Paris, Plon, 1971. 297 p.

First volume of leading Gaullist politician's memoirs concentrates on selected episodes: London, 1940; mission to Warsaw, 1945; work as head of French delegation to European Commission, 1961-62, during which Fouchet Plan was formulated; service as Algerian Haut commissaire, Mar.-July 1962. Interesting inside information on O. A. S.-F. L. N. negotiations, relations of French government representatives with army, police, O. A. S., and role as minister of interior in May 1968, at which time police forces were under his control.

428 FOUGEYROLLAS, PIERRE. Pour une France fédérale, vers l'unité européenne par la révolution régionale. Paris, Denoël, 1968. 215 p. (Collection Grand format. Médiations) Bibliographical footnotes.

Plea for greater regional autonomy, based in part on ethnic lines within French hexagon. Author feels that as it steps beyond national to European framework, France must shed exaggerated centralism and accept historical diversities of cultures to release regional energies and fructify all parts of the country. Discussion of Breton, Basque, Flemish, Catalan, Alsatian, Occitanian populations and proposal for 11 regions and three autonomous areas (Flemish, Basque, Catalan). Distinctions between concept of "nation" and "state" in political theory are carefully examined.

429 FOURASTIE, JEAN. Essais de morale prospective. Paris, Gonthier, 1966. 208 p. (Collection Grand format. Médiations) Bibliography: p. 195. ML

Reflections on crisis of contemporary morality, seen as transition from traditional Christian morality (many examples drawn from French daily life and literary interpretation of recent past) which still in fact permeates much of social practice (e.g., marriage) to a moral consciousness incorporating contributions of experimental science. Most profound changes are rejections of those elements of traditional morality based on scarcity and stability, positive aspects of which are greater tolerance for diversity, affirmation of individual autonomy, and negative aspect of which is refusal of sacrifice, suffering, inequality, which are as unavoidable as before. Potentialities and limitations of scientific knowledge in making decision process more rational are lucidly discussed, in the light of personal involvement in French long-range planning as well as in elaboration of economic Plans.

430 FOURASTIE, JEAN. Faillite de l'université? Paris, Gallimard, 1972. 186 p. (Collection Idées, 257. Sciences humaines) Bibliography: p. 181-183.

Confronts higher education with its major challenges as a mass rather than elite educational institution: how well can it allow its students to make an appropriate professional choice in the face of vastly varying aptitudes and motivations, and how will it prepare them for the transformations taking place in society during their lives? Planner describes in some detail employment forecasts, his concept of life-long learning, need to inculcate the experimental scientific spirit as the only way to give the "technical polyvalence" demanded by ever-increasing accumulated knowledge of our scientific society. So far the French university has failed in these tasks.

431 FOURASTIE, JEAN. Lettre ouverte à quartre milliards d'hommes. Paris, A. Michel, 1970. 167 p. (Collection Lettre ouverte)

Informal summation of major findings in physics, cosmology, biology, demography, economics, psychology, and sociology through modern experimental method, as basis of what human mind knows of reality. Accepted scientific truths can supply only a small fraction of answers to questions vital to human existence, while undermining support to human life hitherto offered by art, morality, religion, and philosophy. These characteristics of modern civilization explain restlessness, protests of youth.

432 FOURASTIE, JEAN, and JEAN-PAUL COURTHEOUX. La planification économique en France. 2e éd. refondue. Paris, Presses universitaires de France, 1968. 316 p. (Collection SUP. L'Economiste, 3) Bibliographical footnotes.

History and methods of French planning. This revised edition has extensive chapter on regional planning, results of Fourth Plan (1962-65), dispositions of Fifth Plan (1966-70), and overall appraisal of forecasting and planning of economic growth in French thinking.

433 FOURNIER, JACQUES. Politique de l'éducation. Paris, Editions du Seuil, 1971. 317 p. Bibliographical footnotes. ML

Well-informed, comprehensive work on major issues in French education, with many useful comparisons with American, Western and Eastern European educational efforts. Among questions particularly well presented are relation between democratization of education and expansion of educational needs, unit cost of education, its effectiveness, interpretation of current educational structure in transition from "selective" to "open" system on primary and secondary level, leading to many more failures than purely selective systems (British) and purely open ones (U. S.). Author is specialist on problems of education at Institut d'études politiques.

434 FOURRIER, CHARLES. Les institutions universitaires. Paris, Presses universitaires de France, 1971. 126 p. ("Que sais-je?" no. 487) Bibliography: p. [127].

Transformations in French higher education through Nov. 1968 "loi d'orientation" and subsequent decrees signed Dec. 1970. Short survey of modifications in education goals and concepts (trends in direction of functional, socially useful American-style universities) and in structure. List of all 56 universities existing as of 1970, their legal status, administrative organs, governing and consultative bodies, degree and nature of autonomy, current organization and administration of individual universities on basis of Unités d'enseignement et de recherche (U. E. R.), extent of student participation, implementation of pluridisciplinarity, pedagogic innovations, modifications in faculty status, student admission rules and academic requirements.

435 FRACHON, BENOIT. Au rythme des jours, rétrospective sur 90 années de luttes de la C. G. T. (Textes choisis). Préf. par Henri Krasucki. . . . Paris, Editions sociales, 1967-68. 2 v. plates.

Vol. 2 covers 1955 to 1967. Chronologically arranged speeches and articles by C. G. T. secretary general on political questions (such as de Gaulle's return to power June 1958 and C. G. T.'s opposition) and problems of labor movement, strikes.

436 La France. Paris, Librairie Larousse, 1967. (Collection Monde et voyages) ML

Survey of French daily life, cities, culture, history. Beautiful photographs.

437 FRANCE. AMBASSADE. U.S. SERVICE DE PRESSE ET D'INFORMATION. French economic and financial aid to the developing countries. New York, 1966. 8 p. (Its French affairs, no. 197)

1962-64 figures for bilateral aid and contributions to international and European aid agencies. In 1964 foreign aid was 2 percent of gross national product.

438 FRANCE. ASSEMBLEE NATIONALE, 1958- SECRETARIAT GENERAL. Recueil des textes authentiques des programmes et engagements électoraux des députés proclamés élus à la suite des élections générales. 1967, v. 1-2; 1968, v. 1-2. Paris, Impr. de l'Assemblée nationale.

Same information as in earlier Recueils (see French Fifth Republic Bibliography, 1, no. 712). Parliamentary groups in 1967 and 1968 National Assembly were: Groupe d'union des démocrates pour la Ve République (Groupe d'union des démocrates pour la république in 1968), Fédération de la gauche démocrate et socialiste, Communiste, Républicains indépendants, Progrès et démocratie moderne. Name index at end of Vol. 2.

FOR FRANCE, ASSEMBLEE NATIONALE..., SEE ALSO NO. 475

439 FRANCE. CENTRE NATIONAL DE LA RECHERCHE SCIENTIFIQUE. GROUPE DE SOCIOLOGIE RURALE. Les collectivités rurales françaises; étude comparative de changement social. Tome 1. Sous la direction de M. Jollivet et H. Mendras. Paris, A. Colin, 1971. 222 p. maps.

Major patterns of change in village life from 19th century to 1960's and identification of 23 regions, briefly characterized. Main part offers case studies of rural communities in 10 characteristic areas: Vendée, Bretagne, Beauce, Lorraine, Jura, Haute-Marche, Rouergue, Gascogne, Provence, Languedoc. Final section summarizes diversity and common trends in French agriculture and rural society.

440 FRANCE. CONSEIL ECONOMIQUE ET SOCIAL. Reconnaissance légale des sections syndicales d'entreprise et garantie de leurs moyens d'action en relation avec le statut de l'entreprise. Rapport présenté au nom du Conseil économique et social par René Mathevet. Paris, 1964. 74, 7 p.

Report and proposed laws for extending trade union rights within plants and assuring greater worker participation.

441 FRANCE. CONSEIL ECONOMIQUE ET SOCIAL. SECTION DE LA CONJONCTURE ET DU REVENU NATIONAL. Appréciation des résultats connus du plan de stabilisation, de ses effets sur l'évolution prochaine de la conjoncture et l'expansion économique. Rapport présenté au nom de la Section de la conjoncture et du revenu national par Jean Mersch. Paris, 1964. 78 p.

Government stabilization plan initiated Feb. 1963 and its impact on economic growth on basis of 1963 figures on output, balance of trade, price stabilization. Report criticizes relative ineffectiveness of plan in reducing inflation.

442 FRANCE. CONSEIL ECONOMIQUE ET SOCIAL. SECTION DE LA PRODUCTION INDUSTRIELLE ET DE L'ENERGIE. Situation des industries de biens d'équipement. Etude présentée par la Section de la production industrielle et de l'énergie sur le rapport de Georges Glasser, le 6 mai 1964. Paris, 1964. 42 p.

Survey of main sectors of heavy industry production (mechanical, agricultural, electrical, and automotive equipment) and level of production, exports, employment, wages, reasons for current stagnation, and proposals for reform.

443 FRANCE. CONSEIL ECONOMIQUE ET SOCIAL. SECTION DE L'AGRICULTURE. I. Le marché du bois de pin maritime dans les landes. II. Le marché de la gemme dans le sud-ouest. Etude présentée par la Section de l'agriculture sur le rapport de Pierre Lemée, le 10 mars 1964. Paris, 1964. 26 p. tables.

444 FRANCE. CONSEIL ECONOMIQUE ET SOCIAL. SECTION DE L'EXPANSION ECONOMIQUE EXTERIEURE. Développement des exportations de biens d'équipement. Etude présentée par la Section de l'expansion économique extérieure, le 21 avril 1964. Paris, 1964. 76 p.

Statistical analysis of exports of capital goods within and outside franc zone, reasons for declines of latter since 1959, proposed changes in credit policy and technical and economic assistance policy.

445 FRANCE. CONSEIL ECONOMIQUE ET SOCIAL. SECTION DES ECONOMIES REGIONALES. Etudes des sociétés d'immeubles industriels. Etude présentée par la Section des économies régionales sur le rapport de René Uhrich, le 24 juin 1964. Paris, 1964. 66 p.

Recommendation for regional body charged with building plants in harmony with regional development plans, then sale of plants to interested companies. Operation and financial problems of several French societies having this function, particularly the Société des immeubles du Bas-Rhin, are outlined.

446 FRANCE. CONSEIL ECONOMIQUE ET SOCIAL. SECTION DU PLAN ET DES INVESTISSEMENTS. Principe et critères d'une politique des revenus: application à la répartition du revenu national dans le cadre des objectifs économiques et sociaux du plan. Projet d'avis présenté au nom de la Section du plan et des investissements par Bernard de Loynes. Paris, 1964. 17 p.

Proposal for government intervention to raise income of groups least favored by economic growth. Proposal was turned down.

447 FRANCE. DIRECTION DE LA DOCUMENTATION. Charles de Gaulle. Paris, 1971. 1 v. (unpaged) of 26 numbered items. illus., ports., map. In portfolio. (Numéro spécial de la Documentation photographique)

Texts, photographs, facsimiles concerning significant events in de Gaulle's life. Materials prior to 1945 are exclusively from files of Documentation française, subsequent ones from other sources as well. For Fifth Republic, pictures cover official receptions, foreign visitors, visits abroad. Useful map showing all foreign trips.

448 FRANCE. DIRECTION DE LA DOCUMENTATION. Composition du gouvernement et des cabinets ministeriels. Sept. 1968, Mar. 1969, July 1969, Oct. 1969. Paris, Documentation française.

List of ministers, secretaries of state, under Couve de Murville, Sept. 1968 and Mar. 1969; under Chaban-Delmas, July and Oct. 1969. Later compilations also available. For permanent ministerial staff, see no. 452 below. See also no. 549.

449 FRANCE. DIRECTION DE LA DOCUMENTATION. Documents relatifs à la politique agricole. Paris, Documentation française, 1962-64. 2 v. (Its Recueils et monographies, no. 41, 52)

Speeches of prime minister, ministers of agriculture; texts of laws related to agriculture. Vol. 1 for Apr. 1960-Mar. 1962, Vol. 2 for Apr. 1962-July 1964.

450 FRANCE. DIRECTION DE LA DOCUMENTATION. L'Institut national de la statistique et des études économiques et le recensement de la population de 1968. Paris, Documentation française, 1967. (Documentation française illustrée, no. 232, déc. 1967)

Historical survey of how I.N.S.E.E. has carried out its census operations. Includes selected significant graphs from earlier census and describes how data collection is currently done.

451 FRANCE. DIRECTION DE LA DOCUMENTATION. Les régimes complémentaires de retraites par répartition. Paris, Documentation française, 1965. 105 p. (Its Recueils et monographies, no. 54) Includes bibliography.

Text of five talks at colloquium of Institut de statistique de l'Université de Paris (June 1965) describing different aspects of retirement insurance outside social security system but complementary to it. As of 1961, it covered over five million salaried personnel.

452 FRANCE. DIRECTION DE LA DOCUMENTATION. Répertoire permanent de l'administration française. Années 1968-1971. 4 v. Paris, Documentation française. maps.

Same type of information as in 1964, 1966 Répertoire (see French Fifth Republic Bibliography, 1, no. 743). In addition there is complete administrative listing for newly created departments in Paris area as well as all new electoral cantons. Under Ministry of Interior, listing of cities with 30,000-100,000 inhabitants, based on 1968 census for 1969- editions. Worldwide list of diplomatic missions and delegations, ambassadors, under Foreign Affairs Ministry. Maps of economic, educational, judicial regional subdivisions. Names of all members of Conseil d'Etat, Cour des comptes. Name index and index of service agencies. See also no. 549.

453 FRANCE. INSTITUT NATIONAL D'ADMINISTRATION SCOLAIRE ET UNIVERSITAIRE. La déconcentration administrative à l'éducation nationale. Poitiers, 1967. 2 v. In folders.

v. 1: La gestion du personnel et sa déconcentration.
v. 2: La gestion financière et sa déconcentration.

Vol. 1 discusses principles involved in educational reorganization through deconcentration and relevant decrees, notably Feb. 1964 decree on civil servants in higher education, as well as other decrees, ordinances, memoranda, 1958-Nov. 1965. As of 1966, there were 10 million students in public education and 600,000 employees of Ministry of Education (150,000 in 1939). Vol. 2 covers same ground with respect fo deconcentration of educational expenditure, 1958-Mar. 1966.

454 FRANCE. INSTITUT NATIONAL DE LA STATISTIQUE ET DES ETUDES ECONOMIQUES. Annuaire statistique de la France. 1955-1970. Paris, Impr. nationale, 1956-71. ML

1969 volume has main results of 1968 census.

455 FRANCE. INSTITUT NATIONAL DE LA STATISTIQUE ET DES ETUDES ECONOMIQUES. Recensement général de la population de 1962. Résultats du sondage au 1/20 pour la France entière: ménages, familles. Paris, Journaux officiels, 1968. 239 p. illus. ML

Statistics and graphs for family size, marital status, by employment categories, cities, rural areas.

456 FRANCE. INSTITUT NATIONAL DE LA STATISTIQUE ET DES ETUDES ECONOMIQUES. Recensement général de la population de 1962. Résultats du sondage au 1/20 pour la France entière: population active. Paris, Journaux officiels, 1964. 183 p. ML

Statistics for employment in different professions, agricultural and non-agricultural, with distribution by sex, age, nationality.

457 FRANCE. INSTITUT NATIONAL DE LA STATISTIQUE ET DES ETUDES ECONOMIQUES. Recensement général de la population de 1962. Résultats du sondage au 1/20 pour la France entière: structure de la population totale. Paris, Journaux officiels, 1965. 129 p. illus., maps. ML

Tables and graphic presentation of results for age and sex distribution, marital state, foreigners, Algerian residents. Figures for age and sex distribution are given for 1776 on.

458 FRANCE. INSTITUT NATIONAL DE LA STATISTIQUE ET DES ETUDES ECONOMIQUES. Recensement de 1968: population de la France; départements, arrondissements, cantons, et communes. Paris, Journaux officiels, 1968. 1221 p. ML

Overall figures for departments, then figures arranged alphabetically by departments subdivided into arrondissements, cantons, communes, and cities with population of over 10,000. Census data for overseas territories and departments are published separately. Reproduces figures for departmental population of 20 previous census reports, 1851-1968. See also no. 450 above.

459 FRANCE. INSTITUT NATIONAL DE LA STATISTIQUE ET DES ETUDES ECONOMIQUES. Recensement général de la population de 1968. Résultats du sondage au 1/4: population, ménages, logements, immeubles. Fascicules départementaux. Paris, Impr. nationale, 1971. ML

460 FRANCE. INSTITUT NATIONAL DE LA STATISTIQUE ET DES ETUDES ECONOMIQUES. Recensement général de la population de 1968. Résultats du sondage au 1/20 pour la France entière: formation. Paris, Impr. nationale, 1971. 246 p. ML

Educational statistics.

461 FRANCE. INSTITUT NATIONAL DE LA STATISTIQUE ET DES ETUDES ECONOMIQUES. Recensement général de la population de 1968. Résultats du sondage au 1/20 pour la France entière: population active. Paris, Impr. nationale, 1971. 217 p. illus. ML

Same contents as 1962 census.

462 FRANCE. INSTITUT NATIONAL D'ETUDES DEMOGRAPHIQUES. INSTITUT NATIONAL D'ETUDE DU TRAVAIL ET D'ORIENTATION PROFESSIONNELLE. Enquête nationale sur le niveau intellectuel des enfants d'âge scolaire. Paris, Presses universitaires de France, 1969. 181 p. (Travaux et documents, Cahier no. 54) ML

Results of 1965 study of I.Q. of 120,000 children ages six to 13, out of 6,550,000 in Metropolitan France, repeating 1944 study. Only samples of 1944 questions are presented, no comparison with results of earlier study.

463 FRANCE. INSTITUT PEDAGOGIQUE NATIONAL. L'enseignement du français à l'école élémentaire; essais et confrontations 1968. Paris, 1970. 80 p. (Recherches pédagogiques, 44) ML

Conference on pedagogic reforms in teaching French in line with extension of general education and its egalitarian mission. Inadaptation of teaching is reflected in the fact that only 25 percent of boys and 30 percent of girls finish elementary cycle in "normal" number of years.

464 FRANCE. INSTITUT PEDAGOGIQUE NATIONAL. La lecture chez les jeunes et les bibliothèques dans l'enseignement du second degré. Paris, 1969. 62 p. (Recherches pédagogiques, 37) Bibliography: p. 59-62. ML

Resources, organization of school libraries, whose growth began after World War II.

465 FRANCE. INSTITUT PEDAGOGIQUE NATIONAL. Loisirs et éducation; les intérêts des jeunes de quinze et seize ans dans les loisirs et dans l'enseignement. Bilan d'une enquête réalisée par le Département de la recherche pédagogique de l'Institut pédagogique national. Compte rendu par Jean Hassenforder. Paris, 1967. 104 p. (Courrier de la recherche pédagogique, mai 1967, no. 30) ML

May 1965 questionnaire study for Grenoble and Montpellier area of over 4,000 students in all types of school on time spent on homework, favorite leisure activities, categorized by sex, type of school.

466 FRANCE. INSTITUT PEDAGOGIQUE NATIONAL. Organisation des premiers cycles secondaires et individualisation de l'enseignement. Paris, 1970. 161 p. tables, diagrs. (Recherches pédagogiques, 41) ML

Description of organization of guidance in secondary education, tables reporting results for aptitude tests, French and mathematics achievement tests for first two years of secondary cycle in different types of schools and for different social background of pupils. Other volumes in this series report on recent changes in elementary and secondary curricula.

467 FRANCE. LAWS, STATUTES, ETC. L'indemnisation des Français dépossédés outre-mer. Par Jacques Ribs. Avec la collaboration de Roland Blanquer. Paris, Dalloz, 1971. 226 p. (Manuel Dalloz de droit usuel)

Presentation of laws passed 1961-70 on compensation for confiscated overseas possession and resettlement aid, treatment of debts to French credit institutions on confiscated property. Complete text of Algerian (1963-68) and French (1961-70) legislation, decisions of Cour de cassation. Major new legislation is that of July 15, 1970, and subsequent decrees. For 1971, 500 million francs were to be paid in compensation, a maximum of 76,000 francs per person.

468 FRANCE. MINISTERE DE LA JEUNESSE ET DES SPORTS. Jeunes d'aujourd'hui; d'après le rapport d'enquête du Ministère de la jeunesse et des sports. Paris, Documentation française, 1967. 338 p. Includes bibliography.

June 1967 report presented to government by François Missoffe, minister of youth and sports. Youth crisis is analyzed on basis of information from youth organizations, current sociological research, public opinion survey. Chapters on professional distribution of young, their psychology, role in society. Summary of needs for educational and athletic facilities. Results of public opinion survey on political attitudes of young, physical and mental health problems. Good bibliography of books, articles, government documents on each topic. This report represented most up-to-date and enlightened official views on youth problems before May 1968, yet Feb. 1968 confrontation between Missoffe and Cohn-Bendit at Nanterre sparked student revolt.

469 FRANCE. MINISTERE DE L'EDUCATION NATIONALE. Le mouvement éducatif en France, principales tendances 1968-1971. Rapport présenté à la XXXIIIe Conférence internationale de l'instruction publique. Paris, Institution nationale de documentation pédagogique, 1971. 127 p. ML

Quadrilingual report on recent changes in all levels of French education.

470 FRANCE. MINISTERE DE L'INTERIEUR. Les élections législatives de 1967. Métropole, départements et territoires d'outre-mer: 12 mars 1967; Polynésie française: 5 et 19 mars 1967; Côte française des Somalis: 23 avril 1967. Paris, Impr. nationale, 1967. 1122 p.

For contents, see French Fifth Republic Bibliography, 1, nos. 783 and 784. Includes new electoral districts organized July 1966, Feb. 1967 regulations on radio-TV election propaganda.

471 FRANCE. MINISTERE DE L'INTERIEUR. Les élections législatives de 1968. Métropole, départements d'outre-mer: 23 et 30 juin 1968. Territoires d'outre-mer: Comores: 23 juin 1968; Nouvelle Calédonie et dépendances et Nouvelles-Hébrides, Saint-Pierre-et-Miquelon, Territoire français des Afars et des Issas: 23 et 30 juin 1968; iles Wallis et Futuna et Polynésie française: 7 juillet 1968. Paris, Impr. nationale, 1969. 1116 p. tables. ML

Results of 1968 elections in same format as in earlier volumes. See French Fifth Republic Bibliography, 1, nos. 783 and 784. Includes electoral maps for U.D.R., P.C.F., F.G.D.S., and Progrès et démocratie.

472 FRANCE. MINISTERE DE L'INTERIEUR. Les élections sénatoriales du 23 décembre 1962. Série A: Métropole, départements d'outre-mer, territoires d'outre-mer, Français établis hors de France. Annexe: élections partielles. Paris, Impr. nationale, 1963. 165 p. tables. ML

Follows same pattern as for earlier election results. See French Fifth Republic Bibliography, 1, nos. 785 and 786.

473 FRANCE. MINISTERE DE L'INTERIEUR. Les élections sénatoriales du 22 septembre 1968. Série C: Métropole, départements d'outre-mer, territoires d'outre-mer, Français établis hors de France. Annexe: élections partielles. Paris, Impr. nationale, 1969. 159 p. tables. ML

As above, no. 472.

474 FRANCE. MINISTERE DES AFFAIRES ETRANGERES. French foreign policy; official statements, speeches and communiqués. 1966-1969. New York, Ambassade de France, Service de presse et d'information. 7 v.

One volume for 1966, half-yearly volumes for 1967-69. Each volume has foreign affairs chronology, followed by text and documents of Council of Ministers sessions, official speeches, interviews, in chronological order. Subject index for each volume. For French version, see nos. 1176 and 1178.

475 FRANCE. PARLEMENT, 1946- ASSEMBLEE NATIONALE. SECRETARIAT GENERAL. Statistiques, 1967-1968. Document établi par le Secrétariat général de l'Assemblée nationale. Paris, Impr. de l'Assemblée nationale, 1968-69. 2 v. ML

Figures on National Assembly's membership characteristics, statistics on oral and written questions, projects and propositions, laws adopted. In appendices, list of laws adopted, by area of legislation and date. Vol. I: Apr. 1967-May 1968; Vol. II: July 1968-Dec. 1968.

FOR FRANCE, PARLEMENT..., ASSEMBLEE NATIONALE..., SEE ALSO NO. 438

476 FRANCE. TREATIES, ETC., 1958-1970 (DE GAULLE). Traité de coopération et accords franco-mauritaniens. [Nouakchott] 1961. 46 p.

477 La France dans la compétition économique; quatre débats à l'Académie des sciences morales et politiques. Par Raymond Aron et al. Introd. par Edmond Giscard d'Estaing. Paris, Presses universitaires de France, 1969. 153 p.

Speakers at this Jan. 1969 discussion were Aron, Louis Armand, Jean Fourastié, and Wilfrid Baumgartner. Aron talks about economic consequences of May 1968 on France's competitive position; Armand and Fourastié discuss obstacles to efficiency in French mentality.

478 FRANÇOIS, MICHEL. L'affaire Guy Robert; ou la revanche de 1968. Caen, Union départementale C.F.D.T. du Calvados, 1970. 126 p. (Supplément au no. 71 d'Informations syndicales)

Instance of harassment of trade union spokesmen who had been active May 1968 and had remained militant thereafter. This is case of young technician representing C.F.D.T. in Caen truck manufacturing plant, whose job was eliminated during his year's military service. C.F.D.T. appealed decision to court, but it was turned down, exemplifying government hostility to trade unions.

479 Frantsuzskii ezhegodnik; stat'i i materialy po istorii Frantsii. Annuaire d'études françaises. Moskva, Akademiia nauk SSSR, 1961-69. 9 v.

Studies on modern history, most of them pre-dating Fifth Republic, except for items on Franco-Soviet relations, but some current topics are treated too (e.g., the French press in 1969 volume). Includes list of books and dissertations on French history for year by Soviet authors. French summaries, French table of contents.

480   FREDERIC, CLAUDE. Libérer l'O. R. T. F. Documents et témoignages recueillis par Claude Frédéric. Paris, Editions du Seuil, 1968. 158 p. (Collection Combats)

Background of government control over television, news coverage of first period of May 1968 uprising, day-by-day history of strike by Office de radio-diffusion-télévision française (O. R. T. F.) personnel voted May 17 and ended June 17, except for 120 news broadcasters, most of whom were eventually fired.

481   FREMONTIER, JACQUES. La forteresse ouvrière: Renault; une enquête à Boulogne-Billancourt chez les ouvriers de la Régie. Paris, Fayard, 1971. 380 p. (Le Monde sans frontières) Includes bibliographical references.

Case study of working-class conditions based on investigation of pace-setting Renault factory at Billancourt outside Paris, with 39,000 workers. Using material from interviews with 120 representative employees, journalist author first describes different types of workers, from unskilled to "cadres," hourly to salaried, immigrant to French. Second section destroys myth that workers are becoming integrated into affluent society by account of working and living conditions, cultural alienation. Final section deals with trade union demands, methods of struggle (C. G. T. has majority representation), political attitudes, negative responses to student appeals for collaboration May 1968.

482   French daily newspapers, May 2-July 3, 1968. Microfilm copy (positive) made by Association pour la conservation et la reproduction photographique de la presse, Paris. 54 reels.

This film is subtitled "Evénéments de mai." Each reel covers complete issue for all papers listed below on date(s) indicated. Most papers have no Sunday issue and nothing was published May 14. See also nos. 485 and 1137.

Reels 1-9:	May 2-10	Reels 28-32:	June 3-7
Reel 10:	May 11-12	Reel 33:	June 8-9
Reel 11:	May 13	Reels 34-38:	June 10-14
Reels 12-14:	May 15-17	Reel 39:	June 15-16
Reel 15:	May 18-19	Reels 40-44:	June 17-21
Reels 16-20:	May 20-24	Reel 45:	June 22-23
Reel 21:	May 25-26	Reels 46-50:	June 24-28
Reels 22-26:	May 27-31	Reel 51:	June 29-30
Reel 27:	June 1-2	Reels 52-54:	July 1-3

Combat (Paris); La Croix (Paris); Le Figaro (Paris); L'Humanité (Paris); Le Monde (Paris); La Nation (Paris); Paris-Presse-L'Intransigeant; Centre-Presse (Poitiers); Courrier de l'Ouest (Anjou); Le Dauphiné libéré (Grenoble, Lyon); La Dépêche du Midi (Toulouse); Les Dépêches (Centre-Est, Dijon); Eclair Pyrénées (Tarbes); L'Est républicain (Nancy); L'Indépendant (Perpignan); L'Informateur Corse (Ajaccio); Midi-Libre (Montpelier); Nice-Matin; La Nouvelle république du Centre-Ouest (Tours); Paris-Normandie (Rouen); Le Progrès (Lyon); Le Provençal (Marseille); La République du Centre (Orléans); Sud-Ouest (Bordeaux); Le Télégramme de Brest et de l'Ouest (Brest); L'Union (Reims); La Voix du Nord (Lille).

483   French Fifth Republic Collection

A: Boxes 31-44 described in detail below continue the collection itemized in French Fifth Republic Bibliography, 1, no. 811, which already listed material for the Mar. 1967 legislative elections. As before, the focus of this collection is on legislative and presidential elections and referenda. It also includes some uncatalogued material issued by political parties and organizations. A substantial collection of material on the events of May 1968 is to be found under French student revolt (no. 484 below).

(1) Box 31-40: Legislative elections, June 23 and 30, 1968. Texts of interviews and debates broadcast over Europe 1 between June 7 and 28 and "professions de foi" of candidates for first and second round of elections by departments, election propaganda of political parties.

Box 31: Interviews and answers to listeners' questions by: V. Giscard d'Estaing, W. Rochet, F. Mitterrand, E. Fajon, A. Chalandon, M. Debré, G. Mollet, M. Rocard, M. Couve de Murville, R. Capitant, F. Gaillard, L. Vallon. Debates between M. Habib-Deloncle and B. Motte; P. Abelin and A. Fanton; J. Baumel and P. Juquin; C.-P. Brossolette and P. Joxe.

Box 32: Interviews and answers to listeners' questions by: J. Lecanuet, J. Duhamel, P. Mendès-France, F. Mitterrand, V. Giscard d'Estaing, J. M. Jeanneney, Y. Guéna, G. Defferre, R. Poujade. Debates between R. Ballanger and R. Frey.

Box 33-39: "Professions de foi" from these departments: Aisne, Allier, Basses-Alpes, Hautes-Alpes, Alpes Maritimes, Ardèche, Ardennes, Ariège, Aube, Aude, Aveyron, Bouches-du-Rhône, Calvados, Cantal, Charente-Maritime, Cher, Corrèze, Corse, Côte-d'Or, Côtes-du-Nord, Creuse, Dordogne, Doubs, Drôme, Eure, Eure-et-Loire, Gard, Gers, Guyane, Haute-Garonne, Ille-et-Vilaine, Indre-et-Loire, Jura, Landes, Loir-et-Cher, Loire, Haute-Loire, Loire Atlantique, Loiret, Lot, Lot-et-Garonne, Lozère, Maine-et-Loire, Mayenne, Manche, Haute-Marne, Martinique, Meurthe-et-Moselle, Meuse, Morbihan, Moselle, Nièvre, Nord, Oise, Paris, Pas-de-Calais, Pyrénées Orientales, Puy-de-Dôme, Réunion, Bas-Rhin, Haut-Rhin, Saône-et-Loire, Sarthe, Savoie, Haute-Savoie, Seine Maritime, Hauts-de-Seines, Deux-Sèvres, Somme. Election results for each department are included.

Box 40: Propaganda distributed by these political parties: Parti communiste français, Parti socialiste unifié, Fédération de la gauche démocrate et socialiste, Union pour la défense de la république, Front populaire. Also includes list of party candidates, special issues of "France-Soir," "Figaro," "Lettres françaises," "Parisien libéré."

(2) Box 41-42: Apr. 1969 referendum on regional reform and June 1969 presidential election.

Box 41: Texts of interviews on Europe 1 prior to referendum by: M. Couve de Murville, F. Mitterrand, E. Faure, C. Fuzier, J. Lecanuet, M. Schumann. Debates between M. Debré and F. Mitterrand; R. Poujade and G. Marchais. Texts of speeches and interviews by candidates for presidency A. Poher, G. Defferre, G. Pompidou, M. Rocard, A. Krivine, J. Duclos, L. Ducatel, as well as by V. Giscard d'Estaing, G. Marchais, M. Debré, P. Armand, F. Mitterrand, J. Duhamel, J. Fontanet, P. Sudreau, R. Leroy, P. Mauroy.

Box 42: Additional material on referendum: official government information on referendum and results, campaign material from Parti socialiste, Union des démocrates pour la république, Centre démocrate, Parti communiste français. Additional material on presidential campaign from Parti communiste français, Parti socialiste unifié, Ligue communiste, Alliance des jeunes pour le socialisme, Union des démocrates pour la république, and Ambassade de France's "Biographies of the Candidates."

(3) Box 43-44: Miscellaneous material from political parties and other organizations.

Box 43: Fédération de la gauche démocrate et socialiste: 1966-67 material; U.N.R.-U.D.T. groupe parlementaire, Conseil national: 1963-64 material; Union des jeunes pour le progrès, Association pour le soutien du Général de Gaulle; students' and women's organizations: U.N.E.F., Fédération des étudiants révolutionnaires, Fédération des étudiants de Paris, Association générale des élèves de l'Institut des études politiques, Mouvement démocratique féminin, Union des femmes françaises.

Box 44: Parti communiste français and related student organizations, 1966-69; Communist opposition groups: Union des jeunesses communistes marxistes-léninistes, with first four issues of "Garde rouge" (Nov. 1966-Feb. 1967), Jeunesse communiste révolutionnaire, Parti communiste marxiste-léniniste, Ligue communiste; Parti socialiste unifié; organizations opposing Vietnam war. Box 44 also contains special newspaper issues on de Gaulle's death: Le Monde, Nov. 13, 1970; Herald Tribune, Nov. 12-13, 1970.

B: Phonographs records

In addition to printed material the above collection includes two sets of phonograph records from the series "Hommes et faits du XXe siècle," nos. H F 09/IB-IVB and H F 11.

(1) La guerre d'Algérie (H F 09) contains four records. The first covers the events of May 13, 1958, in Paris and Algeria, from demonstration at Algiers Forum to de Gaulle's triumphant Algerian visit June 4. The second centers on the "barricades" uprising in Algeria, Jan. 24, 1960, with preliminary political developments such as 1958 referendum and de Gaulle's expositions of his Algerian self-determination policy. The third culminates in the Apr. 20-24, 1961 Generals' Putsch in Algeria and reactions in Paris. The final record documents activities of O.A.S. from Aug. 1961 to Aug. 1962, Evian treaty, shooting at rue d'Isly, trials of Salan, Bastien-Thiry.

(2) Presidentielle 65 (H F 11) contains campaign speeches during 1965 presidential campaign by all candidates: Marcel Barbu, Charles de Gaulle, Jean Lecanuet, Pierre Marcilhacy, François Mitterrand, Jean-Louis Tixier-Vignancour.

All parts of this special collection are located in the Hoover Archives.

484   French Student Revolt, May-June 1968. Special Collection.

A: Envelopes 1-38 preserve a cross section of ephemeral material issued during this period by established and recently founded revolutionary and moderate students groups, revolutionary youth groups, Communist opposition groups, regular political parties, organizations, and clubs, action committees, student worker committees, lycée student committees, strike committees, teachers' unions, trade unions. Of special interest is the extensive documentation on ad hoc student commissions and assemblies at the different faculties of the University of Paris, the University of Poitiers, as well as several specialized schools and institutes. For catalogued items, consult Subject Index under May 1968.

(1) Reference lists, including rough listing of University of Wisconsin holdings on May 1968.
(2) Studies on student uprising, such as Paris police reports for Apr. 29, May 21, and June 11, 1968.
(3) Documents on police repression.
(4) Cartoons.
(5) Action committees, Paris.
(6) Revolutionary worker-student organizations (Comité d'initiative pour un mouvement révolutionnaire, Mouvement de soutien aux luttes du peuple, Comité d'action ouvriers-étudiants, Comité de coordination des cadres contestataires "C 4," Conseil pour le maintien des occupations, Comité de défense contre la répression).
(7) U.N.E.F. leaflets.
(8) and (9) Revolutionary student organizations (Comité d'action "Nous sommes en marche," Fédération des étudiants révolutionnaires, Internationale situationniste, Jeunesses communistes révolutionnaires, Mouvement du 22 mars, Union des jeunesses communistes marxistes-léninistes).
(10) Right-wing and moderate student organizations (Fédération des étudiants de Paris, Front des étudiants pour la rénovation de l'université, Mouvement Jeune révolution, Occident, Fédération générale des étudiants européens, Etudiants européens, Comité de liaison pour la rénovation universitaire, Comité des étudiants pour les libertés universitaires, Mouvement d'organisation des étudiants pour la liberté).
(11) Communist student and youth organizations.
(12) Foreign students and workers (Comité des trois continents, Commission de liaison des travailleurs étrangers, Fédération des étudiants d'Afrique noire en France, Amis du SNCC, etc.).
(13) Miscellaneous student appeals.
(14) Defense organizations against May 1968 uprising (Comité pour la défense de la république, Front national anti-communiste, Union nationale, Comité d'action civique, Union des commerçants du Quartier Latin).
(15) Political organizations and clubs (Club Jean Moulin, Club Démocratie et université, Objectif 1972, Parti libéral de France, Parti socialiste unifié, etc.).
(16) Communist opposition groups (Cercle d'études marxistes de Paris, Parti communiste marxiste-léniniste de France, Tendance marxiste révolutionnaire de la Quatrième Internationale, Tendance révolutionnaire du Parti communiste français, Parti communiste internationaliste, Organisation communiste pour la reconstitution de la IVe Internationale, Organisation révolutionnaire anarchiste, Ligue ouvrière révolutionnaire).
(17) Parti communiste français.
(18) Religious groups (Fédération des groupes "Témoignage chrétien," Communauté chrétienne de St. Germain-des-Prés, Groupe biblique universitaire de Paris, etc.).
(19) Theater and cinema (Etats généraux du cinéma, Université populaire cinématographique, Théâtre de France, Comité révolutionnaire d'agitation culturelle, etc.).
(20) Lycées and "classes préparatoires" (Lycée Jules Ferry, Assemblée générales des étudiants préparatoires, etc.).
(21) Inter-university documents (includes: Commission nationale interdisciplinaire: "Pour une réflexion sur la mutation de l'université, 6 juin 1968").
(22) Ecole nationale de photographie et de cinématographie (Paris).
(23) Ecole nationale supérieure des beaux-arts (Paris) and other schools of arts and architecture.
(24) Institut pédagogique national and Institut universitaire de technologie.
(25) Université de Paris, Faculté de droit.
(26) Université de Paris, Faculté de médecine and Faculté de chirurgie dentaire ("Livre blanc de la réforme," June 14, 1968).
(27) Université de Paris, Faculté des lettres et des sciences humaines (philosophy, history, modern language departments).
(28) Université de Paris, Nanterre.
(29) Université de Paris, Faculté des sciences (material on academic reform).
(30) Université de Paris, Faculté des sciences (election to its Commission centrale, June 28, 1968).
(31) Université de Paris, Faculté des Sciences (strike committee).
(32) Université de Paris, Faculté des sciences (Université d'été).
(33) Université de Poitiers, Faculté des sciences (material on university reform, May 17-June 28, 1968).
(34) Teachers' unions (Fédération de l'éducation nationale-Ecole emancipée, Syndicat national de l'enseignement supérieur, Syndicat national de l'enseignement secondaire, Syndicat national de l'éducation surveillée, Syndicat général de l'éducation nationale).
(35) Office de la radio-télévision française (material on strike).

(36) Factories on strike (Renault-Billancourt C.G.T. and Force ouvrière material, Renault-Flins, Citroën, Simca, Schwartz-Haumont).

(37) Trade unions (C.G.T., C.F.D.T., Force ouvrière's Fédération syndicaliste des travailleurs des P.T.T., Régie autonome des transports parisiens, Hachette, Nouvelles messageries de presse parisienne, Mariniers).

(38) Students on June 1968 elections (Comité d'action révolutionnaire anti-élection, Comité d'action politique travailleurs-étudiants Halle-aux-vins, Comité de coordination des cadres contestataires, etc.).

B: Newspapers and periodicals

Seventy-six different newspapers and periodicals related to May 1968 events form part of the collection. They are short runs or individual issues of ephemeral publications by student, worker, and revolutionary organizations, as well as special issues of regular publications. Typical titles among these ephemeral publications are: Avant-garde, Cahiers de mai, Cahiers marxistes-léninistes, Etudiant révolutionnaire, Hermès, L'Insurgé, Journal des étudiants en médecine de Paris, Labyrinthe 606 (Journal lycéen), Noir et rouge, Le Pavé, Pouvoir ouvrier, Servir le peuple. Itemized list available on request. For Action, Cause du peuple, and Enragé, see nos. 1145, 1157, 1169. Association pour la conservation et la reproduction photographique de la presse's film on ephemeral press is not at Hoover as yet.

C: Posters on French student revolt

Total of 32 posters issued by Union des jeunesses communistes marxistes-léninistes, Voix ouvrière, Parti communiste français, Jeunesses communistes de France, Union des étudiants communistes, Union nationale des étudiants préparatoires, Mouvement étudiant.

D: Tapes on French student revolt

(1) Pierre Grappin, dean of Nanterre's Faculté des lettres et sciences humaines, discusses background of Nanterre explosion and closing of Nanterre May, 1968, post-May university reforms. Interview was taped at Laurence Wylie's seminar on French civilization, Harvard, Jan. 1969.

(2) André Malraux answers questions by Europe 1 journalists on significance of May-June 1968 events in relation to Western civilization, youth crisis. Interview was taped June 21, 1968, from French radio broadcast.

(3) Jean-Pierre Vigier, physics professor and editor of revolutionary journal "Action," comments on revolutionary portents of crisis. Wylie interview taped Sept. 1968.

(4) Jean-Pierre Biondi, O.R.T.F. journalist, describes conditions at O.R.T.F. before and during strike. Wylie interview taped Sept. 1968.

All parts of this special collection are held in the Hoover Archives. For details on tapes, see no. 1137.

485 French weekly journals covering the period May-July 1968. Microfilm copy (positive) made by the Association pour la conservation et la reproduction photographique de la presse, Paris. 3 reels.

Microfilm subtitle is "Evénements de mai." See also no. 482.

Reel 1: "Aspects de la France," Apr. 25-July 4; and "Express," Apr. 22/28—June 24/30.

Reel 2: "Express," July 1/7; "Figaro hebdomadaire," Apr. 25-July 4; "Humanité dimanche," Apr. 28-July 5; "Minute," Apr. 25-July 4/10; and "Le Monde hebdomadaire," Apr. 25/30—July 4/10.

Reel 3: "Nouvel observateur," Apr. 24/30—July 3/9; "Réforme," Apr. 20-July 6; "Témoignage chrétien," Apr. 25-July 4; and "Tribune socialiste," Apr. 25-July 4.

486 FRIGUGLIETTI, JAMES, and EMMET KENNEDY, comps. The shaping of modern France; writings on French history since 1715. Introd. by Crane Brinton. New York, Macmillan, 1969. xiii, 633 p. Includes bibliographies.

Chapter 18, entitled "The Fifth Republic, the final synthesis," has contributions by Douglas Johnson on the political principles of de Gaulle, W. W. Kulski on de Gaulle and decolonization, Alfred Grosser on de Gaulle's foreign policy views, and Louis J. Halle on his European views.

487 FROLKIN, NIKOLAI MIKHAILOVICH. Krest'ianstvo v alzhirskoi revoliutsii, 1954-1962. Kiev, Naukova dumka, 1967. 124 p.

Contribution of Algerian peasants to triumph of nationalists and F.L.N. land reform program.

488 FRONT DE LA JEUNESSE. L'Union de la jeunesse devant les erreurs de la Vème République. Un ensemble de documents sur les interventions récentes de l'Union de la jeunesse et du groupe du Front de la jeunesse dans les domaines de la monnaie, de la banque, de la planification et de l'enseignement. Meudon, 1967. 20 l. (Revue du Front de la jeunesse et de l'externité, avril-mai 1967)

May-June 1967 material including questions by Maurice Lemaître at de Gaulle's May 16, 1967 press conference, proposals to solve unemployment crisis of young, pedagogic innovations such as elimination of baccalauréat, opposition to Missoffe report (see no. 468) and Fouchet reform. Isidore Isou and Lemaître, formerly close to Internationale situationniste movement and now heading Mouvement lettriste, are cosigners of these documents. See also Isou (no. 637) and Lemaître (no. 732).

489 FUENTES, CARLOS. Paris, la revolución de Mayo. México, Era, 1968. 31 p. illus.

Impressions, reported conversations of Mexican journalist in Paris, amplified by some original pictorial material.

490 GALANTE, PIERRE. Le Général. Paris, Presses de la Cité, 1968. 253 p. plates.

Anecdotes, based on conversations with family members and collaborators, on de Gaulle's family and aspects of his military and political career, relations with other countries, glimpses of personal tastes, daily life at Elysée Palace and Colombey. Book completed before May 1968. Many family photographs.

491 GALANTE, PIERRE. Malraux. Avec le concours d'Yves Salgues. Préf. de Gaston Bonheur. Paris, Plon, 1971. 344 p portr. Includes bibliography.

Biography of writer, man of action, art critic. Last third describes his role in R.P.F. and accomplishments as Fifth Republic minister of cultural affairs and propagator abroad of French civilization. Includes his Dec. 1969 interview with Malraux after latter's retirement from office, in which Malraux defines his relations with de Gaulle.

492 GALLANT, MAVIS, ed. The affair of Gabrielle Russier. With a pref. by Raymond Jean and an introd. by Mavis Gallant. New York, A. A. Knopf, 1971. 177 p.

Introduction by American journalist Mavis Gallant sketches background, course of events culminating in suicide of lycée teacher at Marseille because of persecution for her affair with a student, son of Communist professors at Aix University who had brought the matter to the attention of courts. Affair had begun around May 1968, during which boy was active as Maoist, teacher freely sided with students and came to symbolize in eyes of authorities and public the disorders growing out of events. Prosecution initiated in Dec. 1968 led to suicide Aug. 1969. Includes portrait of Mme Russier by friend and colleague

Raymond Jean and her letters to family and friends in last months of her life.

493 GALLO, MAX. Gauchisme, réformisme et révolution. Paris, R. Laffont, 1968. 191 p. (Collection Contestation)

May 1968 student explosion seen as specific instance of "gauchisme," that is, a historically premature revolutionary movement. As history professor, author observed firsthand the inspiration of revolutionary student movement and the hate dividing it from P.C.F. Both gauchisme and orthodox Communism are viewed as impasse for French society by preventing alliance of entire Left.

494 GARAUDY, ROGER. L'alternative. Paris, R. Laffont, 1972. 252 p.

Youth demands for cultural revolution are taken as starting point for a contemporary form of socialism based on "autogestion" compatible with high levels of technology and education. In contrast to his earlier works, the author here evaluates Chinese cultural revolution favorably.

495 GARAUDY, ROGER. De l'anathème au dialogue; un marxiste tire les conclusions du Concile. Paris, Plon, 1965. 126 p. (Les Débats de notre temps)

Recent trends in Marxist and Christian thinking permitting fruitful confrontation rather than mutual anathema.

496 GARAUDY, ROGER. Garaudy par Garaudy; entretiens avec Claude Glayman. Paris, Table ronde de Combat, 1970. 270 p. (La Politique selon . . .)

"Combat" and "Témoignage chrétien" journalist introduces this lengthy questioning on models of socialism and their relation to current status of science and technology, socialism and Christianity, importance of aesthetic creation for ordinary human beings, prospects for the year 2000, and proposals for educational reform, with portrait of this dissident French Communist shortly before his exclusion from P.C.F. First section in particular treats his views on P.C.F., May 1968 events, possibilities for socialism in France, European unification. Although rejection of Russian model is complete, P.C.F.'s position on internal and international questions usually upheld.

497 GARAUDY, ROGER. Le grand tournant du socialisme. Paris, Gallimard, 1969. 315 p. (Collection Idées, 204)

Reviewing student movements and strikes, where technical personnel joined forces with workers, Garaudy sees demand for participation as cause of revolution in highly technical societies. Conflicts between capitalism and Communism are secondary sources of tension, since neither camp has answers to new problems. Strengths and weaknesses of U.S. and U.S.S.R. fairly assessed, as are Yugoslav and Chinese models. Form of socialism creating human model for technical civilization remains to be put forward, but some steps in right direction for France are proposed, necessary changes within P.C.F. indicated. Published in English as "The crisis in communism; the turning point of socialism" (New York, Grove Press, 1972).

498 GARAUDY, ROGER. La liberté en sursis Prague 1968; avec des textes de Alexandre Dubcek [et al.] et des extraits du Programme d'action du Parti communiste tchécoslovaque. Paris, Fayard, 1968. 156 p. (En toute liberté)

Garaudy's introduction to texts by Czech political figures written between Jan. and Aug. 1968 states his hope for a model of democratic socialism in a country with a high technical, economic, and cultural development and tradition of political democracy.

499 GARAUDY, ROGER. Le problème chinois. Paris, Seghers, 1967. 300 p. illus.

Historical explanation of Chinese socialist model (interaction of liquidation of underdevelopment and Confucian tradition with construction of socialism) leads to condemnation of recent cultural revolution as a rejection of humanism.

500 GARAUDY, ROGER. Pour un modèle français du socialisme. Paris, Gallimard, 1968. 386 p. (Idées actuelles, 171) Bibliographical footnotes.

Essays first published under title "Peut-on être communiste aujourd'hui?" by French philosopher and P.C.F. Central Committee member discuss his personal history as Communist, significance of Marx's writings for the present, in particular relevance to current "alienation." Anti-humanist element in dogmatic Marxism such as Louis Althusser's is opposed and affinities with Catholic and Protestant avant-garde brought out. Work concluded spring 1968 includes summary of P.C.F.'s program for French socialism.

501 GARAUDY, ROGER. Reconquête de l'espoir. Paris, B. Grasset, 1971. 146 p.

First part attacks Soviet socialism for perversions growing out of priority of capital goods production and too rapid growth rate, on which he blames repeated revolts in Eastern Europe and wasteful bureaucracy. Second part elaborates alternative model of socialist democracy based on worker administration, grass-roots democracy, in contrast to P.C.F. strategy of party dictatorship combined with short-run parliamentary approach. Final part reverts to mutual enhancement of Marxism and Christianity.

502 GARAUDY, ROGER. Toute la vérité. Paris, B. Grasset, 1970. 196 p.

Indictment of P.C.F. leadership failure to act more decisively May 1968, to condemn Soviet intervention in Czechoslovakia and Polish anti-Semitism, followed by defense of his own position and 1968-70 publications as loyal to real P.C.F. and socialist interests, in contrast to P.C.F.'s distortions. Includes texts of own speeches at party congresses, articles, letters, some of pronouncements of P.C.F. leaders. He was excluded from party at its 19th congress, Jan. 1970.

503 GARAUDY, ROGER, and QUENTIN LAUER. A Christian-Communist dialogue. Garden City, N.Y., Doubleday, 1968. 190 p.

Garaudy's interlocutor is American Jesuit priest. Conflicts between basic Marxist and Christian tenets are freely aired under headings of atheism, moral, historical, political, social problems. On each side gulf between theory and practice on the part of Soviet government and Catholic Church is stressed, but desire to find common ground is genuine. Dialogue took place late 1967, and Garaudy was still defending Soviet Union and P.C.F. actions.

504 GARAUDY, ROGER; METZ, JOHANN B.; RAHNER, KARL. Der Dialog, oder Ändert sich das Verhältnis zwischen Katholizismus und Marxismus. Hamburg, Rowohlt, 1966. 139 p.

Translation of "De l'anathème au dialogue" followed by speeches of German theologians who met Garaudy at 1965 and 1966 Paulus Gesellschaft conferences. No actual exchanges reproduced here.

FOR ADDITIONAL WORKS BY AND ABOUT ROGER GARAUDY, SEE AUTHOR INDEX

505 GARELLI, FRANÇOIS. Pour une monnaie européenne. Paris, Editions du Seuil, 1969. 156 p.

Banker economist's review of past and current methods for harmonizing international monetary flow and proposals for using European Communities as nucleus for adopting common European currency, in which currency itself is federal but economic and fiscal policies remain within local control, as in Swiss federation, which has great disparities in economic and social development between cantons.

506 GASCON, ROGER. La nuit du pouvoir, ou le 24 mai manqué. Paris, Nouvelles éditions Debresse, 1968. 101 p. illus. (Collection Révolte, no. 2)

May-June 1968 events narrated from angle of disillusioned member of Gaullist party's protection service, who was called upon to protect Union des démocrates pour la Ve République headquarters and those of the rue de Solferino, seat of related Gaullist organizations, during and subsequent to May 24 disorders and later to protect Gaullist candidates. Intrigues and demoralization in Gaullist ranks are brought to light, and reliance on secret service to maintain party in power, role of Comités de défense de la république (C.D.R.) discussed.

507 GAUDEZ, PIERRE. Les étudiants; essai. Préf. de Dominique Wallon. Paris, Julliard, 1961. 193 p. ML

Facts on life, attitudes of university students as individuals and members of student unions, U.N.E.F. stand on internal (educational) and political questions.

508 GAULLE, CHARLES DE, PRES. FRANCE. De Gaulle vous parle; choix d'allocutions et de conférences de presse de 1958 à 1967. Montréal, Editions du Jour, 1967. 121 p.

Short unannotated selections from de Gaulle's writings and speeches grouped around: France and Frenchmen, French destiny, politics, war, nations, the state, statesmen.

509 GAULLE, CHARLES DE, PRES. FRANCE. Citations du président de Gaulle. Choisies et présentées par Jean Lacouture. Paris, Editions du Seuil, 1968. 189 p. (Politique, 18)

Excerpts from speeches, press conferences, television interviews, May 1958-Jan. 1968, divided into 30 themes (chronological within themes) illustrating political philosophy, personality, style of political writing. Each theme is preceded by introductory comments. Typical themes are: France, the state, power, greatness, independence, legitimacy, political parties, parliament, decolonization, Atlantic Alliance, succession, arts, God.

510 GAULLE, CHARLES DE, PRES. FRANCE. De Gaulle vous parle; choix d'allocutions et de conférences de presse de 1958 à 1967. Montréal, Editions du Jour, 1967. 121 p.

Selected official speeches given without sources or comments.

511 GAULLE, CHARLES DE, PRES. FRANCE. Discours et messages. Edité par François Goguel. Paris, Plon, 1970. 5 v.

v. 1: Pendant la guerre, 1940-1946.
v. 2: Dans l'attente, 1946-1958.
v. 3: Avec le renouveau, 1958-1962.
v. 4: Pour l'effort, 1962-1965.
v. 5: Vers le terme, 1966-1969.

For Fifth Republic, Vol. 3 covers May 15, 1958-July 8, 1962, Vol. 4 Sept. 4, 1962-Dec. 31, 1965, and Vol. 5 Jan. 1, 1966-Apr. 28, 1969. These complete texts of official speeches, for which handwritten or official stenographic texts exist (radio and television addresses, press conferences, public addresses, messages to parliament), were revised for publication by de Gaulle in last months of his life. Goguel introduces each volume with detailed chronology, identifies circumstances for each speech and annotates it. Vol. 4 has de Gaulle interviews with Michel Droit, Dec. 13, 14, and 15, 1965, and Vol. 5 the lengthy interview with Droit June 7, 1968.

512 GAULLE, CHARLES DE, PRES. FRANCE. Extraits, pour l'avenir. Paris, Livre de poche, 1973. 346 p.

Short excerpts drawn from entire published writings and speeches, prepared by Institut Charles de Gaulle, which succeeded the Centre national d'étude de l'oeuvre du Général de Gaulle, organized during his lifetime. Arrangement by major themes of de Gaulle's message, chronological within each subtopic. Major divisions are: France and Frenchmen (unity and divisions); state, society, and participation; independence and peace (international monetary system, military policy, European policy, international cooperation). Institute has also published list of articles by de Gaulle (available at Hoover Library).

513 GAULLE, CHARLES DE, PRES. FRANCE. Full text of the fourteenth press conference held by French President Charles de Gaulle in Paris at the Elysée Palace on Friday, October 28, 1966. New York, Ambassade de France, Service de presse et d'information, 1966. 13 p. (Speeches and press conferences no. 253a)

514 GAULLE, CHARLES DE, PRES. FRANCE. Mémoires d'espoir. Paris, Plon, 1970-71. 2 v.

First volume, entitled "Le renouveau, 1958-1962," was completed and published Aug. 1970 and is divided into chapters on new political institutions, decolonization, Algeria, economy, Europe, the world, head of state. More ambitious second volume, "L'effort, 1962- . . . ," published posthumously in 1971, is incomplete, consisting of only two out of projected seven chapters, and covers Oct. 1962 constitutional referendum and 1963 economic reforms. For information on composition and publication of these volumes, see nos. 212 and 787. For English translation of both volumes, see next entry.

515 GAULLE, CHARLES DE, PRES. FRANCE. Memoirs of hope: renewal and endeavor. Translated by Terence Kilmartin. New York, Simon and Schuster, 1971. 392 p.

See preceding entry for comments.

516 GAULLE, CHARLES DE, PRES. FRANCE. Le petit livre rouge du général [Charles de Gaulle]. Pensées choisies (et parfois commentées) par Robert Rocca. Paris, Editions de la Pensée moderne, 1968. 253 p.

Brief excerpts from speeches, remarks during travels, press conferences, interviews (some not printed elsewhere) through Dec. 1967, as well as excerpts from writings, seasoned with scattered barbs by editor. Quotations are grouped around topics. Includes de Gaulle's astrological table and a few apocryphal anecdotes. Rocca is pen name of Canavezo (see no. 178).

FOR ADDITIONAL PUBLICATIONS BY AND ABOUT DE GAULLE, SEE SUBJECT INDEX

517 GAUMENT, ERIC. Le mythe américain. Paris, Editions sociales, 1970. 272 p.

Reply to Servan-Schreiber's "Le défi américain" by French Marxist economist who had spent two years in U.S. and concludes that rigorous class struggle lies ahead there. Author is not wholly hostile to U.S. investment in Europe, sees it as internationalization of capitalist economy, which is equalizing industrial sector in all Western countries without eliminating competition between firms.

518 GAVI, PHILIPPE. Les ouvriers: du tiercé à la révolution; enquête. Paris, Mercure de France, 1970. 315 p. (En direct)

Selected interviews, based on hundreds of tape-recorded interviews spontaneously arranged with skilled and unskilled, male and female, French and foreign workers, technicians at Peugeot, Sud-Aviation (Nantes), Rhodiaceta (Lyon), and coal mines in Northern France and Lorraine. Unstandardized interviews range over political attitudes, party affiliations, reactions to

May 1968 events, satisfaction with work and standard of living, housing, leisure activities.

519 GEISMAR, ALAIN, SERGE JULY, and ERLYNE MORANE. Vers la guerre civile. Paris, Editions et publications premières, 1969. 441 p. (Collection Stratégies)

July 1968-Mar. 1969 essays appraising various phases of revolutionary action during May 1968 events from point of view of insiders. Authors are critical of Trotskyist groups, U.N.E.F., S.N.E. Sup., P.S.U., as well as of P.C.F. and C.G.T., for their unrevolutionary caution at critical junctures such as May 24 and June 2. Only Mouvement du 22 mars is praised for efforts to tie in with factory occupations. Other essays deal with weakening of Gaullist regime through anti-authoritarian revolt, prospects for further revolts.

520 GENEVE, PIERRE. Histoire secrète de l'insurrection de mai 1968. Paris, Presses noires, 1968. 317 p. illus. (Les grandes affaires de ce temps)

Blow-by-blow account of events, concentrating on clashes between students and authorities Mar. 22-May 31. Author emphasizes student irresponsibility, thought not wholly favorable to government. No secret documents, only composite of newspaper reports, excerpted texts of speeches introduced as "témoignages" and "documents." Dictionary of student expressions and slogans.

521 GENTIL-BAICHIS, YVES DE, ed. Problèmes des jeunes. Paris, Editions Beauchesne, 1970. 117 p. (Carrefour des jeunes, 1)

Interviews with ten young people, selected response to short questionnaire in Nov. 1969 "La Croix" on attitudes and preoccupations of youth.

522 GENTIS, ROGER. Les murs de l'asile. Paris, F. Maspéro, 1970. 90 p. (Cahiers libres, 163)

Psychiatrist's indictment of mental hospitals as convenient places for getting rid of individuals troublesome to society because of their deviance rather than as a therapeutic setting. Mental hospital is viewed as social utopia, since each patient there accepts his place, has no responsibilities, has all needs cared for.

523 GEORGE, PIERRE. La France. Paris, Presses universitaires de France, 1967. 217 p. illus., plates, maps. (Collection Magellan, la géographie et ses problèmes, no. 11) Bibliography: p. 255-265. ML

Good factual presentation of historical, demographic, economic, and geographic basis for French regions, causes of regional disequilibria, current regional trends in agriculture, major industries, service trade, difficulties of organizing regions around solid urban cores with exception of Lille and Lyon areas. Lengthy section on Paris and vicinity, recent implantations of university, administrative, industrial centers beyond city.

524 GEORGEL, JACQUES. Le Sénat dans l'adversité, 1962-1966. Paris, Editions Cujas, 1968. 219 p. (Collection Vie politique et politique internationale) Bibliographical footnotes.

Origins of conflict between Gaullist regime and Senate in Monnerville's determined opposition to Oct. 1962 referendum and subsequent clashes between Senate and executive, leading to degradation of Senate's function as control organ. Final section summarizes recent proposals for Senate reform and Senators' reactions thereto. These proposals were incorporated in Apr. 1969 referendum.

525 GIANNOLI, PAUL XAVIER. Roger Peyrefitte, ou Les clés du scandale. Paris, Fayard, 1970. 105 p.

Interview with author of several controversial books on French society ("Les Juifs," "Des Français") and recent autobiographic work on homosexuality. Includes excerpts from critics.

526 GICQUEL, JEAN. Essai sur la pratique de la 5e République; bilan d'un septennat. ... Préf. de André Hauriou. ... Paris, Librairie générale de droit et de jurisprudence, 1968. viii, 399 p. (Bibliothèque constitutionnelle et de science politique, t. 33) Bibliography: p. 361-379.

Introduction on genesis of 1958 Constitution, followed by detailed demonstration of how this imprecise and ambiguous document was implemented by unwritten constitutional practices. Part I deals with transformation of constitution by exercise of de Gaulle's mandate (1958-62), describing origins, instruments, and impact of presidential supremacy and downgrading of parliament, relations with cabinet, special powers, referenda. Part II concerns Oct. 1962 reform and acceptance thereof, relations between government and majority Gaullist party and revitalized opposition. Completed fall 1967. Very extensive bibliography of books and articles on political institutions.

527 GILPIN, ROBERT. France in the age of the scientific state. Princeton, N.J., Princeton University Press, 1968. xii, 474 p. illus., map. Bibliographical footnotes.

American political scientist's comparative history of French scientific policy before World War II, during Fourth and Fifth Republic. Specific Gaullist innovations in scientific planning and incorporation into Fifth Plan, impact on science and technology of new military program, current organization of French scientific research, research expenditures, statistics on science students by fields, through 1963, with forecasts to 1971, reforms of scientific education, steps toward European and international scientific cooperation.

528 GIRARD, ALAIN. Le choix du conjoint; une enquête psychosociologique en France. Paris, Presses universitaires de France, 1964. 201 p. tables. (Institut national d'études démographiques. Travaux et documents, Cahier no. 44) ML

Effects of increasing social mobility on choice of spouse. Results show that "homogamy" continues to prevail. Questionnaire method to determine social, geographic, professional, religious background of spouses, occasion for meeting, opinions on marriage. Study based on 5 percent sample of first marriages, as of 1959, when work was done.

529 GIRAUDOUX, JEAN PIERRE. La VIIe République. Paris, B. Grasset, 1969. 160 p. ML

Imaginery dialogue with young revolutionary (author's son?) defending both anti-Marxist and anti-Gaullist views.

530 GISCARD D'ESTAING, EDMOND V. Les finances, terre inconnue. Paris, A. Fayard, 1958. 187 p. (Les idées et la vie)

Arguments in favor of free enterprise system, of which productive U.S. economy is repeatedly cited as model, opposition to obsession with full employment, automatic wage increases for increased productivity. Price stability is given key role in economic and social progress. Author, who is civil servant and industrialist, is father of Valéry Giscard d'Estaing.

531 GISCARD D'ESTAING, OLIVIER. La décentralisation des pouvoirs dans l'entreprise, condition du succès, son application dans les entreprises américaines. ... 2e éd. Paris, Editions d'Organisation, 1967. 140 p. tables. Bibliography: p. 125-139.

Lessons for French industry on effective methods of decentralizing business management based on the experience of U.S. companies. Author is brother of Valéry Giscard d'Estaing.

532 GISCARD D'ESTAING, OLIVIER. Education et civilisation; pour une révolution libérale de l'enseignement. Paris, Fayard, 1971. 244 p. plates, tables. Bibliography: p. 243-244. ML

Proposals for education reform based on practices common in U.S., Sweden: greater decentralization and autonomy of educational establishments, more audio-visual and programmed material, adult education, curricula revision downgrading classics. Democratization is not stressed. Good current statistics on enrollment, cost of education.

533 GIVET, JACQUES. La gauche contre Israël? Essai sur le néo-antisémitisme. [Paris?] J. J. Pauvert, 1968. 199 p.

Repudiation of quoted attacks on the part of left-wing writers against Israel and demonstration that current wave of anti-Zionism is subtler form of neo-anti-Semitism, which wants to keep state of Israel as vulnerable as was the Jewish minority in the past.

534 GLADWYN, HUBERT MILES GLADWYN JEBB, BARON. De Gaulle's Europe, or Why the General says no. London, Secker and Warburg, 1969. 168 p. ML

British diplomat's account of Fourth and Fifth Republic stand on European unification, acceptance of Common Market, with emphasis on de Gaulle's personal views and intervention. Author played active role in 1966-67, offering compromise solution for British admission to Common Market. Last section predicts Gaullist policy after May 1968 (work concluded before Apr. 1969).

535 GLUCKSMANN, ANDRE. Le discours de la guerre. Paris, l'Herne, 1967. 378 p. (Théorie et stratégie). Bibliographical footnotes.

Confrontation of strategies of dissuasion by nuclear weapons (U.S.) and prolonged war of popular national defense (Chinese Communists). Author shows why the two adversaries are speaking in mutually incomprehensible terms.

536 GLUCKSMANN, ANDRE. Stratégie de la révolution; introduction. Paris, C. Bourgois, 1968. 127 p.

July 1968 dissection of student and young worker movement, with many references to Marx and Paris Commune, proving that it was genuinely revolutionary and that its momentum was broken not by government strength but by P.C.F., trade unions, leftist parties.

537 GLUTZ VON BLOTZHEIM, ALEXANDRE. Le plan Rapacki et les propositions Mendès-France; chances et dangers du désarmement régional pour une politique européenne commune. Nancy, 1967. 85 p. (Université de Nancy. Publications du Centre européen universitaire. Collection des mémoires, no. 23) Includes bibliography.

Polish foreign minister's plan for creation of a denuclearized zone in Central Europe was presented Oct. 1957 and offered by Mendès-France in Apr. 1959 in modified form.

538 GOGUEL-NYEGAARD, FRANÇOIS. Modernisation économique et comportement politique d'après un échantillon d'un trentième du corps électoral français. Paris, A. Colin, 1969. 88 p. graphs, tables. (Fondation nationale des sciences politiques. Travaux et recherches de science politique, 1)

Follow-up on Goguel's earlier studies on electoral sociology and based on nine departments (Calvados, Cher, Drôme, Gard, Ille-et-Vilaine, Lot-et-Garonne, Haut-Rhin, Haute-Vienne, Vosges) for 1928 and 1968 elections. Evolution of "classical" (pre-1928) party blocs (i.e., non-Communist Left, moderates) and new parties (i.e., P.C.F. and Gaullists) followed up in relation to economic situation of individual cantons. There is significant correlation between electoral gains of Communists and Gaullists with economic regression or dynamism, but not for other parties.

539 GOLDMANN, LUCIEN. La création culturelle dans la société moderne. Paris, Denoël, 1971. 184 p. (Bibliothèque Médiations, 84) ML

Posthumous collection of 1965-70 articles and talks on contemporary literary and cinematic productions as expression of revolt against dehumanization of contemporary technocratic society.

540 GOLDMANN, LUCIEN. Marxisme et sciences humaines. Paris, Gallimard, 1970. 361 p. (Collection Idées, 228) ML

Reflections on revisions of Marxism in the face of demand of growing technical salaried class for participation in economy (e.g., May 1968) and recognition that human and cultural fulfillment rather than state ownership of means of production is key to socialist revolution. Other essays deal with Marxism and psychoanalysis, contributions of dialectic sociology to study of literature.

541 GOLDSCHMIDT, BERTRAND. Les rivalités atomiques, 1939-1966. Paris, Fayard, 1967. 340 p. plates. (Les Grandes études contemporaines)

Author is atomic physicist, one of founders of Commissariat à l'énergie atomique and presently head of its foreign relations section. For Fifth Republic years, problems of French civilian and military atomic energy programs and negotiations on nuclear weapons and tests are described. Commissariat now has 30,000 employees, as does private industry. Photographs of personalities in atomic energy program.

542 GOMBIN, RICHARD. Le projet révolutionnaire; éléments d'une sociologie des événements de mai-juin 1968. Paris, Mouton, 1969. 143 p. Includes bibliographies.

Political philosophy of major revolutionary groups involved in May 1968 events: Mouvement du 22 mars, Internationale situationniste, the various Trotskyist and Maoist groups. Sociologist establishes relation between ideas and actions during May period. Sources are groups' publications collected by Bibliothèque de documentation internationale contemporaine, Paris.

543 GONCHAROV, ALEKSEI NIKOLAEVICH. Tresty Frantsii v "Maloi Evrope." Pod red. E. P. Pletneva. Moskva, Mezhdunarodnye otnosheniia, 1966. 157 p. Bibliographical footnotes.

Influence of French monopolies in conclusion of Common Market agreement, effects of Common Market on French exports and imports, individual industrial sectors, U.S. investments, trade with African states. Author also examines position of political parties toward European integration and conflict between "Europe des patries" and European unification. Statistical data through 1964.

544 GONIN, MARCEL. Histoire du mouvement et des centrales syndicales en France. Colmar, Editions d'Alsace pour la C.F.D.T. [1968?]. 113 p. ports., photos.

History of labor movement going back to 19th century. Last pages center on C.F.D.T. (formerly C.F.T.C.) and trace this union's responses to political and economic developments, relations with C.G.T., Communist and non-Communist Left through early 1968. Includes text of preamble and first article of its statutes, adopted Nov. 1964.

545 GORZ, ANDRE. Réforme et révolution. Paris, Editions du Seuil, 1969. 248 p. ML

Mainly reprints of earlier "Stratégie ouvrière et néocapitalisme" (1964) and chapter entitled "Réforme et révolution" from 1967 "Le socialisme difficile" (see French Fifth Republic

Bibliography, 1, nos. 984 and 985). Fifty-six-page preface post-dates May 1968 and stresses incapacity of Communist and non-Communist Left to seize power for lack of a coherent revolutionary strategy and relevant critique of capitalism that could have served as support to fragmentary protests of youth. Appeals for new type of non-authoritarian revolutionary body to formulate doctrinal frame of reference and stimulate grass-roots action.

546 GOURDON, ALAIN. Les cadres: essai sur de nouveaux prolétaires. [Par] Julien Cheverny [pseud.]. Paris, Julliard, 1967. 212 p. Includes bibliography.

Polemical rather than scholarly work on the "men in the gray flannel suits"--management and technical personnel in private employment accounting for close to one-fourth of secondary and tertiary sector. Group is portrayed as docile, apolitical mainstay of Gaullist technocratic regime, as represented by Confédération générale des cadres. Author shows working role and ideals of private existence, leisure. Good statistics. Discussion of technocratic-oriented works by Teilhard de Chardin, Bloch-Lainé; "Réflexions pour 1985"; Marxist contribution nil with respect to cadres' self-realization. Reinforcement of caste status of cadres through current educational policy of technical training for cadres, general culture for ruling elite, so that France is becoming "nation cadre" subordinated to needs of American economy.

547 GOURDON, ALAIN. Le temps des obsèques; essai de nécrologie politique. [Par] Julien Cheverny [pseud.]. Paris, Fayard, 1970. 208 p. Includes bibliographical references.

Pessimistic appraisal of French political scene since advent of Fourth Republic, stressing declining respect for laws and rational decision-making by politicians, chaotic political procedure, alongside reinforced technocratic elements, impact of mass media (notably television). Common language is seen as disappearing from political society: there is the "language of the prince" (de Gaulle), that of the "bleeding hearts," the Marxists, and the technocrats. Faced with chaos of values, French may seek new form of fascism.

548 GOUSTINE, LUC DE. 10 mai 1968, manifestation théâtrale en trois points et un schéma. Paris, Editions du Seuil, 1968. 64 p. (Théâtre, 11)

Street theater with anonymous characters commemorating events leading to students' first barricades, May 10.

549 Le gouvernement et les cabinets ministeriels, bureaux des Assemblées, Assemblée nationale, Sénat, Conseil économique et social, Conseil de Paris, avec les membres des Cabinets de leurs présidents, Préfecture de Paris, Région parisienne, Préfecture de la Seine, Préfecture de police, avec les membres des Cabinets des préfets et secrétaires généraux. Paris, Saulgeot, 1962-   ML

Six issues a year, plus revisions when necessary. For each ministry and préfecture, address and telephone are indicated.

550 GOUX, CHRISTIAN. L'économie française; diagnostic 1969, perspectives 1970. Avec la collaboration de Monique Bithorel-Delaby, Jacques Fabian [et] Jean Matouk. 3e éd. Paris, Editions Cujas, 1969. 156, [67] p. tables, diagrs.

Economic survey for Jan.-Apr. 1969, preparation of new economic policies for May-Aug. 1969, and status of production, consumption, European economic policy, government plans for 1970 and prospects for their realization. Tables of statistics on economic conditions, 1960-69.

551 GRANIER, JACQUES. De Gaulle et l'Alsace. 2e éd. Société alsacienne d'édition et de diffusion, 1970. 327 p. plates, ports., facsims.

De Gaulle's visits to Alsatia, 1944-64. Visits of state during Fifth Republic were Sept. 1958, Nov. 1959, July 1960, Nov. 1961, and Nov. 1964. Excerpts of speeches and wealth of photographs (including handshake with General Massu Nov. 1961).

552 GRAVIER, JEAN FRANÇOIS. La question régionale. Paris, Flammarion, 1970. 233 p.

Historical view of French political and administrative divisions and stages of regional reform since introduction of departments by French Revolution, with emphasis on years 1956-69. Geographic and demographic criteria for proper dimensions of different entities (communal and regional) are examined, with proposals for reduction in number of communes to 3,500 and amalgamation of 21 regions into 15 as basic units, suggestions for distribution of political control. Situation of Paris region is studied separately and government plans maintaining rapid growth for region rejected. Author is pioneer French regional planner.

553 GRENOBLE. UNIVERSITE. INSTITUT D'ETUDES POLITIQUES. Aménagement du territoire et développement régional: les faits, les idées, les institutions. Grenoble, 1968-71. 4 v. maps, diagrs. Includes bibliographies.

v. 1: 1965-66. 689 p.
v. 2: 1968-69. 753 p.
v. 3: 1970. 848 p.
v. 4: 1971. 744 p.

Annual volume, with index at end of each volume, offers half a dozen individual studies on regional planning in France and elsewhere from sociological, geographic, economic, political, administrative point of view; selected and annotated bibliography of books and articles on regional planning, urbanism, individual French regions; documents on issues of current interest, official texts, chronology 1964-69, addresses of planning organisms. Among studies of special interest for Fifth Republic are: survey of organization of regional planning, attitudes of French population toward various aspects of regional planning (Vol. 1), Sixth Plan, government decentralization measures with relevant decrees, new urban "communautés" (Vol. 2), methods of selecting departmental Conseillers généraux, municipal finances, report on 1969 referendum, preliminary report on 1968 census, public opinion survey on urban renewal in Paris Halles quarter (Vol. 3), and study of industrial complex of Lyon-St. Etienne-Grenoble, urban planning 1959-69, regional planning and rural life, agricultural cooperatives, development of port of Fos-sur-Mer near Marseille, the Breton language, impact of Maisons de culture on urban culture (Vol. 4).

554 Grèves revendicatives ou grèves politiques? Acteurs, pratiques, sens du mouvement de mai. Par Pierre Dubois et al. Paris, Anthropos, 1971. 550 p. (Sociologie et travail)

Contributions by five C.N.R.S. sociologists (including Daniel Vidal) on political significance of workers' and unions' demands in May 1968. See also nos. 1036 and 1103.

555 GRIGNON, CLAUDE, and JEAN-CLAUDE PASSERON. French experience before 1968. Paris, O.E.C.D., 1970. 137 p. diagrs. (Case studies on innovation in higher education) ML

Work centers on three educational innovations: reform of Faculty of Medicine, 1960-62, that of Faculty of Law, 1959-62, both of them aimed at better adaptation to current professional requirements, and curricula revision of Faculty of Arts and Sciences, 1966, also known as Fouchet reform, which came as response to rapid growth in enrollment in these faculties. Impact of reforms on size, social background of student body in these faculties carefully analyzed. Innovations failed to induce structural change because they were absorbed by highly resistant university system. Extensive statistics for different faculties and universities.

556 GRIOTTERAY, ALAIN. Des barricades ou des réformes? Préf. de Valéry Giscard d'Estaing. Paris, Fayard, 1968. 71 p.

Républicain indépendant and Paris deputy's talk in the wake of June 1968 elections sketches main elements of recent crisis and parliamentary reactions, concluding that student and worker demands for greater autonomy and participation are warranted within realistic limits and that own party must stress decentralization. Partiality of mass media to revolt and blindness to strength of pro-Gaullist, anti-revolutionary elements brought out. Introduction by Giscard d'Estaing explains origin of explosion as inadaptation of minds and customs to modern society.

557 GROSS, BABETTE. Frankreichs Weg zum Kommunismus. Kreuzlingen, Neptun Verlag, 1971. 112 p. (Schriftenreihe des Instituts für politologische Zeitfragen, Bd. 3) Bibliography: p. 110.

Activities of French Communists outside party document infiltration in trade unions, local government, intellectual and cultural circles, peace movements, teacher and student organizations and warn about the tight Communist net over France, notwithstanding recent challenges from extreme Left and ideological split in international Communism. Appendix lists Communist local government association, commercial enterprises, front organizations, as well as radical Left organizations (Trotskyist, Maoist, anarchist), and their publications. Author was active in P.C.F. in 1930's and broke with Communism in 1940.

558 GROSSER, ALFRED. Au nom de quoi? Fondements d'une morale politique. Paris, Editions du Seuil, 1969. 335 p. Bibliographical footnotes.

Political scientist (specialist on Germany) discusses personal, skeptical confrontation with "highest values" in political judgments and actions, proving that generally values are incoherent and inconsistently applied by showing the ambivalence in judging political regimes and their legitimacy, in assessing and punishing political crimes and treason. He also examines the rationale of using the nation as the focus of human solidarity, the complexities of weighing personal against collective aims, conflicting purposes in information dissemination and education.

559 GROSSMANN, ROBERT. Intervention de Robert Grossmann, président national de l'U.J.P., à la journée de la majorité à Lille. Paris, 1967. 9 p.

Head of Gaullist youth organization, Union des jeunes pour le progrès, speaks on history of group (founded 1965) at U.D.-Ve Assises nationales, Nov. 1967.

560 GRUSON, CLAUDE. Origine et espoirs de la planification française. ... Paris, Dunod, 1968. xxviii, 438 p. tables. Bibliography: p. [437]-438.

Lectures on history of French economic policy, 1929-65, based largely on gross national product figures, empirical insertion of first four plans and their successes and failures. Final lectures defend rationale of French planning and efine its future challenges. Purely neutral forecasting agency would not be adequate to reduce uncertainties to bearable level, and social chaos is seen as more dangerous than threat of excessive bureaucratization. European framework is viewed as desirable. Interesting discussion of planning for national and international reduction of economic inequities. Author was active as economic planner, head of I.N.S.E.E., and is now head of Ecole pratique des hautes études, where lectures were given.

561 GUEDJ, AIME, and JACQUES GIRAULT. Le Monde ... humanisme, objectivité et politique. Paris, Editions sociales, 1970. 253 p. (Notre temps)

Guedj's contribution uses "Le Monde"'s treatment of May 1968 events as example of superficiality of its acclaimed objectivity when fate of capitalism is at stake (partisan presentation of last two weeks of May, virulent anti-Communism, systematic denigration of C.G.T.) and sums up its political values. Girault presents views of Editor-in-Chief Beauve-Méry (Sirius) on Fifth Republic, May 1958 through Pompidou's election as president. Both authors are collaborators of Communist "Nouvelle critique."

562 GUELAUD-LERIDON, FRANÇOISE. Recherches sur la condition féminine dans la société d'aujourd'hui. Préf. de Jean Fourastié. Paris, Presses universitaires de France, 1967. 128 p. tables. (Institut national d'études démographiques. Commissariat général du plan d'équipement et de la productivité. Travaux et documents, Cahier no. 48) Bibliography: p. [125]. ML

Demographic characteristics of female population, including fertility, family size, based on 1962 census, educational level and professional activities. Proposals as to what social measures could improve women's condition. Appendices include texts on legal status of women, figures on child-care centers and pre-school establishments as of 1964.

563 GUENA, YVES. Maintenir l'Etat. Paris, Fayard, 1970. 121 p.

Minister of postal services from 1967 through 1968, minister of information during June 1968 gives personal account of experiences in maintaining postal services, then restoring television operation in May-June 1968. Postal strike lasted from May 18 to May 31, O.R.T.F. strike from May 17 to June 25, except for news reporters. Inside information on reaction of government leaders, negotiations with representatives of striking groups, problems within O.R.T.F.

564 GUERIN, DANIEL. Pour un marxisme libertaire. Paris, R. Laffont, 1969. 296 p. (Collection Libertés, 80) ML

1956-69 essays on historical aspects of Communism and anarchism, international experiences in socialist countries. Last three essays comment on May 1968 events as expression of youth's striving for Marxism and personal liberty, a symbiosis of Marxism and anarchy. Author upholds feasibility of combining high standard of living based on modern technology with maximum self-administration.

565 GUERRARD, ROGER HENRI. Lycéens révoltés, étudiants, révolutionnaires au XIXe siècle. Paris, Editions du temps, 1969. 96 p. (Collection Le Pavé)

Features of 19th century lycées and universities such as social discrimination, sexual repression, authoritarian methods, which aroused earlier revolts, 19th century antecedents of student-worker collaboration.

566 GUERRES ET PAIX (periodical). Opinions et motivations des étudiants français. Paris, Presses universitaires de France, 1969. (Its Numéro spécial no. 14-15, 1969/4-1970/1)

Detailed results of study sponsored by Institut français de polémologie (publisher of journal) in which 1,216 students of universities and Grandes écoles were interviewed. Questionnaire covered facts of student background and life, personal, political, cultural values, attitudes toward drugs and sex, career plans, sports and other activities, military service, participation in May 1968 events, views on international student movement, influence of mass media, problem of violence. In addition to presentation of overall results and figures for individual items, there is bibliography of 753 articles, 100 books, about a third on May 1968 events.

567 GUERTIN, PIERRE-LOUIS. Et de Gaulle vint ... Une étude socio-politique sur les répercussions de son voyage au Québec. Avant-propos de Laurent Chevalier. [Montréal?] Claude

Langevin Editeur, 1970. 229 p., illus., facsims. Bibliography: p. 225-227.

French-Canadian political journalist's account of de Gaulle's visit to Quebec, immediate repercussions in Quebec and Canadian press, resulting stimulation of demands for autonomy or independence as an international issue. Conjectures on de Gaulle's purpose at the time of the visit and interpretation of his Nov. 27, 1967 press conference. De Gaulle's Canadian speeches, 1967 press conference in appendix. Cartoons from French-Canadian press.

568 GUICHARD, ALAIN. Les Juifs. Paris, B. Grasset, 1971. 263 p. Bibliography: p. 259-263.

History of French Jewry and composition of present French Jewish community, swelled to 600,000 by influx from North Africa. Effects of these newcomers are analyzed. Jewish organizations, Jewish press (itemized list), Jewish attitudes toward internal political problems, relations with Israel, religious orientation, quest for identity. Author is "Le Monde" contributor.

569 GUICHARD, OLIVIER. Aménager la France. Paris, R. Laffont, 1965. 246 p. illus., maps. (Inventaire de l'avenir) ML

Aims of regional planning for coordinating growth or change of cities, industries, agriculture, communications, teaching and research, tourism, and framework for action, administrative methods initiated under Fifth Republic. Guichard was at time of writing Délégué à l'Aménagement du territoire et à l'action régionale.

570 GUILLAUMONT-JEANNENEY, SYLVIANE. Politique monétaire et croissance économique en France, 1950-1966. Préf. d'Emile James. Paris, A. Colin, 1969. xiii, 168 p. (Fondation nationale des sciences politiques. Service d'étude de l'activité économique. Recherches sur l'économie française, 13) Bibliography: p. 155-165.

State intervention in economy to harmonize demands for economic growth and reduced economic business cycles by manipulating money flow, credit, and fiscal incentives for investment. Wealth of statistics on price level, industrial production, actions of central banking authorities and credit agencies. Based on 1964 doctoral thesis.

571 GUILLE, GEORGES. La gauche la plus bête . . . ? Paris, Table ronde, 1970. 158 p.

Socialist deputy for Aude gives short autobiographic sketch, pleads for unity within socialist party rather than prima donna squabbles and for reaffirmation of its traditional doctrine. Skepticism is expressed about collaboration with politicians like Mitterrand, Hernu, Mendès-France, whose personalities he describes; nor is unstable P.S.U. favored. Inside account of S.F.I.O. mechanisms of party democracy and discipline, foundation of new Parti socialiste.

572 GUILLEBAUD, JEAN CLAUDE, and PIERRE VEILLETET. Chaban-Delmas, ou L'art d'être heureux en politique. Paris, B. Grasset, 1969. 251 p.

Biography completed after Chaban-Delmas' nomination as prime minister. Clue to political success is seen in personal charm, sportsman's sense of fair play, avoidance of virulent controversies. Covers role as Fourth Republic's last defense minister and involvement in de Gaulle's return to power and in founding of U.N.R., role as president of National Assembly, 1959-69, as well as career as mayor of Bordeaux.

573 GUILLEMOTEAU, RENE, and PIERRE MAYEUR. Traité de législation scolaire et universitaire. Tome 1: Organisation générale de l'enseignement. Tome 2: Le personnel de l'éducation nationale. Paris, A. Colin, 1970-72. v. 1, 431 p.; v. 2, 382 p.

Vol. 1 covers original laws and decrees, modifications by laws, decrees, circulars, etc. of government concerning: (1) general principles of public education, relations of Church and state, compulsory education, centralization of administration, awarding of degrees, vacations, scholarships, funding of public and private establishments; (2) powers of central (Ministry of Education, consultative organs), regional, and departmental administrations, with discussion of 1968-72 regional reforms; (3) details on instruction at different levels of education and recent restructuring of secondary level, university organization and curricula (loi d'orientation), specialized, vocational, and adult education, regulations on school construction; and (4) state intervention in and subsidy to private schools. Vol. 2 gives civil service provisions for teachers and other school employees: pay, social security, pensions, vacations. Chronological list of laws and statutes on education at end of volume.

574 GUIN, YANNICK. La commune de Nantes. Paris, F. Maspéro, 1969. 183 p. (Cahiers libres, 154)

History of student, worker, and farmer revolt in industrial city on Atlantic coast at Loire estuary. Revolt exploded May 1 with occupation of Nantes University and Sud-Aviation at nearby St.-Nazaire as focal points, and farmers joined in attack on authorities. General strike May 21 reinforced by farmers' strike, lasting till June 6. Central strike committee, unique in France and embryonic of worker power, took over city hall for several days and functioned as parallel administration, although formally no "commune de Nantes" ever existed.

575 GUITARD, LOUIS. De Gaulle-Mendès, aller et retour. Paris, J. Martineau, 1969. 277 p. Bibliography: p. 181-193.

Memoirs on months of Mendès-France government and decolonization by Vichy sympathizer who still felt that Mendès-France was last hope of stable, efficient government in Fourth Republic, leaving way open to excesses of personal power under de Gaulle. Conclusion raises possibility that Mendès-France might still have a chance after de Gaulle's retirement. Work concluded spring 1969.

576 GUITTON, HENRI. Economie politique. 4e éd. Paris, Dalloz, 1965. 2 v. illus. (fold. table). (Précis Dalloz) Bibliographical footnotes.

Elementary economics textbook for Faculté de droit students. Combines economic history and theory with brief description of economic institutions. Concrete examples based on French economy, so that work has good survey on French economic conditions in early 1960's. Author is economics professor at Paris Faculté de droit et des sciences économiques. Subject and name index.

577 GUITTON, JEAN. Un homme: Weygand. Liège, Editions Dynamo, P. Aelberts, 1966. 10 p.

Commemorative speech on first anniversary of Weygand's death, with characteristic remarks of the aged general at end of Algerian war.

578 GUITTON, JEAN. La pensée et la guerre. Bruges, Desclée de Brouwer, 1969. 225 p.

Based on course given at Ecole de guerre. Philosophy professor draws parallel between catastrophe of nuclear war, which can be caused by absolutely determined small nation with one nuclear weapons, and May 1968 revolt, which could have been set off by one absolutely rebellious student.

579 GUNSBERG, HENRI. Le fascisme ingénu. Paris, Julliard, 1968. 253 p. ML

All but final chapters written in late 1966 and attack political parties of the Left for having swallowed myth that modernization (U.S.-style) rather than removal of social inequities will bring required changes, so that depolitization is accepted.

"Modern" Left is epitomized by Servan-Schreiber, admirer of Kennedy. Title refers to self-satisfied, depoliticized, capitalist U.S. as representing "naive fascism." Conclusions written June 1968 interpret student and worker revolt as rejection of unjust and semi-fascist society, but maintain that political Left's abdication of revolutionary leadership deprived this movement of political sophistication. Simultaneously author defends lycée teachers against "modernist" innovations such as student and parent participation, decentralization, abolition of baccalauréat, upholding traditional culture against Americanization.

580 GUNSBERG, HENRI. Le lycée unidimensionnel. Paris, Mercure de France, 1970. 210 p. (En direct) ML

Warning about dire effects of new pedagogic methods advocated by Ecole nouvelle (active teaching methods, team work, less competitiveness, American-style curricula) and academic decentralization introduced into lycées after May 1968. Author foresees that teacher autonomy and professional standing will gradually vanish, intellectual values fall into disrepute, and students turn into conformist, easily manipulated members of a producer-consumer mass society. Author explains how lycée reform won approval simultaneously from extreme Left and Catholic Left ("juvénilo-marxisme" is his name for cult of youth as new revolutionary class) and efficiency-oriented modernist Right, appealing also to professors who wanted to look progressive.

581 GUSDORF, GEORGES. La nef des fous: Université 1968. Québec, Presses de l'Université Laval, 1969. 209 p. ML

University of Strasbourg philosophy professor currently teaching in Canada explains his own pre-1968 proposals for "pilot" universities and student selection, describes experiences at Strasbourg in 1968, criticizes student demands and demagoguery among colleagues, politicizing of universities. Published in France under title "La Pentecôte sans l'Esprit-Saint: Université 1968."

582 HALLS, W. D. Society, schools, and progress in France. Oxford, Pergamon Press, 1965. xxii, 194 p. (Commonwealth and international library. Education and educational research) Bibliography: p. 190. ML

Good introduction to place of education in French society, its objectives, control, and organization, as well as modifications initiated by Fifth Republic.

583 HALTER, MAREK, illus. Mai; dessins. Commentaire de Jean Cassou et al. Genève, Editions de l'avenir, 1970. 1 v. (unpaged) of illus.

Painter's impressionistic black-and-white interpretation of May 1968 street clashes, with retrospective comments by Jean Cassou, Maurice Clavel, François Revel, and Claude Roy on meaning of events.

584 HAMAOUI, ERNEST. Le régime politique de la Ve République; tableaux de droit constitutionnel et institutions politiques. Paris, Editions Monchrestien, 1970. 174 p. tables. Bibliography and references: p. 127-168.

Set of tables breaking down different components of constitutional law, i.e., power and legitimacy, state sovereignty, division of power, formulation and amendment of constitution, showing how different constitutions and nations have approached these. Another set of tables is devoted to 1958 Constitution: Gaullist solution to power crisis, elaboration of constitution, general principles, nature of presidency as expressed in constitution, amendments, de Gaulle and Pompidou speeches, system of presidential election, nature and political reality of cabinet, parliament, judicial and consultative organs, procedures for legislative action, constitutional revision. Each table has extensive bibliography of books and articles.

585 HAMEL, PHILIPPE, and PATRICE SICARD. Mao ou Maurras? [Affrontement entre] Philippe Hamel et Patrice Sicard. Paris, Beauchesne, 1970. 132 p. (Carrefour des jeunes, 2) Includes bibliography.

Debate confronting ideologies of extreme Left (pro-Chinese Communist) and extreme Right (nationalist monarchist). Sicard is 23-year-old law student and contributor to "Aspects de France." Hamel is 20-year-old student. Both were active May 1968, share concern about bureaucratization.

586 HAMELET, MICHEL P. Pour ou contre la participation; une enquête auprès des syndicats et du patronat. Paris, J. Didier, 1968. 60 p.

Discussions held shortly after May 1968 on possibilities and specific plans for worker participation in industry, in particular Capitant's proposals. Labor leaders were all opposed to participation, employer representatives cautious. Includes list of organizations interested in participation.

587 HAMILTON, RICHARD F. Affluence and the French worker in the Fourth Republic. Princeton, N.J., Published for the Center of International Studies, Princeton University, by Princeton University Press, 1967. 323 p. illus., forms, map. Includes bibliographical references.

Study of workers' political attitudes based primarily on Oct. 1955 public opinion survey by Institut français d'opinion publique of carefully selected sample of 1,039 French workers. Author uses figures to isolate workers' living and working conditions and to correlate them with the radicalism of workers' political views.

588 HAMON, LEO. Acteurs et données de l'histoire. Tome 1. Paris, Presses universitaires de France, 1970. ("A la pensée") Bibliographical footnotes.

Reflecting on underpinnings of what he calls "la pratique gaulliste," political sociologist and Gaullist deputy investigates determining factors (internal and external) in the history of nations, discussing conflicting interpretations of historical determinism and voluntarism and, more specifically, the latitude of action available to great statesmen, elected political leaders, political parties and other groups in accomplishing their goals. Most of examples drawn from Fifth Republic: de Gaulle, P.C.F. as instance of strongly cohesive counter-society and its special relations with global society, students' rejection in May 1968 of global society and its rules of the game.

589 HAMON, LEO. La crise tchécoslovaque et les relations entre l'Est et l'Ouest. Heule, Belgique, Editions UGA, 1968. 28 p. port. (Centre international d'études et de recherches européennes. Conférences, 1968)

Lecture at International University, Luxembourg, Sept. 28, 1968, at which Gaullist deputy regrets resurgence of Stalinism and break in growing collaboration between East and West, while reasserting government determination to seek end of blocs.

590 HANSEN, NILES M. French regional planning. Bloomington, Indiana University Press, 1968. xvi, 319 p. illus., map. (Indiana University international studies) Bibliography: p. 289-292.

On the basis of 1965-66 field work in France, American economist dissects rationale and economic factors behind decentralization, regional development, and urbanization in postwar France. Excellent data on population, regional economies, educational facilities within 21 new "program regions." Distinction is made between social and economic overhead investment on the part of the government, and impact thereof examined, as are objectives of Fourth and Fifth Plans. Good bibliography.

591 HARMEL, CLAUDE. La crise de l'enseignement supérieur en France. La Haye, Centre international de documentation et d'information, 1970. 35 p. (International Documentation and Information Centre, Hague. La Nouvelle gauche, 3)

May 1968 student revolt is explained by juncture of two elements: strengthening of revolutionary groups born of disintegration of Stalinist Communism in France, and unpreparedness of French higher education for the effects of massification on an elite system. To this author adds ideological vacuum of non-Communists, "progressive" posture of Catholic youth, general cult of rebellion among young.

592 HARTLEY, ANTHONY. Gaullism: the rise and fall of a political movement. New York, Outerbridge and Dienstfrey, 1971. 373 p. Bibliography: p. 349-359.

Historical roots of de Gaulle's political doctrine during pre-World War II years, creation of Gaullist movement during war, its role and positions in Fourth Republic. For Fifth Republic, British author discusses Gaullist policy in different areas: Algeria, foreign relations, economy, examines split in Gaullist ranks after 1967 elections (conditional and unconditional Gaullists) and changing relations between de Gaulle and his faithful. Last chapters cover May 1968, de Gaulle's withdrawal, Gaullism after de Gaulle's retirement and death. Gaullism as shaped by de Gaulle is seen as episode in French history.

593 HARTUNG, HENRI. Ces princes du management; le patronat français devant ses responsabilités. Préf. d'Henri Guillemin. Paris, Fayard, 1970. 117 p.

Attack on superficiality and hypocrisy of French business community's commitment to human relations and worker participation programs. Evidence drawn from pronouncements of business leaders, problems of "cadres," alienation of workers and consumers in modern industrial society. Author was successful organizer of business-sponsored management training center, from which he withdrew May 1968.

594 HASQUENOPH, MARCEL. La mort en face. . . . Paris, Editions du Clan, 1967. 154 p. illus. (Les Dossiers du Clan, no. 3)

Biographies with portraits and documents of victims of political execution in different historical contexts: anti-Nazi, Vichyist, and O.A.S. O.A.S. is illustrated by four figures, among them its leaders Roger Degueldre (executed July 1962) and Bastien-Thiry (executed Mar. 1963).

595 HASSNER, PIERRE. Les alliances sont-elles dépassées? Paris, Fondation nationale des sciences politiques, 1966. 42 p. (Centre d'études des relations internationales. Sér. C: Recherches, no. 10)

Recent theories (Raymond Aron, General Beaufré) on dismantling of Atlantic Alliance and simultaneous disintegration of monolithic Soviet-dominated Communism, leading to reinforcement of national independence, more traditional alliances or simple non-alignment. Gaullist views are typified by argument of General Gallois that atomic weapons erase differences between large and small powers. Author considers most probable development a combination of bipolarity under whose shadow small powers will have greater latitude, making alliances more complex and responsive to national situations.

596 HAUPT, JEAN. Le procès de la démocratie. Lisbonne, Cahiers Découvertes, 1971. 203 p.

Attack on ideological principles of democracy (liberty, equality, fraternity) and its political institutions (universal suffrage, parties, government by majority, parliament) leads to plea for authoritarian nationalism as answer to state of permanent civil war accompanying democracy. French author is long-time Lisbon resident and editor of "Découvertes," organ of French nationalists in exile.

597 HEGGOY, ALF ANDREW. Insurgency and counterinsurgency in Algeria. Bloomington, Indiana University Press, 1972. 327 p. illus. (Indiana University international studies) Bibliography: p. 269-280.

History of Algerian nationalism, birth of revolutionary movement, its institutions and organizations, French political, military, and administrative countermeasures to quell revolution, such as pacification program, program of Sections administratives spécialisées, resettlement, counterviolence and torture. Study stops with 1958, when French military superiority over nationalist revolt was clear but defeat came on internal and international propaganda front, demonstrating limitation of counterinsurgency. Documentation from reports at Centre de hautes études administratives sur l'Afrique et l'Asie modernes.

598 HEINZ, GRETE UNGER, and AGNES F. PETERSON. The French Fifth Republic: establishment and consolidation, 1958-1965; an annotated bibliography of the holdings at the Hoover Institution. Stanford, Calif., Hoover Institution Press, 1970. 170 p. (Hoover Institution bibliographical series, 44)

599 HENISSART, PAUL. Wolves in the city; the death of French Algeria. New York, Simon and Schuster, 1970. 508 p. illus., col. maps, ports. Bibliography: p. 483-485.

Vivid, non-partisan reconstruction, based on personal narratives and trial proceedings, of history of O.A.S. in Algeria and France, Jan. 1961 through June 1962, and government efforts to counter subversion. Includes material on Generals' Putsch, Sept. 1961 attempted de Gaulle assassination, Algerian peace negotiations, and final chaos preceding independence.

600 HENZ, JOSEPH. Barricades 68. Le Jas du Revest Saint-Martin, Basses-Alpes, R. Morel [1968?]. 1 v. (unpaged). illus.

Humorous line drawings with revolutionary slogans of May 1968.

601 Les héritiers du Général; recensement et diagnostics. Paris, Denoël, 1969. 235 p.

Individual sketches by "Express" journalists of 13 political leaders in high governmental positions after de Gaulle's retirement, as of late 1969. They are categorized as: Gaullist faithful (Michel Debré, Edmond Michelet, and Jacques Foccart); newcomers to power (Jacques Chaban-Delmas, Olivier Guichard, Robert Poujade, and Albin Chalandon); non-Gaullist pillars of regime (Valéry Giscard d'Estaing, Raymond Marcellin, and Maurice Schumann); and outsiders (René Pleven, Jacques Duhamel, and Joseph Fontanet).

602 HERMANN, LUTZ. Jean Monnet, un portrait. Paris, Dalloz, 1968. 36 p. ports.

Short biography and explanation of his philosophy, activities since leaving European Communities post.

603 HERMET, GUY. Les Espagnols en France, immigration et culture. Paris, Editions ouvrières, 1967. 335 p. (Collection L'Evolution de la vie sociale) Bibliography: p. 285-292.

Sociological study of 100 typical Spanish immigrants out of current 431,000 living in France, selected from Paris and Lille area, including political refugees as well as immigrant workers. Introduction summarizes legal and economic status of Spanish in France. Main focus of study is acculturation process, living and working conditions.

604 HERMONE, JACQUES. La gauche, Israël et les Juifs. Paris, Table ronde, 1970. 288 p. (Collection La Table ronde du Combat, no. 17)

Latest manifestation of anti-Semitism is traced back to Marx's writings and stand of French extreme Left. Activities of certain individual anti-Semitic Jewish publicists are identified and propaganda myths isolated. Anti-Israel bias of "Le Monde" is documented in its stand on Arab refugees, advocacy of binational, non-theocratic Arab state.

605 HERNU, CHARLES. Priorité à gauche. Préf. de Paul Guimard. Paris, Denoël, 1969. 136 p.

Review of contribution of political clubs to French political life in 1960's, possibilities for unified Left and attack on parochialism of S.F.I.O., personal interpretation of "modern socialism." Author, close associate of François Mitterrand and founding member of both Convention républicaine and Fédération de la gauche démocrate et socialiste, writes in wake of non-Communist Left's catastrophic defeat in 1969 presidential election and founding of new Parti socialiste, which took over some of unifying functions of defunct F.G.D.S.

606 HERVO, MONIQUE, and MARIE-ANGE CHARRAS. Bidonvilles: l'enlisement. Graphiques et dessins de Monique Hervo. Paris, F. Maspéro, 1971. 410 p. illus., facsims., maps. (Cahiers libres, 219-220)

Case study of shantytown of La Folie, at Nanterre, sheltering mainly North African workers and their families. Work reproduces 25 out of 40 taped interviews on experience of daily life in the community. Final section criticizes government policy on elimination or upgrading of these shantytowns and progressive social assimilation of immigrant workers, emphasizing gap between promises and implementation of decent housing.

607 HERYTEM; CRITIQUE POLITIQUE DE LA VIE QUOTIDIENNE (periodical). "Le Monde" à la lettre. Paris, 1969. 125 p. facsims. (Août-octobre 1969, no. 2)

Sophisticated satirical attack on "Le Monde" for its distortions and omissions, notwithstanding reputation for objectivity. Arrangement is by capriciously selected key words. One of themes is "Le Monde"'s consistent pro-Israel bias. (For conflicting view, see Hermone, no. 604.)

608 HESS, JOHN L. The case for De Gaulle: an American viewpoint. New York, W. Morrow, 1968. xxii, 154 p.

American journalist's defense of those views of de Gaulle which are most unpopular in the U.S.: condemnation of Israel in 1967 war, proposals for international monetary reform, resistance to over-expansion of direct U.S. investment in Europe, Common Market policy (particularly rejection of British membership), withdrawal from N.A.T.O., build-up of French nuclear weapons, and interference in French-Canadian affairs. Author demonstrates that these views are in long-run American interest. Preface written July 1968 gives personal response to May events.

609 HETMAN, FRANÇOIS. L'Europe de l'abondance. Paris, Fayard, 1967. 319 p. diagrs. (Sciences et techniques humaines) Bibliographical footnotes.

Prospects for an "affluent society" in Europe: its values, implication of rapid economic growth for social and economic structure, distribution of goods in affluent society, nature of new mass society. Wealth of statistics. Northwestern Europe is expected to be 20 years behind in reaching U.S. level.

610 HETMAN, FRANÇOIS. La langue de la prévision. The language of forecasting. Avec un vocabulaire français-anglais-allemand. With a French-English-German vocabulary. Mit einem französisch-englisch-deutschen Wörterbuch. Paris, Futuribles, 1969. 540 p.

Conceptual framework of forecasting (planning) research presented in form of 400 alphabetically arranged terms, to each of which one to two pages are devoted. Most entries also refer to specific books which introduced term. Term given in French, followed by English and German equivalent, then French description. Inverse procedure followed in second part. Trilingual index of terms.

611 HEYMANN, PHILIPPE. La bataille du franc; édition mise à jour de La bataille des monnaies. Paris, Editions et publications premières, 1969. 281 p. (Edition spéciale)

Economic background, 1967-69, of devaluation of franc, international movement of capital, speculation, and broader problems of stabilizing international monetary system. De Gaulle's attitude toward question of devaluation, interviews with Edgar Faure, Giscard d'Estaing, economists Robert Marjolin, Michel Rocard, Jacques Rueff, Raymond Barre. Includes detailed chronology of monetary problems, 1967-Sept. 1969. Franc was eventually devalued 12.5 percent, compared to 1958 devaluation of 17.5 percent.

612 HISTORAMA (periodical). De Gaulle: trente ans d'histoire de France. Réalisé sous la direction de Bernard Michal. Paris, 1970. 193 p. illus. (Its Hors série no. 11)

Individual articles on de Gaulle's political career. For Fifth Republic years, contributions concern his return to power May 1958, handling of Algerian conflict, attempted assassination at Petit-Clamart, intervention in Israel-Arab crisis, and circumstances and stages leading to his retirement.

613 Hommages du monde au général de Gaulle. Paris, Editions du Palais royal, 1970. 305 p. port., facsim.

Hastily assembled collection of tributes to de Gaulle by French government officials, politicians, organizations, journalists, and by foreign personalities. Description of ceremonies at Notre Dame, list of foreign delegations at funeral service. Work completed a week after de Gaulle's death, Nov. 11, 1970.

614 HOMMES ET MIGRATIONS (periodical). En France, un million d'analphabètes. Paris, 1969. 111 p. (Its Cahier 111)

Individual reports on alphabetization of illiterate immigrant workers, 50,000 of whom are enrolled in formal or informal adult education courses. Among million effectively illiterate, Algerians and Portuguese are most numerous.

615 HONORE, SERGE. Adaptation scolaire et classes sociales. Paris, Société d'édition "Les Belles lettres," 1970. 159 p. (Bibliothèque de la Faculté des lettres de Lyon, 16) Bibliography: p. 155-159. ML

Director of school guidance center bases research on three secondary schools in Lyons area, one traditional lycée, one collège d'enseignement général, and one "transitional" school. By use of questionnaires on home life, culture-free intelligence tests, aptitude and achievement tests, as well as school records, characteristics of students 11-14 years of age in different schools were determined and factors most relevant to differential academic success according to social classes identified. Results of this study confirm impact of cultural inequalities on access to higher education.

616 HOSS, JEAN-PIERRE. Communes en banlieue: Argenteuil et Bezons. Paris, A. Colin, 1969. 135 p. graphs, tables, plates. (Fondation nationale des sciences politiques. Travaux et recherches de science politique, no. 4)

Based on Paris Institut d'études politiques thesis, this study describes social conditions in two neighboring industrial suburbs in newly created Département de Val d'Oise north of Paris: Argenteuil with 90,000 and Bezons with 24,000 people, mainly working class. Major part of study focuses on accomplishments and failures, methods of operation, budget of the two Communist-controlled municipal governments, careful analysis of public opinion and elections during Fifth Republic, special characteristics of Communist administration (going back to 1935). Postscript on May 1968 events in communities and results of June 1968 elections.

617 HOSTIOU, RENE. Robert Schuman et l'Europe. Avant-propos de G. Dupuis. Paris, Editions Cujas, 1969. 156 p. Bibliography: p. 145-153.

Biography, conceptions of European integration based on Schuman's speeches and writings, contrasts between his ideas and de Gaulle's.

618 HOURDIN, GEORGES; GANNE, GILBERT. Pour les valeurs bourgeoises [par] Georges Hourdin. Contre les valeurs bourgeoises [par] Gilbert Ganne. Nancy, Berger-Levrault, 1967. 78 p., 78 p. (Collection Pour ou contre, 12)

Hourdin, drawing on personal heritage, credits bourgeoisie with introduction of freedom of thought, education, preservation of cultural traditions, religious tolerance, while Ganne focuses on bourgeois hypocrisy, materialism, impeding of social progress, directing his fire especially on leftist intellectuals, but stressing also vanishing function of bourgeois family and economic values.

619 HOUSSIAUX, JACQUES R. La politique des fusions et des concentrations dans la concurrence européenne. Paris, Centre d'études politiques et civiques, 1969. 31 p. (Cahiers du C.E.P.E.C., 38)

Dinner speech at C.E.P.E.C. on trends toward French industrial mergers, achievement of proper balance between needed structural modifications and maintenance of competition.

620 La huelga generalizada; de las barricadas a la ocupación de fábricas, Francia, mayo-junio 1968. Montevideo, Editorial Acción directa, 1969. 97 p. (Cuadernos del militante, 2)

Economic factors leading to May events, student movement, spontaneous worker actions in individual companies (Compagnie générale de télégraphie, Saclay, Sud-Aviation), and responses of trade union organizations.

621 HUGUES, PHILIPPE, and MICHEL PESLIER. Les professions en France; évolution et perspectives. Préf. de Claude Vimont. Paris, Presses universitaires de France, 1969. 473 p. illus., tables. (Institut national d'études démographiques. Travaux et documents. Cahier no. 51) ML

Results based on 1954 and 1962 (not 1968) census for about 100 professional categories divided by major industrial fields into: workers and artisans; scientific and technical personnel; office employees and cadres; merchants and salesmen; health, education, and law; other service fields (household servants, artists, priests, etc.); farmers and fishermen. Includes evolution from 1954 to 1962, forecasts for 1970.

622 HUMANITE ROUGE (periodical). Face au gauchisme moderne. Paris, 1972. 95 p. (Supplément to its no. 155, July 1972)

Identification and criticism of 14 main "gauchiste" movements in France, 1968-72. Each group is characterized by origins, organization, membership, publications, ideology, long-run objectives and short-run strategy, links with P.C.F., Soviet Union, China. In addition to various anarchist, Trotskyist groups, pamphlet describes Parti socialiste unifié, Gauche prolétarienne, Centre d'initiative communiste (founded by Garaudy and fellow P.C.F. dissidents). "Humanité rouge" is identified with Maoist ideology. See also no. 1187.

623 La imaginación al poder: Paris mayo 1968; la revolución estudiantil. 4. ed. Buenos Aires, Ediciones Insurrexit, 1969. 91 p. plates. (Ediciones Insurrexit Publicación 7) Includes bibliographies.

Spanish translation of published texts important for understanding ideas of student revolt: dialogue between Sartre and Cohn-Bendit, declaration of Marcuse during his Paris stay May 5-9, statement by Cohn-Bendit on student commune at Sorbonne, various manifestos and other documents, wall slogans.

624 INSTITUT DE SCIENCE ECONOMIQUE APPLIQUEE. Philosophie et sciences de l'homme. Paris, Presses universitaires de France, 1967. 180 p. (Its Cahiers. Série M: Economies et sociétés, 24)

Individual articles on methodology of social sciences.

625 INSTITUT FRANÇAIS D'OPINION PUBLIQUE. Les Français devant le communisme. Paris, 1966. 30 l. tables.

Feb. 6, 1966 questionnaire answered by 2,000. Among significant questions were: (1) Has P.C.F. become more conciliatory in last 10 years? (yes 60 percent, no 3 percent, same 22 percent); (2) Would you favor, oppose, not care if government had Communist ministers? (favor 38 percent, oppose 30 percent, don't care 23 percent); (3) Is unity of action between Socialists and Communists easier now than 10 years ago? (yes 55 percent, no 21 percent, don't say 24 percent); and (4) Is Communist take-over in France possible in next 10 years? (possible 29 percent, impossible 49 percent, don't say 22 percent).

626 INSTITUT FRANÇAIS D'OPINION PUBLIQUE. Les Français et de Gaulle. Présentation et commentaire de Jean Charlot. Dessins de Jacques Faizant. Paris, Plon, 1971. 361 p. illus., tables, diagrs.

Begins with 127-page analysis of 25 years' public opinion polls on de Gaulle and Gaullism by Charlot: (1) the French between de Gaulle and political parties, (2) Gaullists' and anti-Gaullists' reactions to main tenets and policies of Gaullism, (3) rises and declines of Gaullism since 1958, and (4) social groups and Gaullism. Conclusion by Goguel that, on the whole, French approved Gaullist political institutions and foreign policy. Facsimiles of relevant polls in appendices.

627 INSTITUT FRANÇAIS D'OPINION PUBLIQUE. L'opinion des Français sur le Marché commun et l'unification européenne de 1950 à 1968; une synthèse des résultats obtenus à différentes questions posées à des échantillons nationaux. Rapport de J. Bissery. Paris, 1969. 134 p. tables, diagrs.

Study undertaken for European Communities' Press Service, giving summaries of results, graphs, actual questions and responses concerning attitudes toward European unification efforts, information on Common Market, attitudes toward Community accomplishments, Common Market expansion, European political union, European security, Gaullist European policy.

FOR ADDITIONAL PUBLICATIONS BY INSTITUT FRANÇAIS D'OPINION PUBLIQUE, SEE AUTHOR INDEX

628 INSTITUT MAURICE THOREZ. La fondation du Parti communiste français et la pénétration des idées léninistes en France; cinquante ans d'action communiste, 1920-1970; compte rendu analytique du colloque scientifique organisé par l'Institut Maurice Thorez, Paris, 31 octobre, 1er et 2 novembre 1970. Paris, Editions sociales, 1971. 334 p.

Conference with short speeches by P.C.F. leaders and representatives from other Communist parties on history of P.C.F. and origins of Communist parties in rest of Europe, Africa, Asia. Closing speech by Georges Marchais reiterates goals of P.C.F. and amplifies on Dec. 1968 party manifesto. See also Institut Maurice Thorez in Author Index.

629 Institutions françaises. Edited by Georges Lannois. Oxford, Pergamon Press, 1970. vii, 94 p. (Pergamon Oxford French series) Bibliography: p. 93-94.

Individual contributions on political institutions, central and local administration, justice, the press, and trade unions, giving up-to-date material as well as brief review of historical evolution.

630 INTERCONTINENTAL PRESS. Revolt in France, May-June 1968; a contemporary record; compiled from Intercontinental Press and the Militant. New York, 1968. 168 p. illus.

Articles from U.S. Trotskyist journals, describing events as they happened from outbreak of student revolt to June election and its aftermath. Some articles by French and Belgian Marxists, including Ernest Mandel and Pierre Frank, interview with latter and Alain Krivine on role of Trotskyists in May events. Activities of Trotskyist Jeunesse communiste révolutionnaire and Parti communiste internationaliste followed closely.

631 INTERNATIONALE SITUATIONNISTE. De la misère en milieu étudiant, considérée sous ses aspects économique, politique, psychologique, sexuel et notamment intellectuel et de quelques moyens pour y remédier, par des membres de l'Internationale situationniste et des étudiants de Strasbourg. Paris, 1966. 31 p. (Supplément à la revue "Internationale situationniste")

Influential pamphlet motivating 1968 student revolt by demonstrating superficiality of traditional student radicalism and need to attack society as a whole rather than university. Student revolt is integrated into global revolt of youth against "société du spectacle." See also no. 311.

FOR ADDITIONAL PUBLICATIONS BY AND ABOUT INTERNATIONALE SITUATIONNISTE, SEE AUTHOR INDEX

632 INTER-PARLIAMENTARY UNION. Parlements; une étude comparative sur la structure et le fonctionnement des institutions représentatives dans cinquante-cinq pays. Rédigée par Michel Ameller. 2e éd. augmentée et mise à jour. Paris, Presses universitaires de France, 1966. 378 p.

Useful compendium for comparing French parliamentary institutions and election procedures, as of 1965, to those of other 54 members of Inter-parliamentary Union. Work organized by topics, not by countries: composition and organization of parliament, legislative and control functions.

633 IRIBARNE, PHILIPPE D'. La science et le prince; essai. Paris, Denoël, 1970. 358 p.

Scientific decision-making as rational process for quantifying objectives and results, dangers and limitations of method in that it may disregard unquantifiable elements important to human satisfaction. Complementary nature of scientific decision process and democratic participation in obtaining best results is demonstrated, with interesting examples clarifying debates on "affluent society." Studies institutional framework for smooth collaboration between politicians and technical experts to avoid technocratic excesses. Appendix contains May 1968 manifesto by representatives of central administration on democratic planning.

634 ISAMBERT-JAMATI, VIVIANE. Crises de la société, crises de l'enseignement secondaire français. Paris, Presses universitaires de France, 1970. 400 p. tables, graphs. (Bibliothèque de sociologie contemporaine) Bibliography: p. 343-373. ML

Evolution of academic, social, and moral objectives of lycée education on the basis of a selection of 450 speeches given at annual distribution of school awards, 1850-1965. Work divided into periods, including two postwar sections, 1946-60 and 1960-65. Themes fluctuate rather than developing linearly. Objectives crisis evident in recent period because of contradiction between goals upheld and actual enrollment figures, time spent on different subjects.

635 ISORNI, JACQUES. L'humeur du jour. Paris, Librairie académique Perrin, 1968. 253 p.

Essays on 1965 trips to Italy, Yugoslavia, Portugal (interview with Salazar), and Brittany (conversation with Bachaga Boualem), reflections on place of man in the universe.

636 ISORNI, JACQUES. Pour dire et juger. Paris, Table ronde, 1967. 255 p.

Final section discusses question of amnesty for political prisoners and support of Lecanuet, then Mitterrand in 1965 presidential election, as well as personal relations with Tixier-Vignancour during their joint defense of political prisoners, 1961-63.

637 ISOU, ISIDORE. La stratégie du soulèvement de la jeunesse, 1949-1968. Paris, Centre international de Création kladologique, 1968. 108 p. mimeographed.

Author documents his claim as main precursor of student revolt, going back to his 1949 book "Le soulèvement de la jeunesse," in which youth rather than proletariat is shown as enslaved and as holding promise for revolutionary force because "external" to system. Excerpts from journals founded by him--"Front de la jeunesse" (see above, no. 488), "Union de la jeunesse," "Soulèvement de la jeunesse," for years preceding 1968--as well as personal propaganda for his ideas among political leaders. Extensive documentation of activities May 1968: pamphlets, letters to de Gaulle, other politicians. Author claims that perversion of his sound ideas and strategies by other revolutionary groups, from Communists of all varieties to anarchists and Internationale situationniste, led to collapse of revolt. Author is also one of founders and leaders of closely related Mouvement lettriste, mainly concerned with artistic creativity.

638 ISRAEL, GERARD. Le dernier jour de l'Algérie française, 1er juillet 1962. Paris, R. Laffont, 1972. 326 p. plates.

Notwithstanding title, this is reconstruction of final months of French Algeria, Mar. 18, 1962, signing of Evian agreements to mid-July 1962, when Ben Bella was welcomed back. Story moves between Algiers, Paris, and Oran through eyes of several minor participants in drama, describing O.A.S. actions, countermoves of French government, secret O.A.S.-F.L.N. negotiations, massive exodus of European settlers.

639 JACQUELIN, ANDRE. La juste colère du Val d'enfer; la révolte de la résistance de la vraie. De Gaulle a-t-il trahi la résistance? Avec, comme préf., une série de hauts témoignages. Paris, Promotion et édition, 1968. 287 p. plates, facsims.

Personal narrative of journalist active in underground press during German occupation, followed by indictment of authoritarian aspects of de Gaulle's government and plea for amnesty for all political prisoners and exiles for sake of national unity (amnesty law was passed July 24, 1968).

640 JALLUT, MAURICE. Où va la République? La France à la recherche de sa constitution. Avec la collaboration de François Buy et de Philippe Prévost. Paris, P. Prévost, 1967. 141 p.

History of French political institutions, with Fifth Republic as example of plebiscitary democracy. Basic trouble of French constitutional instability is seen in concepts of popular sovereignty and strict separation of power, the former leading to personalization of power, the latter to ineffectiveness. Hereditary monarchy combined with Conseil d'Etat serving as sort of Supreme Court would permit stable representation of national interest.

641 JAMET, DOMINIQUE. Chaque jour est un jour J (14 septembre 1967). Paris, A. Michel, 1969. 285 p. (Histoire du XXe siècle)

Twenty-four hours of world-wide events, with a 25-page "Petit tour de France" sketching economic conditions (unemployment, changes in industrial output, status of public services) and political conditions such as status of majority and opposition forces, extinction of M.R.P.

642 JANICKI, JANUSZ. Oblicza studenckiego buntu, Francja 1968. Warszawa, Wiedza Powszechna, 1970. 154 p. (Biblioteka

wiedzy współczesnej "omega," 177) Bibliographical footnotes.

Well-documented history of May 1968 events, confronting French Communist responses with other interpretations.

643 JARRY, ROBERT. Les communistes au coeur des luttes des travailleurs sarthois [1920-1970]. Préf. de Robert Manceau. Le Mans, Fédération sarthoise du Parti communiste français, 1970. v. 1, 320 p.; v. 2, 323 p. illus., ports, facsims.

Vol. 1 covers 1920-May 1958, Vol. 2 May 1958-Dec. 1970. For Fifth Republic, work describes Communist position on national and local elections as well as strikes, with special reference to May 1968 strikes and June 1968 elections. Author is Sarthe federation secretary.

644 JEANNENEY, JEAN MARCEL. Régions et Sénat; déclarations et interventions devant le Parlement. Paris, Documentation française, 1968. 143 p.

Statement before National Assembly Dec. 11, 1968, outlining reforms envisaged by government to strengthen participation in factories and on regional level and announcing referendum on Senate and region. Statement before Senate, Dec. 16, 1968, on referenda. Replies to parliamentary questions further elaborating on reforms and justification thereof. Jeanneney was cabinet member responsible for formulation of reforms.

645 JEGOUZO, Y. L'élaboration de la politique de développement dans l'Europe communautaire. Préf. de Paul Jaquet. Paris, Librairie générale de droit et de jurisprudence, 1970. 521 p. (Bibliothèque constitutionnelle et de science politique, t. 40) Bibliography: p. 491-512.

Economic planning in each of six European Communities' members, central, regional, and local bodies in charge of planning and control, participation of economic groups in process. Part 2 surveys Common Market treaties, provisions on economic matters directly related to economic growth and potential conflict between free trade principles and need for government control, possibilities for economic planning on European level.

646 JOHNSON, DOUGLAS W. J. France. New York, Walker, 1969. 271 p. 28 illus. (incl. ports.), map. Bibliography: p. 252.

Short popular history of France, over half devoted to Fifth Republic, covering events through early 1969 and giving rapid survey of political and economic development, institutions, de Gaulle's personality, French civilization.

647 JOHNSON, RICHARD. The French Communist Party versus the students; revolutionary politics in May-June 1968. New Haven, Yale University Press, 1972. xix, 215 p. (Yale college series, 13) Includes bibliography.

Study by Yale political science student, who spent May 1968 in Paris, uses as its sources French works on P.C.F. and interviews with Communist student leaders. It retraces history of P.C.F.'s problematic relations with intellectuals, growth and decline of Union des étudiants communistes and of other extreme leftist student groups, as well as P.C.F. strategy during May-June and response to attacks from revolutionary Left. Party's failure to support radicalism and its stand in favor of legality and parliamentarism are explained as part of long-range strategy derived from experience of 1930's.

648 JOUHAUD, EDMOND JULES RENE. O mon pays perdu, de Bou-Sfer à Tulle. Paris, Fayard, 1969. 569 p. illus., plates.

Military and political history of Algerian war by Algerian-born air force general. Of particular interest are episodes in which he participated: May 1958 in Algeria; Generals' Putsch, Apr. 1961; O.A.S. activities in Oran, Apr. 1961-Mar. 1962; capture in Oran; trial, incarceration, last-minute reprieve from execution, release Dec. 1967. Appendix gives text of O.A.S. appeal to Oran residents, Sept. 1961, signed by him.

649 JOUSSELIN, JEAN. Les révoltes des jeunes. Paris, Editions ouvrières [1968?]. 272 p.

Survey and chronology of world-wide clashes between students, young workers, and adult society in postwar years, showing May 1968 as one instance of these generational conflicts. Arguments for and against activities and objectives of youth in various countries, followed by sympathetic summation of common elements of different youth movements.

650 JOUVENEL, BERTRAND DE. Arcadie; essais sur le mieux-vivre. Paris, S.E.D.E.I.S., 1968. 390 p. (Futuribles, 9) Bibliographical footnotes. ML

Collection of 1957-67 essays whose central themes are economic growth and well-being, measurement by economic tools of goods and nuisances external to monetary circuit, "productive" orientation at root of Western (capitalist and Communist) societies, in which elite have shared materialistic orientation of population rather than rising above it as privileged group, growth of ecological consciousness. Author has participated in French long-range planning and forecasting.

651 JOYEUX, MAURICE. L'anarchie et la société moderne; précis sur une structure de la pensée et de l'action révolutionnaires et anarchistes. Paris, Nouvelles éditions Debresse, 1969. 227 p.

Principles of a new Parti révolutionnaire based on ideas of Proudhon. Communist and capitalist models rejected as equally repressive and elitist. Includes analysis of failure of May 1968 student movement to keep worker sympathies.

652 JUDRIN, ROGER. Journal d'une monade, du 13 avril au 9 septembre 1968. Paris, Gaillimard, 1969. 215 p.

Personal reflections of essayist and school teacher on life, art, literature, and French civilization, with occasional references to current events but no personal participation.

653 JULLIARD, JACQUES. La IVe République (1947-1958). Paris, Calmann-Lévy, 1968. 370 p. (Naissance et mort) Bibliography: p. 359-368.

Political history of Fourth Republic emphasizing that regime died a natural death resulting from congenital weaknesses, so that it had no real popular support and doesn't deserve Left's nostalgia. Last third of work describes regime's handling of Algerian crises and collapse. Good chronology and bibliography.

654 JULLIEN, JACQUES, PIERRE L'HUILLIER, and JACQUES ELLUL. Les Chrétiens et l'Etat. Paris, Mame, 1966. 188 p. (Eglises en dialogue, no. 3) Bibliography: p. 181-182.

Three contributions on changing role of Church and state: Jullien's on new style of Catholic Church's presence in temporal sphere, L'Huillier's on acceptance of split between evangelical message and action of Christian as citizen, and Ellul's on Christian theories of state and function of Church in evaluating state actions against Christian ethical criteria.

655 JUQUIN, PIERRE. Le sens du réel. Paris, B. Grasset, 1971. 290 p. Includes bibliographical references.

Author speaks as intellectual who has remained within P.C.F. fold, serving as P.C.F. deputy in National Assembly 1967-68 and on party's Central Committee. After examining position of intellectuals in French society, with up-to-date facts, he marshals rational arguments about effectiveness of socialist governments, using economic and social progress in Soviet Union, Bulgaria, East Germany as examples and illustrating current efforts in Communist world to come to terms with problems of advanced industrial societies. Typical objections about Communist countries' achievements are refuted, though shortcomings admitted. Emphasis is on realism, patience, flexibility, in contrast to utopian views of anarchists and nihilist approach of extreme Left in general and with respect to May 1968 in particular. Discusses liberty under socialism, failures and successes in Eastern Europe, and affirms that P. C. F. has learned from foreign experiences and that it believes firmly in religious, cultural, intellectual freedom and democratic traditions, to which it would be committed if it came to power. This is important book for understanding subtler justification of P. C. F.'s slogans of "advanced democracy" and alliance with Catholic and non-Catholic Left, in which intellectuals naturally find their place.

656 JURQUET, JACQUES. Le printemps révolutionnaire de 1968; essai d'analyse marxiste-léniniste. Paris, Editions Gît-le-coeur, 1968. 178 p., 14 p. "Annexe."

Author is secretary of Parti communiste marxiste-léniniste de France (founded 1967, dissolved June 1968) and publisher of "Humanité nouvelle." Demonstrates that economic situation prior to May 1968 was favorable to revolution, blaming both "revisionist" P. C. F. and anarchist, Trotskyist student movement for failure of vast strike movement to overthrow government. Interesting material on farmer unrest. P. C. M. -L. F. is Maoist, sees Chinese cultural revolution as antecedent of French events. In appendix party's Central Committee proclamations of May 5, 6, 11, 17, 23, 24, 25, 28, 30.

657 JUSSEAU, PAUL. Colonisation, décolonisation. Alençon, Firmin-Didot-Imprimerie Alençonne, 1969. 50 p.

Former director of French railroads in Algeria and spokesman for Groupement national pour l'indemnisation gives point of view of this organization of repatriates from former French colonies on financial compensation and ties plea for private investment in underdeveloped areas with compensation by national governments for losses. Main part of work reproduces editorials in Groupement's "Bulletin d'information," Jan. 1965-Jan. 1969. Organization, which is part of Confédération européenne des spoliés d'outremer, was founded 1965.

658 KAES, RENE. Images de la culture chez les ouvriers français. Paris, Cujas, 1968. 347 p. (Collection Caps de l'histoire. Série "Travailleurs") Bibliography: p. 337-344. ML

Results of research carried out 1958-65 synthesizing four separate studies: (1) cultural behavior of workers (use of and attitude toward leisure), (2) workers' conception of school and education, (3) trade union (C. G. T. and C. F. T. C.) functionaries' conception of culture, (4) content analysis of advertisements of cultural products in certain magazines widely read by workers (e. g., "Sélections du Reader's Digest," "Science et avenir"). Work gives information on working conditions, use of leisure time, educational level, relations between work and culture. Trade unionists' cult of productive values contrasts with ideals presented in magazines of leisure society, which many workers accept.

659 KAHN, GILBERT. Paris a brûlé. Photos de Pierre Juillet, Christian Joubert, Michel Hermans. Texte de Gilbert Kahn. Paris, Del Duca, Paris-Jour, 1968. 1 v. (unpaged). illus.

Pictorial history of May 1968 events, and connecting comments. Period actually covered goes from Mar. 22 to June 16.

660 KAHN, JACQUES. La participation; ce que de Gaulle cache. Paris, Editions sociales, 1969. 192 p. (Notre temps) ML

"Humanité" reporter criticizes de Gaulle's proposals for new regional institutions embodied in Apr. 1969 referendum and reproduces "Humanité" articles, July-Aug. 1968, exemplifying fraudulent character of worker participation in individual industries where they are employed. Final section restates P. C. F.'s general stand on worker self-administration as part of humanist democratic socialism, but significant only when workers participate in operation of society as a whole. Until that time, workers must fight for their self-interests in industry rather than participate.

661 KEMP, TOM. May-June 1968: French revolution betrayed. London, The Newsletter, 1968. 63 p. 8 plates, ports. ML

Reprinted from English Trotskyist organ "Newsletter" Aug. 13-Sept. 28, 1968, this account is based on author's personal observations and discussions with members of Organisation communiste internationaliste, Révoltes, Fédération des étudiants révolutionnaires. Analysis of causes of explosion, description of student revolt and strike movements, highlighting interventions of above groups and criticizing Jeunesse communiste révolutionnaire, tied to rival Trotskyist faction. Portraits of Waldeck Rochet, Séguy, Sauvageot, Krivine. Review of early books on May events (Cohn-Bendit, Ziegel, Kravetz, Aron).

662 KEMPF, UDO. Die Kandidatenaufstellung der "Union pour la nouvelle république" und ihrer Koalitionspartner bei den Wahlen zur Nationalversammlung 1967 und 1968 unter Berücksichtigung der Wahlen von 1958 und 1962. Dissertation, Doktor der Philosophie, Eberhard-Karls-Universität. München, Mikrokopie, 1971. 154 p. Bibliography: p. 142-147.

Internal party mechanisms for selection of Gaullist candidates and candidates of affiliated parties examined briefly for 1958 and 1962 elections and in detail for 1967 and 1968 elections, on basis of interviews with central and local party leaders, deputies, ministers, questionnaires sent to deputies and candidates, unpublished 1966 Institut français d'opinion publique study of candidates. Professions de foi of defeated candidates were not consulted.

663 KERBOURC'H, JEAN CLAUDE. Le piéton de mai. Paris, Julliard, 1968. 185 p.

Journalist's view of Paris May 10-June 10, 1968, with side trips to Boulogne-Billancourt and Flins, recording conversations with many spectators and minor participants in ongoing events (students, police, workers, civil servants, merchants, cleaning women, etc.) and conveying convincingly atmosphere of city.

664 KERMOAL, JACQUES. Procès en canonisation de Charles de Gaulle. Paris, A. Balland, 1970. 146 p.

This spoof, written prior to de Gaulle's death, portrays stages of his canonization 10 years after demise, when Gaullism has politically sunk from view. Plot centers on visit of Vatican investigator to Paris and Colombey to judge de Gaulle's sainthood by consulting family, political disciples, local priest, who resurrect de Gaulle as human being and Christian. Satire is gentle and sympathetic, especially toward Mme de Gaulle. Foccart is presented as instigator of plot and succeeds in canonization, which leads to return to power of Gaullist faithful.

665 KERMOAL, JACQUES, and JEAN-PIERRE NICAISE. Le prétendant. Paris, A. Balland, 1969. 137 p.

Satire on Gaullist succession written before de Gaulle's actual retirement. In this fictitious account, de Gaulle includes selection of vice president in Apr. referendum, picks unknown young captain and wins approval for him. Vice president is groomed for highest office by de Gaulle and eventually succeeds him as an alter ego after his death.

666 KESSELMAN, MARK. The ambiguous consensus; a study of local government in France. New York, Knopf, 1967. xii, 201, v p. Bibliography: p. 197-201.

Study based on analysis of municipal election results, 1959 and 1965, and of three departments--Gironde, Calvados, Nord--as well as interviews with mayors. Describes functions of mayors, municipal councils, relations with central government and achievements (or their absence) of local governments, explaining lack of political conflicts on "commune" scale. Interesting information on Gaullist efforts to win allegiance of predominantly antagonistic mayors. Good bibliography.

667 KESSELMAN, MARK. France: the Gaullist era and after. New York, Foreign Policy Association, 1969. 63 p. illus., ports. (Headline series, no. 194)

Rapid survey of French institutions, political parties, as of Apr. 1969, and basic facts on French economy, population, education, current relations with U.S.

668 KESSLER, MARIE CHRISTINE. Le Conseil d'Etat. . . . Paris, A. Colin, 1968. 390 p. (Cahiers de la Fondation nationale des sciences politiques, 167) Bibliography: p. 373-384.

Revised 1967 doctoral thesis drawing not only on published sources but 1963-64 interviews with 32 members of Conseil d'Etat. Though Conseil goes back to Napoleonic era, study begins with Third Republic. Thesis analyzes Conseil's contradictory function as administrative tribunal and advisory body for the state and studies sources of its stability, extent of outside influence, and ties with other administrative, political, and business groups, in view of the fact that members are free to exercise other professions. Data go to 1965.

669 KINSKY, FERDINAND, GRAF. Europa nach de Gaulle. München, G. Olzog, 1969. 244 p. (Geschichte und Staat, Bd. 148/149) Includes bibliography.

Work based on research at Centre international de formation européenne and lectures at Institut européen de hautes études, University of Nice, concluded shortly before Apr. 1969. Three parts: (1) current views of political leaders in France, Germany, Italy, Benelux, England on different plans for European integration as of 1968; (2) European integration in context of current international relations (East-West conflict, two Germanys, Atlantic Alliance, U.S. economic superiority and Third World); (3) answers offered by Federalist model of European unification to these issues, obstacles to its realization. Postscript on student revolt and European ideas by Alexandre Marc. Appendices with statements by European Federalists.

670 KOENG, WERNER F. Duell im Schatten; der Sturz de Gaulles. Bern und Stuttgart, Verlag Hallwag, 1969. 452 p. ports. Bibliography: p. 453.

Background material on Pompidou's pre-1967 role in Fifth Republic, main part of work devoted to period between Mar. 1967 elections and Apr. 1969 referendum, during which de Gaulle and Pompidou held conflicting views. Referendum is treated in great detail, as are de Gaulle's retirement and Pompidou's candidacy as his successor. Swiss-born author's sympathies are with de Gaulle and leftist Gaullists. Fine photographs of leading Gaullist and opposition leaders. Sources are published French works.

671 KOHL, WILFRID L. French nuclear diplomacy. Princeton, N.J., Princeton University Press, 1971. xiii, 412 p. Bibliography: p. [385]-402.

History of nuclear weapons programs in Fourth and Fifth Republic, technical aspects and costs, role of nuclear weapons in Gaullist foreign policy and impact on relations with N.A.T.O., U.S., Germany, England. Overall assessment of policy, current outlook, downgrading of nuclear ambitions under Pompidou, official views and criticism of government policy. Author had personal discussions with government officials, military strategists.

672 KOŁODZIEJCZYK, LESZEK. Paryskie noce barykad. Warszawa, Książka i Wiedza, 1969. 275 p. illus.

History of May-June 1968 events with many photographs.

673 KORNPROBST, BRUNO, JEAN-FRANÇOIS BAZIN, and JEAN-LOUIS FONCINE. Petit lexique de la subversion. Agrémenté de dessins de Pierre Joubert. Paris, Editions Alsatia, 1969. 214 p. illus.

Humorous definitions of terms bandied about by May 1968 revolutionaries and found in books about events, using quotations as illustrations.

674 KOUCHNER, BERNARD, MICHEL-ANTOINE BURNIER, and EQUIPE D'EDITION SPECIALE. Paris, Editions publications premières, 1970. 335 p. (Edition spéciale)

Well-informed survey of May 1968 aftermaths in such areas as university reform and participation or refusal to participate in university administration by various student groups, action of radical leftist organizations such as Gauche prolétarienne and Ligue communiste, protest movements among merchants, and wildcat strikes in industry.

675 KRASUCKI, HENRI. Syndicats et lutte de classes. Préf. de Georges Séguy. Paris, Editions sociales, 1969. 124 p. (Notre temps) ML

Main part of work reproduces 12 articles from "Vie ouvrière," C.G.T. organ, of which author is editor, as well as C.G.T. secretary. Articles were published Feb.-Apr. 1969, explain C.G.T. stand on such questions as participation, "autogestion," "worker power," and defend value of well-organized union apparatus. May 1969 epilogue condemns split in ranks of Left during campaign for presidency.

676 KRAVETZ, MARC, ed. L'insurrection étudiante, 2-13 mai 1968. Ensemble critique et documentaire établi par Marc Kravetz, avec la collaboration de Raymond Bellour et Annette Karsenty. Paris, Union générale d'éditions, 1968. 509 p.

Documentary work limited to events at Sorbonne for dates indicated. For each day events are summarized, texts of appeals, communiqués, manifestos, press responses, and excerpts from all university-connected organizations reproduced. Completed June 1968.

677 KRIEGEL, ANNIE. Les communistes français; essai d'ethnographie politique. Paris, Editions du Seuil, 1968. 319 p. Bibliographical annotations.

Extensively documented sociopolitical analysis of French Communists as members of a "parti-société," a closed minority counter-society, with its outer ring of adherents, the Communist voters (statistics); the readers of its press; party members (about 250,000, analyzed by region, social class, age, sex); its hierarchy in the P.C.F. apparatus (description of some leaders, mechanism of their selection and training organs). Relations with international Communism and inner rationale for secrecy are examined. Conclusion surveys P.C.F.'s strategy in May 1968, related possibilities for integration with non-Communist Left and conflict with "gauchisme," but sees its stability as counter-society as more significant than surface non-revolutionary strategy. List of abbreviations of French Communist organizations, names of members of P.C.F.'s Bureau politique, 1926-67. English translation: "The French Communists, profile of a people" (Chicago, Chicago University Press, 1972). See also Kriegel's earlier study on French Communism (French Fifth Republic Bibliography, 1, no. 1437).

678 KRIVINE, ALAIN. La farce électorale. Paris, Editions du Seuil, 1969. 69 p. (Collection "Combats")

Comments on Apr. 1969 referendum and justification for own candidacy as representative of extreme Left in presidential election June 1969, in spite of his rejection of parliamentary democracy. As Ligue communiste candidate, he can present workers with real revolutionary program and denounce P.C.F. bureaucracy.

679 KROMMENACKER, RAYMOND J. Le gaullisme; état des recherches et guide bibliographique. Paris, Dalloz, 1971. 127 p. (Cahiers de l'Institut d'études politiques, Universités des sciences juridiques, politiques et sociales, Paris VII) Bibliography: p. 69-117.

Bibliography of publications on de Gaulle, drawn primarily from unpublished theses at various French Instituts d'études politiques, which do not get listed in most bibliographies. Introduction gives bibliographic survey of each topic, briefly describing most important works. Main part of bibliography is divided by phases of de Gaulle's career (180 items on Fifth Republic years, 25 of them on May 1958) as well as works on Gaullism's political accomplishments (110 items on institutions, 55 on elections), Gaullist parties, philosophy of international relations, European policy, Algeria (75 items), social and economic achievements (123 items), and recent works on May 1968 and de Gaulle's retirement.

680 KRYN, JACQUES. Lettres d'un maire de village. Paris, Editions du Seuil, 1971. 188 p. (Collection "Histoire immédiate") ML

Municipal councillor and mayor of Vaucluse village deals with institutional problems of local government, role of council, mayor, finances, confrontation with national political events 1965-70, such as regional, communal reform proposals, which he opposes.

681 KUZNETSOV, VIKTOR IVANOVICH. Frantsiia; ekonomika gosudarstvenno-monopolisticheskogo kapitalisma. Otv. red. A. I. Bechin. Moskva, Mysl', 1968. 238 p. Bibliographical footnotes.

Description of French economy (through 1966), based primarily on French sources. Completed prior to May 1968.

682 LABRO, PHILIPPE. Les barricades de mai. Présentation de Philippe Labro. Photographies de l'Agence Gamma. Paris, R. Solar, 1968. 1 v. (unpaged). illus.

Set of 128 shots by Agence Gamma photographers drawn from Agence files, concentrating on the most dramatic days of street fighting--May 3, 6, 7-8, 10-11, 24-25--and May 27 Charléty meeting. Publication almost simultaneous with events.

683 LABRO, PHILIPPE, MICHELE MANCEAUX, and EQUIPE D'EDITION SPECIALE. Mai/juin 68. "Ce n'est qu'un début." Paris, 1968. 273 p. (Edition spéciale)

Text of eight taped interviews with spokesmen for or participants in May revolution, preceded by editors' comments and factual accounts (good chronology). Documentation on: (1) Nanterre. Interviews with Cohn-Bendit, sociological professor Alain Touraine, and anonymous Mouvement du 22 mars militant on background, actual events; (2) month of barricades: short interviews relating to police action and long interviews with Sorbonne physics professor Alfred Kastler, movie director François Truffaut; (3) interpretation of events by André Barjonet, Alain Geismar, Jacques Sauvageot; and (4) government motivation: interview with two inside informants. Final section collects information and statistics on students and faculty, students' proposals on "new" university.

684 LACOMBE, E.-H., ed. Les changements de la société française. Paris, Editions Economie et humanisme, 1971. 239 p. (Collection Initiation sociologique) Includes bibliographical references.

Summation of condition of French society by individual contributors from Economie et humanisme study group. Sections on new production methods in agriculture and industry, new consumption patterns, new features of social life and the family, urbanization, new power structure through effects of economic pressure groups on state and state intervention in economy.

685 LACOUTURE, JEAN. De Gaulle. Paris, Editions du Seuil, 1969. 254 p. illus., ports. Includes bibliography.

Revised edition of 1965 work has new chapters on foreign policy, May 1968, in particular information on de Gaulle's trip to Germany to visit Massu May 28-29, final year of rule. Contains minor revision of earlier text (see French Fifth Republic Bibliography, 1, no. 1051).

686 LAFFONT, PIERRE. L'expiation. Paris, Plon, 1968. 349 p. Bibliographical footnotes.

Balanced personal view of events in Algeria and French Algerian policy from beginning of Algerian war through 1967. Author was publisher of moderate "Echo d'Oran" (suspended Sept. 1963), served in National Assembly Nov. 1958 till resignation May 1961. Interesting account of two interviews with de Gaulle, Apr. 1959 and Nov. 1960. The "expiation" of title refers to suffering endured by European settlers for past wrongs committed both by them and by France as a whole. Some new material on last months in Algeria prior to independence.

687 LAFONT, ROBERT. La révolution régionaliste. Paris, Gallimard, 1967. 250 p. (Idées actuelles, 123)

Critique of Fifth Republic trends toward increasing administrative and economic centralization, regional underdevelopment (e.g., Bretagne or Languedoc) or regional development as form of internal colonialism. Hope for resurgence of regions from below, using ethnic affinities as starting point and ending economic alienation by regional collective ownership, compatible with European federalism.

688 LAFONT, ROBERT. Sur la France. . . . Préf. de Jacques Madaule. Paris, Gallimard, 1968. 267 p. (Les Essais, 134) Bibliographical footnotes.

Distinction between two types of nations, those based on primary (ethnic) unity, such as Albania, and those based on secondary (historical, cultural, intellectual) unity. When the two types of unity are confused, excesses of nationalism and oppression of ethnic minorities by strongest ethnic group within country, imperialism outside, ensues. Main part of work retraces forced integration and alienation of "primary nations" by French monarchy, e.g., Occitania and Brittany, centralizing tyranny of successive republics and nationalist colonization of Algeria, giving all inhabitants fictitious common history. Psychodrama of European settlers in Algeria resulting from this contradiction now resolved, but struggle still continuing within hexagon.

689 LA GORCE, PAUL MARIE DE. La France contre les empires. Paris, B. Grasset, 1969. 365 p.

Journalist's positive assessment of Gaullist foreign policy 1958-68, concentrating on destruction of American hegemony, limited European integration, improved relations with Communist countries, aid to underdeveloped countries. Despite opposition of political elite to de Gaulle's foreign policy, public opinion is favorable to it, even after May 1968, since drive for national independence springs from same psychological forces as experience of modernization and economic growth within France. Results of public opinion polls.

690 LA LANDE DE CALAN, PIERRE DE, VICOMTE; MAROSELLI, JACQUES. Pour les libertés sociales et économiques [par] Pierre de Calan. Contre les libertés sociales et économiques [par] Jacques Maroselli. Nancy, Berger-Levrault, 1968. 80 p., 80 p. (Pour ou contre, 13)

La Lande reiterates arguments in his book "Renaissance des libertés économiques" (see French Fifth Republic Bibliography, 1, no. 1058) on ineffectiveness of state intervention since 1945, reaffirming more limited functions for government. Maroselli states views of F.G.D.S. and S.F.I.O. on economic democracy, democratic planning and its goals, pointing out that political liberties must not be sacrificed and stressing realism of Left's counterproposals to government plan.

691 LANCELOT, ALAIN. L'abstentionnisme électoral en France. ... Paris, A. Colin, 1968. xiv, 290 p. illus., maps (6 fold. in pocket). (Cahiers de la Fondation nationale des sciences politiques, 162) "Sources et bibliographie": p. 279-[288].

Doctoral dissertation defining abstentionism geographically, politically, and sociologically, for different types of elections. Historical survey goes back to 1815, stops before Mar. 1967 elections, which are covered in appendix. Two major underlying factors: voters' integration in society--fairly constant from election to election; nature of political confrontation--varying greatly according to circumstances. On the average, 15 percent abstentions, half due to each factor, plus 6-7 percent unregistered voters. For 1964, 30 million potential voters. Electoral atlases of abstentions Sept. 1958, Oct. 1962, maps of Paris region districts, cantons for France as of 1962.

692 LANCELOT, ALAIN. [Four articles on French elections, 1966-69. Paris, 1966-69.] 4 v. in 1.

Articles from "Projet" (Feb. 1966, May 1967, Sept.-Oct. 1968, Sept.-Oct. 1969) on: (1) results of 1965 presidential election, (2) Mar. 1967 legislative elections, (3) June 1968 legislative elections, and (4) Apr. 1969 referendum and 1969 presidential election results.

693 LANCELOT, MARIE-THERESE, and ALAIN LANCELOT. Atlas des circonscriptions électorales en France depuis 1875. Paris, A. Colin, 1970. 95 p. maps. (Cahiers de la Fondation nationale des sciences politiques. Série "Atlas" [b]) Bibliography: p. 90-95.

Electoral districts and subsequent reapportionments, 1875-1967, with maps indicating approximate number of registered voters for individual districts. For Fifth Republic, list of "circonscriptions" as of Oct. 1958, maps and lists of July 13, 1966, modifications creating new departments in Paris region. For entire period, with special table for Fifth Republic (1958, 1962, 1967), changes in seats per department, as well as in number of registered voters, votes cast, ratio of male and female voters.

694 LANG, ANDRE. Pierre Brisson, le journaliste, l'écrivain, l'homme (1896-1964). Paris, Calmann-Lévy, 1967. 395 p. plates.

Brisson was director of "Le Figaro" from 1949 to 1964. For these years, biography describes his political positions, exchanges of letters with de Gaulle and Louis Joxe. Interesting material on his relations with Mauriac, whom he venerated.

695 LANGLOIS, DENIS. Le cachot. Paris, F. Maspéro, 1967. 144 p. (Cahiers libres, 97)

Prison diary of student jailed at Fresnes prison in 1966 for infraction of military discipline. Appendix describes author's conflicts with military authorities on status of conscientious objector, fate of other victims of military justice, prison conditions at Fresnes.

696 LANGLOIS, DENIS. Les dossiers noirs de la police française. Paris, Editions du Seuil, 1971. 238 p. (Collection Combats)

Cases of police brutality (mainly non-political), infringement of civil liberties, miscarriage or unequal application of justice in treatment at police station during extraction of confession or arrests, indulgence toward police excesses by tribunals. Most cases refer to Fifth Republic.

697 LES LANGUES MODERNES (periodical). Mai-juin 1968. Paris, 1968. 584-651 p. (Its No. 5, septembre-octobre 1968)

Events and proposals concerning foreign language teaching and diplomas at different institutes of Sorbonne May-June 1968, with some recommendations from other universities, information on language teaching in secondary schools.

698 LANTIER, JACQUES [pseud.]. Le temps des policiers; trente ans d'abus. Paris, Fayard, 1970. 333 p.

Former secret agent and high ministry of interior official now turned anthropologist denounces police function and organization in France for its usurpation of paramilitary and judicial roles, serving political objectives of government instead of limiting itself to preventive measures for preservation of individual rights. Appendix contains speech before Académie des sciences morales et politiques on police reform.

699 LANVERSIN, JACQUES DE. L'aménagement du territoire et la régionalisation. 2e éd. entièrement refondue. Paris, Librairies techniques, 1970. 394 p. Bibliographies for each chapter; general bibliography: p. 63-65.

Doctrine, objectives, and content of regional planning, as well as political obstacles thereto, which became one of prime concerns of Gaullist government from 1963 on. Main part of work gives systematic presentation of organs responsible for planning at central and local level (Paris is treated separately) and elaboration and implementation of regional planning policies, with texts of laws, specific examples of urban regulation, incitements to regional investments, large regional developments such as the port of Fos.

700 LAPASSADE, GEORGES. Procès de l'université. Paris, Editions Pierre Belfond, 1969. 158 p. (Collection "J'accuse") Bibliographical footnotes. ML

Incapacity of reforms introduced by "loi d'orientation" to alter class character of higher education is exemplified by how student participation in universities has worked out in practice in current academic year. Positions toward reform of P.C.F., U.N.E.F., and teacher organizations are presented. Author sees abolition of universities as only answer, in line with Maoist position.

701 LAPASSAT, ETIENNE-JEAN. La justice en Algérie, 1962-1968. Paris, A. Colin, 1969. 183 p. (Etudes maghrébines, 9) Includes bibliography.

Includes description of Algerian judicial system prior to independence and transition to "revolutionary" system of justice and attending purges through special tribunals. Detailed chronology of political developments.

702 LAPIE, PIERRE OLIVIER. De Léon Blum à de Gaulle; le caractère et le pouvoir. Paris, Fayard, 1971. 914 p. (Les Grandes études contemporaines)

Political history of Fourth and Fifth Republic, concentrating on successive heads of government. Main part of book presents Fourth Republic prime ministers from Léon Blum to Pflimlin and final crisis leading to de Gaulle's return to power. Last 60 pages devoted to de Gaulle's approach to political power, methods and conceptions of government, praising his strength of character and vision.

703 LAPIERRE, JEAN-WILLIAM. L'information sur l'Etat d'Israël dans les grands quotidiens français en 1958. Paris, Editions du Centre national de la recherche scientifique, 1968. 327 p. illus., map, tables. (Travaux du Centre d'études sociologiques). Bibliographical footnotes.

Study of 17 Paris and 24 provincial dailies (for which statistics on circulation and readers are given) on frequency, length, category, bias, tone of items dealing with Israel. For 10 major dailies--France-Soir, Parisien-Libéré, Figaro, Aurore, Le Monde, Humanité, La Croix, Ouest-France, Progrès, Dépêche du Midi--synthetic picture of Israel as of 1958 is constructed. Basic theme of study is press treatment of foreign affairs and its influence on public opinion.

704 LARUE, ANDRE. Les flics. Paris, Fayard, 1969. 335 p.

Former "France-Soir" crime reporter's account of case histories of crimes, seen through eyes of different branches of French police. Of interest for Fifth Republic is section on judicial police's intervention in political crimes: F. L. N., Bastien-Thiry's assassination attempt on de Gaulle, Ben Barka murder.

705 LA SOUCHERE, ELENA DE. Le racisme en 1000 images. Collection dirigée par Robin Livio. Paris, Pont Royal, 1967. 320 p. illus., ports.

Pictorial history of racism going back to biblical times. For Fifth Republic years, author discusses views of French and other European racists still preaching anti-Semitism and summarizes currently accepted findings on human races.

706 LA TOCNAYE, ALAIN DE. Comment je n'ai pas tué de Gaulle. Paris, E. Nalis, 1969. 377 p. (Documents du mois)

Impenitent personal account of Bougrenet de la Tocnaye's part in attempted de Gaulle assassination. An anti-Gaullist officer in Algeria, 1956-61, author joined O. A. S. in 1961 and reached France in Jan. 1962. Central part of work describes preliminary assassination plots and other O. A. S. activities prior to the abortive Petit-Clamart assassination attempt Aug. 22, 1962, together with Bastien-Thiry. Imprisoned after Jan. 1963 trial, he was amnestied May 1968.

707 Lattrappicipation, ou La chienlit par racine. [Par] Grr et Zzz [pseud.]. Paris, J. J. Pauvert, 1968. 125 p. of illus. (Collection Enragée)

Cartoons and captions satirizing Gaullism, moral hypocrisies of professors, P. C. F., displayed during and after May 1968.

708 LAUDRIN, HERVE. Politique agricole; rapport. Paris, 1967. 12 p.

Gaullist deputy reviews status of French agriculture and agricultural legislation enacted by Fifth Republic, current budget, Fifth Plan, Common Market decisions favoring agriculture. Report presented before Assises nationales of Union des démocrates pour la Cinquième République, Lille, Nov. 1967.

709 LAUNAY, JACQUES DE. De Gaulle and his France; a psycho-political and historical portrait. Translated by Dorothy Albertyn. New York, Julian Press, 1968. x, 316 p. ports. Bibliography: p. [293]-296.

Synthesis of many earlier works on de Gaulle. First part sketches de Gaulle's personality and physical condition, second part his personal and political curriculum vitae; third part defines his views on foreign affairs, decolonization, Atlantic Alliance, European integration 1944-67. Conclusion identifies views of de Gaulle's supporters and opponents on Gaullism and opinions of French youth on regime.

710 LAUNAY, JACQUES DE. Les grandes controverses du temps présent, 1945-1965. Lausanne, Editions Rencontre, 1967. 519 p.

Historian's attempt to do justice to contemporary controversies on basis of presently available sources. For Fifth Republic, controversies center on (1) de Gaulle's return to power, which is a secondary result of U. S. intervention in European affairs and encouragement of Algerian nationalists, and (2) Algerian war as example of decolonization, from outbreak of conflict through Evian Treaty to Ben Bella's overthrow. Survey of sources, list of unresolved questions, notes on author's own encounters with history in the making, such as conversation with General Valluy, Challe's predecessor at N. A. T. O., at outbreak of Generals' Putsch.

711 LAUNAY, JEAN-PIERRE. La France sous-développée: 15 millions de pauvres. Paris, Dunod-Actualité, 1970. 143 p.

Overall facts on poverty through 1966-67, with statistics on wage range, housing, hospital resources, vacation costs, and special poverty-stricken sectors: the aged, the handicapped, farmers, foreign workers.

712 LAUNAY, ODETTE. Politique sociale; rapport. Paris, 1967. 22 p.

Conseil économique et social member summarizes Gaullist social policy: employment, social security, support for medical care and research and for the handicapped and family allowances. Report presented at Assises nationales of Union des démocrates pour la Cinquième République, Lille, Nov. 1967.

713 LAURENT, JACQUES. Au contraire. Paris, Table ronde, 1967. 304 p.

Articles from "Esprit public," journal which literary critic and virulent de Gaulle opponent helped found Dec. 1960 and which ceased publication in 1962. Other articles attacking de Gaulle reprinted from "Combat." Final section evaluates political mood of literary figures of the Right.

714 LAURENT, JACQUES. Lettre ouverte aux étudiants. Paris, A. Michel, 1969. 129 p. (Lettre ouverte)

Sympathetic view of students' libertarian, iconoclastic, antitechnological demands, but criticism of their blind acceptance of Marxism and decolonization. Lengthy dissection of Aron's attack on students and his final support of de Gaulle, whose skill in exploiting internal French divisions author stresses. Students are urged to become critical minority proposing new values to affluent society rather than spokesmen for workers, who share majority values.

715 LAVALLEE, LEON. Pour une conception marxiste de la prospective. Avec la collaboration de G. Duffau [et al.]. Paris, Editions sociales, 1970. 190 p. ("Problèmes") Includes bibliography.

Contribution of forecasting in a period of rapid scientific and technical change to economic growth and competitive advantage of socialist societies. Marxist author, though convinced that socialist societies are better able to integrate forecasting into their plans, sees no convincing evidence so far that "monopolistic state capitalism" is incapable of assimilating new productive forces within the next decades, nor that qualitative changes are about to occur in socialist countries. Main areas of rapid technological change are surveyed, effect on educational needs estimated. P. C. F. position is not presented. Main French source is "Réflexions pour 1985."

716 LE BARDE [pseud.]. La passion de la patrie. Paris, J. Grassin, 1967. 191 p.

Poems glorifying de Gaulle's wartime and political achievements.

717 LEBESQUE, MORVAN. Comment peut-on être Breton? Essai sur la démocratie française. Paris, Editions du Seuil, 1970. 233 p. (Collection L'Histoire immédiate)

Novelist and "Canard enchaîné" contributor born in Brittany devotes major portion of work to history of region's culture, growth of autonomy movement and its climax 1957-64. Defense of ethnic communities is shown to be compatible with Left's goals of grass-roots democracy, in contrast to Right's demands for strong state and centralization.

718 LEBJAOUI, MOHAMED. Vérités sur la révolution algérienne. Paris, Gallimard, 1970. 249 p.

Personal contribution to history of F. L. N. by one of its leaders from 1955 on. Includes episodes such as meeting with Camus and Jacques Chevallier in Algeria, organization and activities of F. L. N.'s Fédération de France, support of French lawyers. Internal conflict and purges within F. L. N. leadership and power struggle after independence (fate of Mohamed Khider, Ait Ahmed, Ben Bella) discussed in detail. Appendix lists F. L. N. leaders and their present status.

719 LEBRET, LOUIS-JOSEPH. Développement = révolution solidaire. Avec la collaboration de R. Delprat, M.-F. Desbruyères. Paris, Editions ouvrières, 1967. 191 p. Includes bibliography.

Posthumous work by Father Lebret, economic planner at C. N. R. S., explaining in simple terms meaning of underdevelopment and Christian responsibility for its elimination.

720 LE CALLOC'H, BERNARD. La révolution silencieuse du gaullisme au pouvoir. Paris, J. Didier, 1971. 316 p.

Gaullism as a coherent, practical, and realistic doctrine of orderly political action rather than as abstract loyalty to one man. Specific rationale of Gaullism is illustrated in conduct of French diplomacy and military affairs (independence, cooperation, pursuit of peace, nuclear strategy), in political institutions of Fifth Republic (strong executive, stability, direct democracy, majority party support), and in its commitment to and achievement of economic growth, cultural, social, and educational transformations. Author is U. D. R. leader long active in party's information division.

721 LECHENE, ROBERT. Tambour battant; la campagne présidentielle de Jacques Duclos. Préf. de René Andrieu; postface de Waldeck Rochet. Paris, Fayard, 1969. 94 p. plates, ports.

Communist candidate's campaign for French presidency, May 5-May 30, 1969, with excerpts from speeches and television interview. Author accompanied Duclos as reporters for "Humanité-Dimanche." Candidacy was result of Left's incapacity to agree on common program, and Duclos ran close third with 21 percent of votes. Extensive photographs.

722 LEDUC, GASTON, ed. Le transfert social, fondement du progrès économique? France, Communautés européennes, tiers monde. Publié par l'Association pour l'étude des problèmes économiques et humains de l'Europe. Paris, Presses universitaires de France, 1969. 134 p.

Joint work of French, Belgian, Italian, German economists. "Social transfers" embedded in French fiscal policy are characterized and shown to be either appropriate to general level of economy or counterproductive. Figures for 1968 are given (26 percent of gross national product at that time). Current social transfers stipulated by Common Market and through various forms of aid to underdeveloped countries.

723 LEFEBVRE, HENRI. L'irruption de Nanterre au sommet. Paris, Editions Anthropos, 1968. 178 p. (Sociologie et révolution)

Marxist professor of sociology at Nanterre analyzes causes of May 1968 explosion, accepting some of explanations drawn from Marx and Marcuse. Main impetus for outbursts of "contestation, spontaneity, and violence" and demands for "autogestion" such as those at Nanterre is seen in French political situation, where absolute state power is imbedded in a political vacuum. Fundamental reason for crisis lies in double out-of-phase state of institutions, notably those devoted to the accumulation and productive use of knowledge, in that they are based partially on "archaic" values of classical humanism and nationalism of pre-capitalist period, and partially on "modernist" values of industrial capitalism and and economic growth, none of which are appropriate to urban society. English translation, "The explosion; Marxism and the French revolution" (New York, 1969), at ML.

724 LEFEBVRE, HENRI. La vie quotidienne dans le monde moderne. Paris, Gallimard, 1968. 376 p. (Collection Idées) ML

Critique of "consumption society" which integrates or neutralizes deviations by repressive mechanism of diffused terrorism, concealed behind ideology of liberty and rationalism. Only cultural revolution can transform existing experience of daily life by means of sexual, urban, and playful revolution. Work completed 1967, was influential in shaping student ideology May 1968.

725 LEFRANC, GEORGES. Essais sur les problèmes socialistes et syndicaux. Paris, Payot, 1970. 264 p. (Petite bibliothèque Payot, 160)

Collection of articles written between 1930's and 1969 on historical aspects of trade unionism and socialism, as well as author's participation in economic plan elaborated by C. G. T. leaders and setting up of worker university in 1930's. Impact of work and automation on individual worker in Fifth Republic also examined.

726 LEFRANC, GEORGES. Grèves d'hier et d'aujourd'hui; histoire du travail et de la vie économique. Paris, Aubier-Montaigne, 1970. 302 p. Bibliography: p. [290]-296.

Strikes occurring in Fifth Republic described here are miners' strike at Decazeville Dec. 1961-Feb. 1962, general miners' strike Mar.-Apr. 1963, and general strike May-June 1968. Discussion of current status of government control over strikes, strike funds, role of strikes in a country like France where trade union movement is divided. Appendix gives comparative statistics on days lost in strikes for different countries.

727 LEFRANC, GEORGES. Le mouvement syndical, de la libération aux événements de mai-juin 1968. Paris, Payot, 1969. 312 p. (Bibliothèque historique) Bibliography: p. [289]-290.

For Fifth Republic, chapters on retrenchment of trade unionism 1959-60, renewed offensive 1963-68, separate study of May-June 1968, with appended documents on trade union interpretation of events. Survey of individual trade union organizations. Trade union weakness is ascribed to fragmentation of trade union movement. As active trade unionist, author had personal contacts with many leaders in different organizations.

728 LEITES, NATHAN CONSTANTIN. Images of power in French politics, 1951-1958. Santa Monica, Calif., Rand Corp., 1962. 2 v. (Rand Corporation. Memorandum. RM-2954-RC, June 1962) Includes bibliography.

Typical attitudes and self-images of Fourth Republic parliamentarians, with exclusion of extreme Right and Communists. Organized by these topics: images of authority, dereliction and tyranny, deceit; attitudes toward authority, revolt and submission, the domain of the individual. The predominantly negative self-image of the political class reflects its low standing in public opinion in final years of Fourth Republic, and attitudes toward authority facilitating take-over by a savior explain mechanism of de Gaulle's resumption of power. Sources are quotations from "Journal officiel," press.

729 LEITES, NATHAN CONSTANTIN. The rules of the game in Paris. Translated by Derek Coltman. With a foreword by Raymond Aron. Chicago, University of Chicago Press, 1969. ix, 355 p. Bibliography: p. [351]-355.

Insights into the psychological tendencies in French private and political life, illustrated loosely by quotations from literary works as well as political pronouncements (mainly 1959-60) in and outside parliament. Original French version: "La règle du jeu à Paris."

730 LEITES, NATHAN CONSTANTIN, and CHARLES WOLF. Rebellion and authority; an analytic essay on insurgent conflicts. Chicago, Markham, 1970. 174 p. (Markham series in public policy analysis)

Analysis by systems approach of factors determining success or failure of rebellions (insurgency) or authorities (counterinsurgency). Authors reject fashionable view that only political factors--i.e., popular support based on sympathies or improvement of living conditions--determine outcome. Military factors also enter in, but not as they do in conventional warfare, since intelligence and information are much more important for authority side. Costs of insurgency are seen as interaction between supply (growth of rebel forces) and demand (extent of grievances). Algerian, Indochinese conflict, O.A.S. are among examples.

731 LE LEU, CLAUDE. Géographie des élections françaises depuis 1936. Paris, Presses universitaires de France, 1971. 353 p. illus., maps. (Thémis. Section Textes et documents) Bibliography: p. 193-208.

Includes all major Fifth Republic elections: legislative elections of Nov. 1958 and 1962, Mar. 1967, June 1968; referenda of Sept. 1958, Jan. 1961, Apr. and Oct. 1962, Apr. 1969; presidential elections of Dec. 1965, June 1969. Results are interpreted verbally and by electoral atlases showing outcome for each department. Separate analysis and maps for major parties. Conclusions on trends in abstentions, age representation, gains and losses for P.C.F., Socialists, Radicals, M.R.P., Independents, Gaullists, Left versus Right. Extensive bibliography on electoral sociology, national and local election studies.

732 LEMAITRE, MAURICE. Les aventures d'El Momo. . . . Paris, Centre de créativité, 1968. i, 20 l. illus. ML

Comic-strip narration and comments explaining Mouvement lettriste view on cultural revolution and aim of giving creative young outside establishment new opportunities. See also Isou, no. 637, for Mouvement lettriste's involvement in youth revolt.

733 LEONEV, ABD ER RAHMAN. De Gaulle devant ses juges; réquisitoire. Paris, Nouvelles éditions latines, 1970. 283 p.

Political biography of de Gaulle serving as framework for pell-mell indictment of his actions, with focus on Algerian war and peace negotiations, violations of constitution through unlawful prosecutions and introduction of direct presidential elections, failures of foreign and domestic policies culminating in 1968 events and final defeat Apr. 1969.

734 LERIVRAY, BERNARD. La mer aussi se mourt; bloc notes d'un aumônier d'étudiants, mai-juin 1968. Coutances, Editions OCEP, Editions de la Mission étudiante, 1969. 110 p.

Diary of Sorbonne chaplain, May 3-June 12, reflecting sympathetic reactions of Christian to daily events, and recording stand of Mission étudiante and Action catholique universitaire, role of Catholic student groups. Includes conclusions of French episcopal commission on student community, May 21.

735 LERNER, DANIEL, and MORTON GORDEN. Euratlantica: changing perspectives of the European elites. Cambridge, Mass., M.I.T. Press, 1969. xii, 447 p. tables. (M.I.T. studies in comparative politics) Includes bibliographical annotations.

Based on extensive personal interviews with 4,000 prominent figures in principal sectors of public life made in 1955, 1956, 1959, 1961, and 1965 in France, Germany, and England. Interviews were complemented by questionnaires and special studies of French business leaders, lycée principals, Communist Party and C.G.T. leaders, most Fourth Republic prime ministers. Main conclusions are that nationalism and socialism are both obsolescent, Gaullism a passing phase in Euratlantic relations. Part 1 establishes trend of European relations with U.S. (acceptance of Atlantic Alliance nexus) and European integration. Part 2 deals with specific issues: military protection, economic prosperity, prestige in world affairs. Part 3 traces shaping of new values, and Part 4 defines prospects of European integration and Atlantic Alliance. Most of tables are comparative by countries but some also record longitudinal changes. Work sponsored by M.I.T.'s Center for International Studies as part of the European Elite Panel Survey.

736 LETOURNEUR, MAXIME, JACQUELINE BAUCHET, and JEAN MERIC. Le Conseil d'Etat et les tribunaux administratifs. Préf. de René Cassin. Paris, A. Colin, 1970. 295 p. (Collection U. Série "Droit public interne") Bibliography: p. 289-290.

History of Conseil d'Etat--recruitment, attributes, typical cases presented before this highest administrative tribunal, and operation as legal advisor to government during Fifth Republic. Authors are themselves members of Conseil d'Etat.

737 LEUWERS, JEAN-MARIE. Un peuple se dresse; luttes ouvrières, mai 1968. Paris, Editions ouvrières, 1969. 370 p.

Thirty-one personal accounts by militant Catholic workers, prepared under sponsorship of Action catholique ouvrière, relating May-June 1968 experiences in different industrial sectors (railroads, large companies like Citroën and Dassault as well as small establishments). Reflections on events based on A.C.O.'s committee meetings in subsequent months, stressing contributions of Christian views of work and society. No specific reference to young workers or students.

738 LEWANDOWSKI, RUDOLF. Seine V. Monarchie; das Frankreich de Gaulles. Graz, Verlag Styria, 1971. 216 p. Includes bibliography.

Main themes are de Gaulle's return to power, the men involved in the government at different stages of regime, political orientation (Algeria, Europe, Atlantic Alliance), non-Gaullist parties and movements, pressure groups, May 1968, and last year before de Gaulle's retirement. Author is Paris correspondent of various German and Austrian newspapers.

739 LEWINO, WALTER. L'imagination au pouvoir. Photographies de Jo Schnapp. Paris, Terrain vague, 1968. 1 v. (unpaged). illus.

Photographs of wall inscriptions in and around Sorbonne reflecting changing student preoccupations, May 6, 10, and 13, 1968. Final section gives text of wall inscriptions of May 6 and 10 and selection of slogans on Sorbonne walls, asterisks identifying those most frequently repeated.

740 LIGUE COMMUNISTE. Les marxistes révolutionnaires dans l'enseignement. Paris, 1970. 28 p. (Document rouge, 5) Bibliography: p. 28.

Interpretation of recently introduced educational reforms from teacher perspective (government aim is to make teachers earn less and become more docile by undermining their civil service status), teacher ideologies and responses to May 1968. Identifies stand of main teacher organization, the Fédération de l'éducation nationale, whose largest faction is dominated by P.C.F., the latter's educational philosophy being seen as harmonious with government plans. A small F.E.N. faction, with 6.5 percent of membership, is Ecole émancipée, which has Ligue communiste sympathy and whose views are presented in detail.

FOR ADDITIONAL WORKS BY AND ABOUT LIGUE COMMUNISTE, SEE AUTHOR INDEX

741 LINDON, DENIS. La longue marche. Paris, Denoël, 1968. 272 p.

Weakness of Left's electoral alliance in June 1968 elections and political alliance of Left generally is seen in absence of common method of reasoning and programming, for which neither short-term agreements on programs nor vaguely held common aspirations toward egalitarianism, democracy, and change are substitutes. Specifically, rational scale is needed for evaluating movement on economic and equalitarian scale, complemented by semi-subjective scale to measure progress toward self-determination. Examples given for such scales in all policy fields, notably education. Municipal government considered most promising area for demonstrating joint Left action. Surveys of SOFRES on political attitudes of persons identifying themselves with Left and voter attitudes toward Left included.

742 LIPKOWSKI, JEAN DE. Politique étrangère et militaire. Paris, 1967. 16 p.

Gaullist deputy and president of Groupe de l'union démocratique européenne of European Parliament gives views on international relations, stressing unified Europe's opportunity for equal power as a third force and proposing economic, military, and diplomatic measures to implement it. Speech at Assises nationales of U. D.-V^e in Lille, Nov. 1967.

743 LOSCHAK, DANIELE. La Convention des institutions républicaines; François Mitterrand et le socialisme. Paris, Presses universitaires de France, 1971. 92, [4] p. map. (Dossiers Thémis, 5. Série Partis politiques et groupes de pression) Bibliography: p. [93].

History of Convention des institutions républicaines (founded June 1964 as federation of political clubs)--its political orientation, structure, social background of members, results of 1967 and 1968 legislative elections for Convention candidates, final fusion with Parti socialiste under Mitterrand's leadership in June 1971. Documents illustrate each section.

744 LOUIS, ROGER. L'O.R.T.F., un combat. Paris, Editions du Seuil, 1968. 192 p. (L'Histoire immédiate)

Inside story of O.R.T.F. strike which idled 13,000 employees May 16 to June 25, 1968, and was continued to July 13 by newsbroadcasters, 102 of whom were fired in Aug. Author is producer of popular current events series "Cinq colonnes à la une" and discusses basic grievances of television staff against government, notably lack of autonomy of production units. Texts of motions by O.R.T.F. strikers in appendices.

745 LUQUET, CHARLES. L'Europe satellisée, ou L'agression permanente. Tournai (Belgium), Casterman, 1970. 140 p. (Collection M.O.)

French general attached to N.A.T.O. command pleads for military policy directed toward independence from U.S. and build-up of European force in light of current international relations and impact of U.S. on European economies and way of life.

746 LUTZ, VERA. Central planning for the market economy; an analysis of French theory and experience. London, Longmans in association with the Institute of Economic Affairs, 1969. xv, 194 p. diagrs. Bibliography: p. 188-192.

Scrutiny of Second, Third, and Fourth Plans to verify how accurate forecasts turned out to be and how well targets were met. Author argues that centralized forecasting as such is damaging to operation of market economy, and that it is hypocritical to speak of "indicative" or non-interventionist planning while French system is heading toward corporative economy, Bloch-Lainé's "économie concertée," with increasing role for government. What economic progress has taken place is ascribed not to planning but to introduction of management American-style, which might be wiped out by greater government intervention.

747 Les lycéens gardent la parole; Comités d'action lycéens. Paris, Editions du Seuil, 1968. 190 p. ("Politique," 23) ML

Short history of Comité d'action lycéen movement, Dec. 1967-June 1968, followed by selected reports from these committees (C.A.L.) in several hundred lycées and technical schools in Paris and the provinces. Reports illustrate student criticism of educational system and concrete proposals for administrative and pedagogic reform. Comments by professors, trade unionists.

748 MABIRE, JEAN. Les hors-la-loi; récit. Paris, R. Laffont, 1968. 333 p.

Fictional episode in Algerian war, Sept.-Oct. 1959, concerning capture of Algerian nationalist fund collector near electrified Tunisian border. Novel reveals degrees of officers' commitment to French Algeria and to de Gaulle. Like their adversaries, certain officers opt for outlaw status in defying government policy, while others prepare to obey orders and give up fight. Author was reserve officer serving near Tunisian border Oct. 1958-Oct. 1959.

749 MACLENNAN, MALCOLM, MURRAY FORSYTH, and GEOFFREY DENTON. Economic planning and policies in Britain, France and Germany. New York, Praeger, 1968. 424 p.

British scholars' comparative analysis of the three countries' economic policies, particularly planning and promotion of economic growth. Includes chapters on French indicative planning and controversies regarding this method. Other tools of economic policy, such as regional planning, monetary, credit, fiscal, income, and price policies, are also compared. Section on Common Market planning.

750 MAIER, CHARLES S., and DAN S. WHITE, eds. The thirteenth of May; the advent of de Gaulle's Republic. New York, Oxford University Press, 1968. 402 p. (Problems in European history; a documentary collection)

Source readings in English translation on inception of Fifth Republic selected from press, memoirs of participants, 1962 trial records. Six topics: institutions and policies of Fourth Republic, military-civilian dissensions and Algerian war, final month of instability of Fourth Republic, insurrection in Algeria and France May 13-19, events leading to de Gaulle's parliamentary confirmation, and eventual liquidation of Algerian question.

751 MAILLET, PIERRE, and MONIQUE MAILLET. Le secteur public en France. Paris, Presses universitaires de France, 1964. 127 p. ("Que sais-je?" 1131) Bibliography: p. 127. ML

Figures for early Fifth Republic years (1959-62) on budget allocation, government personnel, state investment and subsidies, sources of state and local income, organization of social security, nationalized industries, with some international comparisons. Forty to 50 percent of investment is in public sector, 40 percent of gross national product contributed by public sector.

752 MAITAN, LIVIO. L'esplosione rivoluzionaria in Francia. Con una documentazione e una cronologia essenziali. Roma, Samonà e Savelli, 1968. 99 p. (Cultura politica, 22) ML

Text (in Italian) of important political declarations and appeals, chronology, followed by short but clear summary of principal features of the "explosion," its causes and mechanism, assessment of possibilities of overthrow of Gaullism and capitalism, negative role of P.C.F. and C.G.T., historical significance of events as clue to tensions and contradictions in advanced capitalism and rise of anti-bureaucratic forces.

753 MAITROT, JEAN-CLAUDE, and JEAN-DIDIER SICAULT. Les conférences de presse du général de Gaulle. Préf. de Georges Vedel. Paris, Presses universitaires de France, 1969. 143 p. (Travaux et recherches de la Faculté de droit et des sciences économiques de Paris. Série "Science politique," no. 17) Bibliography: p. 139-140; bibliographical footnotes.

Two 1967 political science "mémoires." Maitrot's deals with de Gaulle's conception of political institutions as reflected in his speeches and press conferences 1958-65, in which means evolve but ultimate aims remain unaltered. Sicault studies style and structure of press conferences, their function as a form of direct popular contact, and other functions of press conferences within Fifth Republic institutions. Sixteen press conferences were held 1958-67.

754 MALLET, SERGE. Le pouvoir ouvrier; bureaucratie ou démocratie ouvrière. Paris, Editions Anthropos, 1971. 246 p. (Sociologie et révolution)

Collection of 1964-71 articles by journalist-sociologist currently teaching at newly founded University of Vincennes and one of founders of Parti socialiste unifié who remains active in party. Articles concern problems of self-administration by workers in technically advanced societies, worker councils, trade unions, radicalizing effect of May 1968 on workers in terms of increased strikes, P.C.F. responsibility for failure of May 1968 movement. Text of Jan. 1971 speech before P.S.U. executive committee on stimulating mass revolutionary movement and work in plant councils by P.S.U. locals.

755 MALNOUX, ETIENNE. Animation culturelle et conditionnement révolutionnaire. Paris, Secrétariat d'information et de recherches universitaires et scolaires, 1969. 20 p. ML

Tactics employed at Sorbonne's Faculté des lettres to radicalize students May 1968 both by student groups (U.N.E.F. and revolutionary organizations) and faculty unions (S.N.E. Sup. and Syndicat général d'éducation nationale), their successes and failures as of fall 1968, and danger of converting universities into Communist strongholds as a result of recent university reform because many Unités d'enseignement de recherches are dominated by Communist or pro-Communist lower faculty. Counterrevolutionary organizations are urged to react to this threat.

756 MALRAUX, ANDRE. Antimémoires. v. 2: Les chênes qu'on abat (De Gaulle, Malraux, leur dernière rencontre). Paris, Gallimard, 1971. 236 p.

Distillation of Malraux's last conversation with de Gaulle at Colombey, Dec. 11, 1969, in which for several hours both men range freely over recent and more distant French history in elucidating how lasting de Gaulle's efforts to breathe new life into French civilization are likely to be. Details recreate setting of de Gaulle's final retreat, with side views of Mme de Gaulle. Malraux interview discussing "Les chênes qu'on abat" shortly after its publication is published in Cancnave (no. 195).

757 MALRAUX, ANDRE. Oraisons funèbres. Paris, Gallimard, 1971. 137 p.

Eight funeral orations and commemorative speeches, 1958-64, delivered by Malraux in his capacity as minister of culture, including eulogies of Le Corbusier and Georges Braque. For reprints of selected political writings and speeches during Fifth Republic, see "Espoir," no. 2, Jan. 1973 (no. 1171). For list of published speeches, see bibliography in Mossuz, "André Malraux et le gaullisme" (no. 839).

FOR ADDITIONAL WORKS BY AND ABOUT ANDRE MALRAUX, SEE AUTHOR INDEX

758 MALTERRE, ANDRE. La Confédération générale des cadres; la révolte des mal aimés. Paris, Epi, 1972. 111 p. (Carte blanche) Bibliography: p. 100.

History of trade union federation representing supervisory and technical personnel, founded as separate organization in Oct. 1944, its achievements in gaining social security for its members, stands on economic and political questions and doctrine favoring private ownership, preservation of anti-egalitarian income hierarchies, flexible planning. Detailed presentation of C.G.C.'s role during May 1968 and Malterre's inside account of negotiations with major trade unions at rue de Grenelle, May 25-27, which he attended as C.G.C.'s president.

759 MANCEAUX, MICHELE. Les Maos en France. Avant-propos de Jean-Paul Sartre. Paris, Gallimard, 1972. 254 p.

Preface by Sartre, current editor of Maoist "Cause du peuple" (a journal frequently subject to government seizure), explains revolutionary group's tactic for instigating spontaneous violent mass action on whatever scale feasible. Main part presents nine interviews with Maoist activists, one of them a functionary of Union des jeunesses communistes marxistes-léninistes which he helped form in 1965, who gives history of organization dissolved after May 1968 and reconstituted in late 1968 as Gauche prolétarienne, dissolved in turn in 1970. He describes group's interventions May 1968, subsequent changes in orientation, relevance of Chinese experience to French socialism.

760 MANDEL, ERNEST. Die EWG und die Konkurrenz Europa-Amerika. Frankfurt am Main, Europäische Verlagsanstalt, 1968. 111 p. (Res novae, Bd. 64) Bibliographical footnotes.

Marxist response to Servan-Schreiber's "Le défi américain" (see no. 1026) countering his claim that strengthening of Common Market is only alternative to U.S. control of European economies. Common Market is viewed as unfavorable to European workers' interests, hampering economic growth and democracy, which can be served only by European socialism.

761 MANDEL, ERNEST. Traité d'économie marxiste. Paris, R. Julliard, 1969 (c1962). 4 v. (Le Monde en 10/18) Includes bibliographies.

Widely translated synthesis of world economic history and economic theory, broadly based on Marxist concepts but without direct quotations from Marxist classics and incorporating empirical findings of 20th century research, much of it non-Marxist. Includes 1969 epilogue. A few chapters have been updated and 1964 article on neo-capitalism inserted. Fifty-page bibliography in first volume, though not much of it French. Of particular interest is chapter on nature of a genuine socialist society in last volume. Vol. 1: Work, surplus, money, capital, surplus value, development and contradictions of capitalism. Vol. 2: Trade, credit, money, agriculture, growth of national income. Vol. 3: Business cycles, monopoly capitalism, imperialism, decline of capitalism and neo-capitalism. Vol. 4: Soviet economy, mixed economies, socialist economy.

762 MANDRIN, JACQUES. Socialisme ou social-médiocratie? Paris, Editions du Seuil, 1969. 186 p. (Collection "Combats")

Criticism of S.F.I.O. and its two "bosses" Mollet and Defferre for combining revolutionary phraseology with immobilism. Second part of work gives positive view of rational, plausible socialist "project," describes unproductive P.C.F., P.S.U., S.F.I.O., and extreme leftist approaches, and counters with own promising strategy for achieving it.

763 MANEL, JEAN-PIERRE. La grande aventure de Concorde. Evreux, R. Solar, 1969. 285 p. illus.

History of this technological feat of aeronautics industry from signing of Franco-British agreement Dec. 1962 to production of 400-million-franc jet plane carrying 130 passengers at

2,000 km per hour. Commercial exploitation set for 1972. Many photographs.

764 MANEL, JEAN-PIERRE, and ALOMEE PLANEL. La crise de l'O.R.T.F. Paris, J. J. Pauvert, 1968. 127 p.

Information on political censorship of television prior to May 1968, staff demands for new statutes, comments of leading political candidates before June 1968 election on control over O.R.T.F. Book concluded before end of strike, during which only half-hour daily program appeared. Annual television fee in France per set is Fr. 100.

765 MANFRED, ALBERT ZAKHAROVICH. Traditsii druzhby i sotrudnichestva; iz istorii russko-frantsuzskikh i sovetsko-frantsuzskikh sviazei. Moskva, Nauka, 1967. 329 p.

Very little material on Franco-Soviet diplomatic relations during Fifth Republic.

766 MAOUT, JEAN CHARLES, and RAYMOND MUZELLEC. Le parlement sous la Ve République. Paris, A. Colin, 1971. 119 p. illus. (Collection U2, 191) Bibliography: p. 119.

Operation of Senate and National Assembly in Fifth Republic under de Gaulle and since Pompidou, blockages in legislative and control function. Documentation is drawn from "Journal officiel," debates, critical speeches of parliamentarians. Lists of members of different political groups in National Assembly as of Jan. 1959, Dec. 1961, Dec. 1962, Apr. 1967, June 1968, Dec. 1969, and in Senate as of Apr. 1959, Dec. 1961, Sept. 1965, Sept, 1968, Dec. 1969.

767 MARCELLIN, RAYMOND. L'ordre public et les groupes révolutionnaires. Paris, Plon, 1969. 127 p. (Tribune libre)

Author became minister of interior June 1, 1968, replacing Fouchet. Work identifies most active revolutionary groups— Jeunesse communiste révolutionnaire, Fédération des étudiants révolutionnaires, Union des jeunesses communistes marxistes-léninistes, Voix ouvrière, and Mouvement du 22 mars—documenting their objectives by quotations from leaflets, newspapers (extensive examples in appendix). Tactics of psychological warfare are described, ideological ties with international student movements highlighted, and tentative evidence of international support to French revolutionary groups cited. Government countermeasures illustrated. Includes excerpts from tracts distributed Nov. 1968, mostly from provinces.

768 MARCHAIS, GEORGES. Qu'est-ce que le Parti communiste français? Paris, Editions sociales, 1970. 45 p.

P.C.F. secrétaire général adjoint's statement of party aims and structure at the time of its 50th anniversary.

769 MARCHAIS, GEORGES. Rapport sur les nouveaux statuts. Présenté par Georges Marchais. Paris, 1964. 46 p. (Supplément aux "Cahiers du communisme," no. 5-6, juin-juillet 1964)

Justification of revision of party statutes proposed to P.C.F.'s 17th Congrès national, Paris, May 1964. New statutes aim to strengthen internal participation without challenging principle of democratic centralism. Report contains details on party organization, such as number of party cells (18,500 as of 1964) and local party newspapers (300).

770 MARCHOU, GASTON. Chaban-Delmas. Paris, A. Michel, 1969. 263 p. ports.

Political biography with special emphasis on Chaban-Delmas' views on European integration, political institutions. Interesting chapters on his position during last year of de Gaulle's government and views, as new prime minister under Pompidou, on Gaullism after de Gaulle.

771 MARCUSE, HERBERT. Über Revolte, Anarchismus, und Einsamkeit; ein Gespräch. Aus dem Französischen übertragen von Katrin Reinhart. Zürich, Verlags AG Die Arche, 1969. 48 p.

Conversation with several "Express" reporters in summer of 1968 in southern France, some of it concerning his views on French student revolt.

772 MARIE, CHRISTIANE. L'évolution du comportement politique dans une ville en expansion, Grenoble, 1871-1965. . . . Paris, A. Colin, 1966. 229 p. illus. (Cahiers de la Fondation nationale des sciences politiques, 148) Bibliography: p. 225-[228].

Thesis based primarily on Grenoble election results and voter lists. For Fifth Republic, analysis deals with 1958 and 1962 legislative elections and Mar. 1965 municipal elections. In the latter, influence of new technically oriented voter group put P.S.U.-backed slate into office.

773 MARIN, GERARD. Les nouveaux Français. Paris, B. Grasset, 1967. 317 p. ML

1967 survey of French youth: growing place in society and economy, causes and manifestations of juvenile delinquency, demands on adult world, generation conflicts at home and in school. Several chapters focus on specific groups such as students, young workers, farmers, professionals, and technicians. Opinions of youth on political and moral questions. As of 1967, nearly 11 million in school, over 50 percent of those 16 to 24 years old at work, 12 percent unemployed. No indication that youth is at threshold of revolt. Author is involved in operation of youth centers.

774 MARKS, JOSEPH. The new French-English dictionary of slang and colloquialisms. Rev. and completed by Georgette A. Marks and Albert J. Farmer. New York, E. P. Dutton, 1971 (c1970). 255 p.

Words and phrases under key word, with special emphasis on underworld, sex vocabulary, but also ordinary colloquialisms. Published in England as "Harrap's French-English dictionary of slang and colloquialisms" (London, 1970).

775 MARNY, JACQUES. L'église contestée; jeunes chrétiens révolutionnaires. Paris, Le Centurion, 1968. 253 p. (Collection "Changements")

Testimony collected by team of sympathetic journalists in form of interviews, round tables, documents regarding actions taken by young Catholics in student and worker setting May-June 1968, and unresolved issues such as place of violence, possibility of cooperation with Marxists. One round table on May 11 barricades includes police chief. Among incidents discussed are take-over of Paris church of St. Severin, occupied June 2, events at Catholic student center of Saint-Yves, Paris, unrest at Paris theology faculty and smaller theological seminaries outside Paris, intervention of "Bible et révolution" group at Sorbonne.

776 MARTIN, NICOLAS. L'héritage gaulliste. Paris, Nouvelles éditions Debresse, 1971. 124 p. Includes bibliographical references.

Institutional heritage of Fifth Republic, changes in social and economic structure, international relations attributable to de Gaulle, effects of his personal example. Author is young journalist, editor of Gaullist "Notre République," was active in Apr. 1969 referendum campaign, but is unwilling to support Pompidou. In final section, he joins in discussion with Chinese writer Han Suyin, Gaullists Michel Cazenave, Olivier Germain-Thomas, René Victor Pilhès, Dominique de Roux, and Philippe de Saint-Robert on best strategy for perpetuating de Gaulle's heritage and breaking with Pompidou's version of Gaullism.

777 MARTINET, GILLES. La conquête des pouvoirs. Paris, Editions du Seuil, 1968. 190 p. (L'Histoire immédiate) M L

Lessons to be drawn from May 1968 events and specifically May 29 as to hope for "conquest of power" by democratic socialism. Author stresses ideological background of student and worker movement, its rejections of and affinities with various leftist parties and revolutionary movements. As one of P.S.U. founders and leaders (involved since 1967 in Association "Pouvoir socialiste"), he shows incapacity of this New Left to influence student thinking with its blind faith in both direct democracy and "autogestion." In light of experiences in both Communist and social democratic-ruled countries, author recognizes that problem of socialist democracy has remained unresolved, offering as preconditions for economically advanced countries: recognition of double character of collective property (state ownership and self-administration); democratic determination of planning goals; worker participation in firms; and political pluralism.

778 MASSOT, FRANÇOIS DE. La grève générale, mai-juin 1968. Paris, 1969. x, 311 p. (Supplément au no. 437 d'"Informations ouvrières")

Day-by-day history of May-June 1968 events from point of view of Trotskyist Organisation communiste internationaliste, closely linked with revolutionary student organization Fédération des étudiants révolutionnaires (F.E.R.), many of whose appeals are reproduced. Attacks on P.C.F. and C.G.T., as well as anarchist and Maoist groups, for blocking coordination of general strike. Appendix contains F.E.R., O.C.I. appeals and appeals of worker groups against ending strike. May 1969 preface.

779 MASSU, JACQUES. Le torrent et la digue: Alger du 13 mai aux barricades. Paris, Plon, 1972. 404 p.

Continuation of "La vraie bataille d'Alger" (see next entry). General explains how respite gained by his temporary victory over rebels in Algiers was misused and battle for French Algeria lost. Main episodes are May 1958 in Algiers, gradual transformation of de Gaulle's views on Algeria, clash with de Gaulle in wake of Massu's ill-fated interview with German journalist Kempski from "Süddeutsche Zeitung" Jan. 14, 1960, and his subsequent removal from Algeria. Includes Massu's testimony at Barricades trial. From Oct. 1960 on, he served as military governor of Metz.

780 MASSU, JACQUES. La vraie bataille d'Alger. Paris, Plon, 1971. 391 p. illus.

Battle of Algiers took place Jan.-Oct. 1957, confronting 10th Parachute Division under Massu with F.L.N. organization in Algerian capital. This work is exoneration of French army against excessive use of torture by documenting F.L.N. terrorism and support thereof by certain French personalities (e.g., Germaine Tillion) and Catholic organizations. Massu answers questions as to aims and methods of army, F.L.N., reactions of Algerian masses and pieds-noirs, Communist aid to F.L.N., mechanisms of conflict, how information on rebellion was obtained, use of torture, capture of Saadi Yacef, with documents on these points in appendices, which also include diagrams of F.L.N. and government political-administrative organization of Algiers. For replies to his book, see Déméron (no. 329) and Pâris de Bollardière (no. 883). See also no. 779.

781 MATHIEU, PIERRE LOUIS. La pensée politique et économique de Teilhard de Chardin. Préf. de Jean-Jacques Chevallier. Paris, Editions du Seuil, 1969. 302 p. (Etudes et recherches sur Teilhard de Chardin) Includes bibliography.

Influential Catholic philosopher's views on Marxism (early advocate of dialogue with Marxists), Fascism, compatibility of liberal democracy with Christianity, economic growth, scientific and technical contributions to human civilization. Bibliography of philosopher's own publications, works about him, as well as large number of basic works on questions discussed in book.

782 MAUGUE, PIERRE. Le particularisme alsacien, 1918-1967. Paris, Presses d'Europe, 1970. 261 p. map. (Collection Régions) Bibliography: p. 253-256.

For Fifth Republic years, main issues are region's special linguistic and religious status, since Alsace has church-controlled (Catholic and Protestant) schools. Attitudes of M.R.P., Gaullists, Communists toward this special status identified. Author concludes that unless federalist movement encourages Alsatian identity, the region will inexorably move toward assimilation.

783 MAUPEOU-ABBOUD, NICOLE DE. Les blousons bleus; étude sociologique des jeunes ouvriers de la région parisienne. Paris, A. Colin, 1968. 258 p. plates, tables. (Collection Sciences sociales du travail, 3) M L

Study on several hundred apprentices and young workers, 14-20 years of age, based on two separate investigations, both using questionnaire and interview methods. Apprentice study concentrates on behavior, motivations, values of youth, young worker study on working conditions and professional prospects. Though investigations date back to 1960 and earlier, conclusions apply to current perspective of young workers, relations with adults, place in social hierarchy, convergence of views with middle-class youth.

784 MAURIAC, CLAUDE. Un autre de Gaulle; journal, 1944-1954. Paris, Hachette, 1970. 408 p. (His Le temps immobile)

Diary entries recording encounters with de Gaulle during Mauriac's service in de Gaulle's private secretariat, plus meeting Mar. 19, 1960, when his father, François Mauriac, received decoration, and June 1966 reception at Elysée in honor of Belgian ambassador.

785 MAURIAC, FRANÇOIS. Le nouveau bloc-notes. v. 1: 1961-1964. v. 2: 1965-1967. Paris, Flammarion, 1968-70. 477 p.; 474 p.

Peripatetic comments on literary and political events, appearing more or less weekly in "Figaro littéraire." Political issues followed most closely in Vol. 1 are negotiations to end Algerian war, O.A.S., 1962 constitutional referendum, with defense of de Gaulle policies against onslaught from Catholic and non-Catholic Left. In second volume, focus is on 1965 presidential election, de Gaulle's controversial stands on Israel, Canada, European policy, in which he supports de Gaulle. First volume records reactions to Mauriac's "De Gaulle" (1964). Evolution of Catholic Church followed closely.

786 MAURIAC, FRANÇOIS. Le dernier bloc notes, 1968-1970. Paris, Flammarion, 1971. 339 p.

Diary ends shortly before Mauriac's death Sept. 1970. Few comments on May-June 1968, but long interview July 1969 discussing Apr. 1969 referendum, de Gaulle's withdrawal, Pompidou's election. Mauriac sides with Pompidou against Gaullist purists and predicts stability of regime under de Gaulle's successor. Further comments on modernization of Catholic Church, much of which he condemns.

FOR ADDITIONAL WORKS ABOUT FRANÇOIS MAURIAC, SEE AUTHOR INDEX

787 MAURIAC, JEAN. Mort du général de Gaulle. Paris, B. Grasset, 1972. 183 p.

Younger son of François Mauriac was Agence France-Presse's accredited journalist to de Gaulle, 1944-70. This minutely detailed account of last 19 months of de Gaulle's life, Apr. 27, 1969, to Nov. 9, 1970, is based on testimony of family members and former associates of de Gaulle. Of special interest are the account of de Gaulle's retirement, his work on "Mémoires de l'espoir," trips to Ireland and Spain, personal feelings and political observations expressed in encounters with visitors.

788 MAYER, DANIEL. Pour une histoire de la gauche. Paris, Plon, 1969. 448 p.

Contribution to history of French Left, centering on individual socialist politicians having played a leading role in French history. For Fifth Republic, only François Mitterrand is singled out. Epilogue summarizes position of Left in post-1968 France and gives results of 1967 SOFRES study of opinions of moderate and extreme Left voters.

789 MAYER, RENE. Féodalités ou démocratie? Paris, Arthaud, 1968. 259 p. illus., maps. (Collection Notre temps, 17) Bibliography: p. 255-[258].

Author is regional administrator currently in charge of Provence-Côte d'Azur-Corse construction program. Work describes weaknesses of present administrative structure, changes introduced during Fifth Republic, presenting principles for decentralization and successful counterstrategies for overcoming rigidities by using different approaches simultaneously. Most interesting section on combining ethnic regions in periphery of France with decentralization around middle of country, leaving Paris as its major city. Good bibliography.

790 MEARDI, CARLO. La Chiesa e la lotta di liberazione dal colonialismo: la lezione dell'Algeria. Milano, Jaca Book, 1969. 206 p. (Cronache alla prova: Chiesa e società, n. 13) Includes bibliographical references.

Position of Catholic Church in Algeria regarding colonization and national liberation, with chapters on its stand on Algerian nationalism, use of torture, O.A.S. terrorism, Evian Treaty. Includes statistics for 1958 and 1961 on number of Catholics and Catholic priests, members of religious orders in each of the four Algerian dioceses. In 1961, there were close to one million Catholics.

791 La médecine confisquée. Paris, F. Maspéro, 1969. 44 p. (Cahiers "Rouge," no. 2)

Survey of French medical system under social security provisions, recent hospital and medical school reforms, criticism of P.S.U. and P.C.F. health programs and proposals of Ligue communiste.

792 MEGLIN, ALBERT. Le pari humain. Préf. d'Albert Caquot. Lettres de Roger-Adolphe Lacan et Raymond Lautié. [Tours?] Maison Mame, 1968. 271 p. ML

Industrialist's plea for French moral renewal and specific proposals in areas of industrial management (participation, leadership within firm, productivity).

793 MENAIS, GEORGES PAUL. A la recherche d'une monnaie unique européenne. Préf. d'Edouard Bonnefous. Paris, Editions de Epargne, 1964. 104 p. illus. (De quoi s'agit-il?) Includes bibliography.

Banker's plea for assigning creation of single European currency high priority in European economic unification. Author also describes recent fluctuations in value of European and other currencies, gold reserve, use of Eurodollar, efforts of European Communities' monetary committee, and Common Market problems in maintaining international exchange balance with U.S.

794 MENARD, ORVILLE D. The Army and the Fifth Republic. Lincoln, University of Nebraska Press, 1967. xii, 265 p. illus., ports. Bibliography: p. 239-249.

Scholarly work on political role of French army, seen in historical perspective of "La Grande Muette" and military unity and obedience. Turning point to activism is around 1956 with activist counterrevolutionary doctrine. Military participation in May 1958, intervention in Algerian policy 1958-60, and de Gaulle's successful struggle to regain civilian control are described in detail, as are Jan. 1960 and Apr. 1961 confrontations. Effects of this clash on officer corps after 1962 are symbolized by army's current return to its silent role. Good bibliography of books and articles.

795 MENDES-FRANCE, PIERRE. Pour préparer l'avenir; propositions pour une action. Paris, Denoël, 1968. 121 p.

Stenographic record of campaign speeches for re-election as deputy for Grenoble, June 1968, giving interpretation of recent events, appeal for unity of Left, and a few specific points in program: university, social, and economic reform.

796 MENDL, WOLF. Deterrence and persuasion; French nuclear armament in the context of national policy, 1945-1969. New York, Praeger, 1970. 256 p. (Studies in international politics) Includes bibliographical references and biographical note, p. 230-240.

Based on Ph.D. dissertation concluded just before de Gaulle's retirement. Author analyzes how development of atomic energy and nuclear weapons in Fourth and Fifth Republic was related to foreign, military, and domestic policies of successive governments, through 1968. Although nuclear weapons became operative only during Fifth Republic, continuity of basic options is emphasized. List of ministers in charge of atomic questions 1945-69, results of 1946-65 public opinion polls on French nuclear weapons. As of 1969, half the military budget was devoted to nuclear expenditures. Good compendium of works on political background, foreign, defense, and nuclear policies.

797 MENDRAS, HENRI. La fin des paysans; innovations et changement dans l'agriculture française. Paris, S.E.D.E.I.S., 1967. 361 p. (Futuribles, 6) Bibliography: p. 342-351.

Sympathetic view of daily rural life, farmers' attitudes, resistances against and forces within French agriculture encouraging transition from autarchic, polycultural family farm, based on hard work and respect for local conditions and natural balance to market-oriented agriculture. Two typical innovations are introduction of hybrid corn and tractors. Role of agricultural organizations, political parties, government in transformation is seen as encouragement to semi-industrial methods of rationalization, specialization of labor, leading eventually to a greatly reduced farm population (5-10 percent of work force) and abandonment of traditional support to agriculture on moral grounds. Work is based on sophisticated synthesis of many micro-studies by economists and sociologists on rural society. Author heads C.N.R.S. group on rural sociology.

798 MERCIER VEGA, LUIS. L'increvable anarchisme. Paris, Union générale d'édition, 1970. 185 p. (Collection Le Monde en 10/18) Includes bibliography.

Different currents of anarchist thought throughout the world, past and present, with chapter on "autogestion" and extent to which Mouvement du 22 mars in May 1968 drew on anarchist views.

799 MERLEAU-PONTY, MAURICE. The essential writings of Merleau-Ponty. Edited by Alden L. Fisher. New York, Harcourt, Brace and World, 1969. viii, 383 p. Bibliography: p. 379-383; bibliographical footnotes.

Selections from Merleau-Ponty's writings, arranged topically under: philosophy and phenomenology, philosophy and the sciences of man, philosophical anthropology, philosophy of language, philosophical aesthetics, history and politics, on the problems of God and religion. Bibliography of works, translations, secondary sources.

800 MEYNAUD, JEAN. Technocracy. Translated by Paul Barnes. New York, Free Press, 1969. 315 p. Bibliography: p. 304-306. ML

Referring mainly to the situation in the Fourth and Fifth Republic, but also to the U.S. and Great Britain, political scientist identifies technocrats among civil servants and scientific elite and distinguishes the concept of technocracy as decision-making power granted to experts from bureaucracy and technical specialization. Areas in which power is concentrated and expanding under specific conditions of Fifth Republic, links with business pressure groups outside government, are examined, as are principles of a "technocratic ideology" as best suited for modern society, in contrast to corrupt, incompetent political representation. Meynaud, while admitting technocratic trend, denies possibility of eliminating political choices and fears that weight of efficiency-conscious technocracy will be thrown in conservative, status quo side of balance. Published originally as "La technocratie, mythe ou réalité?" (1964), material here is only slightly updated.

801 MEYNAUD, JEAN, and DUSAN SIDJANSKI. L'Europe des affaires; rôle et structure des groupes. Paris, Payot, 1967. 247 p. (Bibliothèque politique et économique) Bibliographical references included in "Notes" (p. [227]-244).

Mergers and interlocking of firms within Common Market, influence of American investment, take-over of French firms by American companies, fluctuations of French government policy in relation to foreign investments, and position of European Economic Communities Commission.

802 MEYNAUD, JEAN, and DUSAN SIDJANSKI. Groupes de pression et coopération européenne, organisations professionnelles au plan régional européen. Paris, Fondation nationale des sciences politiques, 1968. 73 p. (Fondation nationale des sciences politiques. Centre d'étude des relations internationales. Série C.: Recherches, no. 14) Bibliographical footnotes.

Survey of inter-European organizations affecting French economy and their relations with French pressure groups: Commission économique pour l'Europe (U.N. subsidiary), Organisation européenne de coopération économique (renamed Organisation de coopération et de développement économique after 1960), and Association européenne de libre échange.

803 MICHAL, BERNARD, ed. Histoire du drame algérien. Genève, Editions de Crémille, 1971. 4 v. plates, ports. Bibliography: v. 4, p. 243-248.

History of Algerian war in both its military and political aspects, following up conflict with material on O.A.S. Vol. 1: Nov. 1954-Jan. 1956; Vol. 2: Jan. 1956-May 13, 1958; Vol. 3: May 1958-Dec. 1960; Vol. 4: Dec. 1960-Aug. 1962. Cover title. "Le destin tragique de l'Algérie française."

804 MICHAUD, GUY. Révolution dans l'université. Paris, Hachette, 1968. 144 p. (Classiques Hachette)

Author is professor of French literature and civilization at Nanterre's Centre d'études des civilisations. First part of work retraces events at Nanterre; second part gives inside view of student-faculty discussions at Nanterre on university reform which would lead to institutional autonomy and student participation, new teaching and teacher training methods. Author is in sympathy with these goals.

805 MICHEL, M.L. De Gaulle. 300 caricatures et photographies. Anthologie de la caricature. Nukerke, Belgique, 1968. 143 p. illus., ports.

Photographs of de Gaulle throughout his life, followed by collection of 300 cartoons from the pens of 50 international artists, some hitherto unpublished. Contributors are identified by country and city of origin. Cartoons arranged by topics: grandeur, foreign policy, European policy, Common Market, Atlantic Alliance, Franco-German relations, Communism, Franco-Russian relations, Franco-Chinese relations, nuclear deterrence, cooperation and Third World, Vietnam, Algeria, elections and domestic affairs. Each topic is introduced by editor and quotes from de Gaulle. Stops with 1967.

806 MICHELET, CLAUDE. Mon père Edmond Michelet, d'après ses notes intimes. Comme un feu d'amitié. Paris, Presses de la Cité, 1971. 284 p. illus. Bibliography: p. 284-285.

Last 50 pages of biography related to Fifth Republic and Michelet's role as minister of veterans' affairs (1958), minister of justice (Jan. 1959-Aug. 1961), president of Conseil constitutionnel (Feb. 1962-1967), deputy (Mar. 1967-June 1969), and minister of cultural affairs under Pompidou till his death in Oct. 1970.

807 MINCES, JULIETTE. Le nord; conditions de vie et de travail de la classe ouvrière d'une des régions industrielles de France. Paris, F. Maspéro, 1967. 198 p. (Cahiers libres, no. 102)

1965-67 study of working-class life in Départements du Nord and Pas-de-Calais concentrating on textile workers and coal miners. First part describes region's economic conditions, second part typical personal account of workers' lives, followed by industrial statistics on wages, working conditions, health hazards. Final section reviews inadequate efforts to establish new regional industries absorbing unemployed coal miners.

808 MINCES, JULIETTE. Un ouvrier parle; enquête. Paris, Editions du Seuil, 1969. 88 p. (Combats)

Personal account by machinist in southern France on his life and working conditions, as of 1965, complemented by 1969 interview, in which he expresses reactions to May 1968, criticizing romantic revolutionary aspects but agreeing with basis of protests.

809 MINGUET, RENE. Grandeur et servitudes de l'industrie. Préf. de Georges Villiers. Paris, Des livres pour vous, 1970. 218 p.

Appeal by industrialist to business community for innovative spirit, human and technical adaptations demanded by modern society, such as greater worker participation and research, with U.S. presented as model of productiveness and social peace.

810 MINGUET, RENE. Le tournant à prendre. Préf. de Louis Armand. Paris, Des livres pour vous, 1970. 183 p.

Sympathetic interpretation of May 1968 events as legitimate expression of demands for greater social justice, cultural equality, participation, which industry and trade unions must take into account.

811 MINOT, JACQUES. L'entreprise éducation nationale. Paris, A. Colin, 1970. 431 p. illus., maps. (Collection U. Série Science administrative) Bibliography: p. 384-386; bibliographical footnotes.

Comprehensive work on French educational system viewed from angle of central and regional administration. There are sections on Ministry of Education, reorganization of ministry 1958-70, educational goals and organization of studies and research, with 1958-70 reforms, facts on student enrollment, teaching staff at elementary, secondary, university level, administrators, educational expenditures, new pedagogical approaches. As of 1970, educational expenditures were 17 percent of government budget, 5 percent of gross national product. Historical evolution as well as current situation and statistics. Extensive bibliographies for each section.

812 MISSOFFE, FRANÇOIS. Une politique de la jeunesse: pourquoi faire? Conférence faite le jeudi 19 octobre 1967 au Théâtre des Ambassadeurs sous les auspices des Conférences des Ambassadeurs. Paris, 1967. 19 p. (Les Conférences des Ambassadeurs. Grands discours français et internationaux, n.s., no. 33)

Survey of status of 16- to 24-year-olds by Ministre de la jeunesse, who had just supervised publication of "Jeunes d'aujourd'hui" (see no. 468) and whose clash with Cohn-Bendit at Nanterre a few months later was to spark student revolt.

813 MITTELBERG, T. I., illus. Une certaine idée de la France, 1958-1969. [Par] TIM [pseud.]. [La plupart des dessins réunis dans cet album ont paru dans "L'Express." Textes de Michèle Cotta.] Paris, Tchou, 1969. 101 p. of illus.

Superb cartoons, with subtitles, arranged chronologically to illustrate main incidents in de Gaulle's career as French head of state and political history of Fifth Republic.

814 MITTELSTÄDT, AXEL. Frankreichs Währungspolitik von Poincaré zu Rueff. Frankfurt a. M., Knapp, 1967. xi, 257 p. (Institut für das Kreditwesen. Neue Schriftenfolge) Bibliography: p. 249-255.

Final section presents de Gaulle's monetary policy, 1958-63, beginning with 15 percent devaluation of franc Dec. 1958 and embodying other proposals of Rueff report such as complete convertibility of franc.

815 MITTERRAND, FRANÇOIS. Ma part de vérité; de la rupture à l'unité. Paris, A. Fayard, 1969. 206 p. (Collection "En toute liberté")

Interview with Alain Duhamel covering biographical elements, opinions on political and economic questions, personal views on major events of 1965-69: 1965 presidential election, founding, successes, and final dissolution of Fédération de la gauche démocrate et socialiste, repeated attempts to collaborate with P.C.F., personal intervention in May 1968, June 1968 elections, 1969 presidential election.

816 MITTERRAND, FRANÇOIS. Un socialisme du possible. Avec la collaboration de Jean-Paul Bachy [et al.]. Paris, Editions du Seuil, 1970. 118 p. (Collection Politique, 42)

First part contains interview with Jacques Julliard and Robert Fossaert on false quarrels splitting Left and preventing its unification (paths to socialism, class struggle, democratic liberties). Second part reproduces "Contrat socialiste," a collective work (1969) by members of Convention des institutions républicaines outlining a French model of socialism if Left came to be in a position of political power, incorporating "le socialisme du possible" under actual French conditions and spelling out specific programs. Final section gives short history of Convention des institutions républicaines, founded 1964.

817 MOCH, JULES. Rencontres avec Charles de Gaulle. Paris, Plon, 1971. 406 p. photos.

Encounters during Resistance and immediate postwar years, as well as contacts during last month of Fourth Republic, when Moch was minister of interior and was in charge of combatting subversion against regime. Interesting inside information on police reactions, attitudes of socialist parliamentarians. Further meetings with de Gaulle June 18, Aug., Oct. 1958.

818 MOCKERS, J. P. Croissances économiques comparées: Allemagne, France, Royaume Uni 1950-1967; essai d'analyse structurale. Paris, Dunod, 1969. 273 p. tables, graphs. (Collection du Centre d'économétrie de la Faculté de droit et des sciences économiques de Paris, Association Cournot, 6)

Germany has the highest, England the lowest growth rate. Explanation of differences on the basis of initial conditions, government policy and actions of private industry, internal and external limitations to growth. Prospects of future growth are related to international monetary problems, Common Market, adoption of more advanced production techniques. Author sees incipient excess capacity and overinvestment in all three countries and likelihood of slower future growth.

819 MOGUI, JEAN PIERRE. Révolte des Basques. Paris, J. Martineau, 1970. 99 p. illus. Includes bibliography.

White book on repression suffered by Basque autonomists on both sides of the border, plus history: demands of autonomist movement, the Enbata, details on French government's measures against French section, the Euzkadi Ta Akatazuna, 1960-70. Basque demands for autonomy are presented as compatible with leftist, socialist orientation.

820 Un Mois de mai orageux; 113 étudiants parisiens expliquent les raisons du soulèvement universitaire. Introd. de A. Deledicq. . . . Toulouse, Privat, 1968. xxxi, 167 p. (Epoque)

Students questioned May 9, 1968, by professor of mathematics were attending regular first-year chemistry-physics lecture at Faculté des sciences de Paris. Answers, roughly arranged by topic, concern inefficient and inequitable university conditions, government educational policy, proposed reforms, role of extremist groups May 1968.

821 MOLLET, GUY. Les chances du socialisme; réponse à la société industrielle. Paris, Fayard, 1968. 138 p. (Collection "En toute liberté") M L

Socialist leader's restatement of fundamental socialist objectives, socialism's democratic faith, its internationalism, place of violence and revolution. Final chapter on relevance of socialism in the face of student demands. Appendix reproduces S.F.I.O.'s 1962 "Programme fondamental."

822 MOLNAR, THOMAS. La gauche vue d'en face. Paris, Editions du Seuil, 1970. 153 p.

Wholesale indictment of utopian thinking, characterized as rejection of what exists in favor of future transformation of man, its historical manifestations and current expression in French cultural revolution. Utopian ideas are accepted even by moderate political Left and are also held by Christian progressives, propagated by intellectuals. Author fears that fluid, tolerant environment of Western democracies will be subjected to a corroding, permanent state of revolution, rather than single, violent explosion. Author is Hungarian-born professor of French literature in U.S.

823 MONATE, GERARD. La police, pour qui, avec qui? Paris, EPI, 1972. 109 p. (Collection Carte blanche)

Secretary general of Fédération autonome des syndicats de police, which groups various police unions and represents over 60 percent of police, gives facts on membership, role of police in society, their desire to maintain non-political role. Defends police behavior May 1968.

824 MONDON, RAYMOND. Intervention de Raymond Mondon, député-maire de Metz, président du Groupe des Républicains indépendants à l'Assemblée nationale, lors de la journée de la majorité, Lille, le 26 novembre 1967. [n.p., 1967] 4 p.

Speech defining position of Républicains indépendants as members of majority as well as permanent interlocutors of government at Assises nationales of U.D.-V^e.

825 MONETA, JACOB. La politique du Parti communiste français dans la question coloniale 1920-1963, suivi de "A propos de la critique de M. Suret-Canale" par l'auteur. Préf. de Pierre

Frank. Paris, F. Maspéro, 1971. 307 p. (Collection "Livres rouges")

Final third of work presents P.C.F.'s position on Algerian war and decolonization of Sub-Saharan Africa, on the basis of articles in the Communist press, which are situated in the context of current events, demonstrating that P.C.F. actually served interests of Soviet Union and only paid lip service to anti-colonialism. Domestically, its strength lies in its conformity with narrow working-class interests. Book published originally in German as "Die Kolonialpolitik der Französischen K.P." (1968).

826   MONNEROT, JULES. Démarxiser l'université. Paris, Table ronde, 1970. 179 p. (Collection Table ronde de Combat. "Les Brûlots")

Implantation of a wide spectrum of Marxist views in French universities after World War II, which are as deep-rooted as Catholic dogma in Catholic institutions, but with pretense of being scientific and serving truth. All forms of revolution are freely advocated ex cathedra, except those threatening permanence of professorial tenure. These attitudes are blamed for students' actions in May 1968 and for leading universities to brink of destruction. Government and politicians are responsible for tolerating such excesses. Rather than defying Marxist strength in universities directly, author suggests that student demands for politization of universities be met by letting Marxists run their own Facultés des lettres and by the creation of separate non-Marxist institutions devoted to teaching truth, thus preserving free competition of ideas. Attacks current arguments by Bourdieu and others that education is the monopoly of privileged groups.

827   MONNEROT, JULES. La France intellectuelle. Paris, Raymond Bourgine, 1970. 141 p. (Le Spectacle du monde) ML

Virulent attack on conformist, mindlessly pro-Communist and revolutionary bias among French intellectuals since World War II, whereby all good is identified with the Left and all evil with the Right. Proper role of intellectuals should be to defend political optimum between change and conservation.

828   MONPIED, ERNEST. Terres mouvantes; un maire rural au coeur du remembrement. Paris, Editions ouvrières, 1965. 302 p.

Amusing blow-by-blow account of personal involvement in local land consolidation program, 1959-61, undertaken at suggestion of sous-préfet and with approval of local council.

829   MONTAGNON, BARTHELEMY. De Jaurès à de Gaulle: néo-capitalisme? néo-socialisme? Paris, d'Halluin, 1969. 212 p.

Autobiography of trade union militant and industrial engineer who was also active in socialist politics during Third Republic. Plea for neo-capitalism based on people's savings and a distributive neo socialism. Second part of book criticizes de Gaulle's economic and monetary policies for being out of step with industrial technogy and suggests reforms in organization of firms. Author is skeptical of Gaullist worker-participation schemes.

830   MONTALAIS, JACQUES DE. Qu'est-ce que le gaullisme? Préf. d'Edmond Michelet. Paris, Mame, 1969. 213 p.

Exposition and defense of major tenets of Gaullism by editor of Gaullist newspaper "La Nation." Although European and international policy are mentioned, as is Gaullism after de Gaulle, focus is on de Gaulle's program for social and economic reforms along lines of increased participation. Written just before Apr. 1969 referendum, book shows how de Gaulle consistently sought more human way between capitalism and socialism and worked in same direction as the one students had confusedly been demanding. De Gaulle's press conference of Feb. 4, 1965, on social policy, television address of June 7, 1968, and exchange of letters with René Capitant in appendices.

831   MONTARON, GEORGES, and MARCEL CLEMENT. Le socialisme; dialogue entre Georges Montaron et Marcel Clément. Paris, Beauchesne, 1969. 127 p. (Verse et controverse, 11)

Montaron, editor of "Témoignage chrétien," defends building of socialist community as compatible with Christianity but not derived from Catholic social doctrine, in opposition to editor of "L'Homme nouveau," who claims that existing Catholic social doctrine is more suitable to problems of human existence than either capitalist individualism or socialist collectivism.

832   MORAZE, CHARLES. Le général de Gaulle et la République; ou La République ne civilise plus. Paris, Flammarion, 1972. 300 p. (Etudes politiques)

Historian's enlargement of themes on evolution of French institutions proposed in his influential "Les Français et la république" (1956), in which he predicted confrontation between partisans of radical change and authoritarian order growing out of crisis of centrist rule. This thoughtful and dispassionate study shows how de Gaulle's quest for legitimacy rather than respect for legality manifested itself in methods by which he returned to power and executed his Algerian strategy. Final defeat is explained by de Gaulle's failure to take the lead in restructuring French economy and education and in controlling transformations of French way of life, and, above all, by his inability to infuse French society with his own archaic urge for national greatness. Morazé was on advisory committee for 1958 Constitution and was consulted by de Gaulle on Algerian policy in early years of Fifth Republic, about both of which he gives interesting inside information.

833   MORIN, EDGAR. Autocritique. Paris, R. Julliard, 1959. 285 p.

Autobiography centering on membership in P.C.F. 1941-51 and subsequent rejection of all dogmatism in understanding the human situation. Stops in 1958.

834   MORIN, EDGAR. Commune en France; la métamorphose de Plodémet. Paris, Fayard, 1967. 287 p. plates. (Le Monde sans frontières)

Sociologist's study of rural center of 1,200 inhabitants and surrounding villages in southwest Brittany as part of large-scale multidisciplinary sociological investigation. Author lived in community in 1965 observing and interviewing (methods carefully described). Work gives vivid picture of rural and small-town life in its transition from traditional agriculture to affluent society standards. Trends in agriculture, small industries, political life and personal significance of modernization are highlighted.

835   MORIN, EDGAR. Le vif du sujet. Paris, Editions du Seuil, 1969. 380 p.

Diary for Nov. 1962-Oct. 1963, without later extension or corrections. During this period Morin was active at C.N.R.S. Centre d'études sociologiques, editor of "Revue française de sociologie" and of Marxist "Arguments." Meditations on sociological, psychological, anthropological, ethical, and autobiographical topics and interesting encounters with other French intellectuals, mostly identified only by initials.

836   MORIN, EDGAR, CLAUDE LEFORT, and JEAN-MARC COUDRAY. Mai 1968: la brèche; premières réflexions sur les événements. Paris, Fayard, 1968. 142 p. (Le Monde sans frontières)

One of first interpretations (mid-June) of student revolt by sociologists who see it as a pure and prophetic uprising against all authority and against meaningless and over-bureaucratized lives, introducing new revolutionary methods of spontaneity and direct action.

837 MORIN, VIOLETTE. L'écriture de presse. Paris, Mouton, 1969. 157 p. Bibliographical footnotes.

Case study done in conjunction with Centre d'études des communications de masse on how daily and weekly press reported Khrushchev visit to France, Mar. 21-Apr. 4, 1960, with detailed analysis of "Aurore," "Figaro," "Parisien libéré," "Humanité," and "Le Monde." Selection of events to be reported and quantity of message units on events determine what reader absorbs from modern communications media.

838 MORTIMER, EDWARD. France and the Africans, 1944-1960; a political history. New York, Walker, 1969. 390 p. 3 maps (2 fold.). Bibliographical footnotes.

Parts 4 and 5 cover 1956-60. For Fourth Republic, focus is on legislative activities of French National Assembly and attitude of political parties toward colonial problems, as well as parliamentary representation of African territories and departments after implementation of 1957 "loi cadre." For Fifth Republic, work describes participation of African parliamentarians in establishment of French Community in summer 1958 and stages leading up to independence. Good maps, list of abbreviations.

839 MOSSUZ, JANINE. André Malraux et le gaullisme. Paris, A. Colin, 1970. 313 p. plates. (Cahiers de la Fondation nationale des sciences politiques, 177) Bibliography: p. 291-313.

Malraux's activities as R. P. F. propagandist and years as minister of cultural affairs. Author had five interviews with Malraux between Apr. 1967 and Jan. 1969 in addition to consulting numerous published speeches (complete list in bibliography) to determine his attitude toward French national mission, stand on Algeria, views on Communist and non-Communist French Left and on May 1968 events. There is no material on his personal relations with de Gaulle. Author concludes that his commitment to Gaullism constituted no break in his political faith.

840 MOSSUZ, JANINE. Les clubs et la politique en France. Paris, A. Colin, 1970. 128 p. (Dossiers U2. Politique, 118) Bibliography: p. 126-128.

Typology of political clubs into "pure" organizations, whose main aim is educational, and politically militant clubs, often branches of political parties. Half-page description of each of 12 "pure" and 16 "political" clubs. Information on recent club regroupings into Assises de Vichy, Apr. 1964, Fédération de la gauche démocrate et socialiste, Sept. 1965, Rencontres socialistes, Apr. 1966, and new Parti socialiste, May 1969, with documents on each. Useful table of 31 clubs listing addresses, date of foundation, membership, publications.

841 MOUCHON, JEAN-PIERRE. La crise estudiantine et les émeutes de mai 1968. Préf. de Maurice Lavarenne. Paris, Editions Ophrys, 1969. 87 p.

Unfavorable interpretation by professor at Clermont-Ferrand University of student demands and actions, for which he blames parental abdication and professors' liberalism, which encouraged thoughtless revolutionary turbulence. Police repression is minimized.

842 MOULIN, LEO. La société de demain dans l'Europe d'aujourd'hui. Paris, Denoël; Milan, Ferro, 1966. 259 p. illus. (Collection Europa una) Bibliographical footnotes.

Survey of technical progress in Europe and the undesirable concomitants of technocracy, meaningless work, undemocratic educational systems, which Moulin views hopefully. Includes statistics on French standard of living.

843 MOUNIER, MONIQUE, ed. De Gaulle vu par . . . Paris, Editions et publications premières, 1969. 170 p.

Biography of de Gaulle and characterization of his personality and political methods built on a mosaic of anecdotes, firsthand impressions, judgments expressed in press and memoirs, reflecting a multitude of opinions. Stops with Apr. 1969.

844 MOURIN, MAXIME. Les relations franco-soviétiques (1917-1967). Paris, Payot, 1967. 372 p. (Etudes et documents Payot) Bibliography: p. 365-367.

Last 35 pages on improved Franco-Soviet relations as a result of de Gaulle's initiatives.

845 MOUTON, CLAUDE. La contrerévolution en Algérie. Chiré-en-Montreuil, Diffusion de la pensée française, 1972. 675 p.

History of "counterrevolution" in Algeria, 1953-62, as seen by a participant in the movement, a close collaborator of Robert Martel, proponent of a Catholic monarchist French Algerian movement. Details on Martel's Union française nord-africaine (1956-57), origins and activities of General Chassin's Mouvement du 13 mai (MP 13), and other political manipulations prior and posterior to May 1958 in Algeria, Martel's intervention in Barricades and Generals' Putsch, ties and clashes with O. A. S. leadership. Leaflets of movement, correspondence with Salan, Chateau-Jobert in appendices.

846 MÜNSTER, ARNO. Paris brennt; die Mai-Revolution 1968: Analysen, Fakten, Dokumente. Vorwort: Claude Roy. Fotos: Inge Weth. Frankfurt a. M., Heinrich Heine Verlag, 1968. 181 p. illus. (Streit-Zeit-Bücher, 1) Bibliographical footnotes.

May events seen through eyes of participant in French student groups, with background on student revolt. Interesting material on police repression and problems of French university. Author is member of Sozialistischer Deutscher Studentenbund.

847 MURY, GILBERT. La société de répression. . . . Paris, Editions universitaires, 1969. 335 p. (Citoyens, 2-3. Essai) Bibliographical footnotes. ML

Major effort to apply Marxist concepts and critique of advanced industrial society (société unifunctionelle, société de processus) of East and West, in which dehumanization has extended from production relations to entire human existence. This dehumanization serves to explain student revolt and worker explosion. P. C. F.'s reformist role within system is emphasized and grand alliance between students and workers advocated, party centralism rejected at present stage of social development. Author left P. C. F. in 1956, active in pro-Chinese Communist Mouvement communiste français, participated in revolutionary groups preparing 1968 revolt.

848 MUTH, HANNS PETER. French agriculture and the political integration of Western Europe; toward "an ever closer Union among the European Peoples." Leyden, A. W. Sijthoff, 1970. 320 p. (European aspects, Series C: Politics, no. 22) Bibliography: p. 291-316.

Stages in transformation of French farmers' attitudes toward Common Market and European integration from hostility to outright support, both as individuals and as members of agricultural pressure groups. Interesting section on French farmers' stand during 1965 E. E. C. crisis. Author interviewed agricultural and E. E. C. experts. Good list of agricultural journals in bibliography.

849 NATAF, ANDRE. La révolution anarchiste. Paris, A. Balland, 1968. 225 p.

Lengthy conclusion of this work on anarchist experiences and thought of 19th and 20th century shows anarchist contributions to current libertarian criticism of state and institutions and efforts to organize society from below.

850 NATANSON, JACQUES, and ANTOINE PROST. La révolution scolaire. Avec la collaboration de René Fromageat et Roger Lépiney. Paris, Editions ouvrières, 1963. 163 p. diagrs., tables. ML

Collective work based on research of Syndicat général de l'éducation nationale on education explosion, concentrating on reforms of secondary education, social obstacles to its democratization, and educators' own resistance to expansion of "common trunk" of instruction, new objectives for primary education, pedagogic innovations in individual areas.

851 N'DIAYE, JEAN PIERRE. Enquête sur les étudiants noirs en France. Paris, Editions "Réalités africaines," 1962. 315 p.

1961 interviews and questionnaires administered to sample of 310 persons concerning life of African students in France, adaptation to French conditions, contacts with other Africans there, personality of students, attitude toward France and own country. Excerpts from interviews and statistical results of questionnaires. Author is Senegalese-born, French-trained sociologist.

852 LA NEF (periodical). Les communismes. Paris, J. Tallandier, 1968. 199 p. (Its Cahier n.s., no. 35, octobre-décembre 1968)

Worldwide survey of Communist parties, with chapter by Georges Mamy on narrow path between revolutionary ideology and legality followed by P.C.F., particularly in 1968.

853 LA NEF (periodical). Dix années de gaullisme. Paris, J. Tallandier, 1968. 159 p. (Its Cahier n.s., no. 33, février-avril 1968)

Individual contributions assessing changes in de Gaulle's political methods, his principal objectives, concepts, and achievements, relations with opposition (articles by P. M. de la Gorce, R. Stephane, J. R. Tournoux, P. Viansson-Ponté, J. Ferniot), and institutional, military, economic controversies of Fifth Republic (J. Fauvet, C. Krief, J. Planchais, P. Bauchard). Of special interest is G. Vedel's prognosis on political institutions after de Gaulle's retirement, which does not anticipate May 1968 crisis (nor do any other articles) but does come close to predicting eventual turn of events.

854 LA NEF (periodical). Les "gauchistes." Paris, J. Tallandier, 1972. 197 p. (Its Cahier n.s. no. 48, juin-septembre 1972)

Individual contributions on antecedents and role of revolutionary groups May 1968 and nuclei of "gauchisme" in evidence since that time: the Christian radical Left, Trotskyists, Maoists, Gauche prolétarienne, Vive la révolution, anarchists, and Internationale situationniste. Press organs, confrontations between these groups and P.C.F., trade unions are described, as well as fate of revolutionary student movements.

855 NEGRIN, JEAN PAUL. Le Conseil d'Etat et la vie publique en France depuis 1958. . . . Paris, Presses universitaires de France, 1968. 173 p. (Travaux et mémoires de la Faculté de droit et des sciences économiques d'Aix-en-Provence) Bibliography: p. 159-165.

Conseil d'Etat's role under Fifth Republic as reservoir of top-level civil servants in ministries, central administration, public enterprises, international agencies, the degree of its influence and limitations of its interventive power as consultative and judicial organ. Author feels that Conseil d'Etat is more influential in Fifth Republic as a result of stronger executive.

856 NEWHOUSE, JOHN. De Gaulle and the Anglo-Saxons. New York, Viking Press, 1970. 371 p.

History of Franco-British and Franco-American relations from de Gaulle's return to power to his retirement, as viewed by men in Washington who had to deal with him. Among topics are problems related to N.A.T.O., nuclear weapons sharing, de Gaulle's maneuvering between the two blocs.

857 NICHOLS, PETER, and PIERRE VIBES. Vocabulaire anglais-français, français-anglais de terminologie économique et juridique. Préf. de Pierre Vellas. Paris, Librairie générale de droit et de jurisprudence, R. Pichon et R. Durand-Auzias, 1971. 104 p. (Droit de la coopération économique et sociale internationale)

Separate list of terms for law and economics. For juridical expressions, alphabetical arrangement by English terms, with French equivalent in adjacent column, bilingual explanations, inverse for economic section and complementary index.

858 NIEL, MATHILDE. Le mouvement étudiant, ou La révolution en marche; signification du mouvement étudiant contemporain. Paris, Courrier du livre, 1968. 127 p. (Collection L'Université permanente) Bibliographical footnotes.

Sympathetic presentation of ideas underlying student movement: need for change in mentality, liberation from dogma and revolutionary myths, autonomy and dialogue, enjoyment of the present through creativity and spontaneity, abolition of distinction between work and leisure, pursuit of human solidarity without conflict or hierarchic distinctions. Author fears misunderstanding of student movement not only from authoritarian and technocratic elements but from dogmatic revolutionary Left.

859 NOEL, LEON. Comprendre de Gaulle. Paris, Plon, 1972. 297 p.

Reminiscences of inner-circle Gaullist, already prominent as diplomat before World War II, on encounters with de Gaulle before 1958. There is no material on years of service as head of Fifth Republic Conseil constitutionnel. Main part of work draws on personal memories of meetings with de Gaulle and published literature to extract quintessential features of de Gaulle's personality which made him a great statesman. Among traits highlighted are his will power, realism combined with vision, deep religious faith, extensive culture and literary skill; aspects of his political philosophy treated are his special version of nationalism, respect for legitimacy and popular support, profound pacificism, all of which contradict legends about de Gaulle's thirst for personal and national power. Final section discusses specific aspects of his international and European policies, with separate chapter on Israel.

860 NOONAN, LOWELL G. France: the politics of continuity in change. New York, Holt, Rinehart and Winston, 1970. xv, 528 p. maps. (Modern comparative politics series) Bibliography: p. 456-407; bibliographical footnotes.

Informative, up-to-date survey of main facets of French society and Fifth Republic institutions, following pattern set for other countries. Chapters on demographic, social, and economic elements of French society and recent technological changes; methods of socialization via education, trends in youth attitudes, political opinion; political families and communications media; national and local administration; political parties, unification problems of Left, Gaullists after de Gaulle; electoral process and Fifth Republic election results; pressure groups; policy-making structures and examples of Fifth Republic policy-making; judicial system; Gaullist foreign policy; Fifth Republic after Apr. 1969. Good bibliographies after each chapter. Text of 1958 Constitution and amendments in English.

861 NOSTITZ, SIEGFRIED VON. Algerisches Tagebuch 1960-1962. Düsseldorf, Econ Verlag, 1971. 266 p.

Personal account of West German consul in Algeria, Oct. 1960 to Dec. 1962, describing contacts with French officials, foreign journalists, diplomatic accommodations with independent Algerian government.

862 Notre arme c'est la grève. Travail réalisé par un collectif de militants du comité d'action qui ont participé à la grève de Renault-Cléon du 15 mai au 17 juin 1968. Paris, F. Maspéro, 1968. 128 p. (Cahiers libres, 137)

Thirty-four-day strike of 5,000 workers at Renault automobile plant, documented by leaflets of student-worker groups, administrative directives, newspapers, showing clash between student groups and C.G.T., more neutral role of C.F.D.T. Last part records July 1968 round-table discussion of Cléon trade unionists on effectiveness, political character of strike, relations with students, usefulness of factory-wide Comités d'action.

863 NOURISSIER, FRANÇOIS. The French. Translated from the French by Adrienne Foulke. New York, Knopf, 1968. vi, 309 p.

Journalist's lighthearted and optimistic guide to France of the 1960's, with good chapters on current French family life and education, attitudes toward foreigners.

864 NUNGESSER, ROLAND. Pour une société nouvelle; la révolution qu'il faut faire. Paris, Plon, 1970. 123 p.

Gaullist view on crisis of modern civilization, as exemplified by May 1968, for which neither capitalism nor Communism can provide the answer. New humanist and Christian values are identified, reforms proposed to increase democratic participation in economy, greater local autonomy, civic sense. Author succeeded Missoffe as Ministre de la jeunesse at end of May 1968.

865 OBRADOVITCH, MILETA. Les effets de la dévaluation française de 1958. Paris, Editions d'organisation, 1970. 197 p. (Rythmes économiques. Série Mouvements économiques) Bibliography: p. 193-197.

Effects on foreign trade, domestic price and wage level, savings, budget deficit, and general economic activity 1959-62. Devaluation is presented as turning point for French economy, permitting integration in international trade, economic expansion, monetary stability.

866 Ocherki rabochego dvisheniia vo Frantsii (1917-1967). Otv. redaktor V. V. Liubimova. Moskva, "Mysl'," 1968. 438 p. Bibliographical footnotes.

Last 100 pages deal with trade union activities during Fifth Republic and unification efforts of socialist and Communist parties 1965-67.

867 OELGART, BERND. Idéologues et idéologies de la Nouvelle gauche. Paris, Union générale d'éditions, 1970. 190 p. (Collection Le Monde en 10/18, no. 467) Includes bibliographies.

Only French representative among ideologists of New Left is Louis Althusser, who maintained loyalty to P.C.F. in May 1968 despite following among students.

868 Onze ans de malheur. Publié sous la direction de Henry Coston. Paris, Lectures françaises, 1970. 230 p. (Lectures françaises, numéro spécial, avril 1970) Includes bibliographical references.

Contributions by individual authors arranged to give chronological view of failures and betrayals of Gaullist government, amounting to a political history of Fifth Republic. Stress on covert influence of big business and press. Interesting information on opponents to 1958 constitution on both ends of political spectrum, position of press in 1965 presidential elections, impact of de Gaulle's policy toward Israel on hitherto favorable sections of the population, contributing to May 1968 events and loss of Apr. 1969 referendum.

869 Options humanistes. Paris, Editions Economie et humanisme, Editions ouvrières, 1968. 216 p. (Collection Economie humaine) Bibliographical footnotes.

Work honoring recently deceased sociologist and founder of Economie et humanisme, Father Lebret (see no. 719). Purpose is to redefine "classic" humanism and replace it with humanism taking into account new knowledge of man and society gained by social sciences, technical advances, rejection of many traditional values. Contributions by Pierre Viau (new approach to humanism as technique of intervention in human society through constructive challenges and dialogue), Robert Caillot (action research), Michel Cornation (contributions of social sciences and philosophy), Edmond Blanc (specific option: democratic participation), Jean-Marie Albertini (satisfaction of human needs in affluent societies), and Alain Birou (aid to underdeveloped countries). Despite Catholic orientation of authors, religion is not used as basis for humanist project, though only humanist options are considered compatible with Christ's teaching.

870 Organigrammes des institutions françaises. [Par] G. Dupuis [et al.]. Préf. de Georges Vedel. Paris, A. Colin, 1971. 256 p. diagrs. (Collection U. Série Droit public interne)

Institutions diagrammatically presented are: French constitutions, 1789-1962; organizations (political parties, trade unions, professional and business groups, press, religious groups); legislative power (National Assembly), executive power (cabinet of Chaban-Delmas, June 1969, individual ministries and secretariats); local and regional administration (new regions, Paris administration), typical mechanisms of state intervention in economy and flow of control; judicial institutions; typical large-scale public and private institutions (Electricité de France, Air France, Treasury, Tax Office); and French diplomatic representation. Concluding chart on European Communities.

871 ORMESSON, WLADIMIR, COMTE D'. Présence du général de Gaulle. Paris, Plon, 1971. 199 p.

Fifth Republic diplomat's essays on de Gaulle's foreign policy, comparisons between de Gaulle and Pétain, de Gaulle and Lyautey, defense of de Gaulle's Algerian policy, followed by reprints of 1961-70 newspaper articles, the final ones on de Gaulle's retirement and death.

872 OUSSET, JEAN. Marxisme et révolution. Paris, Montalza, 1970. 283 p.

Revised edition of "Marxisme et léninisme" (1958) arguing that earlier analysis of Marxist subversion had not become outdated because of weakening of Moscow's influence, since basic nature of movement remained hatred of established order and dialectic method, leading to permanent contestation. Preface and postface relate Marxism to May 1968 and independent Communist groups, which are still dangerous varieties of "Marxism-Leninism." Numerous quotations on Communism from conservative Catholic works, whose views are accepted by author.

873 L'ouvrier français en 1970; enquête nationale auprès de 1116 ouvriers d'industrie. [Par] Gérard Adam [et al.]. Paris, A. Colin, 1970. 275 p. illus. (Fondation nationale des sciences politiques. Travaux et recherches de science politique, 13) Includes bibliographical references.

Analysis based on questionnaires sent out summer 1969 to weighted national sample of French (not immigrant) workers from major industries, unskilled, skilled, and foremen, male and female, young and old. Topics investigated are trade union structures and worker attitudes toward them, electoral behavior, religious behavior, social mobility, complemented by a tentative worker typology. Summaries of questionnaire results and statistics.

874 PADO, DOMINIQUE. Les 50 jours d'Alain Poher; l'intérim, la campagne présidentielle. Paris, Denoël, 1969. 305 p. plates, ports. Includes bibliography.

Political biography of Poher, elected president of Senate in 1966, interim president of Republic and then candidate for that office. Campaign begun May 12, 1969, is described in some detail, with chronology. Author is himself a senator. Texts of Poher speeches Apr. 28, May 14, 1969, in appendix.

875 PAILLAT, CLAUDE. Archives secrètes 1968-69; les coulisses d'une année terrible. Paris, Denoël, 1969. 473 p.

Political history of events in Paris, complemented by background material and sidelights: preliminary explosions in other universities, role of revolutionary groups, explosions in Strasbourg, Nantes, and Caen, special crises (journalists, medical schools, Jesuits, Polytechnic), for which original documentation is presented. Concludes with political, economic, and educational sequels to crisis.

876 PAILLAT, CLAUDE. Vingt ans qui déchirèrent la France. II: La liquidation 1954-1962. Paris, R. Laffont, 1972. 796 p. plates.

Political history of "liquidation" of French Empire, the second volume of which is almost entirely devoted to the Algerian war. The main episodes--for all of which authors draws not only on published memoirs but on his own inside information as journalist with access to military figures, politicians favoring French Algeria--are links between Algerian crisis and de Gaulle's return to power, development of de Gaulle's self-determination policy, negotiations with Si Salah, plots surrounding Generals' Putsch, the organization of the O.A.S., and the mad violence of the last months before independence. Thread running through account of intrigues is the desire to prove that the description of events, 1958-62, as presented by de Gaulle in his "Le renouveau" (1970) is contradicted by the facts, and that his stand on Algeria was motivated solely by his personal ambition. Many previously unpublished letters, private communications cited in full. Good name index but no bibliography.

877 PAILLET, MARC. Table rase, 3 mai-30 juin 1968. Paris, R. Laffont, 1968. 251 p. (Collection Contestation)

Interpretation of events from point of view of non-Communist Left, particularly F.G.D.S., of which author is active member. Despite sympathy for student aims, halfhearted reaction of P.C.F. and F.G.D.S. toward revolution was unavoidable. Causes for lack of massive labor support are presented, ideologies of revolutionary Left (Maoist, Trotskyist, Castroist) are lucidly examined, with conclusion that there may be hope for liberalization of Soviet Communism (written before Czech invasion) but that French Left has no choice but to reject violence and choose reformist path.

878 PALACIO, LEO. Les pieds-noirs dans le monde. Préf. par François Missoffe. Paris, J. Didier, 1968. 224 p. plates. Bibliography: p. 219-220.

Exodus of French Algerians to southern France, Corsica, Spain, Canada, Argentina, and Israel. Influx into France is described in detail, as well as governmental and private efforts to integrate pieds-noirs into French community and compensate them for lost property. Missoffe was minister in charge of repatriates in 1963. As of 1968, there were about 1,400,000 repatriates in France. Appendix lists all laws, decrees, etc. concerning repatriates and repatriate associations.

879 PALMIER, JEAN-MICHEL. Wilhelm Reich; essai sur la naissance du Freudo-marxisme. Paris, Union générale d'éditions, 1969. 192 p. (Collection Le Monde en 10/18, no. 400) Includes bibliography.

Life and thought of Austro-Marxist psychoanalyst, with references to the diffusion and acceptance of his ideas May 1968, particularly those on sexual revolution.

880 PAOLETTI, ODETTE, and ODILE DANIEL. Périodiques et publications en série concernant les sciences sociales et humaines, liste de reproductions disponibles dans le commerce (microformes et réimpressions). Periodicals and serials concerning the social sciences and humanities, current list of available reproductions (microforms and reprints). Paris, Maison des sciences de l'homme, Service bibliothèque-documentation, 1966. 2 v. (xxiv, 684 p.).

Alphabetical listing, completed July 1966, of social science periodicals (not newspapers or government documents). Each entry gives title, place of publication, years reproduced, reproduction process, publisher of reproduction, current prices. List of organizations selling reproductions. Most French serials obtainable through Association pour la conservation et la reproduction photographique de la presse (see no. 64 for its catalogues). Vol. 1: A-J; Vol. 2: K-Z.

881 PAPON, MAURICE. Le gaullisme ou la loi de l'effort. Paris, Flammarion, 1973. 260 p. (Textes politiques)

Former Paris police prefect, industrialist, U.D.R. deputy and treasurer, reviews Gaullist heritage with respect to domestic policy. Reflections concern principles of political action, economic doctrine, planning, participation of workers in industry, administrative reform, education, strategy for economic and technological development, demographic and environmental policy.

882 PARANQUE, REGIS. Le malaise français. Paris, Editions du Seuil, 1970. 206 p.

Journalist from Catholic press analyzes weaknesses of French demography, social psychology, unrealistic attitudes of Left, and incapacity of state mechanisms in both the Fourth and the Fifth Republic to carry out necessary reforms and correct disorders of economy, all of which combined acts to block French society and create "malaise" of its citizens.

883 PARIS DE BOLLARDIERE, JACQUES MARIE ROCH ANDRE. Bataille d'Alger, bataille de l'homme. 2e éd. Paris, Desclée de Brouwer, 1972. 167 p.

Autobiographical notes, whose main interest lies in ex-general's experiences as commander of air force reserve unit in Algeria July 1956-Jan. 1957, at which time he vainly protested against Massu's use of torture in combatting F.L.N. terrorism in Algiers, and was forced to leave Algerian command. (For Massu's version of this episode, see no. 780.) Having resigned from army after Apr. 1961, he assumed role in adult education, which is also described here.

884 PARIS. BIBLIOTHEQUE NATIONALE. Repertoire des bibliothèques et organismes de documentation. Paris, 1971. 733 p. ML

Revised edition on 1970 status of French libraries and documentation centers. Like the 1963 edition (for full description, see French Fifth Republic Bibliography, 1, no. 765), listing is divided into Paris region and rest of France, with index by areas of specialization at end of volume. There are now 3,210 libraries in all of France, 1,315 in Paris area.

885 PARIS. INSTITUT CHARLES DE GAULLE. Bibliographie des ouvrages français sur Charles de Gaulle. Paris, avril 1973. 67 p. mimeographed.

Alphabetical listing of several hundred books about de Gaulle and Gaullism by recently founded organization devoted to research and documentation on de Gaulle. Preliminary version, entitled "Liste des ouvrages publiés en France sur le Général de Gaulle" (Sept. 1972), is also available.

886 PARIS. INSTITUT CHARLES DE GAULLE. Liste des ouvrages publiés en Union Soviétique sur le Général de Gaulle. Liste arrêtée en mars 1971. Paris, 1971. 7, 2 l. mimeographed.

List of 21 articles on de Gaulle and Franco-Soviet relations appearing in Soviet press during 1960's and at time of his death. For other Institute material, see Author Index.

887 PARIS. UNIVERSITE. La Sorbonne par elle-même, mai-juin 1968. Documents rassemblés et présentés par Jean-Claude et Michelle Perrot, Madeleine Rebérioux [et] Jean Maitron. Paris, Editions ouvrières, 1968. 414 p. (Mouvement social, no. 64, juillet-septembre 1968)

Collection of texts, introduced, dated, and cited in full, issued at Sorbonne between May 3 and June 16 and published by student groups, the Assemblées générales of different disciplines, and Comités d'action. Part 1: background texts (pre-May 1968); Part 2: response to events such as police at Sorbonne, student occupation, reflux; Part 3: life inside occupied Sorbonne--appeals, reports, motions; Part 4: reform proposals in social sciences. Careful indices listing groups signing texts, organizations cited. Authors are Sorbonne faculty members.

888 Paris, Mai 1968. Dokumentation [von] Gisela Mandel [et al.]. [München, 1968] 136 p.

Gisela Mandel's eyewitness account of student revolt, texts of selected appeals by student, worker, and political groups (German translation), and very small-scale reproduction of dozens of posters. Includes Sartre interview, June 1968, with "Nouvel observateur" reporter, in which he defends students.

889 PARIS-MATCH (periodical). De Gaulle, 1890/1970. Paris, 1970. 168 p. chiefly illus. (part col.), ports.

Political biography, excerpts from published works, final section on funeral rites in Colombey and Paris. Ample illustrations. Includes record with following speeches: June 18, 1940, June 6, 1944, Aug. 25, 1944, June 16, 1946, May 19, 1958, Sept. 16, 1959, Jan. 29, 1960, Apr. 23, 1961, Sept. 5, 1962, Sept. 1, 1966, July 24, 1967, May 30, 1968, and Apr. 25, 1969.

890 PARODI, JEAN-LUC. Les rapports entre le législatif et l'exécutif sous la Ve République, 1958-1962. Paris, A. Colin, 1972. 224 p. tables, diagrs. (Fondation nationale des sciences politiques. Travaux et recherches de science politique, 17)

Revised and expanded edition covers entire first legislative period through Oct. 1962. Includes National Assembly debate on confirmation of Pompidou, Apr. 1962, all censure motions, with names of individual signers, composition of parliamentary groups and commissions. Many long debates are reproduced in full. Public opinion polls on political institutions, Feb. 1959-Oct. 1962. Operation of Senate is also covered. For original edition, see French Fifth Republic Bibliography, 1, no. 1362.

891 PARODI, MAURICE. L'économie et la société française de 1945 à 1970. Paris, A. Colin, 1971. 374 p. tables, diagrs., maps. (Collection U. Série "Sciences économiques et gestion") Includes bibliographies.

Part 1: economic growth, 1945-70; Part 2: major sectors of economy (agriculture, industry, services); Part 3: economic disequilibria (urbanism, regional inequalities, vulnerability to foreign trade movements); and Part 4: structure of French society, inequalities of income distribution. Good up-to-date statistics, bibliographies.

892 PARTI COMMUNISTE FRANÇAIS. Pour le bonheur et l'avenir de nos enfants; recueil de propositions et réalisations du P. C. F. en faveur de la femme, de la famille et de l'enfant. Paris, 1967. 59 p.

Social reform program specifically focused on improvement of women's conditions, advancement of family life, better child care. Includes bills presented by P. C. F. deputies in National Assembly in these areas and accomplishments of Communist-controlled municipalities (e.g., Nanterre).

893 PARTI COMMUNISTE FRANÇAIS. Programme du Parti communiste français, élections législatives, juin 1968. Paris, 1968. 14 p. (Publié dans le no. 166-167, mai-juin 1968, de "Economie et politique.")

For additional campaign material issued June 1968, see French Fifth Republic Collection (no. 483), Box 40.

894 PARTI COMMUNISTE FRANÇAIS. COMITE CENTRAL. [L'union pour une France démocratique indépendante, pacifique et prospère.] Rapport du Comité central, présenté par Waldeck Rochet, Secrétaire général du Parti communiste français. Paris, 1967. 83 p. (Supplément aux "Cahiers du communisme," no. 1, janvier 1967)

Report to P. C. F.'s 18th Congress at Levallois, by party's new secretary general discusses agreement with F. G. D. S. on electoral alliance for Mar. 1967 legislative elections.

895 PARTI COMMUNISTE FRANÇAIS. COMITE CENTRAL. CONFERENCE, IVRY, OCT. 1968. Rapport présenté par Gaston Plissonnier, membre du Bureau politique. Discours de Waldeck Rochet, Sécrétaire général du Parti. Communiqué. Lettre de démission de Jeannette Thorez-Vermeersch. Déclaration de Roger Garaudy. Résolution. Paris, 1968. 22 p. (Supplément à "L'Humanité," no. 7517 du 23 octobre 1968. Dossier, Comité central d'Ivry, 20, 21 octobre 1968)

This is response of P. C. F. Comité central and Bureau politique to Soviet military intervention in Czechoslovakia, Aug. 22, 1968. Speeches by Gaston Plissonnier and Waldeck Rochet discuss internal controversies on this issue and present letter of Jeannette Thorez-Vermeersch and declaration of Roger Garaudy (Oct. 21) on both sides of issue.

896 PARTI COMMUNISTE FRANÇAIS. COMITE CENTRAL. CONFERENCE, DEC. 1968. Manifeste du Parti communiste français. Pour une démocratie avancée, pour une France socialiste! Paris, Editions sociales, 1969. 77 p.

Reaffirmation, in wake of May events, of socialist and revolutionary principles expressed at 1967 P. C. F. congress, and assertion that they alone are suitable for an "advanced political and economic democracy." May 1969 introduction by Waldeck Rochet links this manifesto with impending presidential election.

897 PARTI COMMUNISTE FRANÇAIS. COMMISSION CENTRALE DE TRAVAIL PARMI LES FEMMES. Les communistes et la condition de la femme. Etude rédigée par Yvonne Dumont. Paris, Editions sociales, 1970. 175 p.

Historical statements on place of women (Marx, Engels, Lenin, Bebel, Zetkin, Thorez) are combined with statistics on women's 1968 working conditions, family life. Moderate stand on questions of sexual liberation is backed up by texts of Communist mentors. Includes Feb. 1968 resolution of conference on women's working conditions.

898 PARTI COMMUNISTE FRANÇAIS. CONGRES NATIONAL. Rapports, interventions et documents. 18e-19e Congrès, 1967, 1970. 2 v. illus., ports. (Published as supplementary issues of "Cahiers du communisme," 1967, 1970.)

Complete stenographic record of proceedings. George Marchais' report at 19th Congress, Nanterre, Feb. 1970, reviews party's stand since 1967, with discussions on collaboration with other political parties, intra-Communist splits (Maoists, exclusion of Garaudy).

FOR ADDITIONAL WORKS BY AND ABOUT PARTI COMMUNISTE FRANÇAIS, SEE AUTHOR INDEX AND SUBJECT INDEX

899   PARTI REPUBLICAIN RADICAL ET RADICAL-SOCIALISTE. CONGRES. 63rd, MARSEILLE, 1966. 63e congrès national, Marseille, 18 et 19 novembre 1966. (Bulletin d'information radical-socialiste, no. 62, janvier 1967)

Texts of speeches and resolutions, not complete congress record.

900   PARTI REPUBLICAIN RADICAL ET RADICAL-SOCIALISTE. CONGRES. 64th, TOULOUSE, 1967. 64e congrès national, Toulouse, 15, 16 et 17 décembre 1967. (Bulletin d'information radical-socialiste, no. 70, avril 1968)

901   PARTI REPUBLICAIN RADICAL ET RADICAL-SOCIALISTE. CONGRES. 64th, TOULOUSE, 1967. Discours, 17 décembre 1967. (Bulletin d'information radical-socialiste, no. 71, mai 1968)

François Mitterrand's speech on Fédération de la gauche démocrate et socialiste, to which Radical party belonged at that time.

902   PARTI REPUBLICAIN RADICAL ET RADICAL-SOCIALISTE. CONGRES. 65th, PARIS, 1968. 65e congrès national, Paris, le 22, 23 et 24 novembre 1968. (Bulletin d'information radical-socialiste, no. 76, janvier-février 1969)

Includes statement of withdrawal from Fédération de la gauche démocrate et socialiste, which party joined in 1965.

903   PARTISANS (periodical). Le mouvement des lycées. Paris, F. Maspéro, 1969. 176 p. (Its No. 49, septembre-octobre 1969)

Individual articles on: pre-May 1968 political activity in lycées with Comités Vietnam national, founding of first Comités d'action lycéens, explosion of politization May 1968, and recent decline. Documents on debates within national C. A. L. movement, case study of Lycée Henri IV, Paris, May 1968-May 1969.

904   PARTISANS (periodical). Ouvriers, étudiants, un seul combat. Paris, F. Maspéro, 1968. 260 p. (Its No. 42, mai-juin 1968)

Mainly chronology of events, May 3-June 13, 1968, complemented by short citations from press, texts of leaflets. Articles on Mouvement du 22 mars, Comités d'action lycéens, Comités de liaison étudiant-ouvrier-paysan, with related documents on these groups.

905   PASQUIER, ALBERT. Où va la région? Paris, Dunod, 1970. ix, 141 p. maps. (Dunod Actualité) ML

Background of Apr. 1969 and controversial issues relating to regional reform after voters' negative decision on referendum.

906   PASSERON, ANDRE. De Gaulle 1958-1969. Paris, Bordas, 1972. 319 p. (Collection "Présence politique") Bibliography: p. 291-311.

Reference work on de Gaulle and his 11 years in power. Contains: (1) excerpts from de Gaulle's statements arranged chronologically within topics, with index to certain key words; (2) de Gaulle's political actions (his agenda); (3) de Gaulle's governments (original team, changes over 11 years, lists of persons in different ministries and list of personalities and their government role); (4) censure motions by parliament; (5) table of press conferences, radio-TV addresses, travels inside and outside France; (6) elections and referenda; (7) assassination attempts; (8) 23 Gaullist organizations presently operative, with addresses, publications; (9) rough bibliography of over 200 works on de Gaulle, Gaullism, Fifth Republic; and (10) Passeron's interview with de Gaulle May 1966 in which he discussed his political methods and attitudes.

907   PAUPERT, JEAN MARIE. De Gaulle est-il chrétien? Lettres ouvertes à des chrétiens gaullistes, suivies de Lettres ouvertes à des chrétiens antigaullistes. Paris, R. Laffont, 1969. 216 p. (Libertés, 77) Bibliographical footnotes.

Open letters composed Oct. 1966 to June 1968. Among Gaullists with emphatically Catholic commitments are Edmond Michelet, François Mauriac, Father Bruckberger, whom these letters challenge to disprove that de Gaulle the public figure (his personal religious faith is set aside) and Gaullism as a political philosophy are in direct conflict with Christian ethics in that the "religion of France," of which de Gaulle sees himself as high priest, replaces the religion of Christ. This attack is illustrated by reference to military and foreign policy, attitudes during Resistance period and since return to power. Letters to Christian opponents of the government date from May-June 1968 and virulently attack Catholic Left's support of revolutionary violence, raising many points that coincide with P. C. F.'s criticism of "gauchisme."

908   Pédagogie et crise de la bourgeoisie. Paris, F. Maspéro, 1969. 83 p. (Cahiers "Rouge." Documents de formation communiste, no. 13)

Demythification of pedagogic reforms undertaken since May 1968 and attack on cooperative spirit of main teacher organizations, P. C. F., and P. S. U. with government reforms. Lack of realism of anti-authoritarian pedagogic movements is also analyzed. Ligue communiste's support for "Ecole emancipée," minority tendency within F. E. N., is justified.

909   PENDAR, KENNETH WHITTEMORE. Adventure in diplomacy: the emergence of General de Gaulle in North Africa. [English ed. with new material.] London, Cassell, 1966. xviii, 382 p. 12 plates (incl. ports.), map, table.

Revised edition of American diplomat's 1945 account of his mission to North Africa 1941-42 and futile U. S. opposition to de Gaulle's assuming control of postwar France. 1966 epilogue reaffirms view that British support of de Gaulle was a mistake.

910   PENENT, JACQUES-ARNAUD. Un printemps rouge et noir. Paris, R. Laffont, 1968. 184 p. (Contestation)

"Combat" journalist sympathetic to May 1968 revolt refutes conspiracy theories, showing that all incriminated groups were unprepared for events and giving own explanation of origins, spirit, and meaning of revolt with quotations from his own pieces in "Combat."

911   Permanence et changement dans le système des partis français. Débat introduit par Maurice Duverger et François Goguel. Paris, Association française de science politique, 1967. 41 l. (Entretiens du samedi, no. 8, juin 1968) ML

Debate held shortly after Mar. 1967 legislative elections. Goguel's thesis is that Gaullist party rather than actual centrist parties represents middle of political spectrum, while center has votes of traditional Right. Duverger defends tendency toward bipolarism, sees it as more advanced in public opinion than in party machinery, and views Gaullism as unifier of Right, Center-Right, and some elements of Center-Left. Bipolar influence of presidential election is pronounced, with P. C. F. becoming less messianic and less threatening in the eyes of voters. Among other speakers are Stanley Hoffmann and Léo Hamon, who take issue with Duverger.

912   PERMANENT ORGANIZATION FOR AFRO-ASIAN PEOPLES' SOLIDARITY. La révolution algérienne. Le Caire, R. A. U., Organisation pour la solidarité des peuples afro-asiatiques, 1962. 108 p. (Publications afro-asiatiques, 3)

F. L. N. stand, as of late 1961, on Saharan question and European minorities, reactions to de Gaulle's Algerian policy. Lists U. N. resolutions on Algeria and countries recognizing Gouvernement provisoire de la République algérienne.

913   PEROTTINO, SERGE, ed. Roger Garaudy et le marxisme du XXe siècle; présentation, choix de textes, biographie, bibliographie. Paris, Editions Seghers, 1969. 190 p. ports., facsims. (Philosophes de tous les temps, 55) Includes bibliography.

Sympathetic analysis of main themes in Garaudy's work (aesthetics, religion, models of socialism) followed by anthology of his writings. Detailed biography and list of works. Garaudy was P. C. F. deputy 1945-62, founder of Centre d'études et de recherches marxistes, organizer of Semaine de la pensée marxiste, as well as philosophy professor, beginning his break with P. C. F. after invasion of Czechoslovakia.

914   PERRAULT, GILLES. Du service secret au gouvernement invisible. Paris, Le Pavillon, 1970. 83 p.

Printed version of lecture and answers to questions at Brussels Cercle d'éducation populaire on cancerous growth of secret services during Cold War years. Infiltration of American secret services in France emphasized.

915   PERRAULT, GILLES. L'erreur. Paris, Fayard, 1971. 225 p.

Cloak-and-dagger story of Service de documentation extérieure et de contre-espionnage agent Eugène Rousseau accused of and condemned for leaking secret documents to Yugoslav agents during his term as attaché in Belgrade 1957-59. In the process of explaining this miscarriage of justice, author reveals intricacies of French secret service operations inside and outside the country.

916   PERRET, JACQUES. Inquiète Sorbonne. Paris, Hachette, 1968. 128 p. (Classiques Hachette) Bibliographical footnotes.

Critical view of events at Nanterre and Sorbonne by professor of linguistics who has participated in reform efforts. Existing institutions and government policies are defended, though revolt is in part blamed on confusion caused by recent government reforms, which are nevertheless steps in the right direction. Answers to criticisms of university system (undemocratic nature, immobilism) and own suggestions for selection of students, pre-salary, adaptation to national needs, in preference to unrestricted admission, university autonomy, politization of education. Interesting passages on personal relations with students before and during May 1968.

917   PERROUX, FRANÇOIS. Aliénation et société industrielle. Paris, Gallimard, 1970. 183 p. (Collection Idées, 206)

Discussion of Marxist concept of alienation, showing limited usefulness of class concept for 20th century alienation, which is independent of class or property relations and can thus occur in socialist as well as capitalist societies. Possibility of reducing, though not eliminating, alienation lies in humanizing institutions by dialogue, which prevents men from seeing one another as objects both within a given society and between societies. Positive contribution of modern technology lies in its facilitating "collective creation" by collective action.

918   PERROUX, FRANÇOIS. François Perroux interroge Herbert Marcuse . . . qui répond. Paris, Aubier-Montaigne, 1969. 211 p. (Tiers-monde et développement)

Sociologist's presentation of Marcuse's philosophy based on his writings through mid-1969. Perroux's book reproduces course taught by him at Collège de France in spring 1969, in which he also criticized Marcuse for inciting students to achieve revolution by total rejection of contemporary society rather than by setting specific goals, to which they can apply rationality and energy. Perroux doubts that this path can lead to fruitful revolution or help alleviate underdeveloped countries' misery. Brief reply by Marcuse.

919   PESQUET, JACQUES. Des Soviets à Saclay? Premier bilan d'une expérience de conseils ouvriers au Commissariat à l'énergie atomique, exposé par Jacques Pesquet. Paris, F. Maspéro, 1968. 88 p. (Cahiers libres, 127)

Experiences at Centre d'études nucléaires de Saclay near Paris with 10,000 employees under Commissariat à l'énergie atomique, two-thirds of them white-collar workers and technicians. Strike began May 20, led to establishment of worker council in agreement with government June 12, 1968. Author, who was one of strike instigators, describes council's efforts to keep from being integrated as new organ into bureaucratic machinery and to allow more democratic participation in work process.

920   PETERS, LOUIS-FERDINAND. Kunst und Revolte; das politische Plakat und der Aufstand der französischen Studenten. Fotografien: Patrick Chauvel in Zusammenarbeit mit dem Verfasser. Köln, DuMont Schauberg, 1968. 151 p. with illus. (p. 33-64, p. 81-135 illus.). insert. (DuMont Aktuell)

Reproduction of 34 posters, 200 photographs of posters, wall newspapers, caricatures, leaflets in art faculties. Author discusses political contents of student posters, place of artists and art students in revolt, how posters were designed at Ecole des beaux arts and other art schools. Author is German lawyer who resided in Paris during revolt.

921   PETONNET, COLETTE. Ces gens-là . . . Paris, F. Maspéro, 1968. 256 p. (Cahiers libres, 125-126) Bibliography: p. [247]-249.

Case study of housing project (cité de transit) in outskirts of unidentified metropolis (probably not Paris) for relocated poor from urban slums who are waiting for permanent low-cost housing. Founded 1962 for 176 families or about 1,000 persons, the largest group consisting of North African Moslems, with some North African Jews, French Algerians, foreign workers, and metropolitans. Study investigates family structure, living conditions, relations within project and with rest of society.

922   PEUCHMAURD, PIERRE. Plus vivants que jamais. Paris, R. Laffont, 1968. 176 p. (Contestation)

Student militant's day-by-day chronicle of events at Sorbonne May 1968.

923   PHILIP, ANDRE. André Philip par lui-même, ou Les voies de la liberté. Préf. de Paul Ricoeur. Avant-propos de Loïc Philip. Paris, Aubier-Montaigne, 1971. 284 p.

Biography of Philip, who died July 1970, followed by excerpts from his speeches in areas that were his lifelong preoccupation: meaning of Christianity (Philip was Protestant), spirit of democracy, economic democracy, and tasks of socialism. Selection from speeches, letters, newspaper articles relative to his more immediate involvement in and stand on political affairs (Algerian war, May 1968, disagreements with Socialist party, European unification, aid to Third World). Includes interview, held shortly before his death, with Francis Jeanson on life experiences and opinions.

924   PHILIP, ANDRE. Mai 68 et la foi démocratique. Paris, Aubier-Montaigne, 1968. 141 p. (Histoire du travail et de la vie économique) Bibliographical footnotes.

Based mainly on "Le Monde" articles, June-Sept. 1968, commenting on recent events, in line with his convictions as democrat, socialist, and Christian, which led him to condemn irrational, violent elements in student revolt and reject idea of "creative instinct of the masses" and glorification of "contestation."

925 PHILIPPONEAU, MICHEL. La gauche et les régions. Paris, Calmann-Lévy, 1967. 254 p. (Questions d'actualité)

History of regional development movements, exemplified by Comité d'études et de liaison des intérêts bretons (C.E.L.I.B.), of which author, a geographer and expert in local economic development, is member. Attack on Gaullist reorganization of regional development since 1962, with specific examples from Brittany, where regional disequilibrium has increased under Fifth Plan. Discusses proposals of Left (Mendès-France, Defferre, Rencontres socialistes de Grenoble) and proposes new regional institutions. See also no. 257.

926 PHULPIN, ANDRE. Mai 1968: l'aube d'un nouvel âge de l'humanité! Nancy, Mouvement "Justice et Fraternité [1968?]. 22 p. mimeographed.

Plea to extend student demands for self-administration to society as a whole by giving control to consumers. Proposals of Mouvement "Justice et Fraternité" for organizing this system of cooperatives from smallest unit to international scale.

927 PIERCE, ROY. French politics and political institutions. New York, Harper and Row, 1968. ix, 275 p. maps. (Harper's comparative government series) Bibliography: p. 261-268; bibliographical footnotes.

Short historical introduction to French political tradition. Main part deals with special features of Fifth Republic: presidential government, relations between government and parliament, elections and party affiliations. Good chapter on interest groups. Table of Fifth Republic cabinets, Jan. 1959-Apr. 1967. Topically arranged and briefly annotated bibliography of books and articles, many in English translation. Text of 1958 Constitution in English.

928 PIETTRE, ANDRE. La culture en question; sens et non-sens d'une révolte. Préf. de Pierre-Henri Simon. [n.p.] Desclée de Brouwer, 1969. 226 p.

Nanterre professor reviews general cultural factors underlying May 1968 crisis, specific stimulation to revolt by Catholic progressives, contradictions in position of student rebels, making positive proposals for new humanism accessible to masses and responsive to science. Establishment of European university is suggested as answer to the American challenge.

929 PINILLA DE LAS HERAS, ESTEBAN. Reacción y revolución en una sociedad industrial. Buenos Aires, Ediciones Signos, 1970. 189 p. (Biblioteca El Pensamiento crítico)

Thoughtful essays on causes (economic and educational) of May 1968 revolt, sequel of events, and internal logic of student and government responses, with detailed analysis of direct-action methods of students as exemplified by Mouvement du 22 mars, and mechanism whereby movement spread outside Nanterre and eventually outside universities. Cogent counterarguments to Raymond Aron's interpretation of cultural revolution as psychodrama. 1970 epilogue on degree to which French society has absorbed crisis.

930 PINTO, ROGER, and MADELEINE GRAWITZ. Méthodes des sciences sociales. Paris, Librairie Dalloz, 1964. 2 v. (994 p.). (Collection des Précis Dalloz) Includes bibliography.

Manual for licence de droit students. First volume surveys concepts of political and social philosophy and law and categorizes different social sciences: sociology, anthropology, ethnology, social psychology, psychoanalysis, history, geography, demography, economics, and political science. Second volume deals with specific tools and methodology of social sciences, such as research design, statistics, documentation. First part of Vol. 1 by Pinto, rest by Grawitz. Good bibliography for each chapter.

931 PISANI, EDGARD. La région, pour quoi faire? ou Le triomphe des Jacondins. Paris, Calmann-Lévy, 1969. 231 p. (Questions d'actualité)

Preliminary criticism of government's program for regional reform, which was incorporated in Apr. 1969 referendum. Former Gaullist minister of agriculture and prefect of Haute-Loire and Haute-Marne, who left majority in 1968, had informally consulted Maine-et-Loire's Conseil général, Oct. 1968, for reaction to government proposals. Pisani sees need for combining decentralization and deconcentration, to make way for new form of regional citizenship and participation. Gaullist referendum is attacked as ill-prepared, timid, incapable of overcoming either nation's conservatism or administration's unwillingness to give up prerogatives. In present state of governmental and private opinion, regional reform remains necessary but impossible. The Jacondins of title are cross between Jacobins and Girondins, symbolizing false arguments between defenders of provinces and Paris.

932 PLANETE-ACTION (periodical). JJSS. Paris, 1970. 145 p. illus., ports. (Special issue for Nov.-Dec. 1970)

Articles on Jean-Jacques Servan-Schreiber, photographs, debate between him and P.C.F. Secrétaire général adjoint Georges Marchais, story of his unsuccessful bid as candidate for Radical party to unseat Chaban-Delmas in Bordeaux Sept. 1970, short comments on his writings and political activities by other politicians.

933 POGNON, EDMOND. De Gaulle et l'histoire de France; trente ans éclairés par vingt siècles. Paris, A. Michel, 1970. 350 p.

Bibliothèque nationale archivist and historian takes de Gaulle's "certain idea of France" and many quotations embedded in writings and speeches relating to episodes in French history and tries to see how far they reflect historical developments accurately, going back as far as Middle Ages. Among the most interesting elucidations of de Gaulle's political philosophy are chapters on France's universal mission and de Gaulle's incarnation of French legitimacy. Author evaluates de Gaulle's contributions to French greatness positively.

934 POIGNANT, RAYMOND. L'enseignement dans les pays du Marché commun; étude comparative sur l'organisation et l'état de développement de l'enseignement dans les pays du Marché commun, aux Etats-Unis, en Grande-Bretagne et en U.R.S.S. Paris, Institut Pédagogique national, 1965. 319 p. tables. (Mémoires et documents scolaires)

Report sponsored by Commission européenne d'études pour le développement de l'enseignement et de la recherche, whose French representatives are Etienne Hirsch and Pierre Piganiol. Comparison is divided into three sections: organization and state of development of primary and secondary education; higher and secondary technical and professional education; human, material, and financial resources devoted to education. For each of these topics and sub-topics, comparisons are made with help of 105 tables, carrying data through 1964. Conclusion is that for Common Market countries, too few highly trained specialists are being educated and social basis of higher education is too narrow, but that bottleneck lies in structure of secondary education.

935 POMPIDOU, GEORGES, PRES. FRANCE. Discours aux IVes Assises nationales de l'U.D.-Vème à Lille, le 26 novembre 1967. [n.p., 1967] 10 p.

Prime minister's clear and eloquent statement of essential political ground of Gaullism, with plea to look toward future rather than past and citing these as major Fifth Republic goals: national and later European independence, friendly relations with all governments, peace, aid to underdeveloped countries, economic and social progress through change in structures, rise in standard of living for workers, their association in profits, opposition to Communism. Pompidou refuses to have Gaullism branded as "union des conservateurs." At end of Assises, Gaullist party's name was changed from Union pour la nouvelle république—Union démocratique du travail (U.N.R.-U.D.T.) to Union des démocrates pour la Cinquième République (U.D.-Ve).

936 POMPIDOU, GEORGES, PRES. FRANCE. Press conference at the Elysée Palace, July 10, 1969. New York, Ambassade de France, Service de presse et d'information, 1969. 27 p.

First press conference after election as French president. Covers full range of his foreign and domestic programs.

937 PONIATOWSKI, MICHEL. Cartes sur table. Paris, Fayard, 1972. 250 p. (En toute liberté)

Interview with Alain Duhamel, in which secretary general of Fédération des Républicains indépendants (since 1967) and close associate of Valéry Giscard d'Estaing gives his views on political institutions, problems of scientific and technical civilization, with interesting inside view of relations between his party and Gaullist, Centrist parties.

938 PONIATOWSKI, MICHEL. Les choix de l'espoir. Avec la collaboration du groupe Avenir des jeunes républicains indépendants. Paris, B. Grasset, 1970. 258 p.

Sweeping panorama of contemporary world now faced with adaptation to scientific revolution of computers, data banks, automation, biological engineering, and problems of demography, pollution, urban sprawl, arms race, international inqualities, and disintegration of the family. Final section sets guidelines for new morality to control scientific progress and keep human purposes and choices at center of rational collective framework. Current ideologies of revolutionary Left are seen as totally unsuited for this task.

939 PONS, BERNARD. Aménagement du territoire et équipement. Paris, 1967. 12 p.

History of Gaullist regional planning and current goals for collective equipments. Speech given at U.D.-Ve Assises nationales, Lille, Nov. 1967.

940 POPEREN, JEAN. Une stratégie pour la gauche. Paris, Fayard, 1969. 162 p. (Le Monde sans frontières) Bibliographical footnotes.

Careful dissection of dynamics of political events May 1968 and failure on the part of all political parties of the Left to prepare unified strategy for taking over government, which was realistic possibility in the last days of May. P.C.F.'s problems and failures are elucidated without condemning party. Conclusions on opportunities for and obstacles to unification of Left after May 1968. Author is currently active in laying ground for new socialist party and transformation of F.G.D.S.

941 PORTHAULT, PIERRE. La France accuse [le "plus illustre des Français" mis en accusation face à l'histoire]. Paris, Edition "La France européenne," 1970. 381 p.

Debunking of de Gaulle's legendary position as national savior by reexamination of various episodes in his military career, based on documents received by author from military men after writing book on French combatants 1939-40. Episodes are from World War I, interwar years, participation in early months of World War II, as well as his leadership in Resistance.

942 POSNER, CHARLES, ed. Reflections on the revolution in France: 1968. Harmondsworth, Middlesex, Eng., Penguin Books, 1970. 317, [1] p. (A Pelican original) Bibliography: p. 317-[318].

Editor is English sociologist teaching at Centre universitaire de Vincennes. Contributions, all sympathetic to May movement, written during or shortly after event, except for May 1969 epilogue. Introduction gives general background and chronology. Among 12 contributions are report on events at Lycée Pasteur, Neuilly, inside view of Ministry of the Interior during crisis, psychoanalyst's interpretation of student revolt.

943 Pour nationaliser l'état; réflexions d'un groupe d'études. [Par] C. Alphandéry [et al.]. Paris, Editions du Seuil, 1968. 237 p.

Study group of 19 political scientists and civil servants, including François Bloch-Lainé and Michel Crozier, which concluded its work before May 1968. Topics of report are: weakness of over-centralized, inward-looking state (governmental administration), for which new methods of recruitment are needed, with special analysis on over-centralization in Ministry of Economic Affairs and Finance; areas of governmental involvement such as education, health, and urbanism, for which administrative reforms are proposed to increase effectiveness; bodies to which state could transfer part of its responsibilities (local government, business groups, public interest associations).

944 POURCHER, GUY. Le peuplement de Paris; origine régionale, composition sociale, attitudes et motivations. Avant-propos de M. Raymond Haas-Picard, préfet de la Seine. Paris, Presses universitaires de France, 1964. 310 p. tables, maps, charts. (Institut national d'études démographiques, Préfecture de la Seine. Travaux et documents. Cahiers, no. 43) Bibliography: p. 301-303. ML

Joint 1961 study by Institut national d'études démographiques and Préfecture de la Seine on recent immigrants to Paris region, estimated by 1962 at 7.4 million inhabitants and 4 million voters, of whom one-fourth are immigrants. Questionnaires were sent to sample of 5,400 immigrants with questions on family and geographic origins, reasons for migration, integration into new occupational setting, housing conditions, attitudes toward Paris. Conclusions were incorporated in planning for growth of Paris area. Good overall survey of demographic characteristics of Paris area.

945 PRADEL, PIERRE-MARIE. L'épargne et l'investissement. 5e éd. Paris, Presses universitaires de France, 1970. 128 p. tables, diagrs. ("Que sais-je?" Le point des connaissances actuelles, no. 822) Bibliography: p. 125-126.

Concepts of saving and investment and controversies surrounding them, separate motivations underlying each of these economic activities, in spite of their formal identity, with short section on traditional and current French attitudes toward saving and investment; statistics on ratio of French savings to consumption 1951-70, investments; government role in keeping proper balance of savings and investments.

946 PRELOT, MARCEL. Le libéralisme catholique. Textes choisis et présentés par Marcel Prélot; avec la collaboration de Françoise Gallouedec-Genuys. Paris, A. Colin, 1969. 479 p. (Collection U. Idées politiques) Includes bibliography.

Only final 20 pages of this broad documentary work going back to 18th century deal with Fifth Republic and give texts of papal statements and French Catholic interpretations on democracy, human rights, peace, religious freedom. Chronology.

947 Présence et priorité au monde ouvrier, Athis-Mons, 1966-1967. [Par] P. Barrau [et al.]. Paris, Editions ouvrières, 1968. 184 p. (Dossier "Masses ouvrières") (Supplément à "Masses ouvrières," 253, octobre 1968) Includes bibliography.

Report on 1966 and 1967 meetings of groups of local priests attempting to penetrate workers' world. Individual testimonies, discussion of problems and prospects for better contact with workers.

948 PREVOST, CLAUDE. Les étudiants et le gauchisme. Paris, Editions sociales, 1969. 190 p. (Collection Notre temps)

Revised version of article appearing in summer 1968 issue of "Nouvelle critique," taking into account first wave of interpretive publications. Works discusses ideological themes of student revolt: creative violence, attack on consumer society, glorification of spontaneity, revolution as an imminent phenomenon, education as central force in transforming society. These ideas are demonstrated to approximate those of men designated by Lenin as leftist opportunists and anarchists. Their lack of realism and preference for irrational is unacceptable to working class. Second part of book examines actual student condition, their privileged status, relations with workers. Several P. C. F. and C. G. T. documents on student revolt presented in appendix.

949 PRIAULX, ALLAN, and SANFORD J. UNGAR. The almost revolution: France, 1968. With an introd. by James Jones. New York, Dell Pub. Co., 1969. 177 p. illus. ML

Eyewitness account by two American journalists, Mar. 22-June 30, 1968, on all aspects of crisis. Includes excerpts from interviews with typical students, militants, workers.

950 Problèmes de la recherche en histoire contemporaine.... Strasbourg, Université de Strasbourg, Centre universitaire des hautes études européennes, 1966. 91 p. (Bulletin de liaison de l'Amicale des professeurs européens d'histoire contemporaine, 1)

Twenty-one professors of contemporary history from Western and Eastern Europe discuss means of facilitating research by improving bibliographical tools, coordinating research in progress. Discussions held at meeting sponsored by Amicale des professeurs européens d'histoire contemporaine at Strasbourg's Centre universitaire, Mar. 10-12, 1966.

951 Projets pour la France. Paris, Editions du Seuil, 1968. 144 p. illus. (Société, 28)

Highlights from earlier publications in Editions du Seuil's "Société" series explaining problems of French economy and society relevant to explosion erupting May 1968: economic expansion and Fifth Plan, wage agreements and inflation, labor rights, population and health policy, consumer and credit policy.

952 PROST, ANTOINE. Histoire de l'enseignement en France 1800-1967. Paris, A. Colin, 1968. 524 p. tables, diagrs. (Collection U. Série "Histoire contemporaine") Includes bibliography.

Although only final 50 pages concern education since World War II, work contributes to an understanding of the coherence of different educational systems--aristocratic (1800-1870), secular (1880-1945), with two well-defined branches for the elite and masses, and the contemporary system aiming for a single common school--as well as the political and sociological underpinnings for each system. Excellent statistics on students and teaching staff. For Fifth Republic, measures to democratize secondary education through collèges d'enseignement secondaire and pedagogic resistances to common trunk are described, as is the educational explosion at the secondary and university level. Bibliographies, documents for each section.

953 QUANDT, WILLIAM B. Revolution and political leadership: Algeria 1954-1968. Cambridge, Mass., M.I.T. Press, 1969. xvi, 313 p. (M.I.T. Studies in comparative politics) Includes bibliography.

Based on research in Algeria 1966-67, including interviews with 40 Algerian politicians (25 identified, among them Ben Khedda and Ferhat Abbas) in which they discussed their road to political involvement, social background, experiences in power. Work itself retraces transformation of Algerian nationalists from liberal politicians to revolutionaries, their organization during Algerian war, early relations between revolutionary intellectuals and military leaders and power struggle between these groups in years after independence, culminating in Ben Bella's overthrow because of his inability to weld together this heterogeneous political elite. Boumedienne's subsequent leadership strategy is described through his Dec. 1967 purge of leftist intellectuals. List of members of Revolutionary Council, G. P. R. A. ministers, F. L. N. political bureau, Ben Bella's governments. Good index makes it easy to locate fate of individual political figures.

954 Qu'est-ce que la participation? Ce que proposent les théoriciens ... ce que pensent les salariés et les patrons. Avant-propos d'Alain Peyrefitte. Paris, Plon, 1969. 250 p. (Tribune libre) ML

Minutes of hearing before Commission des affaires culturelles, familiales et sociales of National Assembly, Oct. 16-Nov. 20, 1968, on the problems of worker participation in firms' management, profits, and capital. Peyrefitte served as president of commission. Among witnesses testifying are trade union representatives (C. G. T., C. F. D. T., Force ouvrière, Confédération générale des cadres), representative of employer associations, and individual industrialists. Much of discussion centers on effectiveness of existing comités d'entreprise. Other witnesses include Louis Vallon, François Bloch-Lainé.

955 QUILLIOT, ROGER. La S. F. I. O. et l'exercice du pouvoir 1944-1958. Paris, Fayard, 1972. xiii, 837 p. Includes bibliography.

History of S. F. I. O. during Fourth Republic, based on complete, unpublished party documentation, including comptes-rendus of Comité directeur du groupe parlementaire, party congresses, and national councils. Last 200 pages concentrate on end of Fourth Republic: Algerian war, constitutional reform for French Empire, disintegration of regime, reaction to de Gaulle's return to power and to new institutions, S. F. I. O. split begun May 1958 and consummated Sept. 1958 with founding of Parti socialiste autonome. Information on party membership 1958-60. Author was S. F. I. O. functionary often opposed to Mollet.

956 RATIANI, GEORGII MIKHAILOVICH. Frantsiia: odinnadtsatoe leto Piatoi respubliki, Moskva, Politizdat, 1969. 46 p.

Events in France Apr.-June 1969: referendum and de Gaulle's withdrawal, presidential election.

957 RAVENNES, ALAIN. Le gaullisme: métaphysique; philosophie de l'action; métamorphose de la France. Paris, Editions C. E. S., 1971. 28 p. (Cahiers du gaullisme)

Speeches by Gaullist militant on philosophy of Gaullism, 1970-71.

958 RAVIGNANT, PATRICK. L'Odéon est ouvert. Paris, Stock, 1968. 256 p. ML

History of Odéon occupation May 15-June 10, 1968, during which the theater was transformed into an open forum attended by several hundred thousand people. Author is young novelist and historian who took part in seizure and served on occupants' Comité révolutionnaire. Operating methods of open forum, sample debates, texts of declaration of Revolutionary Committee, internal struggles and eventual infiltration by rowdies, which turned adventure into nightmare and led to end of occupation. See also no. 145.

959 REGUZZONI, MARIE. La réforme de l'enseignement dans la Communauté économique européenne.... Paris, Aubier-Montaigne, 1966. 415 p. (Collection Recherches économiques et sociales, [3]) Bibliography: p. [389]-412.

Based on doctoral thesis on adaptations of educational systems in the six countries to the need for increasing the supply of skilled labor. Seventy pages concern democratization of education in France mainly under Fifth Republic, with detailed account of reforms introduced by Debré law (1959) and Fouchet measures (1963, 1965). Common tendencies of and differences between the six countries are summarized. Good bibliography on French education.

960 REMOND, RENE. La droite en France de la première restauration à la Ve République. 3e éd. rev., augm. et mise à jour. Paris, Aubier-Montaigne, 1968. 2 v. (Collection Historique)

Vol. 2 covers 1940-68, tracing the transformations of main rightist tendencies identified for earlier periods for Fifth Republic years: the legitimist Right becomes counterrevolutionary, extreme Right, appearing as symbiosis of authoritarian Catholicism and nationalism, but no longer monarchist; the Orleanist Right is embodied in moderate, liberal Right represented by M.R.P. and former Indépendants, as well as more recently formed Républicains indépendants (despite Gaullist alliance), together with some of Radicals; the imperialist (Bonapartist) Right is closest to Gaullism, with its aspiration to greatness, national unity, and direct democracy. Includes material on relation to the Right of special social groups, geographic areas, press. Documentation consists of definitions of the Right by political figures, typical passages characterizing each of the three political tendencies. Epilogue interprets Gaullism's June 1968 electoral success as sign that it has become "Federator of the Right" without absorbing moderate Right.

961 RENAULT-ROULIER, GILBERT. Dans l'ombre du maréchal. [Par] Rémy [pseud.]. Paris, Presses de la Cité, 1971. 279 p. illus., ports.

For Fifth Republic years, covers author's relations with aged General Weygand, efforts to persuade de Gaulle to permit moving of Pétain's remains to Douaumont or Verdun, last exchange of letters with de Gaulle Nov.-Dec. 1968.

962 RENAULT-ROULIER, GILBERT. Dix ans avec de Gaulle, 1940-1950. [Par] Rémy [pseud.]. Paris, Editions France-Empire, 1971. 415 p. facsims., ports.

Testimony on relations with de Gaulle during Resistance years and in R.P.F. until Rémy's expulsion from R.P.F. for his defense of Pétain.

963 REVEL, JEAN FRANÇOIS. Lettre ouverte à la droite. Paris, A. Michel, 1968. 100 p. (Collection Lettre ouverte)

Mar. 1968 open letter has as its starting point journalist's unwitting participation in round-table discussion dominated by Vichyist political and literary figures, whose subject was unfair criticism of the Right After World War II by leftist-oriented press. Revel's thesis is that persons having political power gravitate to the Right in that they try to suppress criticism. Amusing section on Gaullistes de gauche and function they play in de Gaulle's political system.

964 REVERDIN, JACQUES. Jean Monnet et le Comité d'action pour les états-unis d'Europe. Genève, 1967. iv, 190 l. (Thesis, Institut universitaire des hautes études internationales) Bibliography: l. 180-189.

Thesis based primarily on published declarations of Comité d'action pour les états-unis d'Europe, describing committee's and Monnet's personal role in construction of Euratom, Common Market, and failure to exert much influence after 1960. Committee was founded 1955, has members representing S.F.I.O., M.R.P., Radicals, Républicains indépendants, major trade unions, but neither Gaullists nor Communists. On microfilm.

965 Revolution Frankreich 1968; Ergebnisse und Perspektiven von André Glucksmann, André Gorz, Ernest Mandel und Jean-Marie Vincent. Aus dem Französischen von Bernd Leineweber und der ad hoc-Gruppe der Romanisten an der FU, Berlin. Frankfurt a. M., Europäische Verlagsanstalt, 1969. 177 p. (Provokativ)

Contributions by Gorz, "L'enseignement révolutionnaire du 13 mai," Mandel, "L'enseignement de mai 1968," and Vincent, "Mai 1968 et après," appeared originally in "Temps modernes." For Glucksmann, see his "Stratégie de la révolution" (no. 536). These are all interpretations of May 1968 events in light of an overall revolutionary strategy.

966 REVUE POLITIQUE ET PARLEMENTAIRE (periodical). De mai 1968 à mai 1970. Paris, 1970. p. 9-45. illus. (Its No. 810, mai 1970)

Three contributions on May 1968 and its sequels, one on reforms in university and secondary education instituted by the government, one on "Le Monde"'s treatment of May-June events, and one a profile of ex-C.G.T. functionary André Barjonet.

967 RIEBEN, HENRI. Jean Monnet. Lausanne, Centre de recherches européennes, 1971. 126 p.

Biography of Monnet and lengthy discussion of his past and current contributions to European unification and of his confrontation with de Gaulle's European policy and philosophy. Includes Feb. 1970 speech at University of Lausanne when awarded honorary doctorate.

968 RIOUX, LUCIEN, and RENE BACKMANN. L'explosion de mai, 11 mai 1968, histoire complète des "événements." Paris, R. Laffont, 1968. 616 p. plates. (Ce jour-là: 11 mai 1968)

Well-rounded, sympathetic history of events, Mar. 22-June 29, divided into three parts: the students (Mar. 22-May 10), students and workers (May 11-May 30), and students, workers, and politics (May 25-June 29). Quotations from important texts. Authors are "Nouvel observateur" journalists.

969 ROBERT, JACQUES-JEAN. Un plan pour l'université du primaire au supérieur. Paris, Plon, 1968. 170 p. ML

Proposals formulated 1966-67 by team of secondary and university professors, students, and civil servants and published nearly unaltered after May 1968 as representative of ideas of democratic Left, many of which were incorporated in 1968 educational reforms. Among main points are extension of compulsory education to age 18, pre-salary for students 18 and up, expansion of continuing education through universities, decentralization of financing and administration, experience in democratic participation for students.

970 ROCARD, MICHEL, ed. Des militants du P.S.U. Paris, EPI, 1971. 223 p. (Carte blanche)

Interviews with 24 P.S.U. activists typical of different professional and regional backgrounds, with emphasis on their personal involvement in local action rather than purely political activity.

971 ROCARD, MICHEL, ed. Le P.S.U. et l'avenir socialiste de la France. Histoire et sociologie d'un parti, par Roland Cayrol. Michel Rocard parle . . . avec J.-M. Domenach, R. Fossaert [et al.]. Les 17 thèses du P.S.U. adoptées au congrès de Dijon de mars 1969. Paris, Editions du Seuil, 1969. 182 p. (Politique, 31)

Work consists of three separate sections: history of P.S.U., geographical implantation, social background of members and voters; May 1969 discussion between Rocard, P.S.U. secretary general since 1967, and sympathetic journalists on his own and party's stand on economic and political reforms, foreign policy, collaboration with Communists, Socialist party, purpose of Rocard's presidential candidacy; P.S.U. theses adopted at Mar. 1969 Dijon congress.

972 ROCHE, JEAN. Le style des candidats à la présidence de la République, 1965, 1969; étude quantitative de stylistique. Toulouse, E. Privat, 1971. 284 p. diagrs.

Stylistic analysis based on final appeals of candidates in first and second rounds of 1965 and 1969 presidential elections (texts reproduced). Elements of style measured statistically are numbers of word units, numbers of sentences, subordinate clauses, numbers of different parts of speech, types of figures of speech. Each of candidates is individually characterized. In addition, comparisons are drawn between de Gaulle and Mitterrand, de Gaulle and Pompidou, and between 1965 and 1969 campaigns.

973 ROCHEFORT, ROBERT. Robert Schuman. Postface du P. A.-M. Carré. . . . Paris, Editions du Cerf, 1968. 384 p.

Final chapter of this political biography covers 1958-63 relations with de Gaulle and distrust in de Gaulle's European and Franco-German policy.

974 ROCHET, WALDECK. L'avenir du Parti communiste français. Paris, B. Grasset, 1969. 189 p.

P. C. F. secretary general reviews events of 1968 to justify party's refusal in May 1968 to follow "adventurist" path (whose risk is exemplified elsewhere in book by fate of Indonesian Communists). Other points are P. C. F. program for economy and foreign policy, possibilities of collaboration with socialists and dialogue with Catholics, discussion of recent party "Manifeste" (see no. 896). Rochet walks delicate tightrope between international Communist solidarity and friendship with the Soviet Union, on the one hand, and opposition to Soviet intervention in Czechoslovakia and defense of non-violent passage to socialism in "advanced democracies," on the other. Revised 1970 edition takes into account recent presidential elections and collaboration with new Parti socialiste and stresses need for flexibility to adapt to French realities without abandoning revolutionary goal.

975 ROCHET, WALDECK. Les enseignements de mai-juin 1968. Paris, Editions sociales, 1968. 95 p. (Notre temps)

Conclusions reached at meeting of P. C. F. Central Committee July 8-9, 1968, exonerating party as betrayer of revolution, placing blame for reinforcing Gaullist regime on leftist violence, and reiterating P. C. F.'s democratic convictions.

976 ROCHET, WALDECK. Qu'est-ce qu'un révolutionnaire dans la France de notre temps? Paris, Editions sociales, 1968. 63 p. (Notre temps)

Two speeches, the first--"Qu'est-ce qu'un révolutionnaire?" delivered Oct. 15, 1967, at Institut Maurice Thorez' Colloque sur la Révolution d'octobre--stressing P. C. F.'s role as only revolutionary French party and at the same time calling for peaceful passage to socialism and cooperation with other democratic parties. Second speech, "Socialisme, paix, et liberté internationale," which served as conclusion for Nov. 1967 Semaine de la pensée marxiste, explains P. C. F. support for peaceful coexistence and other features of its foreign policy stand.

FOR ADDITIONAL WORKS BY AND ABOUT WALDECK ROCHET, SEE AUTHOR INDEX

977 ROIG, CHARLES, and FRANÇOISE BILLON-GRAND. La socialisation politique des enfants; contribution à l'étude de la formation des attitudes politiques en France. Avant-propos de Jean-Louis Quermonne. Paris, A. Colin, 1968. 186 p. (Cahiers de la Fondation nationale des sciences politiques, 163) Bibliography: p. 185-186. ML

1963-64 investigation in Grenoble area of 413 children of both sexes, ages 10 to 14, in private and public primary and secondary schools. On the basis of questionnaire results, author shows stages of development in political attitudes, with findings for major topics such as attitudes toward and information on political institutions, political orientation (party affinities) and views on authoritarianism, anti-Communism. Profiles of 26 children.

978 ROMI, YVETTE. 70 interviews du Nouvel observateur. Paris, Eric Losfeld, 1969. 193 p.

Chronologically arranged interviews, Nov. 1965-Oct. 1968, with artists, musicians, writers, film producers, and movie and stage actors by "Nouvel observateur" journalist.

979 ROMILLY, JACQUELINE DE. Nous autres professeurs, ces maîtres que l'on conteste. Paris, Fayard, 1969. 123 p. ML

Professor of Greek at Sorbonne describes her teaching experiences, including application of Fouchet reform, and defends non-utilitarian values of Greek, traditional methods of teaching against recent attacks.

980 ROSSANDA, ROSSANA. L'anno degli studenti. Bari, De Donato, 1968. 143 p. (Dissensi, 11) Bibliographical footnotes.

Comparative interpretation of Italian and French student movements during academic year 1967-68, centered on Italian students.

981 ROSSEL, ANDRE, ed. Mai 68. Paris, Editions Les Yeux ouverts, 1968. Loose-leaf album of 8 photographs. (Encyclopédie de l'image, 3)

Poster-size photographs of crowd scenes, striking workers, wall posters, graffiti by Bruno Barbey, Janine Niepce Rapho, Pierre Chausson, Henri Cartier-Bresson, Spoer-Donati, Jacques Windenberger.

982 ROUANET, PIERRE. Pompidou. Paris, B. Grasset, 1969. 320 p. illus.

Personal and political biography concluded Jan. 1969, but focused on personality Pompidou might bring to presidential role. Main sections concern Pompidou's career as prime minister, first entirely subordinated to de Gaulle, stirrings of personal ambition after 1965 presidential election, clarification of his political position 1966-67, attitudes and intervention May 1968, and temporary dismissal. Many direct quotes from Pompidou and other politicians, but no sources. Good insights into trends within U. D. R.

983 ROUEDE, ANDRE. Le lycée impossible. Paris, Editions du Seuil, 1967. 315 p. (Collection Esprit. "La Cité prochaine")

Personal experiences, 1954-64, as administrator of high-altitude "lycée de grand air," mainly intended as boarding school for sickly and disturbed children. Successes and final failure of experimental system of limited self-administration in boarding department are described in conjunction with first-hand observations on educational and child psychology and on factors detrimental to mental health of today's young.

984 ROUGEMONT, DENIS DE. Lettre ouverte aux Européens. Paris, A. Michel, 1970. 213 p. (Collection "Lettre ouverte")

Plea for European federalism on the basis of common culture, priority of regions over nation-state.

985 ROUSSEL, JACQUES. Les enfants du prophète; histoire du mouvement trotskiste en France. Paris, R. Lefeuvre, 1972. 108 p. (Spartacus; cahiers mensuels, série B, no. 44, janvier-février 1972) Bibliography: p. 93-94.

Historical survey of Trotskyism in France, followed by detailed account of five groups currently claiming direct descent from Fourth International: Ligue communiste, outgrowth of Parti communiste internationaliste; Organisation communiste internationale (Lambert); Lutte ouvrière; Parti communiste révolutionnaire trotskiste (Frank), and Groupes marxistes révolutionnaires (Pablo). For each information is given on leadership, publications, common ideologies and divergences, role played May 1968. Similar facts are given about several groups only loosely tied with movement: Socialisme ou barbarie (most strongly identified with worker councils, had much influence May 1968), and Programme communiste. See also no. 287.

986 RUDORFF, RAYMOND. The myth of France. [1st American ed.] New York, Coward-McCann, c1970. 248 p. Bibliographical annotations.

Debunking of myths about France as center of civilization radiating culture and liberty. Demythification bolstered by detailed description of odious means used in subjection of colonial empire, heavy hand of French police in Fifth Republic, physical and cultural decline of Paris, narrowness of appeal of France's literary idols, and failure of Malraux's concept of Maisons de culture as way of bringing art to the masses. Myth that de Gaulle restored civic unity to France also attacked by author, who points up split between leftist intellectuals and strong anti-intellectual proto-fascist following, with each side approving of use of violence against the other (e.g., Algerian war, May 1968 revolt).

987 SABATIER, GUY Politique économique et financière; rapport. Paris, 1967. 27 p.

Deputy and vice president of National Assembly's Commission des finances reviews Fifth Republic economic policies, 1958-67, and results in terms of economic growth (statistics). Speech presented before U.D.-Ve Assises nationales, Lille, Nov. 1967.

988 SAINT-PIERRE, FRANÇOIS. La révolution française est à faire. Paris, Piel, 1968. 139 p.

Essays defending French nationalism against European unification and attacking liberalism, Catholic ecumenism and its acceptance of scientific progress.

989 SAINT ROBERT, PHILIPPE DE. Le jeu de la France en Méditerranée. Paris, Julliard, 1970. 302 p. Bibliographical footnotes.

Support for de Gaulle's critical stand on Israel 1967-69 as instance of his general "anti-colonial" orientation. Supporters of Israel are accused of being under U.S. influence, and pro-Zionist elements in French press are charged with helping to defeat Apr. 1969 referendum as anti-Gaullist revenge. Book includes personal accounts of trips to Israel, Algeria, Libya, and Jordan, 1967-69, some of which were originally published in "Notre République." Popularity of de Gaulle, especially in Algeria, emphasized.

990 SAINT ROBERT, PHILIPPE DE. Principes pour une légitimité populaire. Paris, L'Herne, 1970. 221 p. (Les Livres noirs) Bibliographical footnotes.

Articles originally published in "Combat" and "Notre République," 1965-Feb. 1970, defending de Gaulle's political principles and international conceptions in relation to current events (e.g., presidential elections of 1965 and 1969, legislative elections of 1967, and May 1968 revolt, which is somehow presented as American plot!). Concluding plea for continuity of these basic policies after de Gaulle's withdrawal.

991 SALDICH, ANNE. Politics and television during the de Gaulle years. Unpublished Ph.D. dissertation, Paris, June 1971. 223 p. Xeroxed. Bibliography: p. 209-220.

Governmental regulation and control of French television during Fifth Republic, based on interviews with French minister of information, O.R.T.F. administrators, television producers, political scientists, and journalists. Focus is on political television programs, use of medium for Gaullist propaganda during 1962, 1965 election campaigns, and handling of May-June 1968 O.R.T.F. strike.

992 SALEM, DANIEL. Pierre Mendès-France et le nouveau socialisme. Paris, Presses universitaires de France, 1969. 158 p. (Travaux et recherches de la Faculté de droit et des sciences économiques de Paris. Série "Science politique," no. 14) Includes bibliography.

Sympathetic presentation, completed before May 1968, of Mendès-France's political and economic philosophy, based on his speeches and writings. It is seen as special combination of traditions of French radicalism (rationalism, individual rights, democratic participation) and socialist ideals (social justice, planning for efficiency and growth), which differs considerably from Marxism. Novel elements of his philosophy are call for dialogue between state, individuals, and groups and definition of contract between government and governed for carrying out commonly agreed-on actions. Complete bibliography of books and articles by and on Mendès-France.

993 SALINI, LAURENT. Mai des prolétaires. Paris, Editions sociales, 1968. 176 p. (Notre temps)

History of May 1968 events justifying P.C.F. position that radical students represented only a minority, that the government was in no danger of being overthrown, and that revolutionary "spontaneity" prevented joint efforts by worker and student movement. P.C.F.'s role as revolutionary vanguard is reasserted.

994 SALOMON, JEAN-JACQUES. Science et politique. Paris, Editions du Seuil, 1970. 407 p. (Collection Esprit. "La Cité prochaine") Bibliography: p. 375-388.

French head of science policy division of O.E.C.D. bases his discussion on personal experiences as science administrator and on research carried out during recent stay at M.I.T. He deals with interactions between scientific research and government policy, scientists' ambiguous commitments to human and political as against purely scientific objectives, and end of honeymoon between scientific knowledge and power that began with World War II. Many of sources American.

995 SAN CRISTOBAL SEBASTIAN, SANTOS. Españoles en Francia, hoy. Barcelona, Editorial "Tip. C. Casals," 1967. 160 p.

Galician priest with six years' missionary experience in southern France describes Spanish immigrants' reasons for emigration, their way of life, education of youth, ties with religion, recruitment by Communist party.

996 SARAIVA, ANTONIO JOSE. Maio e a crise de civilização burguesa. 2. ed. Lisboa, Publicações Europea-América, 1970. 202 p. (His Obras 3)

May 1968 events seen as spiritual and cultural challenge to "bourgeois civilization," of which Marxist aspect is only a superficial element. Main part of work by Portuguese historian consists of his diary as an "outsider" in Paris, with entries for May 23-June 12, June 31, July 15, 18, and 30, recording his personal reactions to and discussions of events.

997 SARTRE, JEAN-PAUL. Les communistes ont peur de la révolution. Paris, J. Didier, 1969. 64 p. (Controverses, no. 5) "Bibliographie de Jean-Paul Sartre": p. [55]-62.

Interview (undated, probably June-July 1968) with "Der Spiegel" reporter in which Sartre comments on P.C.F. failure to invent revolutionary methods compatible with advanced industrial society and concomitant unwillingness to take over power. Other political parties of Left are equally condemned. Also includes earlier (also undated) interview in which he discusses personal and literary opinions.

998 SARTRE, JEAN-PAUL. Situations, VIII; autour de 68. Paris, Gallimard, 1972. 478 p.

1965-70 articles and interviews, of which one section is devoted to Vietnam war, another to Israel and Arab world, a third to his definition of the intellectual (1965 lecture in Japan, 1970 interview in "Idiot international" on revision of his ideas after 1968 of role of revolutionary intellectual). Main section contains commentary on French politics: 1964-65 articles on depolitization and the Left, Defferre's presidential candidacy, articles on May 1968 events and their aftermath. The latter include defense of student violence against arguments of Aron, interpretation of revolt's significance after victory of Gaullists, explanation of P. C. F.'s failure as revolutionary vanguard and inevitable tension between need for revolutionary leadership and incapacity of Marxist parties to tolerate internal criticism, comments on government measures of university reform and changes really demanded by lycée and university students, instances of censorship and repression after May 1968.

999 SAUVY, ALFRED. De Paul Reynaud à Charles de Gaulle: scènes, tableaux, et souvenirs. Paris, Casterman, 1972. 216 p.

Memoirs deal primarily with 1930's and occupation years during which author served with government statistical institute, now Institut national de la statistique et des études économiques. Between 1945 and 1962 he headed the newly founded Institut d'études démographiques. Interesting sidelights on de Gaulle's awareness of population problems in Algeria and the prospective youth explosion in France for the 1960's. Sauvy's main concern is to break down ignorance of economic and demographic facts among politicians and public.

1000 SAUVY, ALFRED. Les quatre roues de la fortune; essai sur l'automobile. Paris, Flammarion, 1968. 242 p. ("Le Meilleur des mondes")

Demographer and planner's history of French automobile industry, indictment of extravagant public support of this individual mode of transportation, its real costs to the community and urban centers, explanations for psychological attractions of "mobile" home, for which many spend more than for their "non-mobile" residence, and suggestions for alleviating worst excesses.

1001 SAUVY, ALFRED. La révolte des jeunes. Paris, Calmann-Lévy, 1970. 269 p. (Questions d'actualité)

Demographer, who had 10 years earlier in his "La montée des jeunes" (see French Fifth Bibliography, 1, no. 1582) predicted greatly increased needs of youth as a result of changes in birth rate after World War II, gives cogent explanation for May 1968 student revolt. Among contributing factors are latent Malthusianism of French society, expressed in fear of making room for young in production and general distrust of youth, unwillingness to devote enough resources for them in education and productive investments. Explosive factors among university students, in addition to crowding and inadequate material conditions, are abstract orientation hampering transition to active life, absence of physical effort and manual labor, social consciousness paired with factual ignorance, blind acceptance of three myths, shared to a certain extent by adults--myth of abundance and possibility of mechanizing everything; myths of omnipotent science and technology; myth of simplicity--which combine to lead to rejection of affluent society in its present guise. Showing that there is no way to differentiate real from false needs, no question of real abundance, nor any hope of returning to bucolic simplicity, author stresses lack of economic realism among the young, continued need for selection in education, expansion of technically and scientifically trained human beings in contrast to actual academic trends. Seeing no way of adapting society to university rather than inverse, he suggests introducing all adolescents to professional life at an early stage.

1002 SAUVY, ALFRED. Le socialisme en liberté. Paris, Denoël, 1970. 408 p. (Collection du défi) ML

Iconoclastic and anti-mythical survey of economic and social questions, in which the goals of socialism and of maximum individual liberty are confronted and realistically assessed. As economist and planner, author stresses illusory nature of contemporary abundance, impossibility of isolating real from artificially created wants, role of inflation in government policies. Interesting insights on social policies relating to housing, social security, retirement age, population, and family support. His general conclusion: leave the individual freedom of choice wherever different solutions are equally good for collectivity.

1003 SAVARY, ALAIN. Pour le nouveau parti socialiste. Paris, Editions du Seuil, 1970. 178 p. (Collection Politique, 40)

Author is secretary of recently reconstituted Parti socialiste consisting of old S. F. I. O. and several of the clubs belonging to the defunct F. G. D. S., of which he was active member. Two interviews with Jean Lacouture, Jacques Julliard, and Robert Fossaert on socialists' goals and methods, Parti socialiste's program and international affiliations, followed by Savary's well-organized exposition of scope and conditions of up-to-date socialist action and specific proposals for transforming France. Motions of party's founding congress, Issy-les-Moulineux, July 11-13, 1969, in appendix.

1004 SCHEIN, IONEL. Paris construit; guide de l'architecture contemporaine. 2e éd. Paris, Vincent, Fréal, 1970. 307, [24] p. illus., plans, diagrs. (Collection Environnement)

Photographs of new housing developments, individual residences, government, academic, business, and industrial structures in central Paris and outskirts of city. Captions give exact location, construction date, name of architect. List of Paris architects and their buildings in the city. Statistics on current urban conditions.

1005 SCHERK, NIKOLAUS. Dekolonisation und Souveränität; die Unabhängigkeit und Abhängigkeit der Nachfolgestaaten Frankreichs in Schwarzafrika. Wien, W. Braumüller, Universitäts-Verlagsbuchhandlung, 1969. xv, 184 p. map. (Schriftenreihe der Österreichischen Gesellschaft für Aussenpolitik und Internationale Beziehungen, Bd. 3) Bibliography: p. 172-176.

Dissolution of French Community, facts on birth of sovereign African states, nature of subsequent French economic, technical, cultural, and military assistance, legal aspects of cooperation agreements, and realities of independence. Author concludes that African states remain economically but not politically dependent on France.

1006 SCHNAPP, ALAIN, and PIERRE VIDAL-NAQUET, eds. Journal de la commune étudiante; textes et documents, novembre 1967-juin 1968. Paris, Editions du Seuil, 1969. 876 p. (Collection Esprit. "La Cité prochaine") Includes bibliography.

Collection of 362 complete or excerpted texts with well-informed introduction and annotations for each section, extensive topically arranged and annotated bibliography, index of names and organizations connected with documents, comprehensive list of abbreviations. Book is divided into these sections: origins of movement; May 3-15 at Sorbonne; May 16-31 student strike movement; revolutionary groups; political groups; individual rightists; action committees; June reflux; student objectives outside university and proposals for university reform from various student commissions at Sorbonne and other campuses representing whole range of opinions. Appendices contain documents on Comités d'action lycéens, O. R. T. F., workers' and technicians' manifestos. English translation, "The French student uprising, November 1967-June 1968; an analytical record" (Boston, 1972), at ML.

1007 SCHONFELD, WILLIAM R. Youth and authority in France: a study of secondary schools. Beverly Hills, Calif., Sage

Publications, 1971. 79 p. (Sage professional papers in comparative politics, Series no. 01-014, vol. 2) Bibliography: p. 76-77. ML

Jan.-May 1968 study of 69 classes in 13 Parisian and provincial secondary schools (lycées, collèges d'enseignement général, collège d'enseignement secondaire) to determine patterns of student-teacher authority relations and typical alternation between "authority-laden syndrome" and "chahut syndrome." Inter-school and inter-age variations are examined. The alternation between compliance with effective authority and total insubordination when authority's incapacity and weakness become patent is seen as characteristic of French political system.

1008   SCHRÖDER, WOLFGANG. De Gaulle und die direkte Demokratie. Köln, Wison-Verlag, 1969. 248 p. (Kölner Schriften zur sozialwissenschaftlichen Forschung, Bd. 2) Includes bibliography.

Place of "direct democracy" or referenda in constitution and political institutions of Fifth Republic, as illustrated by the four referenda held Sept. 1958, Jan. 1961, Apr. 1961, and Oct. 1962 (work stops with 1968). Discussion on relation between referendum and personalization of power, depolitization, proposals for eliminating referenda from constitution. Good bibliography of books and articles on political institutions.

1009   SCHUMANN, MAURICE. M. Maurice Schumann, aux Assises de Lille, 26 novembre 1967. [n.p., 1967] 5 p.

Speech by minister for research before U.D.-Ve Assises nationales, on common grounds of Gaullism.

1010   SCHWAB, MORTON. The political relationship between France and her former colonies in the sub-Sahara region since 1958. Atlanta, Emory University, 1968. 61 p. Bibliography: p. 57-61.

Brief history of French Community and its dissolution, new forms of control through economic and military ties, cultural assistance, and interference in internal affairs. Prospects for maintaining 14 African states in French orbit are skeptically evaluated for the next decade. Appendices with useful tables on each state's political agreements, economic conditions, aid received through 1966.

1011   SCHWARTZENBERG, ROGER GERARD. La guerre de succession; les élections présidentielles de 1969. Paris, Presses universitaires de France, 1969. 292 p. Bibliographical footnotes.

May-June 1969 presidential campaign preceding elections of June 1 and 15 is described around three axes: role of political parties in selection of candidates, support during campaign and promised support after election; presentation of a "credible" program; personality and aura of reliability of candidates as manifested during meetings and on television. P.C.F.'s boycott of run-off is viewed as appeal against return to centrism and for bipolar system including Communists, rather than rejection of electoral system as such. Work based in part on interviews with Léo Hamon, Mendès-France, François Mitterrand, and Alain Savary.

1012   SCHWOEBEL, JEAN. La presse, le pouvoir et l'argent. Préf. de Paul Ricoeur. Paris, Editions du Seuil, 1968. 286 p.

Journalist, who is currently president of Fédération française des sociétés de journalistes and regular contributor to "Le Monde," describes function and growth of journalists' associations participating in control of press, as is already the case with "Le Monde." Author also presents lucid discussion of problems of state control over information (with relevant laws relating to press), information as a commercial product and a public service, rights of printers, etc. in the face of technical innovations. Journalists' associations are seen as part of trend toward greater self-administration of workers and professionals. Work concluded before May 1968.

1013   Science et conscience de la société; mélanges en l'honneur de Raymond Aron. Paris, Calmann-Levy, 1971. 2 v. (595 p.; 559 p.). Includes bibliography. ML

Collection of essays by French, German, and American contributors in honor of Aron's 65th birthday. Vol. 1: dimensions of historical consciousness; from revolution to secular religions. Vol. 2: industrial society; war and peace among nations. There are several essays on Aron's contributions to political theory, international relations, sociology of industrial societies. Among articles relating to France, topics are: social origins of a group of "polytechnicians" followed for three generations, proposals for reform of higher education, income distribution by age, educational level. Includes bibliography of Aron's works.

1014   LES SCIENCES DE L'EDUCATION; REVUE INTERNATIONALE. La remise en question de l'école, mai-juin 1968. Paris, Didier, 1968. 206 p. (Numéro spécial octobre 1968)

Declaration of Education nouvelle movement (1967) and June 1968 proposals introduced by various local committees May-June 1968 dealing with reforms for primary and secondary education, teacher training, counselling, education in the arts, psychiatric training. This periodical is the organ of Association des groupements pour l'Education nouvelle de langue française.

1015   SEALE, PATRICK, and MAUREEN McCONVILLE. Red flag, black flag; French revolution 1968. New York, Ballantine Books, 1968. 239 p. plates, ports.

History of May-June events by "London Observer" reporters, based in part on interviews with revolutionary leaders such as Marc Kravetz, Alain Krivine, and Pierre Frank. Best informed on different factions of student movement, revolutionary experiments at Sorbonne, impact of Comités d'action. Includes several eywitness reports.

1016   SEMAINE DE LA PENSEE LIBERALE. 2nd, PARIS, 1969. Le renouveau de la pensée libérale; texte intégral des débats. Paris, Nouvelles éditions latines, 1970. 280 p.

Second conference organized by Association pour la liberté et le progrès social. Among speakers are Henri Guitton, Maurice Allais, Robert Marjolin, and Pierre Lalande de Calan. First day devoted to condition of workers in market economy (questions of participation, unemployment insurance), second to Catholic Church and liberal (i.e., free-market) doctrine, third to liberal doctrine and Common Market, fourth to liberal professions (medicine and law) and state control, last to economic growth, planning, monetary policy.

1017   SEMAINE DE LA PENSEE MARXISTE, PARIS, 1971. Problèmes de la révolution socialiste en France; 100 ans après la Commune. Semaine de la pensée marxiste (22-29 avril 1971) au Centre d'études et de recherches marxistes. Paris, Editions sociales, 1971. 285 p.

Topics under discussion are definition of human needs, socialist democracy, possibilities for political alliance between working class and other social groups. Absence of Garaudy, former organizer of these conferences, should be noted. All Marxists present are P.C.F. functionaries; among main speakers is Lucien Sève. Non-Communist speakers include Duverger, Charlot, Chombart de Lauwe, Estier. For earlier conferences, see French Fifth Republic Bibliography, 1, nos. 1612-1614.

1018   SEMAINES FRANCO-AFRICAINES ET MALGACHES, RENNES, 1966. Caractéristiques essentielles du budget 1967 du Secrétariat d'état aux affaires étrangères chargé de la coopération. Paris, 1966. 3 p.

Secrétariat d'état aux affaires étrangères chargé de la coopération gives comparative figures for 1965, 1966, 1967 (anticipated) of different components in French technical and economic assistance budget. (For earlier data, see French Fifth Bibliography, 1, no. 789.)

1019 SEMINAIRE NATIONAL SUR L'EMIGRATION ALGERIENNE. 1st, ALGIERS, 1966. L'émigration algérienne; problèmes et perspectives. Front de libération nationale, Secrétariat exécutif. Paris, Direction centrale de l'Amicale des Algériens en Europe, 1966. 136 p. illus.

Aug. 1966 conference organized by F.L.N., whose reports were prepared by Amicale des Algériens en Europe. At that date there were 800,000 Algerian emigrants, one-fifth of persons employed in Algeria. Economic and demographic commission reports on housing, health care, and education available to emigrants, administrative and legal commission on mechanisms of immigration procedure and clauses for new agreements. Good current data on Algerians in France, comparisons with other foreign workers.

1020 SERANT, PAUL. La Bretagne et la France. Paris, Fayard, 1971. 441 p. maps. (Les Grandes études contemporaines) Bibliography: p. [433]-438.

History of Brittany, its current economic status, degree of present cultural distinctiveness, autonomist and regionalist movements of past and present (period of most intensive activity was 1967-68) leading up to defeat of de Gaulle's regional reform referendum and Pompidou's amnesty for Breton activists after his election as president.

1021 SERFATY, SIMON. France, De Gaulle, and Europe; the policy of the Fourth and Fifth Republics toward the Continent. Baltimore, Johns Hopkins Press, 1968. xiii, 176 p. Bibliography: p. 167-171.

Author's thesis is that during Fourth Republic French foreign policy reflected the country's declining international standing, whereas during Fifth Republic it reflected its ascendancy, which de Gaulle exploited rather than created. Nevertheless, the problems themselves remained unaltered. For Fifth Republic, stress is on de Gaulle's and Gaullism's concepts of Atlantic Alliance, Franco-German relations, European unification, military independence.

1022 SERGENT, PIERRE. Je ne regrette rien; la poignante histoire des légionnaires-parachutistes du 1er R.E.P. Paris, Fayard, 1972. 404 p. plates.

Régiment étranger parachutiste's role in Indochina and in Algeria, where it was integrated into General Massu's 10th Parachutist Division, 1955-61. Of special interest is account of regiment's role during Algiers barricades Jan. 1960 and in Generals' Putsch Apr. 1961, in the wake of which regiment was dissolved. Sergent was captain in 1st R.E.P., later became O.A.S. activist, as described in next entry.

1023 SERGENT, PIERRE. Ma peau au bout de mes idées. Paris, Table ronde, 1967-68. 2 v. facsim., maps, plates.

Autobiography of career officer assigned to Foreign Legion's 1st R.E.P. in Algeria from 1955 on. First volume relates his participation in fighting, reaction to Jan. 1960 events in Algeria, feelings in Foreign Legion about Algerian independence, de Gaulle, and his personal ties with French Algerian politicians. Full account of his participation in Generals' Putsch in Algiers. Second volume describes Sergent's involvement with O.A.S. in close collaboration with Lt. Roger Degueldre.

1024 SERROU, ROBERT. Dieu n'est pas conservateur; les chrétiens dans les événements de mai. Avec la collaboration de Noëlle Namia. Paris, R. Laffont, 1968. 272 p. (Contestation) ML

"Paris-Match" journalist gives sympathetic insights into activities of Catholic militants, organizations, members of religious orders. Documentation of Catholic interventions in May 1968 events is provided by texts of communiqués, appeals, discussions at meetings organized by religious activists, statements by individual priests and members of Church hierarchy.

1025 SERVAN-SCHREIBER, JEAN-JACQUES. Le défi américain. Paris, Denoël, 1967. 343 p. diagr. Bibliographical footnotes.

Widely read work by publisher of "Express" on threat of American takeover of French and European economy and gradual dependence of Europe on American way of life, whose first stages are evidenced in American penetration of European market and investment in European companies. American challenge is seen in superior management, marketing, and research methods, higher expenditures on research and education, through which technological gap between U.S. and Europe is widening. Good comparative figures for research and investment expenditures for major industries. Answer is seen not in imposing restrictions on U.S. investment but in counterattack on Common Market level by pooling technical resources (computer, space technology) and creating European style of growth. On French level, only salvation is seen in Left's becoming a progressive force exploiting confidence and initiative, not a negative force exploiting existing discontent. English version, "The American challenge" (New York, 1968), at ML. See also no. 760.

1026 SERVAN-SCHREIBER, JEAN-JACQUES. J.J.-S.S. par J.J.-S.S. Entretiens avec Jean-Claude Vajou. Paris, Table ronde, 1971. 259 p. (La Table ronde de "Combat." La Politique selon)

Journalist Jean-Claude Vajou's firsthand impressions of Servan-Schreiber at his home in Nancy, notes on autobiographical disclosures, political judgments, including opinions on leading Gaullist and opposition leaders. Final section of book deals with Servan-Schreiber's views on future civilization, role of science, information theory, international relations.

1027 SERVAN-SCHREIBER, JEAN-JACQUES. Le réveil de la France, mai-juin 1968. Paris, Denoël, 1968. 125 p.

Revolt is explained as a response to conditions created by Gaullist regime, such as insufficient stimulation of sense of responsibility and initiative, a lack which hampers France's adaptation to modern world and French economic growth. Continuation of present government is seen as form of "withdrawal," in contrast to Servan-Schreiber's own challenge to accept industrial competition within the European framework, increasing centers of initiative and creating new consensus. Educational problems are not raised. Text of interview with "Life" magazine reporter in appendix. English translation, "The spirit of May" (New York, 1969), at ML.

FOR ADDITIONAL WORKS ABOUT SERVAN-SCHREIBER, SEE AUTHOR INDEX

1028 SEVE, LUCIEN. Marxisme et théorie de la personnalité. Paris, Editions sociales, 1969. 511 p. Bibliographical footnotes.

Lifework of Marxist philosophy professor, a shorter popular version of which appeared in P.C.F. organ "Ecole et la nation" (Nov. 1962, June 1963) as contribution to the controversy about innate abilities and education. Taking this issue, closely related to the democratization of education, as a starting point, he examines Marxist contribution to theory of personality, finds it most deficient, rejects "anti-humanist" structuralist Marxist views of Althusser, and sets aside psychoanalytical and neurobiological findings. His theory of personality has a biographical focus, and its object is the development of the normal adult individual as a resultant of the interaction between his productive role, his productive capacities, and his personal needs, as well as his private and social use of time. Sève shows how the level of production and the level of participation in decisions determine the extent to which human potentials are developed, and how capitalist and socialist societies differ in their impact on human personality.

1029 SIMMONS, HARVEY G. French Socialists in search of a role 1956-1967. Ithaca and London, Cornell University Press, 1970. xi, 313 p. Includes bibliography.

Topics covered are S.F.I.O.'s intervention in 1956, 1958, and 1962 elections, divisions on Algerian policy during Fourth Republic, party split Sept. 1958 leading to founding of Parti socialiste autonome, attempted regroupings of the Left, and Defferre's abortive presidential candidacy June 1965. Chapters on party's internal organization, affiliated groups, leadership styles. Postscript on July 1969 founding of new Parti socialiste, with its more clearly leftist orientation. Appendices on voter statistics for legislative elections, S.F.I.O. representation in local politics, relative strength of departmental federations, social background of Socialist deputies and executive committee members, party chronology.

1030 SIMOEN, JEAN CLAUDE, comp. La France à travers de Gaulle à travers la caricature internationale. Paris, A. Michel, 1969. 190 p. of illus.

Cartoons and satirical comments, with captions often drawn from de Gaulle speeches, by 20 French, English, and American political cartoonists, including Bosc, Tim, Effel, Moisan, Lowe, Levine. Arrangement is loosely chronological.

1031 SIMON, JEAN-PIERRE, comp. La révolution par elle-même; tracts révolutionnaires, de la crise de mai à l'affaire tchécoslovaque. Textes rassemblés et présentés par Jean-Pierre Simon. Paris, A. Michel, 1968. 229 p.

Texts (but not facsimiles) of 160 leaflets, divided into three topics: (1) revolt and protest, which contains 50 leaflets mimeographed at Censier (Faculté des sciences, Paris) with date where ascertainable and chronologically arranged; (2) mass strike, insurrection, repression, for which there are 75 leaflets from the same source showing escalation of revolutionary rhetoric; (3) revolution, in which leaflets reflect revolutionary ideology. Final eight leaflets dated Aug.-Sept. 1968, two of them commenting on invasion of Czechoslovakia.

1032 SINE-MASSACRE (periodical). Numéro 1-7, 20 décembre 1962-31 janvier 1963. Distribué par J. J. Pauvert.

Reprint of first seven issues of anti-establishment, leftist satirical periodical, entirely devoted to cartoons. Among subjects of lampooning in these issues are Algerian repatriates, press censorship, Catholic Church.

1033 SINGER, DANIEL. Prelude to revolution; France in May 1968. New York, Hill and Wang, 1970. xiii, 434 p.

May 1968 events viewed in context of French social and educational problems, characteristics of radical student groups, history of revolt, and its meaning for French and international revolutionary socialism. Marxist author (friend of Isaac Deutscher) is critical of P.C.F. and Soviet Union but rejects Chinese, Cuban models for socialist societies. Europe is seen as ripe for socialist change toward collective property and collective planning, economic equality. Students' merit is to have shown weakness of existing structures. Good list of abbreviations.

1034 SIWEK-POUYDESSEAU, JEANNE. Le personnel de direction des ministères; cabinets ministériels et directeurs d'administrations centrales. Paris, A. Colin, 1969. 144 p. (Collection U. Série "Science administrative") Bibliography: p. 137-140.

Recruitment and jurisdiction of two parallel hierarchies of the executive branch: the politically selected cabinet staff members, personally subservient to the ministers; and the top echelon of the administrative services, the "directeurs d'administration centrale" of the different departments. Trends from Third to Fifth Republic are analyzed, with data on the social, professional, and political background, length of service, age, of both groups for Fifth Republic. Currently the two groups show no marked divergence.

1035 SOCIETE GENERALE POUR FAVORISER LE DEVELOPPEMENT DU COMMERCE ET DE L'INDUSTRIE EN FRANCE. Exercice. 1966-1968. Paris. 3 v. diagrs.

Annual report of investment society's own activities, followed by reviews of French economic trends for the year (output, foreign trade, interest rates, etc.). Comments of special interest for 1968. English translation, "Report," available for same period.

1036 SOCIOLOGIE DU TRAVAIL (periodical). Le mouvement ouvrier en mai 68. Publié avec la collaboration d'Eliane Baumfelder [et al.] Paris, Editions du Seuil, 1970. p. 225-354. (Numéro spécial, douzième année, 3/70, juillet-septembre)

Contributions on specific topics such as labor demands, political interpretations of events by trade unionists and "gauchistes," attempts at "auto-gestion" and "co-gestion" in individual plants, experiences of O.R.T.F., instances of strikes occurring in following year and falling into pattern of May 1968. Collaborators are sociologists Eliane Baumfelder, Sonia Cazes, Sami Dassa, Claude Durand, Danièle Kergoat, Serge Mallet, and Daniel Vidal (see also his works on trade union ideologies, nos. 554 and 1103).

1037 SONDAGES; REVUE FRANÇAISE DE L'OPINION PUBLIQUE. Des jeunes regardent leur avenir; leurs centres d'intérêt, leurs craintes, leurs espoirs. Etude réalisée en 1965. Besançon, 1968. 155 p. (Trimestriel--30e année; 1968, no. 2)

Results of Institut français d'opinion publique's 1965-66 study made for the government on attitudes toward their personal and professional future of four groups of young persons (ages 18 to 24) likely to furnish middle-echelon "cadres" in the future: technicians, military, school teachers, and farmers. The 381 subjects were asked to write essays projecting their lives for 1965-2015 and answer complementary questionnaires. Report covers: major preoccupations, profession chosen, family life, standard of living, expectations of technological and economic changes, moral and religious aims. Purpose was to see whether these attitudes can be conciliated with social dimensions of French long-range planning.

1038 SOUBISE, LOUIS. Le marxisme après Marx (1956-1965); quatre marxistes dissidents français. Préf. de François Châtelet. Paris, Aubier-Montaigne, 1967. 347 p. (Collection Recherches économiques et sociales, 6) Bibliography: p. 327-344. ML

The four dissident Marxists are Henri Lefébvre, Kostas Axelos, François Châtelet, and Pierre Fougeyrollas, whose efforts to up-date Marxist orthodoxy center on concepts of alienation, philosophy of history, class consciousness, and class struggle. Good bibliography of books and articles on Marxian topics.

1039 SOUCHON, LOUIS. Accusé, taisez-vous; les dessous d'une affaire. Préf. de Frédéric Pottecher. Paris, Table ronde, 1970. 252 p. facsims.

Personal account by secret service agent in Service de documentation extérieure et de contre-espionnage on his involuntary involvement in the abduction and murder of Moroccan opposition leader-in-exile Ben Barka Oct. 1965, his trial, conviction to six years in prison, appeals for acquittal with help of lawyer Isorni. Souchon claims that he served as scapegoat for higher-ups responsible for the crime.

1040 SOUCHON, MARIE-FRANÇOISE. Le maire élu local dans une société en changement. Préf. de J.-L. Quermonne. Paris,

Editions Cujas, 1968. 270 p. (Cahiers de l'Institut d'études politiques de Grenoble, no. 3) ML

Impact of large-scale government projects (Bas-Rhône-Languedoc canal, atomic energy center at Marcoule) in Département du Gard is studied through interviews with 30 mayors in two rural districts affected by these projects.

1041 SOULIE, MICHEL. De Ledru-Rollin à J.J.S.S.; le Parti radical entre son passé et son avenir. Paris, EPI, 1971. 198 p. (Carte blanche)

History of Radical party, last 50 pages of which deal with Fifth Republic and focus on party's fusion with Fédération de la gauche démocrate et socialiste, failure of this experiment, renovation initiated Oct. 1969 by Jean-Jacques Servan-Schreiber, and prospects for this reformist party in the current French political constellation.

1042 SOUSTELLE, JACQUES. Vingt-huit ans de gaullisme. Paris, Table ronde, 1968. 479 p. Bibliographical footnotes.

History of early years of Gaullism (Resistance, R.P.F.), followed by a negative appraisal of Fifth Republic in those areas in which Gaullist movement had definite principles and objectives. These include: (1) political reforms perverted through growing personal power of de Gaulle, degradation of parliament and cabinet, direct election of president, threatened elimination of Senate, totalitarian tendencies reflected in highhandedness of justice, parallel polices (as exemplified by O.A.S. prosecutions, Soustelle's own expulsion); (2) anticipated consolidation of French Union negated by loss of Algeria and dismantling of French Community, poorly administered technical aid; (3) foreign policy of anti-Communism, pro-N.A.T.O. stand abandoned in favor of a utopian Europe from Atlantic to Urals, whose failure was confirmed by invasion of Czechoslovakia; (4) price stability and association of workers in ownership of capital sacrificed to growing government appropriations for senseless prestige projects like atomic weapons, technocratization. Neo-Gaullism of Fifth Republic is seen as betrayal of Gaullism. Severity of May 1968 crisis is blamed on regime's authoritarian rigidity. Soustelle's exile was terminated June 1968.

1043 SOUTH AFRICA. TREATIES, ETC. Protocol between the Government of the Republic of South Africa and the Government of the French Republic concerning the installation of a scientific tracking station in South Africa. Place and date of signing: Pretoria, 6th January, 1964. Pretoria, Govt. Printer, 1964. 9 p. ([South Africa] Treaty series, no.: 1/1964)

1044 SPENDER, STEPHEN. The year of the young rebels. London, Weidenfeld and Nicolson, 1969. [6], 186 p. Bibliographical footnotes.

British poet's personal encounters with student revolts in the U.S., Berlin, Prague, and at the Sorbonne, where he attended a number of student meetings. Specific descriptions are followed by reflections on student activism epitomized by these manifestations, contrasts and similarities with irruption into politics of previously ivory-tower intellectual youth of the thirties.

1045 SPILLMANN, GEORGES. Les cas de conscience de l'officier. Paris, Perrin, 1970. 338 p. (Les Cas de conscience) Bibliography: p. 329-[334].

Most of this work on issue of military loyalty--what constitutes legitimate authority and how far should unquestioning obedience be carried in light of highest national interest?--deals with pre-1958 examples. Final chapters present loyalty conflict during Algerian war, followed up by Oct. 1966 decree on military discipline and obedience, to which author is favorable.

1046 STAHL, KLAUS. Die Sicherung der Grundfreiheiten im öffentlichen Recht der Fünften Französischen Republik. Hamburg, Hansischer Gildenverlag, 1970. xv, 339 p. (Veröffentlichungen des Instituts für Internationales Recht an der Universität Kiel, 61) Bibliography: p. 303-317.

Constitutional and institutional protection of civil liberties ("libertés publiques") under Fifth Republic in light of changes such as weakening of legislative power, strengthening of Conseil d'Etat and Conseil constitutionnel, emergency powers of president. Status of individual liberties, such as security of person and property, equality before the law, freedom of the press and opinion, freedom of assembly, religious and educational freedom, freedom of professional and business activity, labor rights to unionize and strike, are examined in detail.

1047 STEHLIN, PAUL. Retour à zéro; l'Europe et sa défense dans le compte à rebours. Préf. d'André François-Poncet.... Annexe chronologique (1939-1968), par Gilbert Gantier.... Paris, R. Laffont, 1968. 387 p. (L'Histoire que nous vivons)

Work based on 1944-68 diary of air force general who had been advocate of common European military strategy. For 1958-68, author shows how de Gaulle weakened Atlantic Alliance without building up an independent European defense force. Stehlin was elected deputy in June 1968, running against Gaullist candidate.

1048 STEPHANE, ANDRE [pseud.]. L'univers contestationnaire, ou Les nouveaux chrétiens; étude psychanalytique.... Paris, Payot, 1969. 308 p. (Petite bibliothèque Payot, 134) Bibliography: p. 301-305.

Interpretation of May 1968 events, that is, the psychological motivations behind the student revolt, by two practicing Freudian psychoanalysts personally involved in Paris academic world. Authors incorporated some material provided by patients (no direct quotes) in their interpretation. Authors claim that attitudes of students represent narcissistic stage of adolescence, with concomitant refusal to integrate reality, face Oedipus complex and take on father's role. Student tendencies are in harmony with those of Christianity, which accounts for wholehearted support of revolt by Catholic intellectuals, while Judaism is seen as stressing law of father. Psychological explanation for paradoxical combination of playful element and ascetic rejection of consumption society is presented. Three of mentors of student revolt--Marcuse, Vaneigem, and Lefebvre--are examined especially closely.

1049 STEPHANE, ROGER, and ROLAND DARBOIS. Mémoires de votre temps. Paris, Calmann-Lévy, 1967. 311 p. illus., plates. (Télé-biliothèque)

Based on television programs conducted by authors, these are interviews with participants in chapters of French history since World War II. For views on Algerian question and Algerian war, interlocutors include Robert Lacoste, who defends his action as Algerian governor general against Jacques Chevallier, Germaine Tillion, and Pierre-Henri Simon. Debré justifies his reversal on Algerian policy. Another discussion centers around May 13, 1958, in which journalist Ferniot and Léon Delbecque are participants.

1050 STOLERU, LIONEL. L'impératif industriel. Paris, Editions du Seuil, 1969. 296 p. illus. Bibliographical footnotes.

Impact of Common Market on competitiveness of French economy, existing government intervention in industrial production (e.g., state subsidies as of 1965), and author's own proposals for a proper dosage of "liberal" and interventionist measures to stimulate competition while compensating for existing weaknesses and moving toward a policy of European rather than French planning. Author is former engineer with economics Ph.D. from Stanford, currently on staff of Commissariat général du plan and technical counsellor of Finance Ministry.

1051 STRASBOURG. BIBLIOTHEQUE NATIONALE ET UNIVERSITAIRE. Bibliographie alsacienne 1965-1966. Etablie par Madeleine Lang. Strasbourg, 1970. viii, 206 p.

Books at Bibliothèque nationale, Strasbourg, concerning Alsatia (geography, population, history, cultural and regional characteristics), published 1965-66. Some of material deals with current regional problems. Arranged by subject, with author and place-name index.

1052 SUDREAU, PIERRE. L'enchaînement. Paris, Plon, 1967. 313 p.

Survey of international relations and military confrontations, with danger of nuclear war. Critical review of French military strategy and plea for French leadership in disarmament proposals and for joint Eastern and Western European defense program. Sudreau had been Gaullist minister, later served as prefect, elected centrist deputy 1968.

1053 SUETONIUS INTRANQUILLUS, C. [pseud.]. Vie d'un treizième César. Traduction et notes de M. François d'Erce. Iconographie de Pinatel. Paris, Faur, 1969. 94 p.

Satirical biography of de Gaulle, in the style of Roman historian Suetonius, ending with presumed assassination after June 1968. Epilogue has more specific indictment of 10 years' failures of Gaullist rule. Author is contributor to "Défense de l'Occident."

1054 SUFFERT, GEORGES. Charles de Gaulle, 1890-1970. Mis en image par André Gobert. Documentation réunie par Colette Ysmal. Paris, Editions du Groupe Express, 1970. 358 p. of illus., ports., facsims.

Pictorial biography, for which Suffert's text provides continuity, with high-quality photographs of de Gaulle from childhood to death. Last 130 pages are a panormama of Fifth Republic events and personalities.

1055 TALBO, JEAN-PHILIPPE. La grève à Flins. Documents, témoignages rassemblés par J.-Ph. Talbo. Paris, F. Maspéro, 1968. 104 p. (Cahiers libres, 121)

Documents on conflict at Renault factory, Flins, between May 16 and June 19, 1968, giving details on June 7-12 incidents, including death of lycée student Gilles Tautin. Descriptions are in words of anonymous workers.

1056 TAVERNIER, YVES. Le syndicalisme paysan: F.N.S.E.A., C.N.J.A. Paris, A. Colin, 1969. 227 p. illus., maps. (Fondation nationale des sciences politiques. Travaux et recherches de science politique. Etudes syndicales, 5) Includes bibliography.

History, organizational structure, statutes, membership, functionaries of the two major agricultural syndical associations. Fédération nationale des syndicats d'exploitants agricoles was founded in 1946 to represent all farmers in France. Centre national des jeunes agriculteurs (originally Cercle national) was founded in 1947 and is officially affiliated with F.N.S.E.A., though effectively independent. Includes chart of main agricultural syndical associations through 1966.

FOR TCHOU, FIRM, PUBLISHERS, PARIS, SEE NO. 1080

1057 TECHNIQUE ET DEMOCRATIE (association). Etude objective d'une politique européenne. Paris [1968?]. 3 v. in 1.

Specific proposals by political club for making European economic integration more effective, based on examination of existing European political institutions, social and economic trends in Common Market countries, international monetary problems, and dangers of U.S. economic control. Proposals stress greater economic coordination and more power for common institutions. Vol. 3 has good statistical survey.

1058 TECHNIQUE ET DEMOCRATIE (periodical). Programme d'action économique pour la France. Paris, 1968. 361 p. (Numéro spécial, avril 1968)

Reports of Technique et démocratie commissions on: (1) basic choices confronting French economy in terms of European integration, economic reform; (2) weaknesses of French economy and the "économie incitée" model; (3) government role in this model; (4) international monetary policy; and (5) small and medium enterprises. Each section contains club's own proposals. Second part devoted to Oct. 1967 conference, a gathering of 400 persons active in politics, business, trade unions (list included). Speeches at each session are summarized and represent wide range of political views, with comments on proposals of first part. See also no. 82.

1059 TENNE, CLAUDE. Mais le diable marche avec nous. Paris, Table ronde, 1968. 256 p.

Personal narrative of young worker who joined Foreign Legion and was sent to Algeria in 1955 with 1er R.E.P. He joined O.A.S. after unit was dispersed Apr. 1961, working with Capt. Sergent, Lt. Degueldre, and Sgt. Dovecar, who were later apprehended and executed. He himself was captured in early 1962, escaped from prison in 1967. Narrative moves back and forth between Algerian war and prison years.

1060 Terre, paysans et politique; structures agraires, systèmes politiques et politiques agricoles. Etudes rassemblées et présentées par un groupe de recherches sous la direction de Henri Mendras et Yves Tavernier. Paris, S.E.D.E.I.S., Futuribles, 1969. 2 v. (608 p.; 301 p.). (Futuribles, 12) Includes bibliography.

Introductory section compares different types of agriculture and shows relations between agricultural structure and national and international economy as well as social and political organization. For French agriculture, 77-page contribution by Claude Servolin and Yves Tavernier, "La France: réforme de structure ou politique des prix," discussing structural changes of French agriculture, trends for 1985, political involvement of agricultural organizations, Gaullist agricultural reforms. As of 1965, 17 percent of active population in agriculture, producing 9 percent of gross national product.

1061 TERRENOIRE, LOUIS. De Gaulle vivant. Paris, Plon, 1971. 309 p.

Though work concluded after de Gaulle's death, bulk of it was written during his lifetime and was about to be submitted for his approval. It gives Gaullist politician's (he was R.P.F. secretary for some years and minister during Fifth Republic) interpretation of de Gaulle's personality and political doctrine, concentrating on his role as Republican monarch, relying on certain forms of direct democracy, his relations with R.P.F. and individual Gaullists (notably Soustelle, Pompidou). Many anecdotes and quotations based on personal encounters with de Gaulle.

1062 TERUEL-MANIA, PIERRE. De Lénine au panzer-communisme. Paris, F. Maspéro, 1971. 233 p. (Cahiers libres, no. 192-193)

Member of political group "Unir" (Amicale des anciens membres du P.C.F.) draws on 1964 history of P.C.F. (see French Fifth Republic Bibliography, 1, no. 62) by this organization, complementing it with many personal experiences, to demonstrate how bureaucratic, monolithic party operates from top down, similar to Soviet model. Of special interest is criticism of current P.C.F. efforts to enhance its image as a patriotic, social-democratic, non-revolutionary party, illustrated by its response to May 1968 crisis. Author pleads for a second Congrès de Tours, where, as in 1920, real revolutionary elements can break away to form a new organization. Conflicts and splits in international Communism seem favorable to this renovation and breakdown of Communist monolithism.

1063 TEUlIERES, ANDRE. L'outre-mer français, hier... aujourd'hui... demain. Paris, Berger-Levrault, 1970. 483 p. maps, tables. Bibliography: p. 463-472.

History of French colonization, stages in dissolution of French Community, current status of remaining four Départements and and six Territoires d'outremer. Detailed economic and demographic survey of these 10 areas (which are small Caribbean and Pacific islands with the exception of French Antarctica, French Guiana, and French Territory of the Afars and the Issas) and government development program, prospects for modernization.

1064 THIBAUDEAU, JEAN. Mai 1968 en France. Précédé de Printemps rouge, par Philippe Sollers. Paris, Editions du Seuil, 1970. 120 p. (Collection "Tel quel")

Introduction by Philippe Sollers explains ideological meaning of play, which is written in Brechtian realist style and was intended for O.R.T.F. but refused by government, finally performed on Westdeutscher Rundfunk May 1969. Play reconstructs 31 days of May 1968 almost as current events sequence, with anonymous student and worker roles.

1065 THIBAULT, PIERRE. Le temps de la contestation, 1947-1969. Cartographie de Guy Arbellot. Paris, Larousse, 1971. 475 p. illus., maps. (Histoire universelle Larousse de poche) Bibliography: p. 457-470.

World history which offers rapid overview of key French developments with respect to economic reconstruction, European policy, changes in political institutions and strength of political parties, decolonization, relations with Third World. Detailed chronology for 1948-69, juxtaposing columns for international relations, Western world, Communist world, Third World, and France.

1066 THOMAS, BERNARD, ed. Ni Dieu, ni maître; les anarchistes. Citations recueillies et présentées par Bernard Thomas. Paris, Tchou, 1969. 187 p. (Collection "Les Murs ont la parole") Includes bibliography.

Short excerpts, with sources, from topically arranged anarchist texts, dating mostly from 19th century, several of which appeared as graffiti in May 1968.

1067 THOMPSON, VIRGINIA, and RICHARD ADLOFF. The French Pacific Islands: French Polynesia and New Caledonia. Berkeley, University of California Press, 1971. 359 p. illus. Bibliography: p. 519-530.

Separate treatment for each of these French overseas territories, covering history of colonial administration and political status in Fifth Republic through 1969, economic life, social conditions. Special section on issue of nuclear testing for Polynesia.

1068 TONKA, HUBERT. Fiction de la contestation aliénée. Paris, J. J. Pauvert, 1968. [14 p.] illus.

June 1968 comic strip on ideology of student revolt, police repression.

1069 TOURAINE, ALAIN. Le communisme utopique; le mouvement de mai 1968. Paris, Editions du Seuil, 1972. 313 p. (Politique, 54)

Slightly abbreviated version of 1968 edition, with epilogue on extent to which subsequent evolution in French labor movement and universities vindicated original interpretation that student revolt was model of conflicts in post-industrial societies.

1070 TOURAINE, ALAIN. Le mouvement de mai ou le communisme utopique. Paris, Editions du Seuil, 1968. 303 p. (L'Histoire immédiate)

Nanterre sociology professor and specialist in industrial sociology sees student revolt as a harbinger of revolutions in modern industrial societies and an expression of the double contradiction in French society between technocrats and operator-consumers, on the one hand, and present technical and cultural realities and past forms of organizations and institutions, on the other. Students' demand for "autogestion" combines social and cultural protest into a positive goal, the "utopian Communism" of the title, which promises to be new focus of social struggle. Major part of book deals with university problems, relations between students and faculty.

1071 TOURAINE, ALAIN. La société post-industrielle. Paris, Denoël, 1969. 319 p. (Bibliothèque Médiations, 61) Bibliographical footnotes.

General theme of these four articles, written 1959-68, is that in our present "programmed" society the locus of conflict is moving away from the economic sector (industry and labor movement) and diffusing through the tissue of society, as economic growth is translated into a certain type of social development. Sociologists therefore bear the main burden of elucidating change. Dec. 1968 articles deals with the international student movement. English translation, "The post-industrial society" (New York, 1971), at ML.

1072 TOURNOUX, JEAN RAYMOND. Jamais dit. Paris, Plon, 1971. 490 p. facsims. Includes bibliographical references.

Elucidation of aspects of de Gaulle's political biography by the publication of new documentation, personal information given to author. For Fifth Republic, items of special interest are: (1) source material on secret military operations designed to support de Gaulle's return to power; (2) background information on withdrawal of French forces from N.A.T.O.; (3) documents about de Gaulle's Algerian policy and handling of rebellious generals; (4) de Gaulle's views on Soviet Union; (5) details on his unannounced visit to General Massu May 28-29, 1968, and reactions of government leaders to his disappearance; (6) de Gaulle's quandaries about Apr. 1969 referendum; and (7) Guy Mollet letter, Nov. 4, 1970, commenting on de Gaulle's "Mémoires d'espoir."

1073 TOURNOUX, JEAN RAYMOND. Le mois de mai du général; livre blanc des événements. Paris, Plon, 1969. 528 p. illus. Bibliographical footnotes.

May events seen from perspective of de Gaulle and government leaders, reporting their opinions on problems of education, causes of uprising, tactical responses as expressed in the course of government conferences. Among unpublished appended documents are letter to author by Mitterrand and note on interview with Mendès-France on their willingness to take over government, text of Minister of the Interior Marcellin's letter to prefects on May crisis (June 4). Includes extensive dictionary of terms used by de Gaulle on political, historical, artistics, and other subjects, with quotations and sources.

1074 TRIBOULET, RAYMOND. Grandeurs et servitudes de la majorité, conférence . . . 17 novembre 1966, au Théâtre des Ambassadeurs. . . . Paris, Les Conférences des Ambassadeurs, 1967. 28 p. (Les Conférences des Ambassadeurs. Grande discours français et internationaux, nouv. sér., no. 28)

Gaullist deputy explains rationale of Fifth Republic's political institutions, particularly need for majority support of government, whose head is both French president and majority leader.

1075 TRICOT, BERNARD. Les sentiers de la paix, Algérie 1958-1962. Paris, Plon, 1972. 443 p.

Important work on de Gaulle's handling of Algerian question by major participant in policy formulation and execution. Author (not a pre-1958 Gaullist and known to favor decolonization) served as cabinet director to secretary general for Algerian affairs in Algiers, June 1958-mid-1959, where he watched over 1958 referendum and elections, economic and social programs, visiting many parts of Algeria. He subsequently served as legal and political advisor on Algeria in Secrétariat général in Paris, playing an active role in de Gaulle's evolving policy for Algerian self-determination, and observing misunderstandings with Algerian politicians, military leaders. "Barricades" and Generals' Putsch were witnessed from Paris. Major portion of memoir deals with peace negotiations 1960-62, in which he was participant, and final months of violence, which he witnessed in Algeria as assistant to Fouchet, giving government views on O.A.S., causes of European exodus. Epilogue comments on chapters in de Gaulle's memoirs devoted to Algeria, which de Gaulle asked him to check.

1076 TRINQUIER, ROGER. Guerre, subversion, révolution. Paris, R. Laffont, 1968. 287 p. illus.

Nature of subversive (or revolutionary) warfare in its varied manifestations from political to military onslaught to seizure of the country, how government in power can defend itself against threat of subversion and even launch counterattack. Examples are largely drawn from Algerian and Indochinese experiences. Final section examines problems of military strategy when traditional military confrontations give way to atomic and subversive conflicts, for which national, non-professional army like that of Israelis or Swiss is seen as most suitable. (See French Fifth Republic Bibliography, 1, nos. 1715-1718, for earlier works.)

1077 TRIPIER, PHILIPPE. Autopsie de la guerre d'Algérie. Paris, Editions France-Empire, 1972. 648 p. maps.

Author served in Secrétariat général de la défense nationale gathering secret information from other ministries for conduct of Algerian war, and it is from this vantage point that he tells history of the war. Contains detailed account of F.L.N. subversive and combat methods, diplomatic offensive, leadership structure and internal conflicts within nationalist camp. F.L.N. is viewed as lacking majority support of Algerian population, which sided with it later only out of opportunism. Political aspects of French response to F.L.N. challenge are presented for Fourth and Fifth Republic. Evolution for Fifth Republic is traced from period when pacification and disintegration of F.L.N. forces seemed at hand (1958-Sept. 1959) to de Gaulle's opening up possibility of self-determination, growing French ambiguity, peace negotiations from Melun to Evian, final period of violence and F.L.N. seizure of power. Appendices contain F.L.N. documents, organizational charts, glossary of Arab terms, list of abbreviations, chronology of Algerian revolution. One appendix gathers typical contemporary arguments from military and political figures favorable to integration of French Algeria. Good battle maps. No list of sources.

1078 TROTIGNON, YVES. La France au XXe siècle. Tome I: Jusqu'en 1968. Tome II: Depuis 1968. Paris, Bordas-Mouton, 1968-72. 2 v. (448 p.; 226 p.). (Collection Etudes supérieures, 51, 51B) Includes bibliography.

Second half of first volume deals with years after World War II and covers demographic and political developments, decolonization, governments' intervention in the economy, new social welfare institutions and other social reforms through June 1968. Final section summarizes structural mutations in agriculture, industry, transportation, housing, foreign trade, nature of regional disequilibria. Second volume has facts and figures for 1968: demographic status, social and professional structure, consumption pattern, economic conditions, place in world economy. Evolution since 1968 is established for economy, population, social conditions, environment (creation of five national and several regional parks, 1963-72), regional planning, European policy, aid to underdeveloped countries. Work is intended as social science textbook.

1079 TRUTAT, JEAN MARIE. Le livre tricolore du gaullisme. Paris, Centre de recherche et d'étude sur le gaullisme, 1969. 152 p.

Highlights generous humanitarianism and pacifism as distillation of Gaullism in the political, economic, and international sphere, with illustrations drawn from Fifth Republic and pertinent citations from de Gaulle's speeches. These are to serve as guide to de Gaulle's successor. Work published in late 1969.

1080 TCHOU, FIRM, PUBLISHERS, PARIS. Mai 68 affiches. Paris, 1968. illus. (part col.).

Album of 31 full-size (49 x 32 cm.) posters, some signed, others the result of collective work at Ecole des beaux arts.

1081 UNION DES DEMOCRATES POUR LA CINQUIEME REPUBLIQUE (political party). Manifeste pour la Ve République. [n.p., 1968] [7] p.

Achievements and program of Gaullist party after 10 years of Gaullist rule. Probably issued before May 1968.

1082 UNION DES DEMOCRATES POUR LA CINQUIEME REPUBLIQUE. ASSISES NATIONALES, LILLE, 1967. [Miscellaneous publications. n.p., 1967] 7 pts. in 1 v.

Concluding motions on social policy, youth and athletics, agriculture, foreign affairs, education and youth, overseas territories and departments. On Nov. 26, 1967, name changed from U.N.R.-U.D.T. to U.D.-Ve. (For reports presented earlier, see Subject Index under Union pour la nouvelle république: congresses.)

FOR ADDITIONAL WORKS BY AND ABOUT UNION DES DEMOCRATES POUR LA CINQUIEME REPUBLIQUE, SEE AUTHOR INDEX AND SUBJECT INDEX

1083 UNION FRANÇAISE POUR L'AMNISTIE. [Miscellaneous leaflets, newsletters, etc., 1964-65. Paris, 1964-65] 1 envelope in folder.

Aim of organization founded May 1964 is to promote release of political prisoners, notably O.A.S. prisoners.

1084 UNION GENERALE DES ETUDIANTS MUSULMANS ALGERIENS. 4e CONGRES NATIONAL, BIR EL BEY, TUNISIE, 1960. IVème congrès national de l'Union générale des étudiants musulmans algériens (UGEMA), Bir el Bey, Tunisie, 26 juillet-1er août 1960. Publié par l'UGEMA avec l'assistance technique du Secrétariat de coordination des unions nationales d'étudiants (COSEC), 1960. 116 p. illus., ports. Printed in Holland.

New statutes of UGEMA, resolution of congress, speech by Ferhat Abbas, long report of organization's president about conditions of Algerian students since 1957 congress and 1958 dissolution of UGEMA by French government, participation of students in Algerian war, relations with other student movements (representatives present at congress).

1085 UNION NATIONALE DES ETUDIANTS DE FRANCE. Le livre noir des journées de mai. Paris, Editions du Seuil, 1968. 95 p. plates. (Combats) ML

Unsigned depositions collected by U.N.E.F. and Syndicat national de l'enseignement supérieur (S.N.E.Sup.) committee documenting police abuses, May 3-13, 1968, with complementary newspaper accounts. See also no. 260.

FOR ADDITIONAL WORKS BY AND ABOUT U.N.E.F., SEE AUTHOR INDEX

1086 URI, PIERRE. Pour gouverner. Paris, R. Laffont, 1967. 272 p.

Former collaborator of Jean Monnet in laying groundwork for French planning and Common Market, Uri is now F.G.D.S. member (via Club Jean Moulin) and participant in Mitterrand's counter-government. These articles, written shortly before Mar. 1967 legislative elections, are critical of Gaullist approach to domestic and international economic questions and appeal to moderate Left by their avoidance of anti-Communist or anti-American demagoguery. Specific topics are Common Market, European political union, American investments in Europe, and relations with U.S.

1087 VALABREGUE, CATHERINE. La condition étudiante. Paris, Payot, 1970. 189 p. (Petite bibliothèque Payot, 149) Bibliography: p. 185-187.

Information on student conditions in these areas: (1) general student demands raised May 1968; (2) specific demands and conditions related to sexual revolution, sex education, contraceptive facilities; (3) married students; (4) self-administration; (5) housing; (6) use of leisure time; (7) aspects of academic life such as exams, teaching methods, guidance; and (8) financial aspects. Work based on interviews with students, reforms proposed by student commissions May 1968, measures initiated thereafter.

1088 VALLON, LOUIS. L'anti de Gaulle. Paris, Editions du Seuil, 1969. 120 p.

Gaullist deputy (Union démocratique du travail) and author of 1966 "Vallon" amendment on worker participation in corporate reinvestment denounces Pompidou's actions from the 1965 presidential elections to the defeat of Apr. 1969 referendum. Pompidou is accused of furthering his personal ambitions and strengthening conservative tendencies within Gaullist party, thereby undermining de Gaulle's efforts to initiate economic and social reform, including the referendum on regional reform. Appendices with de Gaulle statement favoring worker participation, July 1968 directive organizing participation.

1089 VALLON, LOUIS. De Gaulle et la démocratie. Préf. de Frédéric Grendel. Paris, Table ronde, 1972. 177 p.

Further accusations against Pompidou (see also preceding entry) for contributing to de Gaulle's Apr. 1969 defeat and for abandoning most of his predecessor's guidelines in foreign and domestic policy. Title refers to de Gaulle's skeptical attitude toward all political parties, including that of his followers, and his specific conception of democracy, in which participation appears as prime vehicle for economic and social reform.

1090 VANEIGEM, RAOUL. Terrorisme ou révolution. Paris, Editions Champ libre, 1972. 44 p. (Classiques de la subversion, 2/3)

Introductory essay on 19th century French revolutionary Ernest Coeurderoy restates position of International situationniste spokesman on need for "autogestion" and the abolition of the system of "spectacle-merchandise" characterizing modern society and blames "gauchistes" for falsifying and fragmenting his ideas, substituting terrorism for revolution.

1091 VANEIGEM, RAOUL. Traité de savoir-vivre à l'usage des jeunes générations. Paris, Gallimard, 1967. 287 p.

Belgian-born author is closely affiliated with Internationale situationniste. His radical critique of consumer society does not rely on either Christian ethics or Communist ideology. Revolution is to come out of new perspective on daily life, in which key concepts are self-realization, pleasure, play, participation, creativity, spontaneity, and refusal to make sacrifice of oneself or of present enjoyment for the sake of a better future. This work was influential May 1968.

1092 VANUXEM, PAUL FIDELE FELICIEN. Espoir à Saigon. Paris, Table ronde, 1967. 234 p. map. (L'Ordre du jour)

Journalistic report on former general's 1966 visit to Saigon, in which he describes U.S. and South Vietnamese forces and changes in economy, expressing admiration for American technical superiority, which promises military victory.

1093 VAUDIAUX, JACQUES. Le progressisme en France sous la 4e République; les hommes, l'organisation, les électeurs.

Préf. de Léo Hamon. . . . Paris, Editions Cujas, 1968. 263 p. diagrs. (Collections Vie politique et politique internationale) Bibliography: p. [249]-252.

Organization, leadership, militants, and electorate of Union progressiste, which was dissolved in Nov. 1958. This small leftist party was the only electoral ally of P.C.F. during Fourth Republic. Although most of material stops with 1958, work projects problems of unification of the Left implied in collaboration with P.C.F. to Fifth Republic and shows similarities between the Union progressiste's foreign policy and de Gaulle's as an explanation for the fact that Union progressiste leader Emmanuel d'Astier de la Vigerie became Gaullist supporter in 1965. Election results for individual seats held by Union progressiste for Fifth Republic.

1094 VAUJOUR, JEAN. Le plus grand Paris; l'avenir de la région parisienne et ses problèmes complexes. Préf. de Jean Fourastié. Paris, Presses universitaires de France, 1970. xi, 202 p. plates, maps. (Collection Villes à venir) ML

Implementation of regional planning for Paris area, initiated by Feb. 1959 creation of District de la région parisienne and Aug. 1960 decree for the "Plan d'aménagement et d'organisation générale de la région parisienne" and complemented by the creation of six new departments in Mar. 1964 and the appointment of a regional prefect in Aug. 1966. Topics discussed include administrative structures of these new units, planning goals, creation of new towns, major projects for improving transportation, collective equipments, renovation of Paris. Facts on regional budget and taxes, population growth projections to 2000. Author was secretary general of the Paris District, later Préfecture de la région parisienne, under Paul Delouvrier, 1961-69. Good maps and photographs.

1095 VEILLARD, GEORGES. "L'Affaire" Bull. Paris, S.P.A.G., 1969. 248 p. ML

"White book" on Bull Affair, by one of former directors of Bull company. Bull is French computer company founded 1931, whose precarious financial position forced it to let General Electric become majority shareholder at end of 1964. Issue came to public and governmental attention when French atomic energy agency needed a sophisticated electronic computer, which the U.S. refused permission to export and which Bull was then asked to design. Scandal arose over the fact that the only French computer firm of any standing had been allowed to fall into hands of an American company as a result of vacillating government support. Includes correspondence, records of company's general assemblies.

1096 VELLAS, PIERRE. Moyens sociaux du développement économique. Paris, Presses universitaires de France, 1968. 111 p. (Paix, coopération et développement, no. 1) Bibliographical footnotes.

Educational and informational tools for facilitating purely economic forms of investment in underdeveloped areas, which allow population to participate actively in development program. These concepts are also applied to French regional development. Includes proposals for institutions organizing socioeconomic development. Author is head of Toulouse University's Institut d'études internationales et des pays en voie de développement.

1097 VENNER, DOMINIQUE, comp. Ils sont fous, ces gauchistes! Pensées choisies et parfois commentées par Dominique Venner. Paris, Editions de la pensée moderne, 1970. 248 p.

Topically arranged short excerpts from "gauchiste" writings, ranging from Marxist classics through Mao to 1968 books and slogans. Typical topics are: advanced democracy, non-violence, internationalism, strategy, racism, proletariat. Contradictory statements are given prominence to convey flavor of "gauchiste" phenomenon. Venner is journalist for extreme Right press.

93

1098 VERMOT-GAUCHY, MICHEL. L'éducation nationale dans la France de 1975. Monaco, Editions du Rocher, 1965. 332 p. illus. (Futuribles, 2)

Educational planner's closely reasoned and documented history of technical and professional education in France and the way in which it came more and more fully under the sway of the university. Crisis of university is predicted for 1968-69 because of the failure to take into account the diversity of student backgrounds and formative needs of society. Author feels that the Ecole primaire supérieure of early 20th century was much better adapted to present needs than the lycée for democratization and expansion of education. Second part discusses methods for predicting demands for training in different professions, projections for degrees awarded in different fields. Third part shows trends for 1975, with wealth of statistics, making proposals for adapting educational system to real needs of economic growth.

1099 VERRET, MICHEL. Les marxistes et la religion; essai sur l'athéisme moderne. 3e éd. . . . Paris, Editions sociales, 1966. 301 p. (La Nouvelle critique. Les Essais) Bibliography: p. 289-296.

Examination of religious beliefs, stressing tolerance of P.C.F. toward religious faith and institutions, possibility of working with Catholics, followed by justification of atheism as Marxist answer to ethical questions.

1100 VERRON, M. Participation, histoire du travail, développement et doctrines sociales. Paris, Editions polyglottes, 1968. 158 p. Bibliography: p. 154-156. ML

Stand of Catholic Church on social questions and economic and political doctrines (opposition to capitalism, Communism, socialism, but sense of responsibility toward community). In this context, Catholic support of participation of workers in firms is justified. Quotations and references to texts of papal encyclicals through 1967.

1101 VIANSSON-PONTE, PIERRE. Après de Gaulle qui? Paris, Editions du Seuil, 1968. 284 p. (Collection "L'Histoire immédiate")

Political sketches (biography, political career) of major and minor contenders to de Gaulle's succession and characteristics demanded for successor. Carefully portrayed major contenders are Pompidou, Mitterrand, and Giscard d'Estaing. Minor Gaullist possibilities are Michel Debré, Alain Peyrefitte, Jacques Chaban-Delmas, and, for the non-Gaullists, Edgar Faure, Jean Lecanuet, and Gaston Defferre. There are also short portraits of leaders of major political parties--Guy Mollet, Waldeck Rochet, Jacques Duhamel, René Billères, Jean-Louis Tixier-Vignancour, Mendès-France, Gaston Palewski, Charles Hernu, Michel Poniatowski--and very brief sketches of 20 other second-line figures in Communist and non-Communist Left, Center, and among Gaullists. Work concluded before May 1968.

1102 VIANSSON-PONTE, PIERRE. Histoire de la République gaullienne. Paris, Fayard, 1970-71. 2 v. (578 p.; 764 p.). (Les Grandes études contemporaines) Includes bibliography.

"Le Monde" political analyst's comprehensive and minutely detailed political history of Fifth Republic, May 1958-June 1969. Vol. 1: La fin d'une époque, mai 1958-juillet 1962; Vol. 2: Le temps des orphelins, été 1962-avril 1969. First volume focuses on origins and birth of Gaullist regime, many stages in the resolution of the Algerian question. Second volume has three major divisions: (1) period of innovation and greatness, 1962-65; (2) incipient decline of de Gaulle's authority and mounting economic, educational problems, Dec. 1965-Apr. 1968; and (3) "la chute" May 1968-June 1969, with long section on May-June 1968 events in political perspective, background for Apr. 1969 referendum. In the last two sections there is much speculation about de Gaulle's relations with Pompidou and insight into the process whereby the latter emerged as political leader in his own right. Aside from familiarity with published literature, journalist draws on inside information from many government and party sources. Indispensable work for seeing years of de Gaulle's rule through eyes of politically impartial, extremely well-informed French observer. Detailed chronologies for each volume, results of elections and referenda, members of cabinets, including all minor reshuffles. Name index. Bibliographic "orientation" at end of second volume, citing most useful or typical books for (1) entire period, (2) de Gaulle, (3) Gaullism, (4) May 1958 and Algeria, (5) 1965 election, (6) economic and social policy and reform, and (7) May 1968.

1103 VIDAL, DANIEL. Essai sur l'idéologie; le cas particulier des idéologies syndicales. Paris, Editions Anthropos, 1971. 322 p. illus. (Sociologie et connaissance) Includes bibliographical references.

Definition of ideological fields in close accord with structuralist Marxist approach of Althusser, in which ideologies are neither mystification superimposed on reality nor separate reflections of social attitudes. This theory is applied to relation between trade union actions and the predominant ideological orientation of trade union members. Data are based on 1965-68 questionnaire studies of trade union members by several industrial sociologists under the guidance of Alain Touraine and the C.N.R.S. Laboratoire de sociologie industrielle. Five types of trade union action (syndicalisme de métier, syndicalisme de défense économique, syndicalisme de classe, syndicalisme de défense professionnelle, and syndicalisme gestionnaire) are correlated with ideological choices in three areas (integration of working class or working-class consciousness, conflictive or conciliatory social relations, and peaceful or violent social transformations) and personal factors such as social mobility and work satisfaction. These variables are complemented by objective conditions of trade union members (private or public enterprise, declining or growing industry, consumption or capital goods industry, wage level, qualification). The principal distinction is between reformism and radicalism, social integration or rupture, and multi-variate statistical analyses determine crucial and secondary factors for this division, which only partially follows that of the doctrinally revolutionary C.G.T. and the more reformist unions such as the C.F.D.T. Particularly interesting light on ideological meaning of May 1968 crisis, in which the C.G.T.'s slippage in the reformist direction came to the surface, while the demands for "autogestion" represented a radicalization of hitherto better-integrated workers. For further developments on this point, see also nos. 554 and 1036.

1104 VIDAL-NAQUET, PIERRE. La torture dans la république; essai d'histoire et de politique contemporaines (1954-1962). Paris, Editions de Minuit, 1972. 203 p. (Grands documents, 35) Bibliography: p. 187-202.

Insidious intrusion of torture into police, army operations in Algeria, and spread to France in final years of Algerian war, responses of politicians, judicial institutions to these abuses during Fourth and Fifth Republic. Main sources are memoirs, newspaper accounts. Work originally published in English and Italian in 1963; 1972 French edition also assesses impact of this form of violence on different segments of French population, protests among intellectuals, apathy of majority. Author concludes that by May 1968, impact of Algerian conflict on youth was slight and admits that use of torture has not been limited to situations like Algeria where victims were colonials, but can arise whenever society feels threatened by dissidence, even in "classless societies" in which government thinks truth is all on its side. Excellent bibliography (through 1971) of works on Algerian war and torture, listing books by victims of torture, military, lawyers, journalists, intellectuals, churches, government figures, as well as documentaries and fictional reconstructions on film about Algerian war.

1105　La vie extraordinaire de Charles de Gaulle. [Par] Christian Houillion et al. Genève, Editions de Crémille, 1972. 397 p. plates, ports. (part col.), facsims. Includes bibliography.

Handsomely printed and illustrated with a wealth of photographs, many of them unfamiliar, this de Gaulle biography is the work of several contributors for the different periods of his life. For the Fifth Republic years, the contributors are Lucien Viéville (1958-62) and Jean Renald (1962-70), who focus on French history rather than on personal anecdotes about de Gaulle, except in final section on retirement and death. Topics are: return to power and Algerian drama, great political objectives, end of a reign. Includes several photographs of attempted assassination at Petit-Clamart.

1106　VIENET, RENE. Enragés et situationnistes dans le mouvement des occupations. Paris, Gallimard, 1968. 322 p. illus., map. (Collection Témoins)

Personal account by member of Internationale situationniste of events at Nanterre, street fighting, occupation of Sorbonne and factories, and manner in which short-lived revolutionary activity realized philosophy of anti-hierarchic spontaneity and autonomy through workers' councils. The Enragés became known at Nanterre in Jan. 1968 by disrupting lectures and using walls for pop-style frescoes, joined with Internationale situationniste, May 14, 1968. Author denigrates all other revolutionary groups, sparing only the Conseil pour le maintien des occupations founded by the original Comité d'occupation de la Sorbonne, May 17. Appendix has some of its declarations. Includes unusual photographs of street fighting, posters, documents of Internationale situationniste and Enragés. Map locating 60 street barricades in Paris.

1107　VIGUERIE, JEAN DE. Trois semaines vécues à la Sorbonne. Texte de l'exposé fait à la réunion privée d'information du C.E.P.E.C. le mercredi 19 juin 1968. Paris, Centre d'études politiques et civiques, 1968. 27 p. (Dossiers du C.E.P.E.C., 23)

Sorbonne history professor's personal impressions of occupation of the Sorbonne, where he stayed behind to protect libraries from vandalism. Students' actions are viewed as sign of "infantilism" to make adults pay attention to them, and hasty reforms approved to assuage them are condemned.

1108　VILLENEUVE, PAQUERETTE. Une Canadienne dans les rues de Paris pendant la révolte étudiante, mai 1968. Montréal, Editions du Jour, 1968. 192 p. illus. (Cahiers de Cité libre, CL-4) Bibliography: p. 189.

Personal account of Paris-based Canadian journalist living near Sorbonne, who seeks to act as impartial observer. Of special interest are a long interview with Nanterre sociology professor Alain Touraine, who gives her his version of the Nanterre outbreak and early troubles at Sorbonne, discussion with U.N.E.F. Vice President Jacques Sauvageot, visits to occupied Sorbonne, Faculté de médecine, Faculté de droit, Ecole des beaux arts, Lycée Henri IV. Vivid rendition of Latin Quarter mood. Author's own photographs.

1109　VILQUIN, MICHEL. De Gaulle, cet inconnu méconnu. Paris, Pensée universelle, 1972. 119 p.

Plea against turning de Gaulle posthumously into the mythical founder of a doctrinaire sect, when de Gaulle's only wish was to serve as symbol of French unity.

1110　VINCENT, GERARD. Les lycéens. Paris, A. Colin, 1971. 852 p. (Cahiers de la Fondation nationale des sciences politiques, 179) M L

Results of two investigations of French lycée students, Oct. 1967-Dec. 1967, Oct. 1968-Dec. 1969, involving several thousand 12- to 20-year-olds in Paris, Paris suburbs, and provinces. Study used interviews, combined with analysis of students' compositions about school life and imaginary autobiographies. Findings cover all aspects of educational establishments as seen through student eyes, students' personal lives, their career plans, political participation. One 75-page section describes May 1968 in lycées. Results are reflected in typical excerpts from student composition rather than tabulations.

1111　VINCENT, GERARD. Les professeurs du second degré; contribution à l'étude du corps enseignant. Avec la collaboration de Guy Michelat [et al.]. Paris, A. Colin, 1967. 330 p. (Cahiers de la Fondation nationale des sciences politiques, 160) Bibliographical footnotes.

Study of lycée teachers in Paris area based on 1964 questionnaires to 474 teachers and 1965-66 questionnaires to students at Institut d'études politiques, Paris, about their attitudes toward former lycée teachers. This intensively exploited information, combined with author's personal experiences as lycée professor and published literature, produces an impressively well-rounded picture of student-teacher interactions in French lycées, professors' view of their work and place in society, as well as factual data on their social origins. Only this one form of secondary education was explored. At the time of writing, there were 60,000 lycée teachers. Author's concern is with growing imbalance between requisite qualities for pedagogic success on both the academic and the personal level and prevailing pattern of low salaries and social standing.

1112　VIRTON, PAUL. Histoire et politique du droit du travail. . . . Paris, Spes, 1968. 255 p. (Bibliothèque de la recherche sociale) Bibliographical footnotes.

After historical introduction, main labor problems in France in the 1960's are discussed: unemployment, use of foreign workers, special problem of young and old workers and women, on-the-job training, public and private sector of labor force, geographic and professional mobility. Final section on measures for protecting individual workers, collective bargaining, participation of workers in firms and other institutions. No texts of laws.

1113　VIVE LE COMMUNISME (periodical). Vive le 1er mai 70. Paris, Editions Git-le-Coeur, 1969. 24 p.

Autocriticism of Nanterre Marxist-Leninist group for poor organization of a May 1969 demonstration in Paris suburb of Belleville, which showed that they had failed to allow for lack of enthusiasm and conviction of the masses, as well as Communists' fear of jeopardizing chances of Duclos' presidential candidacy by participating in demonstration.

1114　VIVIEN, ROBERT ANDRE. Jeunesse et sports. Paris, 1967, 15 p.

Gaullist deputy cites Fifth Republic accomplishments in education, sports, housing for the young, and calls for separate Ministry for Youth. In appendices are statistics for participation in French athletic leagues for 1958, 1965, and 1966, government athletics budgets 1955-68, Vivien's bill for lowering voting age to 19. Speech delivered at U.D.-Ve Assises nationales, Lille, Nov. 1967.

1115　LA VOIX DU NORD. Un grand journal régional d'information: La Voix du Nord. Lille, 1961. 67 p. illus., maps, diagrs.

Technical aspects of producing and distributing this regional newspaper of northern France with a circulation of 1,400,000 and staff of over 1,000.

1116　VOLCOUVE, VICTOR. La crise du franc. Paris, Editions du Seuil, 1969. 143 p. (Société, 34)

Domestic and international monetary aspects of "franc crisis" in final months of de Gaulle's rule. Author shows effects of Grenelle agreements, June 1968, on price level and misjudgments in monetary and fiscal policy leading to gold drain.

1117 VOLTA, ORNELLA. Diario di Parigi, 1956-1968. Milano, Longanesi, 1969. 318 p. ("La Fronda," v. 96)

Most of the nearly daily diary entries fall between May 1 and June 16, 1968, with scattered entries up to Oct. 1968. Author's main concerns are problems of the universities, opinions and behavior of leftist intellectuals, academic and creative (writers, journalists, film producers), and their links with P. C. F., smaller revolutionary groups. No personal comments of author. Good name index.

1118 VUILLEMIN, JULES. Rebâtir l'université. Paris, Fayard, 1968. 84 p. (Le Monde sans frontières)

Proposals for university reform completed largely before May 1968: student recruitment, decentralization, regional autonomy, greater coordination of student orientation and requirements of the economy. Author is professor at Collège de France.

1119 WADIER, HENRI. La réforme de l'enseignement n'aura pas lieu. Paris, R. Laffont, 1970. 266 p. (Collection "Réponses")

Title refers to perennial shortcomings of French primary and secondary education (excessive discipline, poor organization of school year, overwork, overemphasis on competition and grades, disdainful attitude of professors toward students) as well as to the failures of recent Gaullist reforms in preschool education, development of mass "middle school" system. May 1968 is seen as justified revolt against these shortcomings and failures. Author draws on his many years' experience as primary school inspector and father of five children who have recently completed lycée. Work includes constructive and practical suggestions for teaching of reading and composition, new mathematics. Of particular interest is characterization of primary school "instituteurs" and their unequal relations with "professeurs" issued from universities. Main conclusion is that the best of primary school child-centered pedagogy intended for mass education must be fused with greater intellectual competence of secondary education.

1120 WAITES, NEVILLE, ed. Troubled neighbours: Franco-British relations in the twentieth century. London, Weidenfeld, 1971. 386 p. (Reading University studies on contemporary Europe) Includes bibliographies.

Individual contributions on different periods of Franco-British relations, with final chapter by Guy de Carmoy on such Fifth Republic developments as collaboration on military projects, negotiations over Common Market membership.

1121 WALSH, ANNMARIE HAUCK. Urban government for the Paris region. New York, Praeger, 1968. xvi, 217 p. illus., maps. (International urban studies of the Institute of Public Administration, 1) Bibliography: p. 211-217. ML

Physical, economic, demographic description of Paris region with its 8-1/2 million inhabitants as of 1964. Administrative and political organization, allocation of budget prior to and after 1964-66 regional reorganization and appointment of Paul Delouvrier as regional prefect, planning for Paris area. Details on functioning of main urban services (water supply, mass transportation, subsidized low-cost housing, education) reflect effectiveness of urban government. International comparisons in certain aspects of urban administration.

1122 WASIELEWSKI, PAWEŁ. Francja w roku odejścia De Gaulle'a. Warszawa, Wydawn. Ministerstwa Obrony Narodowej, 1970. 153 p. (Ideologia, polityka, obronność)

Continuity and change in French internal and foreign policy in year following de Gaulle's retirement.

1123 WATERMAN, HARVEY. Political change in contemporary France; the politics of an industrial democracy. Columbus, Ohio, C. E. Merrill, 1969. xiv, 256 p. (Merrill political science series) Bibliography: p. 239-252.

Work by American political scientist completed just before May 1968, demonstrating how French politics is becoming less ideological and violent and how a more stable, consensual political community typical of modern industrial democracies is emerging. Changes both in political style and in political behavior are analyzed. There are chapters on major political ideologies (socialist, Communist, liberal, Catholic, nationalist), relations between voters and politicians, participation in elections, forms of protest. Epilogue clarifies how May 1968 events fit into general analysis by presenting French university as major anachronistic element and therefore out of step with French society.

1124 WEBER, ANDRE-PAUL. Les concentrations industrielles dans la France contemporaine. Paris, Bordas, 1971. 142 p. tables. (Collection Bordas-Connaissance. Série information, 26) Bibliography: p. 139-142.

Statistics on industrial mergers in different sectors of industry, 1950-70, economic factors and government policy encouraging concentration, international comparisons on degree of concentration, impact of monopolistic tendencies on competition, and need for U. S.-style antitrust legislation.

1125 WEBER, PIERRE-ANDRE. Les grandes énigmes de mai 1968. Présentées par Jean Dumont. Enquête et textes de Pierre-André Weber avec la collaboration de Jean Salez. Genève, Editions de Crémille, 1970. 3 v. (248 p.; 240 p.; 238 p.). plates. Bibliography: v. 3, p. [233]-238.

Lengthy introduction on student revolts outside France, followed by straightforward chronological account of events in France beginning with troubles at Nanterre and ending with June elections. Some of material is based on personal interviews with participants (students, Catholic priests, government officials, police) and on radio broadcasts. Detailed accounts of Odéon occupation, O.R.T.F. strike, role of leftist priests. Reproduces text of alarmist confidential report on state of incipient civil war submitted to de Gaulle on his return from Rumania, entitled "La machine infernale." First volume covers events through May 9, second volume through May 15, third volume through June elections. Many photographs.

1126 WEINSTOCK, ULRICH. Regionale Wirtschaftspolitik in Frankreich; eine Auseinandersetzung mit ihren Problemen und Methoden. Hamburg, Verlag Weltarchiv, 1968. 344 p. maps. (Veröffentlichungen des Hamburgischen Weltwirtschafts-Archivs) Bibliography: p. [329]-344.

Regional planning history, concepts, aims, methods, organizations, incorporation into Fifth Plan. Among specific issues examined in detail are relation of regional planning and central budget, private and public investments. Developments in regional planning followed up through 1966. Good statistics on population and economic conditions for different regions. Work based on dissertation, done with help of French planning agencies. Extensive bibliography of books and articles on regional planning.

1127 WEISS, OTTO GEORGES. L'économie française; analyse et étude préliminaire pour la construction d'une seconde base économique fondamentale. Paris, Structures nouvelles, 1969. 31 p.

Addendum to earlier work (see next entry), with further discussion of obstacles to economic growth and detailed plan for Centre national de la recherche, du recyclage et de l'information suggested in main volume. This center would stimulate reemployment of displaced workers and concentrate applied research in laboratory-factories. Construction of the center is proposed for the Lozère department.

1128 WEISS, OTTO GEORGES. L'économie française; réalités et perspectives. Paris, Structures nouvelles, 1969. 194 p. tables.

Survey of French economy with chapters on gross national product, population (historical and regional evolution, immigration), agriculture, energy, raw materials, imports (special discussion of problems of the automobile), productivity, employment, consumption patterns and average income, wages, education, scientific research. French and international statistics for each section, highlighting weaknesses of economy and suggesting alternatives. Author develops proposal for a Centre national de la recherche, du recyclage et de l'information, a combined science, research, and adult education city of about 100,000 to be located in a poor region of central France. See preceding entry for addendum.

1129 WEYGAND, JACQUES. Weygand mon père. Paris, Flammarion, 1970. 503 p. ports.

Biography of General Maxime Weygand, with last chapters on his activities during Fifth Republic. After 1959, he maintained a rigid hostility toward de Gaulle, whose return to power he originally welcomed. He died at 98 in 1965.

1130 WILLENER, ALFRED. L'image-action de la société, ou La politisation culturelle. Paris, Editions du Seuil, 1970. 351 p. (Collection Esprit. "La Cité prochaine") Bibliography: p. 342-346. ML

French social psychologist uses May 1968 explosion as case study for images of society in a period of rapid and irreversible change. May 1968 is characterized as double juncture between anarchism and Marxism, on the one hand, and politics and culture, on the other. Book is divided into: (1) full-length May 25, 1968, interview with female sociology student active in May events; (2) opinion poll of 77 Sorbonne humanities and science students on their image of society, forces leading to change, as exemplified by May 1968; (3) Nov. 1968 discussion with group of young sociologists on May events; (4) ideas paralleling students' image of established society and counter-images based on imagination and action, notably theories of "Situationnisme"; and (5) parallel artistic movements--Dadaism, surrealism, free jazz, experimental cinema and theater. Appendices with typical poems, leaflets, photographs of posters and graffiti, as well as long interview with retired engineer, Nov. 1968, exemplifying antagonistic response to events. Willener believes that the "cultural politization"--that is, turning the individual's experience of daily life and action into an element of his final goals, which rejects technocratic perspective as much as abstract veneration of culture--will be carried over even after political defeat. Its central axes are drives for self-realization through "autogestion" and for permanent change. English translation, "The action-image of society on cultural politicization" (London, 1970), at HL.

1131 WILLENER, ALFRED, CATHERINE GAJDOS, and GEORGES BENGUIGUI. Les cadres en mouvement. Paris, Editions de l'Epi, 1969. 284 p. (Colloques et recherches de la Fondation Royaumont) Bibliography: p. 259-273.

Investigation of "cadres" (technical and administrative white-collar employees) sponsored by Fondation Royaumont, which is supported by 30 French firms and brings together C.N.R.S. sociologists and government and industrial administrators. One study deals with actions and attitudes of union organizations of "cadres," notably the Confédération générale des cadres (C.G.C.) and the recently founded Centre national des jeunes cadres, as well as C.G.T.- and C.F.D.T.-affiliated unions toward May-June 1968 events. A second study concentrates on strike in one (anonymous) company and examines protest movement among "cadres," projects for achieving greater autonomy and participation in decision-making, recognition of technical competence. Final study compares "cadre" attitudes toward unionization in different types of firms.

1132 WILLIAMS, PHILIP MAYNARD. The French Parliament: politics in the Fifth Republic. New York, Praeger, 1968. 136 p. (Studies in political science, 2) Bibliography: p. [125]-126.

Changes introduced by Fifth Republic in operation of parliament, composition of both houses through 1967 elections. Major alterations in functioning studied in parliamentary checks on cabinet, passage of new laws, budget control. There are five legislative case studies: 1960 bill on liquor distilling, 1963 bill on strike limitations, 1964 bill on broadcasting, 1965 bill on value-added tax, 1966 bill on child adoption. Situations with and without Gaullist majority in parliament are compared. Overall judgment on new parliamentary model is favorable.

1133 WILLIAMS, PHILIP MAYNARD. French politicians and elections, 1951-1969. With David Goldey and Martin Harrison. Cambridge, Eng., University Press, 1970. xvii, 312 p. tables, maps.

Mainly collection of articles on current events, by Williams, Harrison, and Goldey published in British press. For Fifth Republic, one section deals with phases of Algerian war and its settlement as reflected in establishment and consolidation of Fifth Republic, 1958-62, another with unsuccessful challenges to Gaullist regime from Left, 1960-65, and a final section with the serious and successful challenges, 1965-69, with articles on 1965, 1967, and 1968 elections, 1969 referendum and election, and long article on May 1968 events. Useful tables and maps on different facets of election results, such as comparative results for 1951-68 legislative elections in 13 selected voting districts. Good list of abbreviations.

1134 WILLIAMS, PHILIP MAYNARD. Wars, plots and scandals in post-war France. Cambridge, Eng., University Press, 1970. 232 p.

Twelve articles on political plots and scandals since World War II, mostly related to decolonization. Introductory article shows role of scandals in attacks by French Right. Three scandals relate directly to decolonization problems: 1956 affaire des fuites, 1959 Mitterrand assassination plot, and 1965 assassination of Ben Barka (described in great detail). Other chapters focus on plots surrounding fall of Fourth Republic, Generals' Putsch of 1961.

1135 WILSON, FRANK L. The French democratic left, 1963-1969; toward a modern party system. Stanford, Calif., Stanford University Press, 1971. 258 p. Bibliography: p. [221]-250.

Study based in part on interviews with 76 political figures associated with French Left (e.g., Mitterrand, Hernu, Estier, Savary, Rocard, Pineau, Pomonti, listed in appendix) on unsuccessful attempts of French Left to counteract its declining popularity in Fifth Republic by constituting a majority-oriented "catch-all" party similar to the German Social Democratic model. Specific manifestations are proliferation of political clubs, Defferre's abortive 1965 presidential candidacy, political efforts of short lived Fédération de la gauche démocrate et socialiste and its failure to become either a centrist or a leftist party. Impact of genuine bipolarism in French politics is assessed negatively for its civil-war potential (e.g., pre World War II Austria). Excellent bibliography.

1136 WYLIE, LAURENCE WILLIAM, ed. Chanzeaux, a village in Anjou. Cambridge, Mass., Harvard University Press, 1966. xx, 383 p. illus., maps.

Sociological study following same design as Wylie's 1950-51 investigation of village in the Vaucluse, but carried out together with a dozen Harvard students. On-the-spot research was done in 1957 and 1965, and book is a joint product. Chanzeaux is located in west-central France, in a notably conservative, Catholic-dominated area hostile to republican tradition. Commune of over 1,000 inhabitants is primarily agricultural and in slow decline; leaders belong to Catholic farm organizations. Special section is devoted to religious behavior, which also determines political divisions; latter are traced back to French Revolution. In 1962 Gaullists had majority of vote, Communist and non-Communist Left together 3 percent! Includes description of patterns of childhood, adolescence, and old age.

1137 WYLIE, LAURENCE WILLIAM, FRANKLIN D. CHU, and MARY TERRALL. France: the events of May-June 1968; a critical bibliography. Cambridge, Mass., Council for European Studies, 1973. iv, 118 p. (Western European Studies, Harvard University)

Annotated bibliography compiled by participants in Wylie's French civilization seminars at Harvard, 1968-72, and edited by Wylie et al. The first part annotates over 200 alphabetically arranged books on May events, most of them available at Hoover and itemized in the present volume. The second part gives alphabetical listing of selected newspapers, magazines, and journals, for each of which articles (about 500 in all) related to May events are chronologically listed and identified by author and content. The following files were completely scrutinized: (1) newspapers (Combat, Humanité, Le Monde); (2) weeklies (Express, Nouvel observateur, Paris-Match); (3) general-interest periodicals (Economie et humanisme, Esprit, Evénement, Nouvelle critique, Pensée, Projet, Temps modernes); (4) scholarly journals (Annales, Cahiers internationaux de sociologie, Revue française de science politique, Revue française de sociologie, Sociologie du travail). For nearly 50 other periodicals, special issues devoted to May events or individual articles of interest are cited. Nearly all periodicals listed in the second part are at Hoover (see Part II in French Fifth Republic Bibliography, 1, as well as in the present volume; however, some of the special periodical issues have been catalogued and can be found in Part I of the present volume). The third part locates and describes special collections of ephemerae, microfilms, and tapes in France and elsewhere. Harvard's own tape collection includes: (1) nine tapes from May-June radio broadcasts (de Gaulle, Malraux, activists' speeches and interviews, etc.); (2) 13 tapes of interviews done by Wylie in France, Aug.-Sept. 1968 (Paul Maucorps, Jean-Pierre Vigier, Jean-Pierre Biondi, Jean-Marie Vincent, etc.); (3) eight tapes of lectures and discussions by French scholars at Harvard 1968-69 (Pierre Grappin, Michel Crozier). Four of these tapes are at Hoover (see no. 484 [D]), as are microfilms made by Association pour la conservation et la reproduction photographique de la presse (see nos. 482 and 485).

1138 YACANO, XAVIER. Histoire de la colonisation française. Paris, Presses universitaires de France, 1969. 127 p. ("Que sais-je?" 452)

Final 15 pages give compact summary of dissolution of French Empire under Fourth and Fifth Republic.

1139 YSMAL, COLETTE. La carrière politique de Gaston Defferre. Paris, Fondation nationale des sciences politiques, 1965. 71 p. (Centre d'étude de la vie politique française. Série: Recherches, no. 3) Bibliographical footnotes.

Concentrates on his activities as socialist politician, government member in Fourth Republic, mayor of Marseille. Topically arranged speeches and statements on major political issues (political institutions, Algeria, Europe). Work concluded June 1965, as Defferre's candidacy for presidential election was under serious consideration.

1140 YSMAL, COLETTE. Defferre parle (18 décembre 1963-25 juin 1965). Paris, Fondation nationale des sciences politiques, 1966. 125 p. Centre d'étude de la vie politique française. Série: Recherches, no. 4)

Defferre's abortive candidacy for 1965 presidential election, withdrawal June 25, 1965, significance of this retreat for Fédération de la gauche démocrate et socialiste, restructuring of non-Communist Left, and pursuit of "modern socialism." Topically arranged and annotated excerpts from speeches under these headings: candidacy; program and relations with "forces nouvelles"; stand on political institutions, foreign and domestic policy. Aug. 1962-June 1965 chronology of major political developments.

1141 ZAMANSKY, MARC. Mort ou résurrection de l'Université. Paris, Plon, 1969. 158 p. (Tribune libre) ML

As dean of Sorbonne Faculté des sciences, author was personally involved in May 1968 events. Student discontent is blamed on incoherence of prior reforms and on professors' encouragement of student irrationalism. Account of Sorbonne occupation and acts of vandalism, based on author's own observations, difficulties created by Oct. 1968 university reform. Selection of students for degree-carrying university curricula is considered imperative; budgetary autonomy of universities and student participation in administration are denounced as impractical slogans.

1142 ZEGEL, SYLVAIN. Les idées de mai. Paris, Gallimard, 1968. 245 p. (Collection Idées)

Well-selected compendium of ideas and proposals emerging from May 1968 revolution, though exact sources are not given for quotations. Book is divided into these topics: (1) Mouvement du 22 mars; (2) students and workers; (3) university reform--letters and sciences, medicine, fine arts and architecture, law and social sciences (Institut d'études politiques, E.N.A.), scientific research; (4) lycée movement; (5) reforms proposed by professors, including May 12 manifesto by 75 professors (with names of signers); and (6) theater and cinema.

1143 ZIEBURA, GILBERT. Die deutsch-französischen Beziehungen seit 1945; Mythen u. Realitäten. Pfullingen, Neske, 1970. 200 p. Includes bibliographical references.

Half of volume deals with Fifth Republic, with emphasis on economic relations and the Common Market, military relations and N.A.T.O. Myths of either perfect collaboration or outright hostility are yielding to coexistence with mutual dependence and unresolved conflicts and, upon de Gaulle's withdrawal, to down-to-earth accommodations.

1144 ZIEGLER, GILETTE G. Le défi de la Sorbonne; sept siècles de contestation. Paris, Julliard, 1969. 191 p. plates, ports. Includes bibliography.

Conflicts at Sorbonne from the Middle Ages through May 1968, with last 20 pages describing incidents during Fifth Republic.

PART II: SERIAL PUBLICATIONS

Serials previously listed in the French Fifth Republic Bibliography, 1, Part II, and cited as 1967+ (currently received) are not repeated here. With the exception of nos. 1171 and 1232 (Espoir, Unité), files whose initial issue postdates 1970 have been omitted.

Publications listed in this section can be located in the French newspaper and serials catalogues, with the following exceptions: serials designated ML (Main Library, Stanford) or BS (Library of the School of Business Administration, Stanford); and serials flagged by an asterisk, denoting that they can be located in other special Hoover Institution catalogues.

Unless specified, the initial date is January and the terminal date December. A broken file is indicated by brackets, but isolated missing numbers are not taken into account.

Separately catalogued individual issues of periodicals (e.g., Défense de l'Occident) are listed in Part I. Two special microfilmed newspaper collections are itemized in Part I, nos. 482 and 485. See also no. 484 (B) for information on another special newspaper collection.

Title changes can be traced through the Title Index.

1145 Action; réalisé au service des Comités d'action avec le soutien de l'U.N.E.F., du S.N.E.Sup. et des Comités d'action lycéens. May 1968-June 1969. Paris.

Paper published weekly in May, nearly daily June 5 through July 1968, irregularly thereafter. Edited by Jean-Pierre Vigier (see no. 484 [D3]). This was the most widely read of the student revolt publications.

1146 Algérien en Europe; organe de l'émigration algérienne. Mar. 1969-1972+. Paris. Bi-weekly.

Closely linked to official Algerian views, with some material on living conditions of Algerians in France.

1147 Anarchisme et non-violence. [1966-1967] 1968-1972+. Marseilles/Paris. Quarterly.

Organ of anarchists and conscientious objectors.

1148 Aux écoutes. Sept. 1958-Feb. 1959; June 1961-June 1962; Feb. 1967-Mar. 1969// Paris. Bi-monthly.

Popular political paper with right-wing, anti-Gaullist orientation.

1149 BANQUE NATIONALE DE PARIS. Revue économique. 1967-1972+. Monthly. BS

Supersedes BANQUE NATIONALE POUR LE COMMERCE ET L'INDUSTRIE. Bulletin d'information économique (see French Fifth Republic Bibliography, 1, no. 1845). Articles on French industries, technology, foreign trade.

1150 Cahier et revue de l'Ours. July 1969-1972+. Paris. Monthly.

Nos. 1-30 entitled Cahier de l'Ours. Supplement to L'Ours (see below, no. 1203). Each issue contains complete presentation on topics such as S.F.I.O. history, economic theory, role of trade unions, social classes by members of Office universitaire de recherche socialiste or O.U.R.S. study groups.

1151 Cahiers de l'Union des démocrates. Sept. 1970-1972+. Paris. 6 a year or irregular.

Organ of Union des démocrates pour la république for party militants and press information.

1152 Cahiers d'histoire de l'Institut Maurice Thorez. Apr. 1966-1972+. Paris. 6 a year.

Title changed 1972 from Cahiers de l'Institut Maurice Thorez. Institut Maurice Thorez serves as P.C.F. political education center concentrating on history of Communism, political and ideological questions of current interest, problems of party's internal organization. Cahiers reproduce texts of P.C.F. leaders' lectures, Institute-sponsored conferences and colloquia. Of special interest is issue no. 5, 1970, with full-length review of Fondation nationale des sciences politiques' "Communisme en France" (see no. 419). See also Institut Maurice Thorez in Author Index.

1153 Cahiers du C.E.R.E.S. Oct. 1967-June 1972. Paris. 2 a year.

Centre d'étude de recherches et d'éducation socialiste founded 1966 by S.F.I.O. dissidents urging unification of Left, but represented in new Parti socialiste. Cahiers have articles on economic and ideological questions, structure and organization of socialist parties, strategy for unification of Left. See also Volonté socialiste (no. 1235). After Dec. 1972 title changed to Frontière, a monthly addressed to wider audience.

1154 Cahiers du communisme révolutionnaire. July-Oct. 1964; Feb. 1967// Paris. Quarterly.

Organ of Parti communiste révolutionnaire de France, which calls itself Marxist-Leninist-Stalinist movement.

1155 Cahiers marxistes-léninistes; organe théorique et politique de l'Union des jeunesses communistes (marxistes-léninistes). July/Oct. 1966-Apr./June 1968// Paris. Quarterly.

Originally organ of Cercle des étudiants communistes de l'Ecole normale supérieure, close to Althusser. Addressed to intellectual elements. The U.J.C.M.-L. was dissolved June 1968.

1156 Le Canard enchaîné. 1966-1972+. Paris. Weekly.

For special issues and publications of this satirical newspaper, see also nos. 176 and 177.

1157 La Cause du peuple, nouvelle série; journal communiste révolutionnaire prolétarien. May-June 1968; Aug. 1969; June-Oct. 1970; 1971-1972+. Paris. Irregular.

Original subtitle "journal du mouvement de soutien aux luttes du peuple," then "journal du front populaire." Nearly daily from end of May to end of June 1968. Important organ for student-worker alliance; later voice of most activist of extreme Left, the Gauche prolétarienne.

99

1158 Confronter. Oct. 1968-1972+. Paris. 6 a year.

Continues Perspectives socialistes (see French Fifth Republic Bibliography, 1, no. 2047). Published by Centre de culture ouvrière.

1159 Contacts européens. Nov. 1969-1972+. Paris. Irregular. Organisation française du Mouvement européen.

1160 Contrepoint. May 1970-1972+. Paris. 3 a year.

Cultural and political topics, middle-of-the-road, with some of same contributors as Esprit.

1161 Croissance des jeunes nations. Mar. 1967-1972+. Paris. Monthly.

Political and economic developments in Third World, status of immigrant workers in France from point of view of Catholic Left. Edited by Georges Hourdin.

1162 Défense de l'Occident. Jan./Feb. 1970-1972+. Paris. Monthly.

Edited by Maurice Bardèche. Extreme Right orientation. See also nos. 4, 81, 319, and 360.

1163 Démocrates; revue d'information de l'Union des démocrates pour la Vᵉ République. Apr. 1968-1972+. Paris. 5 a year.

General interest articles and news of party.

1164 2000; revue de l'aménagement du territoire et du développement régional. 1966-1970. Paris. Irregular. ML

Glossily illustrated articles on regional and city planning, government policy on environmental protection, long-range planning.

1165 Dossiers de l'Entreprise. Feb. 1968+. Paris. Irregular. BS

Supplement to Entreprise (no. 1170), each issue on a special topic such as service industries, business machines, transportation.

1166 Economie et comptabilité; gestion des entreprises. Mar. 1964-1972+. Paris. Quarterly. Institut français des experts comptables. BS

Technical and broader articles on private and public enterprises.

1167 Economie et humanisme. Jan./Feb. 1966-1972+. Lyon. 6 a year.

Social and economic questions, problems of modern civilization. Catholic Left orientation.

1168 Economie et statistique. May 1969-1972+. Paris. Monthly. BS

Issued by I.N.S.E.E.; supersedes Etudes et conjonctures. Articles on economic and demographic trends, with facts and figures on employment, consumption, housing, production, government economic policy. See also Tendances de la conjoncture (no. 1230).

1169 L'Enragé. May 24 [?]-July 8, 1969. Paris. Weekly.

Edited by J. J. Pauvert. Seven issues, of which first two undated. Satirical comments on current events by means of cartoons, poetry, etc.

1170 Entreprise. Apr. 1953-1972+. Paris. Weekly. BS

Business news, developments in French and European economic policy.

1171 Espoir; revue de l'Institut Charles de Gaulle. Sept. 1972+. Paris. 6 a year.

Testimonies about de Gaulle, unpublished de Gaulle documents, papers. No. 2 (Jan. 1973) reproduces unpublished speeches and writings of André Malraux. For other publications of Institut Charles de Gaulle, see Paris. Institut Charles de Gaulle in Author Index.

1172 Evénement. Jan. 1967-Jan. 1969; numéro spécial June/July 1969// Paris. Monthly.

Founded and edited till his death by Emmanuel d'Astier de la Vigerie. Chronology of events, articles. Not anti-Gaullist.

1173 Expansion; mensuel économique. 1969-1972+. Paris.

Business and political monthly published by Servan-Schreiber family with support of McGraw-Hill.

1174 Le Fédéré; Bretagne et démocratie; organe mensuel du Parti socialiste d'Ille-et-Vilaine et Finistère. June 1967-June 1969// Rennes.

1175 Le Figaro; sélection hebdomadaire. June 23, 1966-Dec. 1967. Paris.

Daily Le Figaro available on microfilm through Interlibrary Loan.

1176 FRANCE. COMITE INTERMINISTERIEL POUR L'INFORMATION. SECRETARIAT GENERAL. La Politique de la France. 1970-1972+. Paris. 6 a year. ML

Supersedes La Politique étrangère de la France (no. 1178). Published jointly with Direction de la documentation. Two issues a year on foreign policy (with same title as before) combined with four issues on domestic policy entitled "La politique intérieure de la France; chronologie, déclarations gouvernementales." This is a most useful tool for all French political events. Day-by-day account of domestic events, political activities, followed by speeches, interviews by government members in chronological order. List of laws. Excellent subject index for each issue, including listing of activities by political parties, organizations, business, professional, trade union groups.

1177* FRANCE. DIRECTION DE LA DOCUMENTATION. Documents officiels. 1967-1972+. Paris. Weekly.

Texts of documents on international relations (conferences, military pacts, space, etc.), NATO, European Communities, international economic relations, and French relations with individual countries. Annual index. Published jointly with Ministère des affaires étrangères, Service d'information et de presse. Title changed 1972 to Documents d'actualité internationale.

1178 FRANCE. MINISTERE DES AFFAIRES ETRANGERES. SERVICE D'INFORMATION ET DE PRESSE. La Politique étrangère de la France; textes et documents. 1966-June 1969// Paris. 2 a year. ML

Published jointly with Direction de la documentation. Superseded by France. Comité interministériel pour l'information's La Politique de la France (no. 1176). For English version for 1966-69 and fuller description, see no. 474.

1179* FRANCE. MINISTERE D'ETAT DES AFFAIRES CULTURELLES. Bulletin des nouvelles acquisitions. 1968-1972+. Paris. Annual.

Archives nationales, Section d'outre-mer's annual acquisitions list, topically arranged. Includes general works on French politics, decolonization, reference works.

1180   France informations. Oct. 1967-1972+. Paris. Monthly.

English edition published by Ministère des affaires étrangères. Service d'information et de presse. Material of general interest on French society.

1181   France moderne. Jan. 1967-Sept. 1968; May 1969-1972+. Paris. Monthly. Fédération nationale des Républicains Indépendants.

Between Oct. 1968 and Apr. 1969, publication changed title to Réponses--France moderne (see no. 1216).

1182   French-American commerce. May-June 1958-1972+. Paris. 6 a year. French Chamber of Commerce in U.S. BS

Articles in French and English. Information on U.S. firms in France and French firms in U.S., foreign trade regulations, descriptions of individual French industries.

1183   FRONT DU PROGRES. Notes d'information. Mar. 1968-1972+. Paris. Fortnightly or weekly.

Supplement to Télégramme de Paris (see French Fifth Republic Bibliography, 1, no. 2109). Organ of left-wing Gaullists currently grouped under Union travailliste, founded 1971.

1184   Guerres et paix; revue trimestrielle de l'Institut français de polémologie. 1966-1970// Paris.

Problems of violence, international relations. For special issue on student revolt, see no. 566. Continued July 1971 under title Etudes polémologiques.

1185   L'Homme et la société; revue internationale de recherches et de synthèses sociologiques. Oct. 1966-1972+. Paris. Quarterly. M L

Focus on Marxism, Marxist sociology.

1186   L'Humanité nouvelle; organe central du Parti communiste marxiste-léniniste de France. Mar. 1966-June 6, 1968// Paris. Weekly.

Dissolved by government order and continued by L'Humanité rouge. Maoist views.

1187   L'Humanité rouge; hebdomadaire d'information et d'etudes marxiste-léniniste au service des luttes des ouvriers, paysans et intellectuels. Sept. 18, 1969-1972+. Paris.

Continues L'Humanité nouvelle.

1188   I.T.C. actualités; revue mensuelle du Parti communiste français. Jan. 1970-1972// Paris.

P.C.F.'s organ addressed to "ingénieurs, techniciens, cadres," but intended for wider educated audience and treating social and economic questions in less dogmatic fashion than other party publications.

1189   Idiot international. Dec. 1969-Nov. 1972// Paris. Monthly.

Appeal to whole range of revolutionary Left from Marxist-Leninist to anarchist, libertarian, with news coverage of French and international events. Among editors: Gilbert Mury, Simone de Beauvoir. Frequent judicial pursuits. Superseded by Tempêtes--Idiot international.

1190   Idiot liberté. Dec. 1970-June 1971. Paris. Bi-monthly.

Alternated with Idiot international during this period, concentrating on French social problems.

1191   Informations ouvrières; organe de la Fédération d'Alliance ouvrière. June 1970-1972+. Paris. Weekly.

Linked with Trotskyist Organisation communiste internationaliste and Alliance des jeunes pour le socialisme. See also La Vérité (no. 1233) and no. 778.

1192   Internationale situationniste. July 1958-Sept. 1969. Paris. Irregular.

One-volume reprint of all twelve issues. Final two issues were published Oct. 1967 and Sept. 1969. Important organ for controversies surrounding cultural revolution and attacks on modern civilization. See also Internationale situationniste in Author Index.

1193   Jeune révolutionnaire; organe mensuel de l'Alliance des jeunes pour le socialisme. Dec. 1968-1972+. Paris. Monthly or bi-monthly.

Linked to Organisation communiste internationaliste (Trotskyist), which was dissolved June 1968, and addressed to students and young workers. See also no. 1201.

1194   Lettres françaises. Mar. 1968-May 1970. Paris. Weekly.

Edited by Louis Aragon. Communist-oriented cultural weekly, split with P.C.F. after 1968.

1195   Ligne rouge; journal communiste (marxiste-léniniste). Sept.-Oct. 1969. Paris. Monthly.

Maoist student publication critical of L'Humanité rouge.

1196   Lutte communiste. Jan. 1968-Sept. 1969. Paris. Weekly or fortnightly.

On microfilm (one reel). Organ of Parti communiste révolutionnaire, tendance Posadas (Trotskyist).

1197   Le Monde. June 1966-1972+. Paris. Daily.

1198   Le Monde juif; revue du Centre de documentation juive contemporaine. Jan./Mar. 1964-Apr./June 1964; Dec. 1965-1972+. Paris. Quarterly.

Mainly international Jewish affairs, some information on French Jewry. For other publications of Centre de documentation juive contemporaine, see nos. 197 and 198.

1199   Le Monde uni. Dec. 1967-Mar. 1972// Paris. Bi-monthly.

Organ of Mouvement mondialiste, concerned with problems of world poverty. Message continued by Terre entière (no. 1231).

1200   Le Nouveau Clarté; mensuel de l'Union des étudiants communistes de France. Feb. 1969-1972+. Paris.

Orthodox organ of P.C.F.'s student organization.

1201   Nouvelles études marxistes; revue de l'Alliance des étudiants révolutionnaires. 1970-1972+. Paris. Irregular.

Published by Centre d'études marxistes and closely linked to Trotskyist Alliance des jeunes pour le socialisme. Some news about U.N.E.F. activities.

1202   Objectif 72. Jan. 1969-1972+. Paris. Monthly.

Organ of leftist political club of same name initiated by Robert Buron.

1203   L'Ours. July 1969-1972+. Paris. Monthly.

Organ of Office universitaire de recherche socialiste founded by Guy Mollet in 1969 after dissolution of S.F.I.O. Publication still under his control. See also Cahier et revue de l'Ours (no. 1150).

1204 PARIS. UNIVERSITE. BIBLIOTHEQUE DE DOCUMENTATION INTERNATIONALE CONTEMPORAINE. Nouvelles acquisitions. Jan.-Dec. 1967. Paris. Bi-monthly.

Bibliothèque de documentation internationale contemporaine, like Hoover Institution, specializes in political crises of 20th century. Listing of new acquisitons only, organized topically: international problems (political, social, economic, military, intellectual, religious, regional), World Wars I and II, national problems, with section on France. Library is now located at Centre universitaire de Paris-Ouest.

1205 Paris-Match. 1966-1972+. Paris. Weekly. ML

1206 Politique aujourd'hui. Jan. 1969-1972+. Paris. Monthly.

Largest circulation periodical of leftist intellectuals. Founded by P.C.F. dissidents connected with P.C.F.'s Démocratie nouvelle. Not tied to any party at present.

1207 Politique hebdo. Oct. 1970-Mar. 1971; Oct. 1971-1972+. Paris. Weekly.

Weekly with same editor as Politique aujourd'hui but with few Communist dissident contributors. Forced to close because of financial troubles in Mar. 1971, rescued Oct. 1971. Concentrates on current events.

1208 Le Populaire de Paris; organe central du Parti socialiste S.F.I.O. Jan. 1967-Dec. 1969// Paris. Twice weekly.

Function of this venerable socialist organ, whose publication ceased after S.F.I.O.'s demise, has been taken over by Parti socialiste's (1969-) Unité (see no. 1232).

1209 Problèmes politiques et sociaux; articles et documents d'actualité mondiale. 1970-1972+. Paris. Weekly.

Supersedes Direction de la documentation's Articles et documents (see French Fifth Republic Bibliography, 1, no. 1839). Each issue is devoted to a special topic, mainly international. Annual index.

1210 Progrès et liberté; bulletin mensuel du Mouvement national Progrès et liberté. June 1970-1972+. Neuilly-sur-Seine.

Organ of party of same name founded by Jacques Soustelle Apr. 1970 and edited by him.

1211 Propos; revue des jeunesses radicales. Nov. 1967-Apr. 1968. Paris. Monthly.

Organ of Parti républicain radical et radical-socialiste youth group.

1212 Quatrième internationale. 1956-1972+. Paris. 5 a year.

Edited by Pierre Frank. Trotskyist organ. Mainly international issues.

1213 Que faire? Cahiers du Centre d'études et d'initiative révolutionnaire. Feb. 1970-1972+. Paris. 5 a year.

Centre d'études et d'initiative révolutionnaire founded 1970 by P.S.U. dissidents. Each issue devoted to one topic, e.g., national minorities in France (Dec. 1971).

1214 Raison présente; revue trimestrielle editée par les Editions rationalistes. Feb./Apr. 1967-1972+. Paris. ML

General interest articles on all aspects of French political and intellectual controversies, many on Marxist thought, as well as articles on education.

1215 RENCONTRES SOCIALISTES DE GRENOBLE. Bulletin de liaison. Apr. 1968. Paris.

For conference itself, see French Fifth Republic Bibliography, 1, nos. 1509-1511.

1216 Réponses--France moderne. Oct. 15, 1968-Apr. 22, 1969. Paris. Weekly. Fédération nationale des Républicains indépendants.

Continues France moderne (see no. 1181). Original title resumed May 1969.

1217 Le Réveil de Djibouti. 1966-1972+. Djibouti. Weekly.

Newspaper of Territoire français des Afars et des Issas (formerly French Somaliland) which voted 1967 to stay part of France.

1218 Revue des droits de l'homme; revue de droit international et comparé. Jan. 1958-1972+. Paris, Strasbourg. Quarterly.

Scholarly juridical publication.

1219 Revue des études coopératives. Mar. 1970-1972+. Paris. Quarterly. Institut français de la coopération.

Organ of world-wide cooperative movement (agricultural, labor, consumer) and of French Groupement national de la coopération, founded 1968.

1220 Revue économique de la Banque nationale de France. 1967-1972+. Paris. Quarterly.

Studies on international trade, French investment, economic conditions in different regions of France. Good economic statistics.

1221 Revue française de l'élite européenne. 1956-1972+. Paris. Monthly. ML

Lavishly illustrated general interest magazine with good coverage of education, cultural affairs, technology. Special issue Feb.-Mar. 1969 on Algeria since independence: French-Algerian cooperation, economic, agricultural, educational, and cultural developments.

1222 Revue française du marketing. 1969-1972+. Paris. Quarterly. BS

Published by Association pour le développement des techniques du marketing. Articles on techniques of marketing, forecasting, advertising. English abstracts.

1223 Rouge; hebdomadaire de la Ligue communiste. Oct.-Nov. 1968; July 1969-June 1971; Jan. 1972+. Paris.

Important organ of Trotskyist Left founded by Cercles rouges Sept. 1968. For additional publications of Ligue communiste, see Ligue communiste in Author Index.

1224 S.N.E.SUP. Bulletin du syndicat national de l'enseignement supérieur. Feb. 1970-1972+. Paris. Monthly.

Reports on congresses, activities within universities, economic status of university personnel, adjustment to newly created university institutions.

1225 SOCIETE D'ETUDES ET DE DOCUMENTATIONS ECONOMIQUES, INDUSTRIELLES ET SOCIALES. Analyse et prévision. 1966-1972+. Paris. Monthly. ML

Supersedes Bulletin SEDEIS (see French Fifth Republic Bibliography, 1, no. 2096). Edited by Bertrand de Jouvenel.

1226 SOCIETE D'ETUDES JAURESIENNES. Bulletin. 1967-1972+. Paris. Quarterly.

Totally devoted to Jaurès studies.

1227　Société nouvelle. Dec. 1969; Jan. 1970. Paris. Monthly.

　　　Social and educational topics.

1228　Le Soleil; journal d'action nationaliste. Feb. 1966-Feb. 1967. Paris. Monthly.

　　　Edited by Pierre Sidos. Organ of nationalist Right and addressed to same audience as Europe-Action.

1229　Statistiques et études financières. 1966-1972+. Paris. Monthly. Ministère de l'économie et des finances. BS

　　　Also monthly supplement. Statistical survey of monetary and fiscal conditions, reports on government economic policy and new legislation.

1230　Tendances de la conjoncture; graphiques mensuels. Apr. 1969-1972+. Paris. BS

　　　Issued by I.N.S.E.E. Charts showing trends in industrial production, wages, housing, consumption, foreign trade, prices, etc. Complements Economie et statistique (no. 1168).

1231　Terre entière. July/Aug. 1964; Mar./Apr. 1969-1972+. Paris. Bi-monthly.

　　　Edited by Robert de Montvalon. Concerned with role of Catholic Church in aid to underdeveloped countries, plight of immigrant workers in France, problems of education. Closely linked to Le Monde uni (no. 1199).

1232　Unité; hebdomadaire socialiste. 1972+. Paris.

　　　Organ of Parti socialiste (1969-) under Mitterrand's leadership. Addressed to wider audience (like defunct Le Populaire de Paris).

1233　La Verité; organe du comité central de l'organisation communiste internationaliste (pour la reconstruction de la IVe Internationale). Nov. 1969-1972+. Paris. Irregular.

　　　Not only international aspects of Trotskyism but French political issues, controversies with other French Marxist groups. Linked with Informations ouvrières (no. 1191).

1234　Vie française; la semaine économique et financière. 1965-1972+. Paris. Weekly. BS

　　　French business and financial newspaper.

1235　Volonté socialiste; bulletin du C.E.R.E.S. 1970-1972+. Paris, Irregular.

　　　Notes on current political issues, complementing Cahiers du C.E.R.E.S. (no. 1153).

SUBJECT INDEX

See Introduction for discussion of most important subject headings. Unless specified, all headings refer to France under the Fifth Republic.

ADMINISTRATION, BUSINESS. See Industrial management; Industrial relations

ADMINISTRATION, GOVERNMENTAL, 20, 188, 233, 297, 362, 376, 698, 870, 943; bibliography, 188; civil service, 20, 187, 302, 309, 453, 751, 855; decentralization, 453, 699, 789 (see also Decentralization); decision-making, 633, 800; directories, 448, 452, 549; in education, 453, 573, 811; information services, 991; local level, 73, 110, 140 (see also Local government); ministries and other divisions, 448, 452, 549, 906, 1034; regional, departmental, and local units, 73, 452, 1094, 1121 (see also Local government; Regional reform); technical experts, 800 (see also Science and state; Technocracy)

AFRICA, FRENCH. See Assistance, technical and economic: Africa; Decolonization; Foreign relations: African states; French Community; French Union

AFRICA, NORTH: bibliography, 29; European minority, 392; political developments, 29; reference works, 29. See also Algeria; Algeria, post-independence; Decolonization

AFRICANS IN FRANCE, 484 (A 12), 851. See also Students, African

AGRICULTURE, 135, 259, 328, 439, 708, 797, 848, 891, 1060; bibliography, 86; Gaullist policy, 86, 449, 708, 1060; land reform, 828; lumber, 443. See also Organizations, agricultural; Pressure groups: farmers; Rural and village life

ALGERIA: agriculture, 273; history, 3; Jewish minority, 223; judicial system, 701; organizations, 1084; political parties, 845; press, 686; sociological studies, 273

-- European settlers, 392; and Catholic Church, 790; personal narratives and fiction, 55, 105, 263, 686, 845; political attitudes, 638

-- Gaullist policy, 183, 283, 638, 779, 1077; documents, 296; personal narratives, 119, 296, 427, 1075; phonograph records, 483 (B 1)

-- independence, 638, 861; exodus of European settlers, pro-French Moslems and Jews, 223, 392, 878

-- political developments, 119, 283, 845, 876, 1075; elections and referenda, 1075; in 1958 (May-June), 283, 483 (B 1), 779, 845; 1960 (Jan.) barricades, 200, 183 (B 1), 779, 1022; 1961 (Apr.) Generals' Putsch, 283, 483 (B 1), 876, 1022; phonograph records, 483 (B 1)

-- political figures: European settlers, 686, 845

ALGERIA, POST-INDEPENDENCE, 1221; agriculture, 273; bibliography, 29; chronology, 29; economic development, 340, 355; education and culture, 340; emigration from, 1019; European minority, 392, 912; expropriation of French property, 467; foreign relations, 29, 340, 861; French aid and cooperation, 62; governmental documents, 29; judicial system, 701; opposition to government, 718; political developments, 29, 109, 340, 392, 701, 718, 953; political leaders, 718, 953; reference works, 29; relations with France, 989

ALGERIAN NATIONALISM: leadership, 953

ALGERIAN QUESTION, 392, 688; bibliographies, 392; pro-French Algerian polemics, 1077

ALGERIAN REVOLUTION: and Algerian students, 1084; Algerians' support of, 1077; French support of, 718, 780; history, 283, 597, 718; international aspects, 912, 1077; leadership, 191, 718, 780, 953, 1077; military aspects, 730, 780; and peasantry, 487. See also Front de libération nationale

ALGERIAN WAR (major works), 283, 803, 876, 1077; abbreviations, 1077; bibliographies, 283, 392, 1104; documents, 780; fiction, 748; final months of violence, 55, 119, 263, 296, 427, 483 (B 1), 599, 638, 648, 686, 876, 1075; maps, 1077; military strategy, 597, 780, 794, 883; movies on, 284, 1104; opposition to, by French intellectuals, 380, 1104; peace agreement, 392, 483 (B 1); peace negotiations, 427, 599, 912, 1075; phonograph records of speeches, 483 (B 1); pictorial works, 284

-- atrocities: torture, 329, 780, 883, 1104; terrorism by F.L.N., 780

-- military operations: air commando, 282; battle of Algiers (1957), 780

-- pacification program, 597; resettlement centers, 273

-- personal narratives: French civilians, 119; German diplomat, 861

-- personal narratives, French military, 353, 779, 780; air force, 174, 282, 648, 883; Foreign Legion, 128, 1022, 1023, 1059

ALGERIANS IN FRANCE, 62, 457, 614, 921, 1019, 1146; persecution, 1104

ALIENATION, 238, 847, 917

ALSACE, 551, 782, 1051

ANARCHISM, 350, 564, 651, 798, 849, 1066, 1147

ANARCHIST GROUPS, 484 (A 16), 854. See also Mouvement du 22 mars; Internationale situationniste

ANTI-AMERICANISM, 391, 579, 580

ANTI-COMMUNISM, 397, 557, 826, 827, 872

ANTI-SEMITISM, 48, 197, 198, 275, 300, 533, 604, 705. See also Foreign relations: Israel; Jews in France

ARCHITECTURE, 1004

ARCHIVES. See Libraries and archives

ARMY: educational programs, 356; Foreign Legion, 1022; history, political, 794, 1045; legal responsibilities, 100. See also Algeria: political developments--1961 (Apr.); Civilian-military relations; Fifth Republic: inception--military intervention; Military . . . ; Organisation de l'armée secrète

ARMY IN ALGERIA, 353, 356, 648, 748, 789; Foreign Legion, 128, 1022, 1033; and Generals' Putsch, 174, 648

ARTS. See Cultural life, arts; May 1968; and art world

ASSISTANCE, TECHNICAL AND ECONOMIC, 200, 356, 719, 1096; African states, 1005, 1010; bibliography, 189; Gaullist policy, 189, 264, 437, 444, 476, 1018

ATHEISM, 281, 325, 1099

ATHLETICS, 468, 1114

ATLANTIC ALLIANCE, 595; Gaullist policy, 13, 1021, 1047; and public opinion, 735

ATOMIC ENERGY AND RESEARCH. See Nuclear technology

ATOMIC WEAPONS. See Nuclear weapons

AUTOGESTION. See Industrial relations: worker participation; Marxism: and "autogestion"

AUTONOMIST MOVEMENTS, 143, 170, 1020. See also Minorities, ethnic; Basque autonomy movement; Brittany; Occitanian autonomy movement; Regionalism

BARBOUZES, 119

BARRICADES IN ALGIERS (JAN. 1960). See Algeria: political developments--1960 (Jan.) barricades

BASQUE AUTONOMY MOVEMENT, 143, 819

BIBLIOGRAPHIES: acquisitions lists of libraries, 1179, 1204; Alsace, 1051; de Gaulle, 679, 885, 886, 906; Fifth Republic, 598, 679, 906, 1102; Gaullism, 679, 885, 906; Jewish question, 197, 198; May 1968, 14, 484 (A 1), 1137; political parties, 217; Russian works on France, 479; serials, 1179, 1204; of social science reference works, 421, 930

BIOGRAPHICAL DICTIONARIES, 276, 337

BIOGRAPHIES: political figures, 65, 601, 1101

BRITTANY, 170, 257, 553, 717, 834, 925, 1020, 1174

BUDGET, 751; education, 57, 304

BUREAUCRACY, 297

CABINETS, 448, 906, 1034

CARTOONS, POLITICAL, 24, 72, 132, 147, 177, 600, 707, 732, 805, 813, 1030, 1032

CATALOGUES, 64, 197, 198, 217, 418, 421, 880

CATHOLIC CHURCH: aggiornamento, 312, 313, 396, 785, 786, 988; in Algeria, 790; and Algerian war, 790; and atheism, 495, 504; and censorship, 196; clery, 363; clergy, leftist, 313; and colonial questions, 790; and de Gaulle, 123; and economic doctrine, 1016; educational institutions, 386; integrist groups, 312; and Marxism, 281, 312, 313, 325, 358, 495, 503, 504, 781, 872; and May 1968, 306, 734, 737, 775, 1024 (see also Catholics and May 1968; May 1968: and Catholic Left); and pacifism, 32, 946; and revolution, 224, 312, 775; social doctrine, 312, 503, 719, 737, 831, 1100, 1231; and state, 654, 946; and students, 734; and violence, 224, 380, 775; and working class, 947

CATHOLIC INTELLECTUALS, 196, 380, 396, 781, 785, 786, 907; and education, 580

CATHOLICS AND MAY 1968, 306, 484 (A 18)

CENSORSHIP, 196, 764, 998, 1012, 1032, 1189

CHILDREN: disturbed, 326, 983; political attitudes, 977

CHRONOLOGIES, 27, 226, 286, 1065, 1176

CIVIL LIBERTIES, 186, 196, 260, 696, 698, 946, 1012, 1046

CIVILIAN-MILITARY RELATIONS, 210, 353, 381, 779, 794, 1045; bibliographies, 794; Generals' Putsch, 174, 599, 648, 1072, 1134

CIVILIZATION, FRENCH, 37, 297, 374, 391, 436, 528, 652, 684, 728, 729, 832, 834, 860, 863, 882, 986, 1007, 1123, 1136, 1180. See also Daily life in France; Fifth Republic (general)

CIVILIZATION, FUTURE, 82, 1026, 1037

CIVILIZATION, MODERN, 39, 49, 52, 98, 106, 111, 136, 239, 297, 303, 346, 348, 354, 372, 377, 382, 391, 399, 429-431, 481, 494, 496, 497, 546, 547, 580, 609, 618, 633, 650, 658, 781, 797, 832, 842, 869, 928, 937, 938, 996, 1000-1002, 1071, 1167; critique of, 238, 311, 378, 539, 724, 822, 847, 864, 917, 918, 1091, 1192

CLUBS, POLITICAL, 82, 166, 240-243, 252, 389, 398, 484 (A 15), 605, 743, 816, 840, 1057, 1058; serials, 1202. See also Club Jean Moulin; Club Nouvelle frontière; Convention des institutions républicaines; Objectif 72; Technique et démocratie in Author Index

COLLOQUE D'AMIENS, 58

COLLOQUE DE CAEN, 58

COMMON MARKET, 168, 1016; and African states, 543; British membership, 51, 534; and French agriculture, 86, 259, 328, 848; and French economy, 543, 818, 1050; Marxist view, 760; and public opinion, 627. See also European integration, economic

COMMUNISM. See Anti-Communism; Communist opposition groups; International Communism; Marxism; Parti communiste français

COMMUNIST FRONT ORGANIZATIONS, 84, 167, 557

COMMUNIST INTELLECTUALS, 167, 244, 913

COMMUNIST OPPOSITION GROUPS: Maoist, 319, 483 (A 3), 484 (A 8, A 9, A 16), 484 (B), 542, 585, 622, 656, 759, 847, 854, 898, 1113, 1154, 1155, 1186, 1187, 1195; Trotskyist, 41, 102, 266, 287, 484 (A 8, A 9, A 16), 484 (B), 542, 622, 630, 767, 778, 854, 985, 1191, 1193, 1196, 1201, 1212, 1223, 1233 (see also Ligue communiste in Author Index)

COMMUNIST VOTERS, 419, 677

CONCORDE (airplane), 331, 763

CONFERENCES, CONGRESSES, COLLOQUIA, MEETINGS, ETC.: academic, 58, 61, 253, 370, 393, 419, 420, 950; political, 200, 224, 264, 628, 1016, 1017, 1215; political--Algeria, 62, 1019. See also individual political parties, e.g., Parti communiste français: congresses

CONSCIENTIOUS OBJECTORS. See Military service: conscientious objectors

CONSTITUTION (1958), 584, 860; and civil liberties, 1046; French Community, 838; genesis, 526; implementation, 526; opposition to, 868; planning agencies, 272; presidency, 77; prime minister, 233; proposed reform, 38; revision of, 526

CONSTITUTIONAL COUNCIL (CONSEIL CONSTITUTIONNEL). See Political institutions: Constitutional Council

CONSTITUTIONAL LAW, 584, 870

COOPERATIVE MOVEMENT, 926, 1219

COUNCIL OF STATE (CONSEIL D'ETAT). See Political institutions: Council of State

COUNTERINSURGENCY. See Military doctrine: counterinsurgency; Revolutionary warfare

COUNTERREVOLUTION, 134, 318, 845

CRIMES, POLITICAL. See Trials, political

CULTURAL LIFE, 65, 307, 354, 436, 539, 757, 785, 786, 978, 986, 1117, 1130; arts, 56; cinema, 229, 484 (A 19); diffusion of French culture abroad, 78, 491; French language, 391; Gaullist policy, 78, 382, 491, 986; pen names of writers and artists, 277; serials, 1192, 1194; and working class, 658

DAILY LIFE IN FRANCE, 37, 291, 436, 863, 1178

DECENTRALIZATION, 110, 111, 453, 553, 590, 943. See also Administration, government: decentralization

DECISION-MAKING PROCESS, 429, 633, 800

DECOLONIZATION, 2, 113, 191, 575, 710, 1063, 1133, 1138

DEMOCRACY, 596, 633

DEMOCRACY, ECONOMIC. See Industrial relations: worker participation

DEMOGRAPHY, 455, 457, 459, 523, 562, 944, 999, 1001, 1168. See also France. Institut national d'études démographiques in Author Index; Population

DEPOLITIZATION, 379, 546, 579, 691, 1123

DICTIONARIES: biographical (see Biographical dictionaries); juridical terminology, 857; May 1968 terms, 161, 177, 673; slang terms, 774; social sciences, 610, 857

DIPLOMACY, 117, 452

DISARMAMENT, 537, 1052

ECOLOGY, 650, 1078, 1164

ECONOMETRICS, 6, 1225

ECONOMIC CONDITIONS, 27, 37, 146, 264, 341, 576, 681, 684, 891, 1128; agriculture (see Agriculture); archival sources, 175; automobile ownership, 1000; consumption, 112; devaluation of franc,

611, 865, 1116 (see also Economic policy: monetary and fiscal measures); disequilibria, 891; employment, 456, 461, 621, 1112, 1127; foreign trade, 42, 43, 444, 1149, 1220 (see also International economic relations); industries (see Industries); international comparisons, 16, 609, 818, 1128; investment and banking institutions, 225, 235, 278, 294; investment motivation, 945; investments, foreign, 517, 760, 801, 1025, 1095, 1182; monopolistic concentration, 96, 235, 619, 801, 1124; price level, 6, 1002; productivity, 477; by region, 299, 523, 590, 1126, 1220; savings motivations, 945; serials, 1149, 1164-1166, 1168, 1170, 1182, 1220, 1225, 1229, 1230; social transfers, 722; standard of living, 6, 239, 291, 348, 354, 481, 650, 842, 1000; statistics, 43, 79, 133, 162, 225, 299, 357, 442, 454, 456, 461, 523, 550, 560, 621, 751, 891, 945, 987, 1078, 1128, 1168, 1220, 1229, 1230; strikes, 16, 146, 435, 674, 726, 754; U.S. investments in France (see Economic conditions: investments, foreign); vacations, 291; wages, 264, 403

-- in 1967: 641

-- in 1968: 248, 268, 1035, 1078

-- in 1969: 269, 550

ECONOMIC DOCTRINE: free enterprise, 530, 690, 746, 1016

ECONOMIC GROWTH, 570, 590, 609, 650, 749, 797, 818, 891, 1127. See also Planning; Planning, regional

ECONOMIC POLICY, 550, 749, 936, 951, 1002; banking and credit, 235, 294; chronology, 43; history, 560, 1078; income distribution, 446; industrial mergers, 1124; international comparisons, 749; investment in research, 527; investments, 570; investments, foreign, 801, 1086, 1095; monetary and fiscal measures, 42, 43, 133, 225, 441, 530, 570, 611, 722, 751, 814, 865, 1116, 1229 (see also Budget); participation of workers in firms, 181, 440, 660, 954, 1088; proposed reforms, 829, 943, 1025, 1050, 1058, 1086, 1127, 1128; serials, 1164, 1167-1169, 1229; structural reform of economy, 330. See also Fifth Republic: economic development; Planning; Planning, regional; State and economy

ECONOMIC THEORY, 112, 610, 761, 945

ECONOMICS: terminology (French-English), 857; textbooks, 168, 375, 576, 761

EDUCATION (major works), 137, 295, 433, 573, 811, 952, 1098; administration of, 573, 811, 1119; bibliographies, 185, 811; Catholic schools, 386 (see also Education: private schools; Education, higher: private institutions); civics instruction, 32; coeducation, 153; conferences, congresses, 58; democratization of, 94, 185, 304, 433, 842, 934, 959, 1098; documents, 952; economic aspects, 57, 433, 453, 532, 934; and economy's requirements (see Education: and society); equipment (school construction, etc.), 57, 573; examinations, 159 (see also Education: guidance and testing; Education, secondary: baccalauréat); Gaullist policy, 58, 295, 304, 317, 342, 453, 468, 488, 573, 582, 811, 952, 959, 1119; government expenditures, 57, 453; guidance and testing, 159, 430, 462, 466, 615; history, 317, 565, 811, 952, 1098; intelligence tests, 462, 465, 615; international comparisons, 185, 433, 532, 934, 959; laws and statutes, 234, 317, 573, libraries in schools, 464; Marxist views on, 94, 908, 1028; objectives, 45, 137, 430, 1098; pedagogic principles and innovations, 106, 137, 153, 303, 488, 580, 850, 983; personal narratives, 979, 983, 1119; and political parties, 580, 969; private schools, 573; proposed reforms, 58, 92, 382, 463, 488, 532, 747, 928, 943, 969, 1014, 1098; psychological factors, 220; reforms, post-May 1968, 469, 573, 674, 740, 908; science teaching, 527; and society, 430, 433, 582, 952, 1001, 1098; sociology of, 49, 94, 137, 371, 615, 658; statistics, 57, 94, 295, 304, 342, 460, 527, 811, 934, 952, 1128; teacher salaries, etc., 573; teacher training, 58, 484 (A 24); teachers' attitudes, 1111, 1119; teachers' organizations, 234, 293, 484 (A 34), 740, 850, 908, 1224; and working class, 658

EDUCATION, ADULT, 159, 354, 430, 573, 614, 1127

EDUCATION, HIGHER, 232, 591, 934, 1087; administration of, 30, 415, 453, 1141; classical studies, 979; Communist influence on, 755, 826; democratization of, 30, 53 (see also Education: democratization of); foreign-language study, 697; Gaullist policy, pre-May 1968, 453, 555; Gaullist policy, post-May 1968, 59, 141, 221, 310, 400, 401, 434, 573, 916, 966, 998; Grandes écoles, 388, 415, 1013; history of, 1144; humanities, 44, 979; international comparisons, 107, 211; laws and statutes, 59, 310, 573; medicine, 159; objectives, 343, 401; personal accounts, 30, 44, 415 (see also May 1968 student revolt: personal accounts--professors, students); private institutions, 305; professors, 211, 213, 305, 387, 979; reforms, May 1968 (see May 1968 student revolt: university reforms); reforms, pre-May 1968, 30, 53, 114, 213, 400, 581, 1118 (see also Education, higher: Gaullist policy, pre-May 1968); reforms, post-May 1968, 33, 211, 221, 258, 305, 415, 434, 484 (D 1), 674, 700, 755, 826, 966, 1141, 1124 (see also Education, higher: Gaullist policy, post-May 1968); science teaching, 527; serials, 59, 1224; social science teaching, 930; sociological aspects, 107, 192, 261, 555, 1013; statistics, 310, 527, 555, 683; student syndicalism, 410 (see also Union nationale des étudiants français in Author Index); student views on, 250, 484 (A 21-33), 820, 1087; teachers' organizations, 211, 484 (A 34), 1224 (see also Syndicat national de l'enseignement supérieur in Author Index); teaching methods, 211, 979; theological faculties, 775

EDUCATION, PRIMARY, 92, 94, 462-464, 934, 1119; laws and statutes, 573

EDUCATION, SECONDARY, 92, 94, 274, 371, 465, 466, 634, 934, 1119; baccalauréat, 274; Comités d'action lycéens, 293, 747; foreign-language teaching, 697; history of, 634; laws and statutes, 573; lycée students, 76, 293, 492, 903; objectives, 634; reforms, pre-May 1968, 850; reforms, post-May 1968, 580, 966; social factors, 466, 615, 850; special schools for sickly children, 983; student-teacher relations, 1007, 1110, 1111; teachers, 1111, 1119; teaching methods, 580, 1007

EDUCATION, SPECIAL (for the handicapped, etc.), 326

EDUCATION, VOCATIONAL AND TECHNICAL, 95, 371, 573, 1098

ELECTIONS: abstentionism, 691; Algeria (see Algeria: political developments--elections and referenda); atlases, 691, 693; bibliographies, 679, 731; campaigns on television and radio, 483 (A 1, A 2), 991; candidate selection, 662; results, 27, 131, 691, 693, 731, 772, 860, 1029, 1132; voter statistics, 693; voting districts, 452, 693

ELECTIONS, LEGISLATIVE (NATIONAL ASSEMBLY):

-- 1967 (Mar.), 389, 438, 691, 894, 1086, 1133; campaign, 470; results, 68, 88, 171, 470, 692. See also French Fifth Republic Bibliography, 1, no. 811m-o

-- 1968 (June), 209, 241, 438, 1133; campaign, 483 (A 1), 506, 795, 893; results, 471, 538, 692; student intervention, 484 (A 38)

ELECTIONS, LEGISLATIVE (SENATE):

-- 1962 (Dec.): results, 472, 772

-- 1968 (Sept.): results, 473

ELECTIONS, MUNICIPAL, 666, 772

ELECTIONS, PRESIDENTIAL:

-- 1965 (Dec.), 9, 88, 389, 422, 483 (B 2), 636, 982, 1133; bibliography, 422; campaign, 483 (B 2), 972, 991; candidates, 104, 183 (B 2), 1029, 1139, 1140; issues, 417; results, 692

-- 1969 (June), 9, 35, 70, 164, 178, 269, 349, 389, 426, 675, 896, 956, 1011, 1133; campaign, 483 (A 2), 972, 1113; candidates, 483 (A 2), 678, 721, 874, 971, 982; results, 692

ELECTORAL LAW, 470-473, 693; voting age, 405, 1114

ELECTORAL SOCIOLOGY, 215, 216, 538, 691, 772; bibliographies, 731

ELECTORAL SYSTEMS, 68, 279

ESPIONAGE, 913, Soviet, in France, 397

ETHICS, 869

ETHNIC MINORITIES. See Minorities, ethnic

EUROPEAN INTEGRATION, 39, 40, 51, 156, 168, 201, 327, 346, 602, 617, 669, 923, 964, 984; after de Gaulle, 669; Fouchet Plan, 36, 427; Gaullist policy, 36, 156, 183, 286, 327, 427, 534, 742, 1021; and interest groups, 417; and May 1968, 669; organizational chart, 870; organizations supporting (see Organizations, political: pro-European unification); and political parties, 417, 543, 669;

EUROPEAN INTEGRATION (continued)
    and public opinion, 328, 417, 627, 735; serials, 201; socialist views, 292; student views, 669

EUROPEAN INTEGRATION, ECONOMIC, 156, 168, 505, 801, 1025, 1057, 1086; currency unification, 793; and French social policy, 722; planning coordination, 645. See also Common Market

EUROPEAN INTEGRATION, MILITARY, 1047

EUROPEAN INTEGRATION, NUCLEAR, 156

EXISTENTIALISM, 238. See also Philosophy

FEDERALISM, 170, 352, 428

FICTIONAL WORKS: May 1968, 205, 395, 548, 1064; O.A.S., 298

FIFTH REPUBLIC (general), 37, 336, 357, 374, 646, 667, 860, 863, 906, 1054, 1102, 1180; appraisal, 158, 314, 561, 626, 720, 776, 832, 853; appraisal, negative, 38, 413, 547, 868, 986, 1042 (see also Gaulle, Charles de: indictments of)

FIFTH REPUBLIC: Algerian conflict (major works), 283, 381, 648, 686, 710, 750, 804, 876, 1049, 1075; bibliographies, 368, 598, 679, 906, 927, 1102; cartoons, 72, 805, 813, 1030; chronologies, 27, 1102; economic developments, 336, 987, 1078 (see also Economic conditions; Economic policy); foreign affairs (major works), 183, 286, 474, 689, 1021 (see also Foreign policy; foreign relations; International relations); government organs and their members, 448, 452, 549, 870, 906, 927; phonograph records, 483 (B 1); pictorial works, 1054, 1105 (see also Fifth Republic: cartoons); political chronicles and diaries, 8, 25, 27, 72, 237, 347, 435, 510, 785, 786, 990, 998; political history, 9, 54, 69, 88, 149, 216, 227, 228, 233, 336, 368, 398, 483 (B 1), 511, 514, 515, 670, 738, 813, 815, 868, 906, 982, 1042, 1102, 1105, 1133; political parties, 368, 398, 860, 1123, 1133 (see also Political parties); and public opinion, 158, 216, 890; reference works (see Reference works: Fifth Republic); regional reform, 140 (see also Regional reform); social problems, 1078, 1088 (see also Social conditions; Social policy)

-- Gaullist policies, 181, 336, 413, 486, 592, 608, 853, 906, 935, 1081; public opinion on, 158. See also Algeria: Gaullist policy; Assistance, technical and economic: Gaullist policy; Economic policy; Education: Gaullist policy; Education, higher: Gaullist policy; European integration: Gaullist policy; Foreign policy; Laws and statutes; Military policy; North Atlantic Treaty Organization: Gaullist policy; Planning, regional: Gaullist policy; Regional reform: Gaullist policy; Social policy

-- inception, 750, 1049; Algerian crisis, 283, 483 (B 1), 710, 780, 876; Gaullists' role, 572, 1049; military intervention, 353, 381, 794, 1072; opposition to de Gaulle, 333, 435, 817; and political parties, 955; sources, 750

-- political institutions, 12, 20, 74, 77, 181, 233, 309, 368, 374, 526, 584, 629, 855, 860, 890, 927, 1008, 1123; bibliographies, 526, 584; polemics on, 38, 547, 640

FORECASTING, 650, 1225; bibliography, 610; manpower needs, 430, 715, 1098; political, 97, 98; terminology, 610

FOREIGN LEGION. See Army in Algeria: Foreign Legion

FOREIGN POLICY, 183, 285, 286, 474, 742, 936, 1009, 1176-1178; chronology, 474; cultural exchanges, 78; documents, 474, 1176-1178; evaluation, 116, 245, 689, 735; military aspects, 671, 796; and public opinion, 253, 689; socialist views, 292

FOREIGN RELATIONS, 1176-1178; African states, 1005, 1010; Arab states, 300, 989; Canada, 245, 321, 567; Germany, 370, 1143; Ghana, 1; Great Britain, 7, 331, 671, 856, 1120; Israel, 4, 11, 48, 63, 275, 300, 533, 604, 703, 868, 989; Mauritania, 476; South Africa, 1043; Soviet Union, 397, 479, 589, 765, 837, 844, 886; United States, 391, 667, 671, 856, 1182; Vietnam, 208

FOURTH REPUBLIC, 357, 653; Algerian policy, 165, 183, 333, 381, 1049; bibliography, 653; colonial policy, 575, 838; European policy, 183; foreign policy, 183, 1021; military policy, 796; political chronicles, 24, 165, 333, 435; political history, 702, 955, 1133; political institutions, 728; political parties, 955, 1093 (see also Political parties)

-- collapse, 165, 381, 653, 702, 728, 750, 817, 955, 1134; plots, 572

FRENCH ABROAD, 78, 101

FRENCH COMMUNITY, 189, 838, 1010; dissolution, 838, 1005, 1010, 1138

FRENCH SOCIETY. See Civilization, French; Social classes

FRENCH UNION, 838, 1138

FRONT DE LIBERATION NATIONALE, 780, 912, 1077; activities in France, 718; documents, 1077

GAUCHISME, 250, 350, 493, 622, 853, 948, 1090, 1097

GAULLE, CHARLES DE: and Alsace, 551; anecdotes about, 87, 117, 195, 516, 843, 859, 1061, 1171; and Army, 381, 779, 794; assassination attempts on, 193, 599, 706, 906; bibliographies on, 679, 885, 886, 906; biographies, 31, 71, 154, 207, 214, 226, 227, 447, 490, 612, 685, 709, 733, 843, 889, 1054, 1072, 1105; and Canada, 567; and Catholic Church, 123, 664; choice of successor, 665, 1101; chronology, 226; death, 152, 212, 394, 483 (A 3), 613, 787, 871; documents on, 447, 1171; eulogies and homages, 152, 195, 613, 716; historical place, 69, 394, 756, 832, 933; indictments of, 413, 733, 868, 907, 941, 1042, 1052; interviews with, 756; and Jews, 48, 989; judgments on, 832, 843, 871, 933 (see also Gaulle, Charles de: indictments of); and Marshal Juin, 210; language and style, 195, 280, 509, 516, 753, 972, 1073; and Malraux, 195, 491, 756; and Mauriac, 784; and May 1968, 9, 10, 53, 87, 395, 1073; memoirs on, 859, 1061, 1171; military career, 941 (see also Gaulle, Charles de: biographies); military conceptions, 671; and Monnet, 967; personality, 509, 516, 664, 702, 709, 756, 784, 843, 859, 1061; and Pétain, 871, 961, 962; pictorial works on, 31, 132, 214, 447, 551, 805, 813, 889, 1030, 1054, 1105; poetic works on, 207, 716; political methods, 9, 394, 702, 753, 843, 853, 906, 1072; and Pompidou, 9, 87, 164, 670, 982, 1061, 1088, 1102; and public opinion, 152, 158, 626, 709, 843; and R.P.F., 962, 1061; reference works on, 906; and religion, 664, 907; research on, 1171; in Resistance and Liberation, 120, 282, 639, 817, 909, 941, 962; return to power, 817; satires, cartoons, etc., on, 132, 207, 664, 665, 805, 813, 1030, 1053; and social reforms, 830, 1088, 1089; and Soustelle, 1042, 1061; and Soviet Union, 886; travels inside France, 226, 551, 906 (see also Visits of state [de Gaulle]); and U.N.R., U.D.R., 164, 1061, 1089; and United States, 608, 856, 909; writings, 154, 195, 508, 512, 514, 515, 787

-- political philosophy, 69, 120, 154, 195, 289, 316, 324, 394, 486, 509, 512, 514-516, 592, 608, 702, 709, 753, 756, 785, 805, 813, 832, 859, 907, 933, 990, 1042, 1061, 1088, 1089; Algeria, 686, 779, 832, 871, 876, 1072, 1075 (see also Algeria: Gaullist policy); democracy, 1089; European integration, 327, 534, 689, 973, 1021 (see also European integration: Gaullist policy); Franco-German relations, 332, 973, 1021; international relations, 332, 689, 871, 1021; legitimacy of rule, 832, 933

-- retirement (Apr. 1969), 9, 87, 164, 212, 394, 670, 756, 787; constitutional aspects, 77. See also Gaulle, Charles de: death

-- speeches and press conferences, 27, 71, 154, 280, 483 (B 2), 510, 511, 513, 567, 753, 906; excerpts from, 321, 508, 509, 512, 516, 551, 906, 972, 1073; phonograph records of, 483 (B 1, B 2), 889; witticisms, 87

GAULLISM, 216, 316, 679, 720, 776; bibliographies, 679, 885, 906; and Christian ethics, 907; documents, 75, 215; economic and social doctrine, 181, 830, 881; history, 9, 75, 592, 839, 962, 1042; internal conflicts, 670, 1088, 1089; objectives, 935; political philosophy, 957, 960, 990, 1074, 1079, 1171; and public opinion, 215, 216, 626; publications, 217; and World War II, 289. See also Gaulle, Charles de: political philosophy; Press, political: Gaullist; Union des démocrates pour la république; Union pour la nouvelle république

GAULLISM AFTER DE GAULLE, 8, 38, 118, 181, 195, 216, 237, 267, 315, 316, 394, 592, 601, 664, 665, 770, 776, 786, 853, 860, 881, 957, 982, 990, 1011, 1079, 1088, 1089, 1101, 1109, 1122, 1171

GAULLIST VOTERS, 215, 216

GAULLISTS, 9, 315, 427, 569, 572, 601, 670, 720, 770, 806, 839, 859, 864, 881, 1061, 1074, 1101; outside U.N.R.-U.D.T. (later

108

U.D.R.), 181, 316, 396, 559, 588, 589, 776, 963, 989, 990, 1088, 1089, 1183

GENERALS' PUTSCH. See Civilian-military relations: Generals' Putsch

GOVERNMENT: executive branches. See Administration, governmental; Cabinets

GOVERNMENT DOCUMENTS. See France . . . in Parts I and II

GRENOBLE, 772

GUIDE BOOKS, 129

HEALTH CARE, 173, 256, 522, 711, 791, 943

HISTORIOGRAPHY, 60, 244, 479, 588, 710, 832, 950

HOUSING, 173, 239, 606, 921, 1002, 1004. See also Architecture; Urbanism

HUMANISM, 869

IDEOLOGIES, 52, 66, 76, 124, 125, 134, 148, 190, 311, 324, 334, 350, 361, 542, 585, 596, 622, 637, 651, 713, 798, 800, 822, 826, 827, 845, 849, 867, 869, 926, 948, 960, 963, 985, 988, 1066, 1090, 1091, 1097, 1103, 1123. See also Anti-Communism; Anarchism; Communist opposition groups; Cooperative movement; Federalism; Gauchisme; Humanism; Marxism; Monarchism; Nationalism; Socialism; Technocracy; Utopianism in Subject Index; and Internationale situationniste in Author Index

ILLITERACY, 614

IMMIGRANTS: illiterates, 614; North African, 104, 606, 921 (see also Algerians in France); Spanish, 603, 995. See also Social conditions: immigrant workers; Social groups: workers, immigrant

INDOCHINA. See Vietnam

INDUSTRIAL MANAGEMENT, 79, 297, 531, 792, 809, 1025, 1166, 1219, 1222

INDUSTRIAL RELATIONS, 593, 726, 792, 809, 1103, 1112; and May 1968, 203, 248, 403, 478, 1036, 1103; worker participation, 136, 202, 254, 440, 586, 593, 660, 754, 919, 954, 1012, 1036, 1100

INDUSTRIES, 37, 90, 96, 235, 248, 341, 442, 444, 801, 1058, 1124, 1149, 1165, 1170, 1182; aircraft, 331, 763; automotive, 481, 484 (A36), 862, 1000; coal mining, 807; computer firms, 1095; foreign participation in, 1182 (see also Economic conditions: investments, foreign); location of, 445; metallurgy, 254. See also Nationalized industries

INFORMATION MEDIA, 1012

INSURANCE: retirement, 451. See also Social security system

INTELLECTUAL LIFE, 1160, 1194, 1214

INTELLECTUALS: and Communism, 827, 833, 835, 1117; and revolutionary groups, 1117; and utopianism, 822. See also Catholic intellectuals; Communist intellectuals; Social groups: intellectuals

INTERNATIONAL COMMUNISM, 200, 264, 319, 494, 496, 497, 501-503, 564, 628, 655, 852, 1062; Chinese cultural revolution, 499, 656; Fourth International (see Communist opposition groups: Trotskyist); Soviet invasion of Czechoslovakia, 498, 502, 589. See also International relations

INTERNATIONAL ECONOMIC RELATIONS: Eurodollars, 294; inter-European organizations, 802; international finance, 278; monetary aspects, 42, 505, 611, 793, 814, 865, 1058, 1116 (see also Common Market; Economic conditions: devaluation of franc, foreign trade; Economic policy: monetary and fiscal measures; European integration, economic); U.S. preponderance, 760, 1025, 1086, 1182 (see also Economic conditions: investments, foreign; Economic policy: investments, foreign)

INTERNATIONAL LAW, 1218

INTERNATIONAL RELATIONS, 80, 97-99, 134, 144, 200, 208, 245, 253, 286, 288, 344, 535, 537, 589, 595, 669, 735, 1013, 1052,
1065; documents, 1177; Gaullist views, 595, 742, 745; serials, 1177, 1184, 1209

INVESTMENTS. See Economic conditions: investments; Economic policy: investments

INVESTMENTS, FOREIGN, IN FRANCE. See Economic conditions: investments, foreign; Economic policy: investments, foreign

JEWISH QUESTION, 703. See also Anti-Semitism; Foreign relations: Israel

JEWS IN FRANCE, 4, 11, 48, 63, 104, 197, 198, 275, 568, 604, 989, 1198; North African immigrants, 104, 223, 568

JOURNALISM, 28, 277, 694, 837, 1012. See also Press

JUDICIAL INSTITUTIONS, 452, 696, 860, 870, 1046, 1104

JUDICIAL REFORM, 19

JURISPRUDENCE: terminology (French-English), 857

JUSTICE. See Trials, political

LABOR. See Economic conditions: employment, wages; Industrial relations; Labor movement; Social groups: workers; Trade unions

LABOR MOVEMENT, 146, 435, 544, 725, 727, 754, 866, 1158. See also Organizations, political: socialist; Political parties: Left; Socialism; Trade unions

LAWS AND STATUTES: agriculture, 449; civil service, 309, 453; education, 59, 221, 310, 317, 434, 453, 573; elections, 470-473; military affairs, 100, 1045; nuclear installations, 157; organizations, subversive, 260; planning, regional, 699; press, 1012; regional administration, 140; repatriation aid and compensation, 467, 878

LEISURE OCCUPATIONS, 291, 308, 354, 465, 658, 842

LIBRARIES AND ARCHIVES: catalogues of holdings, 197, 198, 418, 421, 1179, 1204; directories, 60, 175, 884; school libraries, 464

LOCAL GOVERNMENT, 73, 110, 129, 142, 240, 420, 553, 616, 680, 828, 1040, 1121; finances, 133

MARXISM, 50, 375, 393, 500, 503, 585, 715, 761, 847, 867, 1038, 1214; and alienation, 238, 917; and anti-Semitism, 604; and "autogestion," 136, 501, 540, 564, 754; bibliography, 1038; and Christianity, 281, 325, 358, 495, 496, 500, 501, 503, 504, 913, 1099; conferences, 393; critique of, 238, 377, 399, 872; and education, 94; history of, 402, 564; and linguistics, 393; and personality development, 1028; and psychoanalysis, 393, 540; serials, 1185; and sexual liberation, 897; and universities, 826; updating of, 358, 540, 545. See also Communist opposition groups; International Communism; Parti communiste français: ideology; Socialism

MAY 1968 (major works), 210, 301, 484, 663, 875, 929, 968, 1006, 1125, 1130; abbreviations, 1006; action committees (Comités d'action), 484 (A5, A6, A38), 1015, 1146, antecedents, ideological, 149, 211, 879, 918, 1091, 1130; and art world, 56, 229, 484 (A 19, A 22, A 23), 683, 920, 1130, 1142; and Catholic activists, 306, 737, 775, 1024; and Catholic Church (see Catholic Church: and May 1968); and Catholic Left, 907, 928, 1048; causes, 111, 122, 163, 405, 409, 484 (A 2), 951, 1073 (see also May 1968: interpretations); chronicles, 127, 218, 236, 630, 663, 778; chronologies, 15, 25, 260, 904, 942; defense committees against uprising, 484 (A 14), 506; and de Gaulle, 9, 395, 1073; economic aspects, 163, 951; economic sequels, 477, 550, 611, 1035, 1116; educational reform, 386, 1014 (see also Education: proposed reforms; Education, higher: reforms; May 1968 student revolt: university reform); and farmers, 656; fictional works, 205, 395, 548, 1064; Grenelle agreements (see May 1968: strikes--agreements); historical parallels and antecedents, 244, 565; ideology (see May 1968 student revolt: ideology); interviews, taped, 484 (D), 683, 1137; and labor movement (see May 1968: strikes, trade unions, workers' and technicians' attitudes); and Malraux, 395, 484 (D2); medical reforms, 256; Odéon occupation, 145, 484 (A 19), 958; and P.C.F., 250, 350, 484 (A 11, A 17), 493, 519, 536, 642, 647, 847, 877, 940, 948, 975, 993 (see also Parti

MAY 1968 (continued)
   communiste français: and May 1968); Paris atmosphere, 663; participants in revolt, 85, 103, 139, 145, 161, 218, 250, 519, 683, 775, 847, 958, 1015; poetry, 206, 322, 365, 1130; police intervention, 205, 484 (A 2); police repression, 260, 484 (A 3), 846, 1085; and political clubs, 484 (A 15); and political parties, 389, 426, 484 (A 15), 506, 519, 545, 556, 777, 815, 877, 940, 960 (see also Elections, legislative [National Assembly]: 1968 [June]; May 1968: and P. C. F., revolutionary groups); and politicians, 10, 218, 795, 815, 1073; posters, 67, 231, 484 (C), 888, 920, 1080; and press, 47, 176, 231, 236, 385, 482, 484 (A 37), 484 (B), 485, 561, 966, 1137, 1145, 1157, 1169; press, ephemeral, 484 (B), 1145, 1157, 1169; in provinces, 209, 408, 416, 574, 616, 875; and public opinion, 484 (A 14); and radio-TV, 177, 260, 480, 484 (A 35, D 4), 744, 764; reference works, 14, 149, 161, 484 (A 1); religious groups, 484 (A 18), 775 (see also Catholic Church: and May 1968); satires, 127, 147, 177, 182, 385, 395, 673, 1169 (see also May 1968: pictorial works--cartoons); sequels, 34, 477, 674, 875, 929, 1069 (see also May 1968: economic aspects, economic sequels); street fighting, 682, 1106; and trade unions, 10, 15, 83, 85, 218, 248, 403, 404, 481, 484 (A 36, A 37), 554, 620, 675, 727, 862, 1036, 1103; violence, 1055 (see also May 1968: street fighting); vocabulary and terminology, 161, 182, 673, 1097; wall inscriptions (see May 1968: documents and sources--graffiti); worker-student collaboration, 484 (A 6, B), 862, 904, 1157; workers' and technicians' attitudes, 481, 518, 554, 737, 808, 1036, 1055; workers' councils, 919, 1106

-- bibliographies, 14, 145, 204, 261, 484 (A 1), 566, 1006, 1137; audio-visual material, 14, 145, 1137

-- documents and sources, 14, 149, 260, 386, 416, 484, 542, 683, 752, 767, 778, 875, 888, 904, 920, 1006, 1031, 1073, 1085, 1125, 1137, 1142; graffiti, 115, 739, 1066; quotations, 231, 904, 1097. See also May 1968 student revolt: documents and sources

-- government response, 10, 218, 683, 767, 942, 982, 1073, 1102, 1125; personal accounts, 427, 563, 767

-- history, 25, 103, 155, 232, 301, 404, 409, 520, 672, 968, 993, 1015, 1033, 1125; inside, 10, 218, 875, 1073, 1125; pictorial, 265, 414, 659

-- interpretations, 122, 125, 192, 204, 238, 297, 345, 423, 484 (D 3), 493, 529, 556, 578, 579, 877, 910, 924, 928, 929, 942, 996, 1027, 1130; anarchist, 18, 564; anti-revolutionary, 53, 872; Communist (see May 1968: and P. C. F.); Gaullist, 316, 484 (D 2), 864, 1073; industrialist, 810; nationalist Right, 81, 116, 360, 714; revolutionary, 519, 536, 545, 630, 723, 752, 771, 847, 965, 998, 1033, 1090

-- personal accounts by foreign observers: Belgian, 888; British, 17, 661, 1015; German, 232, 846; Italian, 206, 1117; Mexican, 489; Polish, 642, 672; Portuguese, 996; U. S., 630, 949

-- pictorial works: cartoons, 147, 177, 385, 414, 484 (A 4), 600, 707, 732, 1068, 1169; drawings, 414, 583; frescoes, 322; photographs, 114, 265, 323, 489, 659, 672, 682, 739, 981; posters, 14, 67, 231, 484 (C), 888, 920, 1080

-- revolutionary groups, 81, 103, 139, 149, 184, 260, 359, 360, 484 (A 6, A 8, A 9, A 16, B, C), 519, 591, 637, 647, 767, 854, 910, 1006, 1117; documents, 484, 637, 778; ideology, 542; international support, 767; publications, 359, 484 (B), 542; tactics, 929. See also Communist opposition groups

-- revolutionary groups (individual): Enragés, 1106, 1169; Internationale situationniste, 148, 542, 1106; Maoist, 34, 319, 484 (A 8, A 9, A 16), 542, 656, 759; Mouvement du 22 mars, 271, 484 (A 9), 542, 798, 904, 929; Trotskyist, 102, 359, 484 (A 8, A 9, A 16), 542, 630, 661, 778, 985

-- strikes, 15, 16, 203, 229, 248, 384, 484 (A 36, A 37), 554, 620, 737, 778, 1036, 1131; agreements, 248, 403, 758; cinema, 229, 484 (A 19); factory occupations, 403, 484 (A 36), 519, 1036; Hachette, 384, 484 (A 37); journalists, 875; Nantes, 574, 875; O. R. T. F., 260, 480, 484 (A 35), 563, 744, 764, 991, 1036; postal workers, 484 (A 37), 563; Régie autonome des transports parisiens, 484 (A 37); Renault, 481, 484 (A 36), 862, 1055; Saclay (atomic energy center), 919

MAY 1968 STUDENT REVOLT (major works), 484, 676, 887, 1006, 1142; antecedents, 114, 149, 250, 387, 631, 637, 683, 724, 879, 918; art students, 67, 484 (A 19, A 22, A 23); 920; Catholic schools, 386, 775, 875; causes, 141, 192, 303, 484 (A 2), 591, 826, 1001 (see also May 1968: causes); chronicle, 922; chronology, 676; Comités d'action lycéens, 76, 484 (A 20), 747, 903, 904; and cultural revolution, 149, 204, 724, 858, 879, 1001, 1090, 1091; documents and sources, 115, 139, 149, 199, 301, 484, 623, 676, 683, 887, 1006, 1142 (see also May 1968: documents and sources); Ecole des beaux arts (see May 1968 student revolt: art students); and elections (June 1968), 484 (A 38); fiction and poetry, 322, 395, 548; Grandes écoles, 415, 875; historical parallels and antecedents, 1144; ideology, 149, 858, 948, 1069, 1070 (see also May 1968: antecedents, ideological; May 1968 student revolt: and cultural revolution); international dimensions, 141, 155, 359, 649, 767, 980, 1044, 1071; Latin Quarter atmosphere, 395, 1108; Latin Quarter maps, 232, 1106; in lycées, 76, 199, 293, 484 (A 20), 492, 747, 942, 1110, 1142; Nanterre, 114, 250, 297, 322, 387, 484 (A 28, D 1), 683, 723, 804, 1106, 1108; participants (see May 1968: participants in revolt); pictorial works (see May 1968: pictorial works); police repression (see May 1968: police repression); and press, 676, 1145; press, student, 484 (B); professors' views, 53, 141, 211, 297, 387, 484 (D 1, D 3), 493, 581, 683, 723, 841, 916, 1069, 1070, 1141; and revolutionary groups (see May 1968: revolutionary groups); student reactions to, 364, 387, 484 (A 13), 566, 820, 1087, 1130; views, hostile, 33, 47, 53, 141, 258, 377, 425, 493, 755, 841, 916, 918, 1107 (see also May 1968: interpretations--anti-revolutionary); vocabulary and terminology, 149, 161 520

-- interpretations: demographic, 1001; psychoanalytical, 942, 1048; sociological, 261, 588, 836, 1069, 1070, 1130. See also May 1968: interpretations

-- Paris, University of (Sorbonne), 484 (A 21-A 32), 676, 887, 922, 1006, 1106-1108; Faculté de droit, 484 (A 25); Faculté de médecine et de chirurgie dentaire, 256, 484 (A 26), 875; Faculté des lettres et des sciences humaines, 484 (A 27), 697, 755 (see also May 1968 student revolt: Nanterre); Faculté des sciences, 484 (A 29-A 32)

-- personal accounts: foreign observers, 1044, 1108 (see also May 1968: personal accounts by foreign observers); professors, 22, 44, 114, 141, 297, 387, 484 (D 1), 581, 804, 916, 1107, 1141; Sorbonne chaplain, 734; students, 364, 820, 922

-- provincial universities, 22, 199, 408, 875; Grenoble, 22; Poitiers, 484 (A 33); Strasbourg, 408, 581

-- student groups: conservative and moderate, 33, 258, 484 (A 10), 755; revolutionary Left, 484 (A 7-A 9) (see also May 1968: revolutionary groups (individual) in Subject Index; and Fédération des étudiants révolutionnaires; Jeunesses communistes révolutionnaires; Union des jeunesses communistes marxistes-léninistes in Author Index); revolutionary Right, 361, 484 (A 10)

-- university reform, 22, 33, 53, 159, 199, 222, 387, 401, 484 (A 21, A 26, A 27, A 29), 683, 697, 804, 820, 887, 916, 1006, 1069, 1070, 1087, 1142; proposals, 1142. See also Education: proposed reforms

MILITARY DOCTRINE: counterinsurgency, 597, 730, 780, 1076

MILITARY LEADERS, 5, 97, 210, 353, 356, 381, 577, 745, 779, 780, 883, 1092, 1129

MILITARY ORGANIZATION: laws and statutes, 1045; proposed reforms, 1076

MILITARY POLICY: embargo on arms to Israel, 300; nuclear weapons, 5, 13, 671, 796, 856

MILITARY SERVICE, 41, 255, 308, 566; conscientious objectors, 695, 1147

MILITARY STRATEGY, 97, 99, 144, 253, 535, 578, 595, 730, 745, 795, 1047, 1052

MILITARY TECHNOLOGY, 527. See also Nuclear weapons

MINORITIES, ETHNIC, 101, 143, 170, 424, 428, 553, 687, 688, 717, 782, 819, 1020. See also Autonomist movements

MINORITIES IN FRANCE. See Africans in France; Algerians in France; Immigrants; Jews in France; Social conditions: immigrant workers; Social groups: workers, immigrant

110

MINORITY PROBLEM. See Anti-Semitism; Race prejudice

MONARCHISM, 845

MUNICIPAL GOVERNMENT. See Elections, municipal; Local government

NATIONAL ASSEMBLY, 632, 728, 766, 870; Algerian deputies, 686; Communist deputies, 407; elections (see Elections, legislative [National Assembly]); legislation, 475, 1132; membership, 438, 475, 549, 890; operation, 475, 890, 1132; parliamentary groups, 407, 438, 890; and planning, 272; presiding officer, 572; and social policy, 954. See also Political institutions: executive-legislative balance, parliamentary functions; Senate in Subject Index; and France. Assemblée nationale; France. Parlement in Part I

NATIONALISM, 124, 361, 585, 596, 640, 688, 988, 1162, 1228

NATIONALIST OPPOSITION TO DE GAULLE, 116, 361, 713, 868, 1042

NATIONALIZED INDUSTRIES, 96, 362, 751, 1166

NEW CALEDONIA, 1067

NEWSPAPERS. See Press; Press: directories; Press, general information: daily

NORTH ATLANTIC TREATY ORGANIZATION: French withdrawal from, 13, 1072; Gaullist policy, 671, 856. See also Atlantic Alliance; International relations; Military strategy

NUCLEAR TECHNOLOGY, 157, 388, 541, 796, 919, 1040

NUCLEAR WEAPONS, 100, 535, 541, 671, 796; and public opinion, 796; tests, 1, 5, 1067

OCCITANIAN AUTONOMY MOVEMENT, 424

ORGANISATION DE L'ARMEE SECRETE, 599, 730, 803, 876; documents, 406, 594; exiled leaders, 193, 406; in French politics, 361; government sympathizers, 193; leadership, 594, 648, 845; operations in Algeria, 119, 283, 296, 406, 638, 648, 845, 1059; operations in France, 193, 706; personal narratives, 298, 406, 1023, 1059; phonograph records, 483 (B 1). See also Algeria: political developments; Algerian war: final months of violence; Nationalist opposition to de Gaulle; Trials, political

ORGANIZATIONS, ACADEMIC AND RESEARCH: documentation centers, 60, 884; Gaullism (research on), 226, 512, 885, 886, 1079 (see also Paris. Institut Charles de Gaulle in Author Index); historical studies, 60, 950, 1226; Jewish history, 197, 198; industrial relations, 162, 593, 1131; social sciences, 61, 158, 200, 222, 261, 303, 911, 999, 1184 (see also Fondation nationale des sciences politiques in Author Index)

ORGANIZATIONS, AGRICULTURAL, 328, 848, 1056, 1060

ORGANIZATIONS, BUSINESS AND PROFESSIONAL, 580, 954, 1012, 1035, 1131, 1166. See also Pressure groups: business

ORGANIZATIONS, CATHOLIC, 196, 224, 386, 484 (A 18); social action, 106, 601, 603; students, 230, 734; workers, 737

ORGANIZATIONS, COOPERATIVE MOVEMENT, 926, 1219

ORGANIZATIONS, EDUCATIONAL, 58, 92, 293, 484 (A 24), 1014

ORGANIZATIONS, EUROPEAN UNIFICATION. See Organizations, political: pro-European unification

ORGANIZATIONS, FRANCO-ALGERIAN, 62

ORGANIZATIONS, FRANCO-GERMAN, 335, 370

ORGANIZATIONS, FRANCO-U.S., 1182

ORGANIZATIONS, JEWISH, 11, 63, 197, 198, 568, 1198

ORGANIZATIONS, JURIST, 19

ORGANIZATIONS, LABOR. See Trade unions

ORGANIZATIONS, POLITICAL, 217, 276, 840, 1176; amnesty for political prisoners, 1083; anarchist, 484 (A 16); Communist (see Communist front organizations; Communist opposition groups; Parti communiste français); Centrist, 217, 1016; Gaullist, 216, 217, 226, 483 (A 3), 484 (A 14), 506, 512, 559, 885, 886, 906, 1079, 1171, 1183 (see also Political parties: Gaullist); Left (see Organizations, political: socialist); Left, revolutionary, 287, 293, 484 (A 6, A 8, A 9, A 16), 488, 557, 622, 661, 674, 759, 854, 985, 1062, 1106, 1154, 1192 (see also Anarchist groups; Communist opposition groups); nationalist, 361; nationalist opposition to de Gaulle, 1210; pro-European unification, 201, 669, 964, 1159; pro-French Algeria, 361; Right, extreme, 361, 484 (A 10, A 14), 845; Right, moderate, 217, 305, 484 (A 15); socialist, 217, 366, 1150, 1153, 1235. See also Clubs, political; Political parties

ORGANIZATIONS, PROFESSIONAL. See Organizations, business and professional

ORGANIZATIONS, REGIONAL, 257, 553

ORGANIZATIONS, REPATRIATES FROM NORTH AFRICA, 657, 878

ORGANIZATIONS, RESEARCH. See Organizations, academic and research

ORGANIZATIONS, STUDENT, 33, 148, 167, 230, 258, 361, 410, 483 (A 3), 484 (A 6-A 12, C), 507, 631, 647, 674, 755, 1200, 1201. See also Comités d'action lycéens; Union nationale des étudiants de France in Author Index

ORGANIZATIONS, TEACHERS'. See Education: teachers' organizations

ORGANIZATIONS, WOMEN'S, 484 (A 3)

ORGANIZATIONS, YOUTH, 335, 483 (A 3), 484 (A 9, C), 488, 637

OVERSEAS DEPARTMENTS AND TERRITORIES, 2, 1063, 1067, 1217

PACIFISM, 32, 80

PARIS, 307, 347, 549, 553, 986, 1004, 1094, 1121; election material for, 483 (A 1); population of, 944

PARIS REGION, 21, 37, 140, 162, 388, 420, 452, 523, 549, 552, 606, 616, 944, 1094, 1121

PARLIAMENT. See National Assembly; Political institutions: executive-legislative balance, parliamentary function; Senate

PARTI COMMUNISTE FRANÇAIS (major works), 419, 677; and Algerian war, 825; anti-colonialism, 825; bibliography, 419; and "cadres," 1188; and Catholic Church, 325, 503, 1099 (see also Marxism: and Christianity); commercial enterprises related to, 557; conferences, congresses, etc., 200, 264, 628, 769, 895, 896, 898, 1017; departmental federations, 643; economic and social questions, 264, 892; and education, 740, 908, 1028; elections and referenda, 171, 407, 483 (A 1, A 2), 643, 721, 893, 894, 974, 1011; European and foreign policy, 976; and "gauchisme," 184, 250, 350, 948; and Gaullist regime, 23; history, 351, 419, 628, 1062, 1152; ideology, 23, 246, 251, 351, 419, 647, 655, 896, 976, 997, 998, 1062, 1152; and intellectuals, 84, 184, 647, 1194; internal opposition, 84, 383, 496, 497, 502, 647, 895, 898, 1062 (see also Communist opposition groups); and international Communism, 200, 502, 895, 974; leadership, 217, 351, 500, leaflets, 483 (A 3); and local government, 130, 325, 557, 616, 892; and May 1968, 23, 84, 85, 251, 350, 351, 383, 404, 484 (A 11, A 17, C), 502, 643, 647, 655, 677, 896, 948, 974, 975, 993, 997 (see also May 1968: and P.C.F.); in National Assembly, 407; and non-Communist Left, 23, 88, 130, 171, 228, 251, 351, 894, 898, 974, 1017, 1093 (see also Political parties: unification of Left); organization and finances, 84, 419, 557, 677, 769, 1062, 1152; political strategy, 501, 655, 677, 852, 997; posters, 484 (C) (see also Parti communiste français: elections and referenda); program, 500, 768, 974; and public opinion, 419, 625; publications, 84, 217, 251, 1152, 1188, 1200; and regional reform, 299; research and documentation centers, 628, 913, 976, 1017, 1152; research on, 419; in Resistance, 289; and sexual revolution, 897; and Soviet invasion of Czechoslovakia, 502, 895; and Soviet Union, 895; and strikes, 643; and student movement, 167, 483 (A 3), 484 (A 11, C), 647, 1155, 1200; and women, 172, 892, 897; and worker participation in industry, 660; and youth, 84, 484 (A 11). See also Anti-Communism; Communist opposition groups; International Communism; Marxism

111

PARTI SOCIALISTE (S.F.I.O.), 571, 762, 821, 923, 955, 1029, 1153; and Algerian question, 333, 1029; congresses, 217; departmental federations, 1174; elections, 483 (A2); and European integration, 292; publications, 217, 1150, 1174, 1203, 1208

PARTICIPATION. See Industrial relations: worker participation

PARTIES, POLITICAL. See Political parties

PEASANTRY. See Agriculture; Organizations, agricultural; Pressure groups: farmers; Rural and village life; Sociology, rural

PHILOSOPHY, 118, 238, 781, 799, 918, 1091, 1214

PHONOGRAPH RECORDS, 483 (B1, B2), 889

PLANNING, 37, 93, 160, 249, 373, 432, 560, 590, 746; bibliographies, 249, 373; and Common Market, 645; critique of, 746; cultural projects, 382; democratic participation in, 249, 633; of educational investment, 57 (see also Forecasting: manpower needs); and European integration, 645; Fifth Plan, 93, 432, 527, 690; financial aspects, 225; forecasts and achievements, 746; Fourth Plan, 160, 432; history, 560; long-range projections, 259, 362, 429, 609, 650, 715, 938, 1002, 1037, 1164, 1125; objectives, 560, 690; parliamentary control over, 272; Sixth Plan, 93, 162, 382; theory of, 160, 373, 610, 749; in Western Europe, 645

PLANNING, LOCAL, 110, 420. 553. See also Planning, urban

PLANNING, REGIONAL (AMENAGEMENT DU TERRITOIRE), 37, 135, 140, 243, 257, 299, 366, 420, 432, 445, 553, 569, 590, 699, 749, 789, 925, 1096, 1126, 1164; bibliographies, 553, 590, 1126; documents, 553; Gaullist policy, 569, 699, 925, 939; new industries, 807; organization of, 699, 1121; and public opinion, 553. See also Regional reform

PLANNING, URBAN, 420, 553, 1121, 1164; and public opinion, 553

POLICE, 26, 186, 260, 549, 696, 698, 704, 823, 986; in Algeria, 119, 296, 1104; and Algerians in France, 1104. See also Barbouzes; May 1968: police intervention, police repression; May 1968 student revolt: police repression; Secret services

POLITICAL ATTITUDES, 12, 158, 215, 252, 374, 422, 558, 625-627, 860, 1123; children's, 977; of Communist voters, 419; of elite, 735; of politicians, 728, 729; of students, 566, 585; of voters, leftist, 741; of workers, 518, 587, 873, 1103. See also Ideologies; Public opinion polls

POLITICAL INSTITUTIONS, 12, 74, 369, 374, 584, 800, 870; administrative organs (see Administration, governmental); bibliography, 1008; bi-party system, 89, 911, 1135; cabinet, 1034; and civil liberties, 1046; Constitutional Council (Conseil constitutionnel), 806; Council of State (Conseil d'Etat), 668, 736, 855; electoral system (see Electoral system); executive-legislative balance, 272, 524, 766, 890, 1132; executive organs, 20, 309; local government, 666, 1121; and mass media, 547; parliamentary functions, 632, 766 (see also National Assembly; Senate); personalization of power, 1008; planning authority, 272; political vs. administrative jurisdiction, 1034; presidency, 77; presidential election, 524; presidential regime, 35, 526, 753; prime minister, 233; proposed reforms, 73, 240, 241, 243, 267, 399, 524, 644, 931, 1008; and public opinion, 890; referenda, 1008; regional administration, 140; regional reform (see Regional reform); technical experts' role, 376, 546, 547, 633, 800. See also Fifth Republic: political institutions; Fourth Republic: political institutions

POLITICAL LEADERS. See Biographies; Gaullists

POLITICAL PARTIES, 12, 131, 217, 276, 369, 374, 870, 1176; bibliographies, 217, 1135; bipolarization, 368, 911; candidate selection, 662; congresses, 217 (see also congresses under individual parties); and decolonization, 838; election campaigns (see Elections and under individual parties); election results, 538, 731 (see also Elections: results); financial support, 278; Gaullist, 75, 216, 217, 679 (see also Gaullism; Union des démocrates pour la république; Union pour la nouvelle république); leadership, 1101; Left, Communist (see Communist opposition groups; Parti communiste français); Left, non-Communist, 118, 320, 333, 334, 389, 398, 426, 571, 579, 690, 741, 762, 777, 788, 816, 822, 1003, 1025, 1029, 1041, 1093, 1135; Left, revolutionary, 266, 270, 985 (see also Communist opposition groups; Organizations, political: Left, revolutionary); and May 1968 (see May 1968: and political parties); parliamentary representation, 890; and political clubs, 840; publications, 217; reference works on, 217, 276; regrouping of, 89, 911, 1123, 1135, 1140 (see also Political institutions: bi-party system; Political parties: unification of Left); Right, 66, 361, 960, 1134 (see also Monarchism; Nationalism; Nationalist opposition to de Gaulle); unification of Center, 89; unification of Left, 88, 228, 389, 493, 605, 625, 741, 815, 816, 866, 894, 940, 1093, 1135, 1140, 1153 (see also Parti communiste français: and non-Communist Left); unification of Right, 960. See also Fifth Republic: political parties; Fourth Republic: political parties; Organizations, political; Sociology, political; political parties listed individually in Author Index: Centre démocrate; Centre national des Indépendants et paysans; Centre progrès et démocratie moderne; Fédération de la gauche démocrate et socialiste; Ligue communiste; Mouvement républicain populaire; Parti libéral de France; Parti républicain radical et radical-socialiste; Parti socialiste (S.F.I.O.); Parti socialiste (1969-); Parti socialiste autonome; Parti socialiste unifié; Progrès et liberté; Rassemblement du peuple français; Républicains indépendants; Républicains sociaux; Union de la gauche socialiste; Union démocratique du travail; Union des démocrates pour la Ve République; Union des démocrates pour la république; Union pour la nouvelle république–Union démocratique du travail; Union progressiste; Union travailliste

POLITICAL PHILOSOPHY, 82, 318, 324, 352, 372, 377, 379, 428, 547, 558, 588, 633, 688, 832, 992, 1123

POLITICAL SCIENCE, 1013; dissertations, 679; in France, 61. See also Electoral sociology; Sociology, political

POLITICS: practical aspects, 728, 729

POLYNESIA, 1067

POPULATION, 523, 1128; census, 450, 454, 456-461, 553, 621; migration, 944; statistics, 133, 173, 450, 452, 1078, 1168. See also Demography

POSTERS. See May 1968: posters

POVERTY, 711

PREFECTURES, 483 (A1); Préfecture de la Seine, 944

PRESS, 28, 629; case studies, 561, 607, 1115; corruption of, 275, 868; directories, 28, 64, 418, 880; excerpts from, 321; financial control over, 278; governmental regulation, 1012; history of, 390; and journalists' association, 1012; microfilms, 64, 482, 485, 880; and public opinion, 703, 837; reference works on, 28, 276; and rightist figures, 963. See also Journalism; May 1968: and press

PRESS, AGRICULTURAL, 86, 848

PRESS, BUSINESS, 1149, 1165, 1170, 1173, 1182, 1222, 1234

PRESS, CATHOLIC, 1161, 1167, 1231

PRESS, GENERAL INFORMATION: daily, 64, 482, 694, 703, 837, 1115, 1137, 1197; weekly and monthly, 64, 65, 485, 1148, 1160, 1172, 1173, 1175, 1189, 1190, 1194, 1205-1207, 1217, 1221, 1234

PRESS, JEWISH, 568, 1198

PRESS, POLITICAL, 217, 276; centrist, 1181, 1216; Communist, 1152, 1188, 1200; Communist opposition (Maoist), 759, 1155, 1186, 1187, 1195; Communist opposition (Trotskyist), 985, 1154, 1191, 1193, 1196, 1201, 1212, 1223, 1233; Communist-oriented, 1194; Gaullist, 1151, 1163, 1171, 1181, 1183; leftist, 1150, 1153, 1206-1208, 1211, 1232, 1235; leftist, revolutionary, 148, 1157, 1189, 1190, 1192, 1213 (see also Press, political: Communist opposition); nationalist, 361, 1162, 1228; nationalist European, 361; nationalist opposition to de Gaulle, 361, 713, 1148, 1210

PRESS, SATIRICAL, 385, 1032, 1156, 1169

PRESSURE GROUPS, 234, 374, 800, 870; business, 801, 802, 868; farmers, 86, 848, 1056; labor (see Trade unions); technocrats, 800 (see also Technocracy). See also Organizations, agricultural; Organizations, business and professional; Social groups

PRISONERS, POLITICAL: African nationalist, 2; amnesty for, 636, 639, 1083; Basque autonomists, 819; conscientious objectors, 695; O.A.S., 412, 594, 1059, 1083. See also Trials, political

PROTESTANTS IN FRANCE, 380, 923

PSYCHIATRY, 326, 522

PUBLIC OPINION POLLS, 158, 357, 468, 566, 587, 625-627, 689, 741, 796, 890. See also Political attitudes

RACE PREJUDICE, 705

RADICAL PARTY. See Parti républicain radical et radical-socialiste in Author Index

RADIO-TELEVISION, 28, 118, 151, 236, 237, 480, 744, 764, 991, 1049; and May 1968 (see May 1968: and radio-TV); political broadcasts, 483 (A1, A2), 991. See also Office de la radio-télévision française in Author Index

RECORDS (PHONOGRAPH), 483 (B1, B2), 889

REFERENCE WORKS, 27, 276, 421, 454; administration, governmental, 28, 448, 452, 549; Algeria, 29; biographical dictionaries, 276, 337; de Gaulle, 906; dictionaries, 161, 177, 276, 277, 774, 857; economic conditions, 454; European integration, 201; Fifth Republic, 27, 276, 336, 448, 452, 598, 679, 906, 1102, 1176; libraries, 60, 884; North Africa, 29; pen names, 277; political institutions, 870; political parties, 217, 276, 361; press, 28, 276, 880

REFERENDUMS, 367, 1008

-- 1962 (Oct.), 367, 524, 526

-- 1969 (Apr.), 9, 140, 164, 242, 243, 299, 366, 367, 483 (A2), 524, 553, 644, 660, 667, 670, 678, 786, 830, 905, 931, 956, 1072, 1102, 1133; results, 692

REGIONAL DIVISIONS, 439, 523. See also Alsace; Brittany; Economic conditions: by region

REGIONAL PLANNING. See Planning, regional

REGIONAL PROJECTS, 699, 1040. See also Planning, regional

REGIONAL REFORM, 20, 73, 140, 240, 242, 243, 257, 299, 309, 362, 366, 428, 523, 552, 590, 687, 789, 905, 931; Gaullist policy, 366, 644, 660, 789, 807, 931, 1094; history, 552; new departments, 388, 1094; Paris area (see Paris region). See also Administration, governmental: decentralization; Decentralization; Planning, regional; Referendums: 1969 (Apr.)

REGIONALISM, 129, 143, 170, 258, 291, 352, 424, 428, 688, 782, 819, 925, 1020; and political parties, 717, 782. See also Autonomist movements

REPATRIATION OF FRENCH ALGERIANS AND COLONIAL SETTLERS, 686, 878; compensation for lost property, 467, 657; government aid, 878; Jews, 104; laws and statutes, 467, 878; personal narratives, 105

RESEARCH: economics, 175, 189; historical studies, 60, 950; scientific and technical, 118, 189, 527, 541, 715, 994, 1043, 1128 (see also Science and State); social sciences, 222, 834, 835, 930. See also Organizations, academic and research

REUNION ISLAND, 2

REVOLUTION, 318, 376, 1013

REVOLUTIONARY WARFARE, 1076. See also Military doctrine: counterinsurgency

RUEFF REPORT, 330

RURAL AND VILLAGE LIFE, 21, 129, 209, 439, 797, 828, 834, 1040, 1136

RUSSIAN AND OTHER EASTERN EUROPEAN WORKS, 130, 227, 228, 479, 486, 543, 642, 672, 681, 765, 866, 956, 1122

SATIRE, POLITICAL. See Cartoons, political; Gaulle, Charles de: satires, cartoons, etc., on; May 1968: satires; Press, satirical

SCHOOLS. See Education

SCIENCE. See Education, higher: science teaching; Research: scientific and technical; Science and state

SCIENCE AND STATE, 527, 541, 994

SECRET SERVICES, 397, 914, 915, 1039

SEINE, DEPARTMENT OF. See Paris; Paris region; Prefectures: Préfecture de la Seine

SELF-MANAGEMENT (AUTOGESTION). See Industrial relations: worker participation

SENATE, 472, 473, 524, 549, 766, 890, 1132; proposed reform of, 644

SOCIAL CLASSES, 378, 405, 618, 891, 1071

SOCIAL CONDITIONS, 37, 173, 354, 684, 712; immigrant workers, 606, 921, 1161, 1231; marriage, 528; mental hospitals, 522 (see also Psychiatry); old persons, 262, 711; poor, 711; women, 562, 892, 897 (see also Women); youth, 308, 773 (see also Youth). See also Health care; Social policy

SOCIAL GROUPS: "bourgeoisie," 378; businessmen, 90, 96, 593; "cadres," 184, 348, 546, 554, 593, 1131; Catholic clergy, 363; civil servants, 96, 187, 302, 573, 1034; intellectuals, 126, 184, 655, 822, 827, 998; managers, 96; old persons, 262, 711; physicians, 256; by profession, 621; scientists, 994; statistics, 621; students, 308, 410, 465, 507, 631, 773, 948, 1110 (see also Students); teachers, 573, 1111 (see also Education: teachers . . . ; Education, higher: professors; Education, secondary: teachers)

-- workers, 481, 518, 587, 616, 658, 807, 808, 873, 1112; immigrant, 456, 461, 711; young, 95, 783

SOCIAL MOBILITY, 528, 873, 1013

SOCIAL POLICY, 173, 606, 712, 951, 1002, 1167; education, 57 (see also Education: Gaullist policy); health care, 256, 791 (see also Health care); proposed reforms, 943; retirement insurance, 451; social transfers, 722; working conditions, 1112; youth, 468, 812, 1114

SOCIAL SCIENCES: methodology, 624, 930; periodicals, 880; textbooks, 930. See also Economics: textbooks

SOCIAL SECURITY SYSTEM, 173, 451

SOCIALISM, 166, 287, 333, 496, 497, 545, 571, 579, 725, 821, 923, 992, 1017, 1150, 1153, 1203, 1215; and Christianity, 831, 923; history, 829, 1150, 1226; renovation of, 426, 494, 498, 501, 605, 762, 777, 816, 1002, 1003 (see also Marxism: updating of; Political parties: unification of Left); in underdeveloped countries, 355. See also Labor movement; Marxism; Organizations, political: socialist; Parti socialiste (S.F.I.O.); Political parties: Left, non-Communist in Subject Index; and Parti socialiste (1969-) in Author Index

SOCIOLOGY, 46, 138, 540, 834, 835, 918, 1013, 1069-1071, 1130, 1214; serials, 1184

SOCIOLOGY, CASE STUDIES: African students in France, 851; children's intelligence, 462; children's political attitudes, 977; civil servants, 302; Jews from North Africa in France, 104; marriage choices, 528; old persons, 262; Paris immigrants, 944; rural and village life, 21, 439, 834, 1136; shantytown (bidonville) dwellers, 606; Spanish immigrants, 603; students, secondary and university, 107, 308, 410, 465, 566, 615, 1007, 1110, 1130; suburban dwellers, 239, 921; teachers, 1111; workers, 481, 518, 658, 807, 873; young professionals, 1037; young workers, 95, 783

SOCIOLOGY, EDUCATIONAL. See Education: sociology of

SOCIOLOGY, INDUSTRIAL, 1036, 1103

SOCIOLOGY, PENAL, 19

SOCIOLOGY, POLITICAL, 12, 588, 960, 977, 1011, 1135. See also Electoral sociology

SOCIOLOGY, RURAL, 797, 834

SPECIAL COLLECTIONS AT HOOVER INSTITUTION, 482-485

STANDARD OF LIVING. See Economic conditions: standard of living; Leisure occupations

STATE AND ECONOMY, 225, 264, 362, 530, 570, 746, 749, 751, 818, 870, 943, 1002, 1016, 1050, 1058, 1124. See also Economic policy; Nationalized industries; Planning; Technocracy

STRASBOURG. See May 1968: in provinces

STRIKES. See Economic conditions: strikes; May 1968: strikes

STUDENTS, 107, 566, 631, 948, 1001, 1048, 1087, 1110, 1130; international movements (see May 1968 student revolt: international dimensions); political participation, 230, 566, 1044 (see also Education, secondary: lycée students; May 1968 student revolt). See also Education: statistics; Education, higher: statistics; Organizations, student; Social groups: students

STUDENTS, AFRICAN, 484 (A 12), 851

STUDENTS, ALGERIAN, 1084

SYNARCHY, 344

TECHNOCRACY, 126, 349, 376, 377, 546, 547, 633, 800, 994

TECHNOLOGY. See Civilization, future; Civilization, modern

TECHNOLOGY, INDUSTRIAL, 331, 725, 763, 1149. See also Industries; Nuclear technology

TELEVISION. See Radio-television

TORTURE. See Algerian war: atrocities--torture

TOURISM, 129, 142, 291

TRADE UNIONS, 16, 83, 108, 146, 169, 179, 180, 234, 384, 435, 440, 478, 481, 544, 554, 629, 658, 675, 725, 727, 758, 823, 870, 1131; history, 725, 727, 866; ideologies, 1103; political activities (see May 1968: and trade unions); publications, 1158; and worker participation in industry, 954 (see also Industrial relations: worker participation); workers' attitudes toward, 873. See also Confédération des travailleurs chrétiens; Confédération française démocratique du travail; Confédération générale des cadres; Confédération générale du travail; Fédération autonome des syndicats de police; Fédération de l'éducation nationale; Fédération française des travailleurs du livre; Force ouvrière; Syndicat national de l'enseignement supérieur in Author Index

TRANSPORTATION, 1000

TREATIES AND AGREEMENTS, 476, 1005, 1010, 1043

TRIALS, POLITICAL, 558, 594, 636; Algerian nationalists, 1104; bazooka affair, 411; Ben Barka affair, 55, 704, 1039, 1134; Jouhaud, 648; Petit-Clamart (de Gaulle assassination attempt), 483 (B 1), 704, 706; Russier affair, 492; Salan, 483 (B 1)

UNION DES DEMOCRATES POUR LA REPUBLIQUE (U. D.-Vᵉ and U. D. R.), 75, 216, 935, 982; bibliography, 679; congresses (see Union pour la nouvelle république: congresses); elections, 483 (A 1, A 2), 506, 662; political philosophy, 720; and prime minister, 233; program, 1081; publications, 1151, 1163. See also Gaullism; Gaullism after de Gaulle; Gaullists; Organizations, political: Gaullist; Political parties: Gaullist; Press, political: Gaullist in Subject Index; and Union des démocrates pour la Cinquième République; Union des démocrates pour la république in Author Index

UNION POUR LA NOUVELLE REQPUBLIQUE (U.N.R. and U.N.R.-U.D.T.), 75, 216, 572, 935; bibliography, 679; congresses, 285, 314, 338, 483 (A 3), 559, 708, 742, 824, 935, 939, 987, 1009, 1114; elections, 662; internal organization, 662; political philosophy, 720, 935; and prime minister, 233; publications, 217. See also Gaullism; Gaullists; Organizations, political: Gaullist; Political parties: Gaullist; Press, political: Gaullist in Subject Index; and Union pour la nouvelle république; Union pour la nouvelle république-Union démocratique du travail in Author Index

UNIVERSITIES. See Education, higher

URBANISM, 239, 257, 388, 420, 553, 590, 699, 921, 1000, 1004, 1094; new towns, 420, 1094; shantytowns, 606

UTOPIANISM, 822

VIETNAM, 208, 1092; opposition to war in, 483 (A 3), 903

VIOLENCE, 192, 224, 372, 380, 566, 1104, 1184

VISITS OF STATE (DE GAULLE), 321, 447, 567, 906

VISITS OF STATE TO FRANCE, 837

WAGES. See Economic conditions: wages

WOMEN, 172, 562, 897

WOMEN'S RIGHTS, 153, 219, 483 (A 3)

WORKERS. See Social groups: workers

YEARBOOKS, 27-29, 454, 479

YOUTH, 95, 118, 173, 405, 465, 468, 488, 521, 773, 812, 1001, 1110, 1114; apprentices, 783; bibliography, 468; expectations of future career, 1037; international comparisons, 649; pictorials works, 335

AUTHOR INDEX

Indexed names include:

(1) All authors, editors, and compilers not listed in the alphabetical position in Part I.

(2) All co-authors, co-editors, participants in colloquia, etc., and other important contributors mentioned either bibliographically or in the annotations.

(3) Pen names when work is listed under author's real name.

(4) Persons or organizations (political parties, clubs, academic institutions, etc.) responsible for or connected with issuing a work but not listed as authors in Part I. These have been indexed only when relevant to the Fifth Republic.

For 1-4, entry numbers are underlined. For example: Giscard d'Estaing, Valéry: 40 indicates that the name is that of the author.

(5) Persons or organizations mentioned either bibliographically or in the annotations, when substantial information about them is provided. (However, the following names will also be found in the Subject Index: Gaulle, Charles de, Front de libération nationale, Organisation de l'armée secrète, Parti communiste français, Parti socialiste, and Union pour la nouvelle république.) In this case entry numbers are not underlined, as in Giscard d'Estaing, Valéry: 65.

Abelin, Pierre 483 (A1)
Action catholique ouvrière 737
Adam, Gérard 873
Adloff, Richard 1067
Allais, Maurice 1016
Alliance des étudiants révolutionnaires 1201
Alliance des jeunes pour le socialisme 484 (A2), 1191, 1193, 1201
Alphérandy, C. 943
Althusser, Louis, 50, 402, 500, 867, 1154
Ameller, Michel 632
Amicale des algériens en Europe 1019
Amicale des anciens membres du Parti communiste français 1062
Amicale des professeurs européens d'histoire contemporaine 950
Amis du SNCC 484 (A12)
Amouroux, Henri 54
Anderson, Barbara G. 21
Aragon, Louis 1194
Arendt, Hannah 192
Armand, Louis 39, 40, 477
Aron, Raymond 45-53, 477, 714, 929, 1013
Association de la presse étrangère 118
Association française des sciences politiques 61, 253, 911
Association générale des élèves de l'Institut des études politiques 483 (A3)
Association nationale pour le soutien de l'action du Général de Gaulle 483 (A3)
Astier de la Vigerie, Emmanuel d' 65, 120, 1093, 1172
Avril, Pierre 35, 73-75
Axelos, Kostas 1038
Ayache, Alain 231

Backmann, René 26, 968
Badiou, Alain 270

Ballanger, R. 483 (A1)
Banque nationale de France 1220
Banque nationale de Paris 1149
Banque nationale pour le commerce et l'industrie. See Banque nationale de Paris
Barbu, Marcel 65, 483 (B2)
Bardèche, Maurice 4, 81, 319, 360, 1162
Barjonet, André 83-85, 264, 683, 966
Barrau, Paul 947
Barrès, Maurice 124
Bastien-Thiry, Jean-Marie 483 (B2), 594, 704
Bauchet, Jacqueline 736
Baumel, Jacques 483 (A1)
Baumfelder, Eliane 1036
Baumgartner, Wilfrid 477
Bazin, Jean-François 673
Beauvoir, Simone de 1189
Bellour, Raymond 676
Benguigui, Georges 1131
Berge, André 92, 106
Bertin, Francis 76
Beuve-Méry, Hubert 56, 561
Bibliothèque de documentation internationale contemporaine. See Paris. Université. Bibliothèque de documentation internationale...
Billon-Grand, Françoise 977
Bin Barakah, al-Mahdi 55, 704, 1039, 1133
Biondi, Jean-Pierre 484 (D4)
Bissery, J. 627
Blanquer, Roland 467
Bloch-Lainé, François 943, 954
Boualam, Bachaga. See Boualam, Said Benissa
Boualam, Said Benissa 635
Boudon, Raymond 192

115

Bougrenet de la Tocnaye. See La Tocnaye, Alain de

Bourdieu, Pierre   53, 58, 137, 138, 185, 826

Brisson, Pierre   694

Bromberger, Serge   156

Brossolette, C. P.   483 (A 1)

Bull Company   1095

Burnier, Michel-Antoine   126, 127, 164, 674

Buron, Robert   166, 1202

Buy, François   167, 640

C.E.R.E.S.   See Centre d'étude de recherches et d'éducation socialiste

C.F.D.T.   See Confédération française démocratique du travail

C.F.T.C.   See Confédération française des travailleurs chrétiens

C.G.T.   See Confédération générale du travail

C.N.R.S.   See France. Centre national de la recherche scientifique

Calan, Pierre de.   See La Lande de Calan, Pierre

Calvi   72, 178

Canavezo, Robert   178, 516

Capelle, Jean   274

Capitant, René   181, 370, 483 (A 1), 830

Cardonnel, Jean   312

Carmoy, Guy de   183, 1120

Cassou, Jean   56, 583

Cayrol, Roland   971

Cazes, Sonia   1036

Centre de documentation juive   197, 198, 1198

Centre de recherche et d'étude sur le gaullisme   1079

Centre démocrate   217, 483 (A 2)

Centre d'étude de recherches et d'éducation socialiste (C.E.R.E.S.)   1153, 1235

Centre d'étude et d'initiative révolutionnaire   1213

Centre d'études et de recherches marxistes   200, 913, 1017

Centre d'études marxistes   1201

Centre d'études politiques et civiques   305, 330, 619, 1107

Centre d'études socialistes   366

Centre d'initiative communiste   622

Centre international d'études bio-sociales   303

Centre national de la recherche scientifique.   See France. Centre national de la recherche scientifique

Centre national des Indépendants et paysans   217

Centre national des jeunes agriculteurs   328, 1056

Centre national des jeunes cadres   1131

Centre national d'étude de l'oeuvre du Général de Gaulle   512

Centre national d'information pour la productivité des entreprises   162

Centre Progrès et démocratie moderne   217

Cercle des étudiants communistes de l'Ecole normale supérieure   1155

Cercle d'études marxistes   484 (A 16)

Cercles rouges   1223

Chaban-Delmas, Jacques   233, 290, 572, 601, 770

Chalandon, Albin   483 (A 1), 601

Chamboredon, Jean-Claude   138

Charlot, Jean   215-217, 626

Charras, Marie-Ange   606

Châtelet, François   1038

Chazelas, Geneviève   390

Chevallez, Georges André   288

Chevallier, Jacques   221, 1049

Cheverny, Julien [pseud.].   See Gourdon, Alain

Chu, Franklin   1137

Claude, Henri   235, 264

Clavel, Maurice   236-238, 583

Clément, Marcel   831

Club démocratie et université   484 (A 15)

Club Jean Moulin   240-242, 484 (A 15)

Cohn-Bendit, Daniel   18, 139, 149, 250, 623, 683

Cohn-Bendit, Gabriel   250

Comité d'action civique   484 (A 14)

Comité d'action "Nous sommes en marche"   484 (A 8)

Comité d'action ouvriers-étudiants   484 (A 6)

Comité d'action pour les états-unis d'Europe   964

Comité de coordination des cadres contestataires "C 4"   484 (A 6)

Comité de défense contre la répression   484 (A 6)

Comité de liaison pour la rénovation universitaire   484 (A 10)

Comité des étudiants pour les libertés universitaires (C.E.L.U.)   258, 484 (A 10)

Comité des trois continents   484 (A 12)

Comité d'études et de liaison des intérêts bretons   257, 925

Comité d'initiative pour un mouvement révolutionnaire   484 (A 6)

Comité Enragés-Internationale situationniste   1106

Comité national de l'enseignement catholique   386

Comité pour la défense de la république   484 (A 14), 506

Comité révolutionnaire d'agitation culturelle   484 (A 19)

Comités d'action lycéens   199, 293, 484 (A 20), 747, 903, 904, 1145

Commission de liaison des travailleurs étrangers   484 (A 12)

Commission nationale interdisciplinaire   484 (A 21)

Communauté chrétienne de St. Germain-des-Prés   484 (A 18)

Confédération française démocratique du travail (C.F.D.T.)   169, 384, 403, 478, 484 (A 37), 544.   See also Confédération française des travailleurs chrétiens

Confédération française des travailleurs chrétiens (C.F.T.C.)   169, 544.   See also Confédération française démocratique du travail

Confédération générale des cadres   546, 1131

Confédération générale du travail (C.G.T.)   83, 85, 130, 248, 339, 383, 384, 404, 435, 484 (A 36, A 37), 675, 948

Conseil national de la Résistance   193

Conseil pour le maintien des occupations   484 (A 6), 1106

Convention des institutions républicaines   217, 389, 743, 816

Coston, Henry   275-278, 868

Cotta, Michèle   813

Coudray, Jean-Marc   836

Courthéoux, Jean-Paul   432

Couve de Murville, Maurice 233, 285, 286, 483 (A1, A2)
Cras, Hervé 288
Crozier, Michel 261, 297, 943, 1137

Daniel, Odile 880
Darbois, Roland 1049
Dassa, Sami 1036
Dauvergne, Alain 25
Debelle, Jean 343
Debré, Michel 233, 314, 315, 483 (A1, A2), 601, 1049
Défense de la jeunesse scolaire 92
Defferre, Gaston 483 (A1, A2), 1139, 1140
Degueldre, Roger 594, 1023
Delbecque, Léon 1049
Deledicq, A. 820
Delouvrier, Paul 420, 1094
Denton, Geoffrey 749
Desmottes, Jean-Michel 95
Dubois, Pierre 554
Ducatel, Louis 483 (A2)
Duclos, Jacques 350, 351, 483 (A2), 721
Duhamel, Jacques 483 (A1), 601
Duigou, Daniel 293
Dumont, Jean 1125
Dumont, Yvonne 897
Duprat, François 4, 81, 319, 359-361
Dupuis, Georges 870
Durand, Claude 1036
Duverger, Maurice 368, 369, 911

Ecole des beaux-arts. See Ecole nationale supérieure des beaux-arts
Ecole émancipée. See Fédération de l'éducation nationale—Ecole émancipée
Ecole nationale d'administration (E.N.A.) 309, 376
Ecole nationale de photographie et de cinématographie (Paris) 484 (A22)
Ecole nationale supérieure des beaux-arts (Paris) 484 (A23)
Ecole normale supérieure (Paris) 415
Economie et humanisme (study group) 372, 684, 869, 1167
Effel, Jean 24
Egen, Jean 255
Ellul, Jacques 192, 377-380, 654
Emeri, Claude 279
Enragés 1106
Erce, François d' 1053
Establet, Roger 94
European Elite Panel Survey 735

F.G.D.S. See Fédération de la gauche démocrate et socialiste
Fajon, Etienne 483 (A1)
Fanon, Frantz 191

Fanton, A. 483 (A1)
Farmer, Albert J. 774
Faure, Edgar 65, 304, 310, 399-401, 483 (A2)
Fauvet, Jacques 118
Favre, Monique 402
Fédération autonome des syndicats de police 823
Fédération d'Alliance ouvrière 1191
Fédération de la gauche démocrate et socialiste (F.G.D.S.) 88, 121, 194, 217, 389, 398, 483 (A1, A3), 605, 690, 815, 840, 877, 894, 901, 902, 1003, 1041, 1086, 1135
Fédération de l'éducation nationale (F.E.N.) 234, 740
Fédération de l'éducation nationale—Ecole émancipée 484 (A34), 740, 908
Fédération des étudiants d'Afrique noire en France 484 (A12)
Fédération des étudiants de Paris 483 (A3), 484 (A10)
Fédération des étudiants révolutionnaires (F.E.R.) 360, 483 (A3), 484 (A8), 661, 767, 778
Fédération française des sociétés de journalistes 1012
Fédération française des travailleurs du livre 339
Fédération générale des étudiants européens 484 (A10)
Fédération nationale des Républicains indépendants. See Républicains indépendants
Fédération nationale des syndicats d'exploitants agricoles (F.N.S.E.A.) 328, 1056
Ferniot, Jean 404, 1049
Fisher, Alden L. 799
Floud, Jean 371
Foccart, Jacques 601
Folliet, Joseph 66
Foncine, Jean-Louis 673
Fondation nationale des sciences politiques. Bibliographies françaises de sciences sociales 217, 418, 421
Fondation nationale des sciences politiques. Bibliothèque 418, 421
Fondation nationale des sciences politiques. Cahiers 86, 419, 422, 668, 691, 693, 802, 839, 977, 1110, 1111
Fondation nationale des sciences politiques. Centre d'étude de la vie politique française 194, 1139, 1140
Fondation nationale des sciences politiques. Centre d'étude des relations internationales 595
Fondation nationale des sciences politiques. Service d'étude de l'activité économique 42, 43, 570
Fondation nationale des sciences politiques. Travaux et recherches de science politique 280, 328, 420, 538, 873, 890, 1056
Fondation Royaumont 1131
Fontaine, Pierre 4
Fontanet, Joseph 483 (A2), 601
Force ouvrière 108, 484 (A36, A37)
Fouchard, Georges 308
Fouchet, Christian 36, 427
Fougeyrollas, Pierre 428, 1038
Fourastié, Jacqueline 6
Fourastié, Jean 429-432, 477
Forsyth, Murray 749
France. Ambassade. U.S. Service de presse et d'information 474, 513

France. Archives nationales. Section d'outre-mer 1179
France. Centre national de la recherche scientifique (C.N.R.S.) 222, 439
France. Conseil économique et social 440-446, 549
France. Direction de la documentation 447-452, 468
France. Direction de la documentation. Recueils et monographies 449, 451
France. Direction de la documentation. Serials 173, 1176-1178, 1209
France. Institut national de la statistique et des études économiques (I.N.S.E.E.) 450, 454-461, 999, 1168, 1230
France. Institut national d'études démographiques (I.N.E.D.) 95, 239, 262, 462, 528, 562, 621, 944, 999
France. Institut pédagogique national 463-466, 484 (A 24)
France. Ministère de l'économie et des finances 1229
France. Ministère des affaires étrangères. Service d'information et de presse 474, 1177, 1178, 1180
France. Ministère d'état des affaires culturelles 1179
France. Secrétariat d'état aux affaires étrangères chargé de la coopération 1018
Frank, Pierre 630, 1212
Frey, Roger 483 (A 1)
Front de libération nationale 718, 780, 912, 1077
Front des étudiants pour la rénovation de l'université 484 (A 10)
Front national anti-communiste 484 (A 14)
Fuzier, Claude 483 (A 2)

Gadjos, Catherine 1131
Gaillard, Félix 483 (A 1)
Gallois, Pierre (Général) 595
Gallouedec-Genuys, Françoise 946
Ganne, Gilbert 618
Garaudy, Roger 281, 358, 494-504, 622, 895, 898, 913, 1017
Gauche prolétarienne 622, 759, 854, 1157
Gaudy, Jean-Charles 390
Gaulle, Charles de 508-516. See also Subject Index
Geismar, Alain 58, 139, 519, 683
Gérard, Jacques 293
Gheysen, R. 288
Girault, Jacques 561
Giscard d'Estaing, Valéry 40, 65, 91, 252, 483 (A 1, A 2), 556, 601, 1101
Glasser, Georges 442
Glayman, Claude 496
Glucksmann, André 535, 536, 965
Goguel-Nyegaard, François 511, 538, 626, 911
Goldey, David 1133
Gorden, Morton 735
Gorz, André 238, 545, 965
Gourdon, Alain 546, 547
Grappin, Pierre 484 (D 1)
Grawitz, Madeleine 930
Grenoble. Université 22
Grosser, Alfred 370, 486, 558

Groupe biblique universitaire de Paris 484 (A 18)
Groupement national de la coopération 1219
Groupement national pour l'indemnisation 657
Groupes marxistes révolutionnaires 985
Guéna, Yves 483 (A 1), 563
Guichard, Olivier 135, 569, 601
Guilhem, Jean 6
Guitton, Henri 576, 1016

Habib-Deloncle, M. 483 (A 1)
Halle, Louis J. 486
Halsey, Arthur 371
Hamon, Léo 118, 253, 290, 588, 589
Harrison, Martin 1133
Hauriou, André 35
Houillion, Christian 1105
Hourdin, Georges 618, 1161
Huguenin, Daniel 79
Hurtig, Serge 61

I.N.E.D. See France. Institut national d'études démographiques
I.N.S.E.E. See France. Institut national de la statistique et des études économiques
Institut Charles de Gaulle. See Paris. Institut Charles de Gaulle
Institut français de la coopération 1219
Institut français de polémologie 566, 1184
Institut français des experts comptables 1166
Institut français d'opinion publique (I.F.O.P.) 158, 625-627, 1037. (For French Fifth Republic Bibliography, 1, see Paris. Institut français d'opinion publique)
Institut Maurice Thorez 628, 976, 1152
Institut national de la statistique et des études économiques (I.N.S.E.E.). See France. Institut national de la statistique . . .
Institut national d'études démographiques. See France. Institut national d'études démographiques
Institut pédagogique national. See France. Institut pédagogique . . .
International Institute for Social History (Amsterdam) 14
International Students' Union 167
Internationale situationniste 148, 261, 311, 408, 484 (A 8), 488, 542, 631, 854, 1090, 1091, 1106, 1192
Isou, Isidore 488, 637, 732

Jancovici, H. 270
Jaurès, Jean Léon 1226
Jeanneney, Jean-Marcel 483 (A 1), 644
Jeunesse étudiante catholique 230
Jeunesses communistes révolutionnaires (J.C.R.) 360, 483 (A 3), 484 (A 8), 630, 767
Jeunesses radicales 1211
Joannès, Victor 247
Johnson, Douglas 486
Johnsson, Philippe 323
Jollivet, Marcel 439

Joxe, P.   483 (A 1)

Jouvenel, Bertrand de   650, 1225

Juin, Alphonse Pierre (Maréchal)   210

July, Serge   519

Juquin, Pierre   483 (A 1), 655

Karsenty, Annette   676

Kastler, Alfred   683

Kennedy, Emmet   486

Kergoat, Danièle   1036

Koenig, Pierre   11

Krasucki, Henri   248, 675

Krivine, Alain   483 (A 2), 630, 678

Kulski, Wladyslaw Wszebor   486

Lacoste, Robert   1049

Lacouture, Jean   509, 685

Lagoutte, Louis-Marie   25

La Lande de Calan, Pierre   690, 1016

Lancelot, Alain   691-693

Lang, Madeleine   1051

La Tocnaye, Alain de   706

Lauer, Quentin   503

Launay, Jacques de   288, 709, 710

Lazard, Francette   264

Leblanc-Dechoisay, Pierre-Yves   367

Lebret, Louis-Joseph   719, 869

Lecanuet, Jean   483 (A 1, A 2, B 2)

Lefebvre, Henri   402, 723, 724, 1038, 1048

Lefort, Claude   836

Legoux, Yves   371

Lemaître, Maurice   488, 732

Lemée, Pierre   443

Leprince-Ringuet, Louis   118

Leroy, R.   483 (A 2)

L'Huillier, Pierre   654

Libertés universitaires régionales   33

Ligue communiste   41, 102, 180, 266, 483 (A 2, A 3), 678, 740, 792, 908, 985, 1223

Ligue ouvrière révolutionnaire   484 (A 16)

Loynes, Bernard de   446

Lutte ouvrière   985

McConville, Maureen   1015

Maillet, Monique   751

Maisl, Herbert   407

Maison des sciences de l'homme   880

Maitron, Jean   887

Mallet, Serge   754, 1036

Malraux, André   65, 195, 395, 484 (D 2), 491, 756, 757, 839, 1171

Mamy, Georges   852

Manceaux, Michèle   211, 683, 759

Mandel, Ernest   238, 630, 760, 761, 965

Mandel, Gisela   888

Maout, Jean-Charles   77, 766

Marc, Alexandre   669

Marcel, Gabriel   66

Marcellin, Raymond   601, 767

Marchais, Georges   171, 483 (A 2), 628, 768, 769, 898, 932

Marcilhacy, Pierre   483 (B 2)

Marcuse, Herbert   623, 771, 918, 1048

Marjolin, Robert   1016

Marks, Georgette   774

Maroselli, Jacques   690

Martel, Robert   845

Massé, Pierre   135

Massu, Jacques (Général)   329, 412, 779, 780, 883

Mathevet, René   440

Mauriac, François   396, 785, 786, 907

Mauroy, Pierre   483 (A 2)

Mayeur, Pierre   573

Mazoyer, Marcel   355

Mendès-France, Pierre   10, 65, 537, 575, 795, 992

Mendras, Henri   439, 797, 1060

Menetry, D.   270

Méric, Jean   736

Mersch, Jean   441

Metz, Johann B.   504

Metzger, Joe   184

Michal, Bernard   612, 803

Michelet, Edmond   601, 806, 907

Millet, Louis   22

Mindu, Patrick   367

Missoffe, François   468, 812

Mittelberg, T. I.   813

Mitterrand, François   10, 120, 194, 483 (A 1, A 2, B 2), 743, 788, 815, 816, 901, 972, 1101, 1232

Moliterni, Claude   323

Mollet, Guy   483 (A 1), 821, 1150, 1203

Monheim, Francis   340

Monnerville, Gaston   524

Monnet, Jean   156, 602, 964, 967

Montvalon, Robert de   1231

Morane, Erlyne   519

Mordal, J.   See Cras, Hervé

Moreau, René   280

Morin, Edgar   261, 833-836

Motte, Bernard   483 (A 1)

Mouriaux, René   179

Mouvement de soutien aux luttes du peuple   484 (A 6), 1157

Mouvement démocratique féminin   483 (A 3)

Mouvement d'organisation des étudiants pour la liberté   484 (A 10)

Mouvement du 22 mars   271, 484 (A 9), 519, 542, 767, 798, 929

Mouvement étudiant   484 (C)

Mouvement européen   1159

Mouvement jeune révolution   484 (A 10)

Mouvement lettriste   488, 637, 732

Mouvement mondialiste   1199

Mouvement national Progrès et liberté.   See Progrès et liberté

Mouvement pour la coopération en Algérie   119

Mouvement républicain populaire (M. R. P.)   217, 641

Mury, Gilbert   1189

Muzellec, Raymond   77, 766

Naville, Pierre   371

Objectif 1972 (political club)   166, 484 (A 15), 1202

Occident   361, 484 (A 10)

Oelgart, Berndt   155, 867

Office de la radio-télévision française   151, 260, 480, 484 (A 35, D 4), 563, 744, 764, 991, 1036.   See also Radio-television in Subject Index

Office franco-allemand pour la jeunesse   335

Office universitaire de recherche socialiste   1150, 1203

Offredo, Jean   166

Organisation communiste internationaliste   661, 778, 985, 1191, 1193

Organisation communiste pour la reconstitution de la IVe Internationale   484 (A 16), 1233

Organisation française du mouvement européen   1159

Organisation révolutionnaire anarchiste   484 (A 16)

Paillat, Paul   262

Paris. Institut Charles de Gaulle   226, 512, 885, 886, 1171

Paris. Institut français d'opinion publique.   See Institut français d'opinion publique. (For French Fifth Republic Bibliography, 1, see Paris. Institut français d'opinion publique)

Paris. Université.   See May 1968 student revolt: Paris, University of in Subject Index

Paris. Université. Bibliothèque de documentation internationale contemporaine   542, 1204

Parti communiste français   171, 217, 483 (A 1, A 2, A 3), 484 (A 11, A 17, C), 502, 643, 769, 892-898.   See also Parti communiste française in Subject Index

Parti communiste internationaliste   630, 985

Parti communiste marxiste-léniniste de France   483 (A 3), 484 (A 16), 656, 1186

Parti communiste révolutionnaire   1196

Parti communiste révolutionnaire de France   1154

Parti libéral de France   484 (A 15)

Parti républicain radical et radical-socialiste   89, 121, 217, 344, 398, 899-902, 932, 992, 1041, 1211

Parti socialiste (S. F. I. O.)   217, 483 (A 2).   See also Parti socialiste (S. F. I. O.) in Subject Index

Parti socialiste (1969-), 605, 840, 1003, 1029, 1153, 1232

Parti socialiste autonome (P. S. A.)   217, 333, 955

Parti socialiste unifié (P. S. U.)   217, 270, 287, 333, 483 (A 2, A 3), 484 (A 15), 622, 754, 777, 970, 971, 1213

Passeron, Jean-Claude   30, 137, 138, 185, 555

Pauvert, J. J.   385, 1032, 1169

Perrot, Jean-Claude   887

Perrot, Michelle   887

Peslier, Michel   621

Pétain, Henri Philippe Bénoni Omer   961

Peters, Louis-Ferdinand   232, 920

Peterson, Agnes F.   598

Peyre, Christiane   371

Peyrefitte, Alain   58, 954

Peyrefitte, Roger   525

Piret, J.   158

Planel, Aloméé   764

Pleven, René   601

Plissonnier, Gaston   895

Poher, Alain   483 (A 2), 874

Poirier, Odette   384

Poitiers. Université   484 (A 33)

Pompidou, Georges   9, 70, 178, 233, 670, 935, 936, 972, 982, 1088, 1089, 1101, 1102

Pontaut, Jean-Marie   193

Poujade, Robert   483 (A 1, A 2), 601

Prévost, Claude   184, 948

Prévost, Philippe   640

Programme communiste   985

Progrès et liberté   1210

Prost, Antoine   850, 952

Rahner, Karl   504

Rassemblement du peuple français   217

Rassinier, Paul   4

Rebérioux, Madeleine   887

Reich, Wilhelm   879

Rémond, René   66, 960

Rémy [pseud.].   See Renault-Roulier, Gilbert

Renault-Roulier, Gilbert   961, 962

Républicains indépendants   91, 216, 217, 252, 556, 824, 937, 938, 960, 1181

Républicains sociaux   217

Revel, François   583

Révoltes   661

Ribaud, Guy   116

Ribs, Jacques   467

Ricoeur, Paul   118, 211

Robin, Gilbert   106

Rocard, Michel   483 (A 1, A 2), 970, 971

Rocca, Robert [pseud.]   178, 516

Rochet, Waldeck   171, 264, 483 (A 1, A 2), 894, 896, 974-976

Roux, Dominique de   508

Roy, Claude   583

Rueff, Jacques 330
Russier, Gabrielle 492

S. N. E. Sup. See Syndicat national de l'enseignement supérieur
Sabatier, Alain 162
Saint-Pierre, Michel de 313
Salan, Raoul 406, 411, 483 (B 2)
Salez, Jean 1125
Salgues, Yves 491
Sartre, Jean-Paul 50, 318, 623, 759, 888, 997, 998
Sauvageot, Jacques 139, 683, 1108
Sauvy, Alfred 118, 999-1002
Savary, Alain 118, 1003
Scalabrino, C. 102
Scheinman, Lawrence 12
Schnapper, Dominique 302
Schuman, Robert 617, 973
Schumann, Maurice 483 (A 2), 601, 1009
Schwartz, Laurent 114
Semaine de la pensée marxiste 976, 1017
Servan-Schreiber, Jean-Jacques 89, 344, 517, 579, 760, 932, 1025-1027, 1041, 1173
Servolin, Claude 1060
Sève, Lucien 1017, 1028
Sicard, Patrice 585
Sicault, Jean-Didier 753
Sidjanski, Dusan 801, 802
Sidos, Pierre 1228
Simon, Pierre-Henri 1049
Sirius [pseud.]. See Beuve-Méry, Hubert
Socialisme ou barbarie 985
Société internationale de défense sociale 19
Sollers, Philippe 1064
Soustelle, Jacques 1042, 1061, 1210
Steiner, Léon David 303
Sudreau, Pierre 483 (A 2), 1052
Sueur, Jean-Pierre 230
Sylvester, H. 147
Syndicat général de l'éducation nationale (S. G. E. N.) 484 (A 34), 850
Syndicat national de l'éducation surveillée 484 (A 34)
Syndicat national de l'enseignement secondaire 234, 484 (A 34)
Syndicat national de l'enseignement supérieur (S. N. E. Sup.) 260, 484 (A 34), 1085, 1145, 1223

Tavernier, Yves 1056, 1060
Technique et démocratie (political club) 82, 1057, 1058
Teilhard de Chardin, Pierre 781
Témoignage chrétien 484 (A 18)
Tendance marxiste révolutionnaire de la Quatrième Internationale 484 (A 16)
Tendance révolutionnaire du Parti communiste français 484 (A 16)

Terrall, Mary 1137
Terray, E. 270
Thomas, Olivier Germain 195
Thorez, Maurice 247
Thorez-Vermeersch, Jeannette. See Vermeersch, Jeannette
Thuillier, Guy 188
Tillion, Germaine 1049
Tim. See Mittelberg, T. I.
Tixier, Jean-Louis 483 (B 2), 636
Tixier-Vignancour, Jean-Louis. See Tixier, Jean-Louis
Touraine, Alain 683, 1069-1071, 1103, 1108
Truffaut, François 683
Tubiana, Raoul 10

U. D. -Ve. See Union des démocrates pour la Cinquième République
U. D. R. See Union des démocrates pour la république
U. D. T. See Union démocratique du travail
U. N. E. F. See Union nationale des étudiants de France
U. N. R. See Union pour la nouvelle république
U. N. R. -U. D. T. See Union pour la nouvelle république–Union démocratique du travail
Uhrich, René 445
Ungar, Sanford J. 949
Union de la gauche socialiste 217
Union de la jeunesse 488
Union démocratique du travail 75, 181, 217. See also Union pour la nouvelle république in Subject Index
Union des commerçants du Quartier latin 484 (A 14)
Union des démocrates pour la Cinquième République (U. D. -Ve) 1081, 1082, 1163. See also Union des démocrates pour la république in Subject Index
Union des démocrates pour la république (U. D. R.) 484 (A 1, A 2), 1151, 1163. See also Union des démocrates pour la république in Subject Index
Union des étudiants communistes de France 484 (A 11, C), 647, 1200
Union des femmes françaises 483 (A 3)
Union des jeunes pour le progrès 484 (A 3), 559
Union des jeunesses communistes marxistes-léninistes (U.J.C.M.-L.) 310, 360, 400 (A 3), 484 (A 9, C), 759, 767, 1155
Union nationale 484 (A 14)
Union nationale des étudiants de France (U. N. E. F.) 260, 410, 483 (A 3), 484 (A 7), 507, 1085
Union nationale des étudiants préparatoires 484 (C)
Union pour la défense de la république 483 (A 1)
Union pour la nouvelle république 217. See also Union pour la nouvelle république in Subject Index
Union pour la nouvelle république – Union démocratique du travail (U. N. R. – U. D. T.) 217, 285, 314, 338, 342, 483 (A 3), 559, 708, 712, 742, 824, 935, 939, 987, 1009, 1114. See also Union pour la nouvelle république in Subject Index
Union progressiste 1093
Union travailliste 1183
"Unir" (political group) 1062
Université populaire cinématographique 484 (A 19)
University of Wisconsin 484 (A 1)

Vajou, Jean-Claude 1026
Vallon, Louis 65, 483 (A 1), 954, 1088, 1089
Vaneigem, Raoul 1048, 1090, 1091
Vedel, Georges 259, 853
Veilletet, Pierre 572
Vergès, Paul 2
Vergez, Gabrielle 390
Vermeersch, Jeannette 895
Viansson-Ponté, Pierre 54, 1101, 1102
Vibes, Pierre 857
Vidal, Daniel 1036, 1103
Vidal-Naquet, Pierre 1006, 1104
Vigier, Jean-Pierre 484 (D3), 1145
Vimont, Claude 95

Vincent, Jean-Marie 965, 1137
"Vive la révolution" 854
Voix ouvrière 767

Walter, François 92
Weber, Henri 103
Weygand, Maxime (Général) 577, 961, 1129
White, Dan S. 750
Wibaux, Claudine 262
Wolf, Charles 730
Wylie, Laurence 484 (D), 1136, 1137

Yacef, Saadi 780

TITLE INDEX

Indexed titles include:

(1) Book titles for works with complicated or ambiguous author entries, such as publications listed under compilers or organizations. Normally, book titles have not been indexed.

(2) Serial titles listed under the publishing agency (e.g., "Revue économique," which is listed under Banque nationale de Paris)

(3) Serial titles where title changes have occurred, or where supplements are listed under different titles.

(4) Selected serial titles for which special issues are listed under other headings.

(5) Serial titles about which substantial information is given elsewhere than under the serial heading in Part II.

(6) Selected series or collection titles of special significance for the Fifth Republic (e.g., Cahiers libres, Tribune libre).

"L'abominable vénalité de la presse française" 275
"Action" 484 (B, D3), 1145
"The affair of Gabrielle Russier" 492
"Ah quelle année!" 72
"Allemagne, actualités et perspectives" 370
"Aménagement du territoire et développement régional" 553
"Analyse d'un vertige" 192
"Analyse et prévision" 1225
"Arguments" 835
"Articles et documents" 1209
"Aspects de la politique sociale française" 173
"L'avant-garde" 390
"Avant-garde" 484 (B)

"Barodet" 438
"Bibliographie alsacienne" 1051
"Le bilan social de l'année 1968" 248
"Bulletin des nouvelles acquisitions" 1179
"Bulletin SEDEIS" 1225

"Cahier de l'Ours" 1150
"Cahiers de l'Herne" 195
"Cahiers de l'Institut Maurice Thorez" 1152
"Cahiers de mai" 484 (B)
"Cahiers des universités françaises" 59
"Cahiers du C.E.P.E.C." 305, 330, 619, 1107
"Cahiers libres" 94, 103, 256, 271, 522, 574, 606, 695, 807, 862, 919, 921, 1055, 1062
"Cahiers marxistes-léninistes" 484 (B), 1155
"Cahiers 'Rouge'" 41, 102, 180, 266, 268, 269, 375, 791
"Le capitalisme monopoliste d'état" 264
"Carrefour des jeunes" 76, 521, 585
"Cause du peuple" 484 (B), 759, 1157
"Ce n'est qu'un début" 271, 683
"Ce qu'ils ont dit de lui" 152

"Le centenaire du Capital" 393
"Les changements de la société française" 684
"Chanzeaux, a village in Anjou" 1136
"Charles de Gaulle" 195
"Charles de Gaulle, 1890-1970" 1054
"La chienlit de papa" 182
"Citations du Général de Gaulle" 508
"Citations du président de Gaulle" 509
"Les collectivités rurales françaises" 439
"Les communismes" 852
"Conférences des Ambassadeurs" 152, 307, 812, 1074

"De la misère en milieu étudiant" 631
"De l'université aux universités" 59
"La déconcentration administrative à l'éducation nationale" 453
"Défense de l'Occident" 4, 81, 319, 360, 1162
"De Gaulle vu par . . ." 843
"Demain la politique; réflexions pour une autre société" 166
"Des jeunes regardent leur avenir" 1037
"Des militants du P.S.U." 970
"Des Soviets à Saclay?" 919
"Le destin tragique de l'Algérie française" 803
"Dictionnaire de la politique française" 276
"Documentation française illustrée" 450
"Documentation photographique" 447
"Documents officiels" 1177
"Documents pour l'élaboration d'indices du coût de la vie en France" 6
"La droite?" 66

"Echo d'Oran" 686
"Economie et politique" 264
"Education, développement et démocratie" 185
"Elaboration de la politique étrangère" 253
"Les élections législatives de mars 1967" 171

123

"L'émigration algérienne" 1019

"En France, un million d'analphabètes" 614

"Enragé" 385, 484 (B), 1169

"Entretiens du samedi" 61, 911

"Esprit public" 713

"Essays in economic history" 175

"The essential writings of Merleau-Ponty" 799

"L'état de la science politique en France" 61

"Etudes et conjonctures" 1168

"Etudes polémologiques" 1184

"Etudiant révolutionnaire" 484 (B)

"Europäer in Frankreich" 417

"Evénement" 65, 1172

"Evénements de mai" 482, 485

"Evénements de mai et l'enseignement catholique" 386

"Les évènements de mai-juin 1968 vus à travers cent entreprises" 203

"Face au gauchisme moderne" 622

"Le Figaro" 694

"La fondation du Parti communiste français" 628

"Les Français devant le communisme" 625

"Les Français et de Gaulle" 626

"La France à travers de Gaulle à travers la caricature internationale" 1030

"France under de Gaulle" 336

"French affairs" 437

"Frontière" 1153

"Futuribles" 362, 610, 650, 797, 1060, 1098, 1225

"Garaudy par Garaudy" 496

"Garde rouge" 483 (A 3)

"Les gauchistes" 854

"Les grandes énigmes de mai 1968" 1125

"La grève à flins" 1055

"Grr et Zzz" 707

"Guide de la recherche en histoire contemporaine" 60

"Hermès" 484 (B)

"Histoire illustrée du plus illustre des Français" 207

"L'Homme nouveau" 831

"Hoover Institution publications" 13, 598

"Ils accusent" 260

"Indemnisation des Français dépossédés outre-mer" 467

"Ingénieurs, techniciens, cadres" 1188

"L'Insurgé" 484 (B)

"L'insurrection étudiante" 676

"JJSS" 932

"Jeunes d'aujourd'hui" 468

"Journal de la commune étudiante" 1006

"Journal des étudiants en médecine de Paris" 484 (B)

"Les journées de mai" 265

"Les journées de mai; rencontres et dialogues" 364

"Labyrinthe 606" 484 (B)

"Lectures françaises" 275, 277, 278, 868

"Livre noir des journées de mai" 1085

"Il maggio di Parigi" 416

"Mai 68" 981

"Mai 68 affiches" 1080

"Mai 1968; la prise de la parole" 261

"Mai-juin 68" 683

"Manifeste pour la Ve République" 1081

"Masses ouvrières" 947

"The May days in France" 18

"Médecine" 256

"Le Monde" 118, 561, 604, 607, 966, 1012

" 'Le Monde' à la lettre" 607

"Le mouvement des lycées" 903

"Le mouvement ouvrier en mai 68" 1036

"Mouvement social" 887

"Les murs ont la parole" 115

"La Nation" 830

"Ni dieu, ni maître" 1066

"Noir et rouge" 484 (B)

"Notes d'information [du] Front du progrès" 1183

"Notre république" 181

"Nous sommes en marche" 484 (A 8)

"Les nouveaux communistes" 319

"L'opinion des Français sur le Marché commun . . ." 627

"Opinions et motivations des étudiants français" 566

"Ouvriers, étudiants, un seul combat" 904

"Le P.S.U. et l'avenir socialiste de la France" 971

"Parijs mei-juni '68" 14

"Paris, mai/juin 1968" 323

"Parlements; une étude comparative . . ." 632

"Le Pavé" 484 (B)

"Périodiques et publications en série" 880

"Perspectives socialistes" 1158

"Le petit livre rouge du Général" 516

"Philosophie et sciences de l'homme" 624

"Le Plan Mansholt" 259

"Poèmes de la révolution" 365

"Pour ou contre" 106, 255, 274, 618, 690

"Pour une réflexion sur la mutation de l'université . . ." 484 (A 21)

"Pourquoi des examens" 159
"Pouvoir ouvrier" 484 (B)
"Problèmes de la révolution socialiste en France" 1017

"Quelle université? Quelle société?" 199

"Le rapport Vedel" 259
"Reflections on the revolution in France" 942
"La remise en question de l'école" 1014
"Le renouveau de la pensée libérale" 1016
"Revolt in France" 630
"La révolte étudiante" 139
"La révolution algérienne" 912
"La révolution par elle-même" 1031
"Revue du Front de la jeunesse et de l'externité" 488
"Revue économique [de la] Banque nationale de Paris" 1149
"Revue française de sociologie" 835
"Roger Garaudy et le marxisme du XXe siècle" 913
"Le rôle du président" 35
"Rouge" 484 (B), 1223

"Le secret des dieux" 278
"Servir le peuple" 484 (B)
"La Sorbonne par elle-même" 887

"Télégramme de Paris" 1183
"Témoignage chrétien" 485, 831
"The thirteenth of May" 750
"Le transfert social, fondement du progrès économique?" 722
"Trente ans d'histoire de France" 612
"Tribune libre" 48, 88, 251, 401, 767, 954, 1141
"Troubled neighbors: Franco-British relations" 1120

"L'Union de la jeunesse devant les erreurs de la Vème République" 488
"L'univers rural et la planification" 135

"Vie ouvrière" 675
"Violences et société" 372
"Vive le 1er mai 70" 1113